WITHDRAWN

TOWARDS INDIA'S FREEDOM AND PARTITION

BY THE SAME AUTHOR

India and the Commonwealth 1885-1929 (1965)
The Emergence of the Indian National Congress (1971)
The Commonwealth and the Nation (1978)

Towards India's Freedom and Partition

S. R. MEHROTRA

VIKAS PUBLISHING HOUSE PVT LTD
New Delhi Bombay Bangalore Calcutta Kanpur

VIKAS PUBLISHING HOUSE PVT LTD
5 Ansari Road, New Delhi 110002
Savoy Chambers, 5 Wallace Street, Bombay 400001
10 First Main Road, Gandhi Nagar, Bangalore 560009
8/1-B Chowringhee Lane, Calcutta 700016
80 Canning Road, Kanpur 208004

COPYRIGHT © S.R. MEHROTRA, 1979

ISBN 0 7069 0712 4

1V02M1403

DS
475
M43

Printed at Delhi Printers, 21 Daryaganj, New Delhi 110002

PREFACE

The essays included in the present volume deal with the political history of India during the nineteenth and the first half of the twentieth century, with particular reference to the problems of national independence and unity. They were written on various occasions and for various audiences. They are now being put together and published in the form of a book in the belief that they have stood the test of time and proved to be of more than transient interest. It is also hoped that their publication in this form would be of use both to the student of modern Indian history and to the general reader.

Recent history is familiarly known, but it is seldom properly known. What is familiar becomes valid; knowing only goes along the surface. There is yet another reason why recent history is generally not properly known. It is an area where publicists rush in but historians fear to tread. By the time historians arrive on the scene, the damage has been done and a lot of bad history has been produced and popularized which no amount of good history can ever succeed in driving out. It is my firm belief that recent history is too serious a matter to be left to the publicists alone, for it plays an extremely important role in determining both public opinion and public policy.

Indians were the first non-white people in recent times to have struggled successfully for emancipation from the white yoke. Their struggle was hard and long, and it occupies a prominent place in the annals of modern Asia and Africa. Though Indians were undoubtedly influenced by foreign models, their movement for national freedom was in many ways autochthonous. I have tried to bring out the uniqueness not only of the Indian national movement, but also of the British response to it.

The story of India's struggle for national independence deserves to be better studied and known than it has so far been. It was marked by a good deal of courage, heroism and sacrifice on the part of the Indian people. It had leaders who were both valiant and wise and of whom posterity may well be proud. The partition of the country in 1947 diminished to some extent the glamour and the glory of their achievement. But even the partition was not an unmitigated evil. In fact, it may well be argued that the partition of 1947 made it easier for the leaders and the people of independent India to continue pursuing the ideals of the Indian national movement—which are now embodied in the Indian Constitution—and to preserve and promote the unity of a major part of the subcontinent.

I should like to thank the following for permission to make use of the material which was first published by them as articles:

George Allen and Unwin ('The Congress and the Partition of India' in C.H. Philips and M.D. Wainwright (eds), *The Partition of India: Policies and Perspectives 1935-1947*, 1970);

Indian Council of World Affairs ('The Early Organization of the Indian National Congress, 1885-1920', *India Quarterly*, October-December 1966);

Frank Cass & Co. Ltd. ('The Development of the Indian Outlook on World Affairs before 1947', *Journal of Development Studies*, April 1965).

Indian Institute of Advanced Study S.R. MEHROTRA
Rashtrapati Nivas, Simla
August 1977

CONTENTS

1 THE GROWTH OF INDIAN NATIONALISM IN THE NINETEENTH CENTURY 1

2 INDIAN POLITICAL THOUGHT IN THE NINETEENTH CENTURY 17

3 ALLAN OCTAVIAN HUME AND THE INDIAN NATIONAL CONGRESS 44

4 THE ORGANIZATION OF THE INDIAN NATIONAL CONGRESS, 1885-1920 67

5 THE OBJECTIVES AND METHODS OF THE INDIAN NATIONAL CONGRESS, 1885-1920 91

6 THE MORLEY-MINTO REFORMS 115

7 THE HOME RULE MOVEMENT IN INDIA 124

8 GANDHI AND THE INDIAN NATIONAL MOVEMENT 135

9 THE GROWTH OF LEGISLATIVE COUNCILS IN INDIA, 1833-1935 158

10 THE CONGRESS AND THE PARTITION OF INDIA 181

11 THE PARTITION OF INDIA: SOME MYTHS AND MIGHT-HAVE-BEENS 223

12 THE PROBLEM OF THE INDIAN STATES IN HISTORICAL PERSPECTIVE 233

13 THE DEVELOPMENT OF THE INDIAN OUTLOOK ON WORLD AFFAIRS BEFORE 1947 251

Biographical Notes 277

Notes 286

Index 315

1

THE GROWTH OF INDIAN NATIONALISM IN THE NINETEENTH CENTURY

In 1884 Sir John Strachey, who had recently retired from the Indian Civil Service after a long and distinguished career, delivered a series of lectures on India at the University of Cambridge. He began by telling his audience: 'This is the first and most essential thing to learn about India—that there is not, and never was an India....'[1] Nor need it be feared, Strachey added, that the bonds of union fashioned by British rule could ever 'in any way lead towards the growth of a single Indian nationality'. 'However long may be the duration of our dominion,' he remarked, 'however powerful may be the centralizing attraction of our government, or the influence of the common interests which grow up, no such issue can follow.' To Strachey it seemed impossible 'that men of Bombay, the Punjab, Bengal and Madras should ever feel that they belong to one great Indian nation'.[2]

Strachey testified to the truth contained in Lord Palmerston's famous epigram that if one wished to be misinformed about a country, he should ask the man who had lived there for thirty years. Strachey lacked sympathy and understanding. He was blind to the changes taking place in India before his very eyes. Even while he was speaking at Cambridge in 1884 there were thousands of Panjabis, Bengalis, Marathas and Madrasis who had already started feeling that they belonged to one great Indian nation. And next year, in 1885, the growing spirit of Indian nationalism found a body in the Indian National Congress. But let us not be too hard on Strachey. He was not unique in thinking that India could never become a nation, and he apparently had good reasons for believing that the idea of a united Indian nation was an impossibility.

If there was any country in the world where the prospect of a united nationhood seemed hopeless in the nineteenth century, it was India. It was a vast country, almost a continent. Its area was as large as that of Europe, minus Russia. It had a huge population of about 250 million. And this huge population was divided by almost every conceivable division—linguistic, racial, religious and political. The babel of tongues in India was notorious. It had more than a dozen major languages and hundreds of dialects. From very early times peoples of different races and climes had been entering India. They came and added to the variety of its population. India contained followers of almost all the major religions of the world—Hindus, Muslims, Christians, Jains, Buddhists, Sikhs, Parsis, and Jews. Even the followers of any particular religion were not united. The Hindus, for example, who formed the majority of the population, were divided into innumerable sects, castes and sub-castes. Administratively, the country was not one unit even under British rule. The provinces enjoyed a good deal of autonomy and there were over five hundred semi-independent princely states.

The British were able to conquer India because it was divided. They were very conscious of this fact. They knew that their rule in India would last only as long as India remained divided. The ease with which the British were able to conquer and govern India encouraged them to harbour many illusions about the Indian people. These illusions were reinforced by their almost total incapacity or unwillingness to penetrate the Indian mind. For example, the British generally believed and openly asserted that Indians had no sense of patriotism, that they did not mind being ruled by foreigners, because they had been accustomed to foreign rule for centuries, and that they had no capacity for self-government. Now, all this was bunkum.

There are no people on earth, however primitive, who are totally lacking in patriotism. We all love the soil which gives us birth and nourishes us. We all love our own people more than other people. We all prefer our own language, literature, traditions, religion and way of life to those of others. We all dislike foreigners to some extent. No people love to be governed by foreigners. No people are entirely lacking in the capacity for self-government. Congenital and willing slaves are rare.

For most people patriotism is synonymous with hatred of the foreigner. 'The only patriotism', wrote the Anglo-Indian *Friend of India* in January 1857, 'we have yet encountered [in Asia] is in Canton. The rabble of that city seems to have a genuine heartfelt contempt for the barbarians, which in Spartans we should admire.'[3] It probably never occurred to the editor of the *Friend of India* that if Indians, for example, did not have the same 'genuine heartfelt contempt for the barbarians' as did the Chinese, it was mainly because the former had had greater experience of 'the barbarians' than the latter. That the rabble in some of the Indian cities had no more love for 'the barbarians' than had that in Canton was a fact of which the editor of the *Friend of India* and his countrymen were made painfully aware only a few months later.

Nations, it has been said, are made in solitude. Until the middle of the nineteenth century, India seldom had the solitude to become a nation. Moreover, the country was too vast. All-India empires were a rare phenomenon and they were short-lived. The integrative process in India was again and again interrupted by foreign invasions. Even if there had been no foreign invasions, it is doubtful whether a country of the size of India could have become a nation before the development of the modern means of communication in the nineteenth century. It is, therefore, not at all surprising that India was not a nation when the British first arrived there as traders. (In fact, modern nationalism itself is a very recent phenomenon. Even in Europe it did not emerge until the beginning of the nineteenth century.) But it would be wrong to conclude, as so many British observers tended to do, that India was entirely lacking in the essentials of nationalism, or that the vastness and diversity of India ruled out the possibility of the emergence of a united Indian nation.

Nature has made the peninsula of India probably the most compact territory in Asia. It has given India a distinct geographical unity and well-defined frontiers. And from very early times the people of India have been conscious of this fact.[4] Communication between different parts of India was frequent. Pilgrims travelled great distances to visit shrines distributed throughout the country. So did merchants and scholars. The physical and administrative barriers within the country seldom impeded the free flow of men or goods or ideas. The two major religious communities in India—the Hindu and the Muslim—were dispersed all over the subcontinent. The sense of belonging to an all-India community cut across regional and linguistic loyalties. Despite the apparent diversity of language, custom, race and religion, India, from the Indus to the Brahmaputra and from the Himalayas to Cape Comorin, possessed a certain underlying uniformity of life which distinguished it from the rest of the world. The web of Indian life was woven of diverse but interlocking patterns. The divisions of India were many, but they were neither rigid nor exclusive. A Bengali Muslim, for example, though he differed from his Hindu neighbour in religion, spoke the same language as did the latter and shared with him in a common regional culture, while as a Muslim he was part of a wider community. Similarly, though the Maharashtrian and the Tamil Hindu were linguistically and racially different, they belonged to the same religion. Nor was the ideal of Indian political unity entirely lacking. The ancient Hindu ideal of a *chakravartin* was that of a monarch who ruled over the entire subcontinent.[5] This ideal was only briefly realized under the Mauryas in the fourth century B.C. and under the Guptas in the fourth century A.D., but what is significant is the fact that the ideal was firmly implanted in the Indian mind. The result was that later when the Mughals succeeded in the sixteenth century in bringing almost the entire subcontinent under one political umbrella, the emperor of Delhi began to be looked upon by the people as the paramount ruler of India. If the East India Company kept up for long the fiction of being the agent of the Mughal emperor in Delhi, it was mainly because the fiction was useful to it and acceptable to the people of India. When the sepoys mutinied in 1857, they, both Hindu and Muslim, naturally turned, as the *Hindoo Patriot*, 21 May 1857, remarked, 'towards the ancient capital of the country where resides the remnant of the former dynasty to which are turned in times of political commotion the eyes of all Indian legitimists'.[6] Reflective Indians hailed the political unification of India brought about by British rule as the realization of India's age-old aspiration for political unity. It is significant that the Indian press compared the Delhi Darbar of 1877, marking the assumption by Queen Victoria of the title of Kaiser-i-Hind, to the *rajasuya yajna* of Yudhisthira and the assemblage of nobles from all parts of India at the Mughal court.

The Growth of Indian Nationalism in the Nineteenth Century

India was far from being a nation in the nineteenth century—she is even to this day only a nation in the making—but she was not entirely lacking in some of those basic elements which are essential for the making of any nation, and given favourable circumstances she could become a nation. Some of these favourable circumstances were provided by British rule.

The British once again gave political unity to India. They re-created a sort of all-India state. By 1849 the military conquest of India was almost complete and though the numerous princely states were allowed a good deal of autonomy, by and large, the whole country came under British sway. Common subjection, common laws and institutions began to shape the people of India in a common mould. Indian patriotism could now fix upon a single state system. Communal, linguistic and regional loyalties did not disappear. In fact, they were reinforced and reinvigorated in many ways. But pan-Indianism also grew and it acquired a new meaning and content.

British rule gave India a long period of peace and security. India was, in a way, isolated and insulated from the rest of the world. The integrative process had now full operation within India. To borrow Edwyn Bevan's famous analogy, the British Raj was like a steel frame which held the injured body of India together till the gradual process of internal growth had joined the dislocated bones, knit up the torn fibres, and enabled the patient to regain inner coherence and unity.[7]

The introduction of the modern means of communication—the press, the new postal system and the railways—which followed the establishment of British rule in India, linked the metropolitan centres with the *mofussil* and one province with another in a closer, more intimate and living unity. Like their Anglo-Indian counterparts, Indian newspapers, particularly those in English, took note of happenings in all parts of the country and circulated freely throughout India. The practice of exchanging free copies enabled the editor of, say, a paper in Madras to easily obtain dozens of other newspapers published in different parts of the subcontinent. The people of one part of India had no difficulty in knowing what was happening in other parts of the country. The importance of the press in promoting a pan-Indian consciousness cannot be over-estimated. More than any other single factor it helped in uniting the country and in creating a community of thought and feeling. Thanks to the press, an Ishwarchandra Vidyasagar of Calcutta, a Dadabhai Naoroji of Bombay, and a Syed Ahmed Khan of Aligarh became all-India figures. Thanks to the press, local happenings and grievances began to attract the attention of the whole country. A famine in the 1870s in Madras or Maharashtra, for example, attracted the sympathy and help of people from all over the country. Similarly, the news of a protest meeting against the income tax in one town encouraged other towns to follow suit. The press thus broke down internal barriers and encouraged inter-regional solidarity. It enabled the people in one part of the country to become aware of the existence of those in other parts of the country and of their feelings and aspirations.

The steady improvement of the postal system in India under British rule, notably the introduction of a cheap and uniform rate of postage in 1854, served to unify the country. It annihilated distance and lessened isolation. It helped in enlarging the circulation of newspapers, in extending commerce, and in promoting the social and intellectual advancement of the people. It enabled public men in different parts of the country, who had few opportunities of meeting together, to remain in close and regular contact with each other.

Railways were another potent means of unifying the country. The construction of railways began in India in the early 1850s and by the mid-1880s about 12,000 miles of railway had been constructed. The coming of the 'steam horse' to India not only meant increased and rapid communication between different parts of the country, it also brought about a profound change in the habits of the people. Noticing, on 25 January 1855, how all the seventeen carriages of the Pandua-Calcutta train were 'full to the brim' with Indian passengers, the *Friend of India* remarked: 'It is one of the wonders of the age to see how the people of India have suddenly changed the stereotyped habits of twenty centuries.'[8] Indeed, the railway compartment, in which people of all castes and creeds and provinces were huddled together, became the symbol of a new and united India in the making. 'Railways may do for India', the prescient Edwin Arnold wrote in 1865, 'what dynasties have never done—what the genius of Akbar the Magnificent could not effect by government, nor the cruelty of Tippoo Saheb by violence; they may make India a nation.'[9] Twenty years later Madhav Rao remarked: 'What a glorious change the railway has made in old and long neglected India!...populations which had been isolated for unmeasured ages, now easily mingle in civilized confusion. In my various long journeys it has repeatedly struck me that if India is to become a homogeneous nation, and is ever to achieve solidarity, it must be by means of the Railways as a means of transport, and by means of the English language as a medium of communication.'[10]

Travel over one's country is usually a great education in patriotism. It heightens one's awareness of the geography, history and culture of one's native land. The knowledge gained through books, newspapers and hearsay acquires a new meaning and definitiveness. There is a widening of sympathy and a broadening of outlook.[11] One's understanding of and attachment to one's country and people grow. This was specially true of the travels in India of English-educated Indians in the latter half of the nineteenth century. We can see it clearly in the cases of Bhau Daji, Keshavachandra Sen and Surendranath Banerjea in the 1860s and 1870s. Their extensive travels in India, which were made easy by steamers and railways, helped them, so to speak, to discover their own country, and added a new dimension to their sense of patriotism. Visits by prominent Indian public men to places outside their own provinces were comparatively rare in the 1860s and 1870s. But probably because they were so rare, they were given wide publicity by the press and attracted a great deal of attention throughout the country. Distinguished visitors from other parts of India were lionized and feted by the local people. Friendships were easily made and they often proved enduring, being constantly renewed through correspondence and return visits. There was a quality of freshness, cordiality and innocence about these early contacts between Indian patriots of different provinces. The condition of India and the means to ameliorate it formed the staple of their conversation and correspondence. On the death of Ganesh Vasudev Joshi in 1880, Shishir Kumar Ghose, the editor of the *Amrita Bazar Patrika*, recalled an episode which is extremely revealing. In the autumn of 1877 Ghose had paid a visit to Poona and stayed with Joshi, whom he had known for long 'by fame' and whose acquaintance he had made during the latter's visit to Calcutta earlier in the same year. 'When leaving that historical city [Poona]', Ghose recalled three years later, 'Mr. Joshi took hold of our arm and inquired:

"You are going away; but tell me, before you go, what will become of India?" When he told this, tears began to trickle down his wrinkled cheeks. What could we say in reply? The destiny of India was not in our keeping and we could not, therefore, give a satisfactory reply to his earnest query. "What will become of India?" and this thought oppressed him all the days of his life."[12] The number of public men was not large in India in the 1860s and 1870s, but the fact that at least some of them were known to their counterparts in the other provinces proved to be of great consequence, for it was the network of interprovincial contacts and friendships which provided the basis for the organization of the Indian National Congress in 1885.

History is replete with examples of common subjection to foreign rule having welded together people of different races, religions and regions into one nation. A common subjection to British rule produced the same result in India. The people of India had known many foreign rulers, but none so foreign, and determined to remain foreign, as the British. Other foreign rulers of India settled in the country and gradually became parts of Indian society. The British came to India from thousands of miles away and they always remained mere sojouners in this country. And the longer they ruled India the more the gulf between them and the people of India widened. With all their differences, the people of India had far more in common with each other than with their foreign rulers. And occasions were not wanting when the 'Natives' were united in common opposition to the 'Feringhees'. By subjecting the people of India to a common yoke, the British themselves aided, however unwittingly, the development of a sense of national unity in the country. A common yoke imposed common disabilities and occasioned common grievances. Common disabilities and grievances, in their turn, created common interests and sympathies, and served to unite the heterogeneous population of India in a common hatred of its foreign rulers.

History knows of few conquerors who treated the conquered, especially if the latter differed in race, language or religion, as their equals and liked them. It is probably impossible to conquer and rule over an alien people without treating them as inferiors and hating them to some extent. The British rulers of India were no exception to this general rule. The ordinary Briton in India behaved as if he was a demigod. He had an ill-concealed contempt for Indians and for their character, customs and religions. He resented travelling in the same railway compartment with an Indian or being tried by an Indian magistrate. He expected to be *salaamed* by Indians, high or low. He went about cuffing and kicking Indians, and if, as it occasionally happened, the Indian succumbed to his injury, the assailant generally escaped his due punishment on the ground that the victim had an enlarged spleen. Those who were thus abused and insulted naturally united in their common humiliation and even developed a xenophobia of their own.

There was another aspect of British rule which aided the growth of Indian nationalism. The British came to India not only as traders and rulers, but also as bearers of an alien religion and culture. Repeatedly in the 1830s, 1840s and 1850s various parts of India were thrown into a state of great alarm because of some action of Christian missionaries which was interpreted by the Indian people as an attack upon their ancient religions and customs, and the common dread of Christianity tended to unite not only the Hindus, Muslims and Parsis of a particular province, but also the people of one province with those of another. It was the feeling that their religion was at stake which lay at the root of the revolt of 1857. The great fear of forcible conversion to Christianity decreased after the revolt of 1857, but the threat of Christianity and of western culture remained and it continued to aid the growth of what is generally known as religious revivalism or cultural nationalism.

Reaction to British economic and fiscal policies gave rise to economic nationalism in India. Concern about the rapid decline of Indian handicrafts, about the inordinate expensiveness of the foreign civil and military establishments, about the 'home charges' and the drain of Indian capital began to be expressed in the first half of the nineteenth century. In the 1860s an Indian indigenous capitalist enterprise began to grow in India. This alarmed the British manufacturers, who started clamouring for a revision of the Indian tariffs in order to suit their interests. The British government yielded to their pressure tactics. The result was that the nascent Indian industrial community grew up in sullen resentment to foreign rule. In the meantime the number of the educated unemployed had begun to grow in India and the evils of an exclusively literary education had begun to be felt. Attention was, therefore, naturally directed towards the promotion of indigenous arts and industries. While other provinces only talked of *swadeshi*, Bombay took the lead in the early 1870s in organizing societies for the promotion of indigenous manufactures and the boycott of foreign goods.

The highly centralized character of British rule in India in the nineteenth century, especially after the Charter Act of 1833, also promoted the growth of a pan-Indian nationalism. Centralization meant not only the subordination of the governments of the various provinces and princely states to the central government at Calcutta, it also meant uniform, and sometimes even common, laws, institutions and taxes for the whole country. 'The very fact that we have established a central government for India,' Ripon pointed out in 1885, 'and that with the present facilities for communication and the spread of news, the eyes of men from the Punjab to Adam's Bridge and from Bombay to Madras, are turned upon the Supreme Government as the final arbiter of their fate, brings them more together among themselves, and gives, as it were, a common centre for their political thoughts, and a rallying point for their political action.'[13] The government of India was 'one and indivisible', and its actions had often the effect of encouraging its subjects to feel that they too were, or should be, one and indivisible. How an action of the central government in India could serve to unite the people of various classes, creeds and provinces in common protest against it was illustrated by the imposition of the income tax. When the income tax was first levied for a temporary period all over British India immediately after the rebellion of 1857, there was a general outcry against it from various parts of the country. The same phenomenon was witnessed in an aggravated form when the tax was reintroduced, after a lapse of five years, in 1869. The *Indian Daily News* of Calcutta noted at the time: 'Amongst so many different tribes in India, using different tongues, there is a radical divergence of interests, which reduces the chances of a general combination to a minimum. . . . In the mutiny we were not more loved in Bombay and Madras than in Bengal. But those presidencies had no sympathy with such centres as Delhi and Lucknow, and no interests to serve by an alliance with the rebel leaders. Even a community of religion has not been able to bind the Mussulmans of the South to the co-believers of the North. Diversity of race, of language, religion, and interests has, however, been powerless before the spell of the Income-tax.... The Income-tax has afforded the native races of the Empire a common point of union—a thing never before known in the history of India The men of the Deccan—no less than the men of Behar, the ryots of Bengal, the peasants of the Punjab, and Guzerat—have one common and all-absorbing illustration of the oppression of the stranger who rules over them all, to engage their attention and guide their conversation.'[14]

British rule had another peculiarity which served to unite the people of India in common opposition to it. Probably no foreign rule in India ever excluded the sons of the soil so completely from higher offices in the state—both civil and military—as did the British in the nineteenth century. Here was a common grievance which united Indians of all creeds and provinces against their alien rulers. What made the exclusion particularly galling to Indians was the fact that it was practised by a government which solemnly and repeatedly professed that it made no distinction, in the matter of employment, on grounds of race, colour, or creed. It is true that from 1853 on, appointment to the Indian Civil Service was, in theory, thrown open to all classes of Her Majesty's subjects, who were all invited to compete for the privilege. But the conditions of the competition were such as practically to exclude Indians therefrom altogether. The examination for the Civil Service was held in London and the sacrifices and expense of sending Indian youths to appear thereat were such as not one man out of a million would think it wise to incur. This palpable injustice did more than anything else to weaken the moral basis of British rule in India. Here at least was a point on which the British could not claim superiority over the Mughals or the Marathas, the Russians or the Austrians. It provided Indians with one of their most potent, persistent and popular demands, in favour of which they could easily mobilize public opinion all over the country. The fact that what Indians demanded was not patronage or favour, but equality of treatment and a fair field, that is the holding of the Civil Service examinations simultaneously in India and in Britain, only served to increase the efficacy of their demand as a rallying point of Indian nationalism. It united men of different classes, creeds and provinces in India by providing them with a genuine grievance and a righteous cause. Moreover, educated Indians throughout the country felt very strongly about it, because with it were associated not only their ambitions for place and power but also their dreams of ultimate self-government.

Probably the greatest contribution of British rule to the growth of Indian nationalism lay in the encouragement which it gave to the dissemination of English education in the country. English education familiarized a steadily increasing number of Indians in the nineteenth century with European history, literature and political thought. It inculcated in them new European ideas of patriotism and public service, of the duties of governments and the rights of subjects. It did not create in India the love of country, the consciousness of nationality or the desire for liberty, for these already existed, but it did stimulate them and give them a new direction. As early as 1838 C.E. Trevelyan had noted how English education, which was then confined to the presidency towns, was giving an entirely new turn to the Indian mind. Those Indians, he had written, who had been educated in English schools ceased to strive for independence according to the old indigenous model. They did not continually meditate and hatch plots and conspiracies with the object of sweeping the infidel usurpers of their country off the face of India in one day by force. Instead, they subscribed to the new British model of political change and aimed at the ultimate establishment of constitutional self-government in India by gradually improving and regenerating their country with the help of their foreign rulers.[15]

Those whose minds had been nurtured on the writings of John Milton, J. S. Mill and Gieuseppe Mazzini, who read about the War of American Independence, the French Revolution, the development of constitutional freedom in Britain and her white colonies, and the struggles for national independence and unity in Europe, could not but be encouraged to cherish aspirations for the ultimate emergence of an independent and united India. These aspirations had begun to be expressed even in the first half of the nineteenth century. They were only more frequently and generally expressed in the second half of the nineteenth century. They were encouraged by the pronouncements of some liberal-minded British statesmen themselves about the ultimate result of their rule in India.

English education not only enabled Indians to absorb European ideas, it also provided them with new and powerful means of inter-regional solidarity. The system of English education was more or less uniform throughout India, and it imposed a common set of standards and a common cultural discipline. English-educated Indians in the different provinces thus came to possess a common stock of ideas and aspirations. They also had a common medium of intercourse. English steadily replaced Sanskrit, Persian, or Hindustani as the lingua franca of the educated classes in India. The number of English-educated Indians in the early 1880s probably did not exceed 500,000. In relation to the teeming millions of the country they were undoubtedly a 'microscopic minority', but in absolute terms the number was fairly large, and it was rapidly increasing. Moreover, as a rising social group, concentrated mostly in the towns, imbued with common ideas and aspirations, controlling the professions, educational institutions and newspapers, and capable of concerted action, English-educated Indians wielded an influence in society which was out of all proportion to their numerical strength.[16] Even in the first half of the nineteenth century there had been signs of nascent solidarity within the ranks of the widely scattered English-educated class in India, as was evidenced by the agitation against the Lex Loci Act and that in connexion with the renewal of the Company's charter. With the rapid spread of education and the increase in the circulation of newspapers in the 1860s, 1870s and 1880s the English-educated class in India began to display greater unity of thought and action. This found an impressive demonstration in connexion with the Indian Civil Service question in 1877-8, the Ilbert Bill issue in 1883 and the farewell demonstrations in honour of Ripon in 1884.

The growth of a national feeling in India was a fact of which even some of the Anglo-Indians were beginning to be aware in the 1860s and 1870s. An ex-judge of the high court of Agra, William Edwards, wrote in 1866 that 'a feeling of nationality has sprung up in India'. 'The result of long years of internal tranquillity and good order, under a powerful government', he added, 'has been to fuse into a whole the previously discordant elements of native society, and to bind together, by a bond of common country, colour and language, those whom we have been in the habit of considering as effectually and for ever separated by diversity of race and religion, and the insurmountable barrier of caste.'[17] William Knighton, late assistant commissioner in Avadh, observed in 1867: 'The educated Bengalee and the educated Sikh, the educated alumnus of the Canning College in Lucknow, and the educated native of Travancore, all alike regard themselves as natives of India, and are all ready to make common cause against foreigners.... It is entirely a new feature, and will lead in the future to great results.'[18] W.B. Jones, the commissioner of Berar, wrote in 1878: '... within the 20 years of my own recollection, a feeling of nationality, which formerly had no existence, or was but faintly felt, has grown up....Now...we....are beginning to find ourselves face to face, not with the population of individual provinces, but with 200 millions of people united by sympathies and intercourse which we have ourselves created and fostered. This seems to be the great political fact of the day.'[19] Anglo-Indians had reason to get alarmed at the growth of a pan-Indian nationalism, or to continue indulging, as most of them did, in the make-believe that such a thing was impossible. They already knew what the Regius Professor of Modern History at Cambridge, John Robert Seeley, was at pains to emphasize in the second course of his celebrated lectures in the spring of 1881, namely that 'if the feeling of a common nationality began to exist there [in India] only feebly, if, without inspiring any active desire to drive out the foreigner, it only created a notion that it was shameful to assist him in maintaining his dominion, from that day almost our Empire would cease to exist'.[20]

Literary and debating societies, where the young English-educated Indians talked patriotism, had begun to grow up at the metropolitan centres in the 1820s and 1830s. These soon flowered into 'Patriotic Associations' and 'Societies for the Amelioration of India'. Following the example of resident Britons, interest groups began to be organized in the 1830s. The first interest group to be organized was the Landholders' Society of Calcutta in 1838. The interesting thing about the Landholders' Society was that it had pretensions of speaking on behalf of the whole country and aimed at establishing branches all over India. Then in 1851-2 came the local associations in Calcutta, Poona, Madras and Bombay. What was being aimed at was a central organization in Calcutta, with branches elsewhere. This did not materialize, but the associations did occasionally correspond and co-operate with each other and there was a striking similarity in their demands and methods of work. These associations were the creation of English-educated Indians. They contained landlords, merchants and professional men. The English-educated professional men—

The Growth of Indian Nationalism in the Nineteenth Century 15

lawyers, teachers, journalists, doctors and clerks—though they were active in these associations in the 1850s, were yet not very numerous or influential. But in the succeeding decades they grew rapidly in numbers and became influential. The result was that scores of middle-class associations grew up in the 1860s, 1870s and 1880s in the larger towns of India. These associations had a wider outlook, their demands were far-reaching and, instead of appealing to the government, they began to appeal to the people. The ideal of a united and independent India began to be openly preached in the press and on the streets. The need for some sort of concert and co-ordination between the activities of these various associations began to be widely felt and expressed. By the mid-1870s the Indian nationalist movement had clearly reached the take-off stage.

In 1876 Queen Victoria assumed the title of Kaiser-i-Hind or Empress of India. In order to mark the occasion, the viceroy of India, Lord Lytton, announced a grand *darbar* to be held at Delhi on 1 January 1877. Sensing the unique significance of the forthcoming event—when distinguished men from all walks of life and from all parts of India were to assemble in the old imperial city of Delhi—and anxious to turn it to some national advantage, the leaders of the Poona Sarvajanik Sabha addressed, on 5 December 1876, a circular letter to the princes, chiefs and gentlemen who had been invited to the great imperial assemblage. The letter, which was also given wide publicity in the press, exhorted the Indian invitees to the Delhi Darbar not to look upon the coming event as an occasion for gaiety and pageantry but as one symbolizing the growing unity of India as a nation and to take advantage of it for furthering that unity. 'The honour that has been paid to you in your personal or representative capacity [in being invited to the gathering at Delhi]', said the Sabha's letter, 'is regarded by us, as an honour to the nation, to which you belong, and we have no doubt that the gathering of so many representative men from all parts of India is an event of national importance, and that it will be regarded, in all future history, as the commencement of that fusion of races and creeds, the second birth of the great Indian nation, for which we have so long prayed and dreamed, and which has been so wonderfully brought about by Providence through strange agencies. On such an occasion, it behoves you to sink the individual and the temporary in the national and permanent concern of the event, and to prove to the world that you are fully alive to the greatness of the responsibilities thrown on you by being thus singled out to represent all that is great and good, true and hopeful, in this vast country ... you should not be dazzled by the gaieties of the gathering, but learn the great moral lesson of healthy, self-sustained, and joint political action, which such an event is so well-calculated to teach. You are the great Notables of the land, the first Parliament of the united Indian nation, the first Congress of the representatives of the diverse states and nationalities which make up the body politic of India .... We pray that you will make it a point of duty to see each other individually during your stay in Delhi, and bid welcome to each other, forgoing all reserve and petty misunderstandings, which have separated us long enough to our ruin. We propose further that you will all meet together in private gatherings, and discuss with each other our present situation and future prospects.'[21]

It was at Delhi in December 1876-January 1877 on the occasion of the Delhi Darbar that Indian nationalists took the first practical steps to draw together the various scattered forces of the growing national life in the country which ultimately resulted, nine years later and under more favourable circumstances, in the organization of the Indian National Congress.[22] They began very modestly, which shows how politically mature and sophisticated they had already become. All that they attempted to do was to bring together once or twice a year in a conference in some central place representatives of the press and political associations to exchange ideas and focus public opinion on demands which represented the highest common factor in the programme of the politically-alert Indians. They aimed at an indirect, federal sort of national organization. A different kind of attempt was being made almost at the same time by a more idealistic group in Bengal, namely to have a central national association in Calcutta with its branches all over the country, but it failed.[23] The organization of the Indian National Congress in 1885 foreshadowed, in a way, the kind of nation India was going to be. The Congress became both the symbol and the instrument of a nation in the making.

2

INDIAN POLITICAL THOUGHT IN THE NINETEENTH CENTURY

'The aegis of British protection is an acknowledged necessity [for India], and none feel its need with greater emphasis than the leaders of native thought. But it is not as the representative of brute force, but of the order and genius of equal law, that we bow down to this supreme necessity. The argument of force, if it is resorted to as a justification for denying concessions in time, necessarily weakens itself for want of sanction. It cannot, therefore, be in the true interests of the Empire that the British rulers of the country should be allowed to isolate themselves in this fashion. The iron hand must be concealed under the soft glove, and the sword sheathed in the scabbard of wise policy....There can be no question that a nation of 250 millions can never be permanently held down by sheer force, and sooner or later in God's Providence, and under the encouragement of British example and discipline, the people of this country must rise to the status of a self-governed community, and learn to control their own affairs in subordinate alliance with England. The transfer of power is inevitable, and the duty of statesmen is to graduate it in a way to make the transfer natural and easy, so as to keep up the continuity of national growth.'
Quarterly Journal of the Poona Sarvajanik Sabha, April 1883, pp. 29-30.

Introductory

Indian political thought in the 19th century, like most other aspects of Indian life and thought during the period, was a strange mixture of the old and the new, the indigenous and the alien, and it was marked by regional and sectional variations. But the central thesis of this paper is that the historically most significant and decisive political thought in India in the 19th century (and even later) was that of the English-educated intelligentsia and that it was largely determined by the fact that almost the entire country came, directly or indirectly, under British sway. The British domination of India determined not only the new foreign influences to which the country became exposed, it also determined the context, content and idiom of Indian political articulation.

Two Models of Political Change

Sir Charles E. Trevelyan, who had helped his brother-in-law, T.B. Macaulay, and the then governor-general, Lord William Bentinck, in inaugurating the system of English education in India in 1835, was asked by the Indian committee of the House of Lords in 1853 to give his opinion 'as to the effect of [English] education upon the probable maintenance of the British Government in India'.[1] In his reply, Trevelyan more or less repeated what he had said in a celebrated pamphlet[2] fifteen years earlier: 'According to the unmitigated native system, the Mahomedans regard us as Kafirs, or infidel usurpers of some of the finest realms of Islam, for it is a tenet of that dominant and warlike religion constantly to strive for political supremacy, and to hold all other races in subjection. According to the same original native views, the Hindoos regard us as mlechas, that is, impure outcasts, with whom no communion ought to be held; and they all of them, both Hindoo and Mahomedan, regard us as usurping foreigners, who have taken their country from them and exclude them from the avenues to wealth and distinction. The effect of a training in European learning is to give an entirely new turn to the native mind. The young men educated in this way cease to strive after independence according to the original native model, and aim at improving the institutions of the country according to the English model, with the ultimate result of establishing constitutional self-government.' Trevelyan added that English-educated Indians considered their British rulers to be persons under whose protection their schemes for the regeneration of their country might be worked out, whereas according to the original Indian view of political change, it was possible to sweep the British off the face of India in a day 'and as a matter of fact, those who look for the improvement of India according to this model are continually meditating and hatching plots and conspiracies with that object; whereas, according to the new and improved system, the object must be worked out by gradual steps, and ages may elapse before the ultimate end will be obtained, and in the meantime the minority, who already regard us with respect, and aim at regenerating their country with our assistance, will receive continual accessions, until in the course of time they would become the majority; but when that will be, no one can say'.[3]

Trevelyan maintained that the British Raj in India could not last for ever. It was bound to die one day, either at the hands of those Indians who subscribed to the indigenous model of political change, or at the hands of those who had been educated in English and subscribed to the new British model of political change. If it was to die at the hands of the latter, it would take a long time and the severance of the British connexion with India would be neither violent nor harmful to Britain, for cultural and commercial bonds would continue.[4]

Trevelyan had very correctly diagnosed the likely effects of English education on the continuance of British rule in India. It was the English-educated class which adopted 'the new and improved system' and took to modern politics in India.[5] It tried to meet the west with the weapons borrowed from the west. It conducted newspapers; it held public meetings; it organized pressure groups, patriotic societies and political associations in the western style. The old indigenous model of political change did not entirely disappear—in fact it was at times reinforced by revolutionary currents from Europe; nor did the old, traditional methods of playing politics die down—they occasionally got mixed up with modern methods of playing politics. But in this paper I propose to confine myself to a discussion of the political ideas of English-educated Indians who subscribed mainly to the new British model of political change.

The revolt of 1857 and the attitude adopted towards it by contemporary English-educated Indians in general provided a remarkable confirmation of the prognostication made by Trevelyan. The revolt of 1857 represented an attempt to gain independence according to the old Indian model, while the activities of the pressure groups and political associations, which were already growing up in India, represented the influence of the new British model.

Meredith Townsend, the famous journalist and author, who was in India during the revolt of 1857, recalled in 1882: 'There was not an Indian on the vast continent who did not consider the Sepoys Nationalists, and did not, even if he dreaded their success, feel proud of their few victories. An old Hindoo scholar, definitely and openly on the English side, actually cried with rage and pain, in the writer's presence, over a report that Delhi was to be razed. He had never seen Delhi, but to him it was "our beautiful city, such a possession for our country".'[6] The attitude of contemporary English-educated Indians towards the revolt of 1857 was far more ambivalent than Townsend's remark would suggest. They thought the rebels to be misguided, but they sympathized with them as their brethren and admired their courage for rising in a just cause They too disliked the British and, though not wishing to see them swept into the sea, derived some satisfaction from their troubles.

Probably the most sophisticated and revealing comment on the revolt of 1857 was provided by the Calcutta *Hindoo Patriot*, which wrote on 21 May 1857: 'How slight is the hold the British Government has acquired upon the affection of its Indian subjects has been made painfully evident by the events of the last few weeks ... it is no longer a mutiny, but a rebellion. Perhaps, it will be said that all mutinies, when they attain a certain measure of success, rise to the dignity of a rebellion. But the recent mutinies of the Bengal army have one peculiar feature—they have from the beginning drawn the sympathy of the country. The Sepoys who, in accepting service under the British Government, neither relinquished their rights of citizenship nor abnegated national feelings have been led to believe their national religion in danger. [They] are deemed by their countrymen justified in sacrificing a minor obligation to a paramount one. They have hazarded all their most valuable interests; and their countrymen view them as martyrs to a holy cause and a great national cause. The mutineers have been joined and aided by the civil population. They have hastened towards the ancient capital of the country where resides the remnant of the former dynasty to which are turned in times of political commotion the eyes of all Indian legitimists.... There is not a native of India who does not feel the full weight of the grievances imposed upon him by the very existence of the British rule in India—grievances inseparable from subjection to a foreign rule. There is not one among the educated classes who does not feel his prospects circumscribed and his ambition restricted by the supremacy of that power. At the present moment, the conviction is ineradicably strong in the mind of every native—save the small circle in Bengal of those who have been indoctrinated into the mysteries of European civilization—that the British Government is actuated by a fixed purpose of destroying the religion of the native races and of converting them to Christianity. Women and children talk of it. The delusion may seem strange to our [Anglo-Indian][7] readers, but it prevails nevertheless. Delusions as strange prevail among Europeans respecting the character and motives of Asiatic communities. Yet the grievance felt and the delusion believed in have not neutralized in the mass of the Indian population the feeling of loyalty which the substantial benefits of the British rule have engendered. We believe the prevailing feeling is that any great disaster befalling the British rule would be a disastrous check to national prosperity. We do not deny that a pettish desire to see the high-handed proceedings of its officials rebuked and the insolence, as it is thought, of the Anglo-Indian community checked to some degree countervails the more sober deduction. But, on the whole, the country is sound.'[8]

The attitude of English-educated Indians to the revolt of 1857 was perhaps nowhere more clearly and frankly expressed than in a letter by 'A Loyal Bengali' to the editor of the Anglo-Indian *Friend of India*, dated 4 June 1857. After referring to the idea widely prevalent in Anglo-Indian society that educated Bengalis were rejoicing at the rebellion and would be glad to see the British driven out of India, the correspondent remarked: 'Young Bengal is not hostile to the British Government. Young Bengal has no wish whatever to see the British Government overthrown under existing circumstances. How could he wish otherwise? Were the British Government in India overthrown, Young Bengal would, doubtless, be buried in its ruins.' The correspondent added that, though Young Bengal was 'by no means satisfied with it', he had no desire to exchange the comparatively mild rule of Britain for 'the horrors of the house of Tamerlane' or 'the barbarism of the Russian Autocracy'. Self-interest alone, therefore, induced Young Bengal to desire the continuance of British rule for the time being 'simply because if it were overturned, a better one could not take its place'. 'He would rather have done with it, and become free (and what man will blame another man for wishing to be free?), but the gods have not decreed so, at least in our days. The load must be endured, and it is Young Bengal's wish to make it as light as possible.' Young Bengal, however, looked upon the rebellion 'as a retribution of Providence' for the atrocities perpetrated by the British in India, and 'as tokens for good'. 'Young Bengal', wrote the correspondent, 'has certain grievances.... For getting these grievances redressed he has had recourse to constitutional means, but in vain. He himself would never resort to unconstitutional means (neither, indeed, has he the power to do so); but he hopes that the unconstitutional efforts of others would produce a salutary effect on the Government. He hopes that the mutinies would exert a wholesome moral influence on the Government...that, in consequence of the mutinies, the Government would be more conciliating towards the natives than it has hitherto been—less injustice would be done to them—and the odious distinctions of colour and creed become obsolete in practice as they have become in theory and in the Company's Regulations.' The correspondent concluded by saying: 'Blessed with an English education, having imbibed the spirit of English literature from my childhood, with English feelings, English tastes and predilections, I am to all intents and purposes an Englishman. Though as a patriotic native I cannot accord the Indian Government in the language of Father Paul to his country "*Esto perpetua*" yet, fully appreciating the blessings (such as they are) of British rule, I can wish for its stability up to the time when we are able to govern ourselves without any fear of foreign invasion.'[9]

English-Educated Indians: Composition, Conditioning and Character

Before going on to discuss in detail the political thought of English-educated Indians in the 19th century, we should try to have some idea of their composition, conditioning and character. English-educated Indians in the 19th century came mainly from the higher castes among the Hindus, especially those which had a tradition of learning. They were largely urban-based, though they were not entirely divorced from land. They were either government servants or employed in independent professions like law, teaching, journalism and medicine. They contained few representatives of the traditional aristocracy and trading community, or of the peasantry and the working classes.

The number of English-educated Indians grew steadily in the 19th century. In the 1830s they numbered only a few hundred and were confined to the coastal metropolitan centres of Calcutta, Madras and Bombay. By the end of the century they were about 500,000 and spread almost all over the country, every town of any size having its own quota, big or small. In relation to the teeming millions of India they were undoubtedly a 'microscopic minority'.[10] But in absolute terms their number was fairly large, and it was rapidly increasing. Moreover, as a rising social group, concentrated mostly in towns, imbued with common ideas and aspirations, controlling the professions, educational institutions and newspapers, and capable of concerted action, English-educated Indians wielded an influence in society which was out of all proportion to their numerical strength.

It was a common accusation of Anglo-Indians, as well as of some Indians, that English-educated Indians were 'denationalized' and isolated from the mass of their countrymen. There is some truth in the accusation, though it was very often made by those who were antipathetic to English-educated Indians. Foreign acculturation was implicit in the whole system of English education in India. Those Indians who imbibed the exotic flavour of English education became ostensibly, even ostentatiously, anglicized in their thought, speech and action, and were to that extent 'denationalized'. Not every English-educated Indian became necessarily 'denationalized'. Nor was the process of 'denationalization' confined to the English-educated in India. The impact of western culture was felt, to a greater or lesser degree, by almost every class in India. Even those in India who had never crossed the portals of an English school and were otherwise considered quite orthodox were not infrequently found drinking imported liquor, using foreign-made goods, or criticizing the established political, religious and social institutions of their own country. However, as a class, English-educated Indians did tend to differ from the mass of their countrymen in their food, dress, manners, language, religious beliefs, social practices and political ideas. But a certain degree of nonconformity and 'denationalization' is probably necessary in the making of a nationalist. It is true that not all 'denationalized' Young Indians were nationalists. In fact, many of them were known to despise their country, their people and their culture. But it is equally true that Old Indians, who had not directly or indirectly imbibed western ideas of nation and state, and who had not learnt to put their country before their caste, creed, community and region, could not become Indian nationalists in the modern sense of the term. In 1868 Rajendralal Mitra gave a fitting reply to those who maintained that English education tended to 'anglicize' or 'denationalize' Indians. 'If they mean thereby', he said, 'that we learn to think like Englishmen... to exert our best to import into our country all that is good and great among Englishmen; if they mean that we should try to make our civilization progressive like that of Englishmen, that we wish our countrymen should rise above the idols of custom and prejudice, that we long for the day when they should rend asunder the bonds of ignorance and priestcraft—I plead guilty to the charge, and most devoutly wish that every man in India may think and act in the same way. But if by Anglicism be meant an insensate aversion to all that is indigenous, a neglect of our language and our country; if it be meant that by learning English we denationalize ourselves—I repel the charge as false and calumnious.' Even *a priori*, Mitra remarked, 'it would be absurd to say that the poetry of Shakespeare and Milton, the philosophy of Bacon, Stewart and Reid, the science of Newton and Herschell and Faraday would make men forget their duty to their nation', but he would appeal to facts: the greatest living Bengali poet was Madhusudan Datta, who had received English education in the late Hindu College, accepted Christianity, lived in Europe for many years and married an English woman; the foremost Bengali novelist of the day was Bankimchandra Chatterji, one of the first B.A.s of Calcutta University; the best contemporary Bengali prose writer was Pandit Ishwarchandra Vidyasagar, who had improved his Sanskrit and Bengali by a liberal study of English language and literature.[11]

The educated have, in all ages and climes, been more or less isolated from the uneducated. The isolation is increased when education is combined with economic and political power. In traditional Indian society the isolation of the educated from the uneducated was mitigated by the fact that the former were not always wealthy or politically influential, and also by the absence of class divisions similar to those in the west. As E.C. Bayley remarked in 1870: 'The one feature of oriental life which strikes all European observers most forcibly and pleasantly, is the comparative social equality of rich and poor, and the close identity of their feelings and sympathies. Even in India, inhabited as it is by "men of many races, languages and religions", and in spite of barriers of some peculiar customs, I think that this remark holds good; and that within the various circles into which society is divided, there is far less distance between the highest and the smallest than is commonly the case in the Western world.'[12] English education brought about a change in the situation in the 19th century, first, because it was foreign, and secondly, because it became increasingly the passport to positions of profit and influence. But even English education did not succeed in completely divorcing its recipients in India from their family and social matrix. Moreover, the every fact of their relative alienation from the mass of their countrymen seems to have prompted the English-educated in India to seek new modes of identifying themselves with the latter.[13] This was encouraged not only by the new ideas of rights and responsibilities which they had imbibed from English education, but also by the necessity of competing with both indigenous and foreign rivals for influence with the bulk of the population.

In an ably written article in October 1876 the *Hindoo Patriot* tried to refute the allegation that English education tended to estrange its beneficiaries in India from the mass of their countrymen. 'It is true', said the paper, 'that English education saps the foundation of old-world notions and prejudices, and draws the man, who receives the benefit of it, nearer to the level of the enlightened intellect of the civilized world of the present day, but instead of destroying in him the love of his country it strengthens and intensifies it, instead of diminishing his sympathy "with the mass of his countrymen" it increases and vivifies it, instead cf weakening his hold upon the confidence of his poor and uneducated countrymen, it gives him a stronger hold upon it, than ever, because it enables him to give a tongue to their voice, and to defend their rights, interests and character with greater ability and power.'[14] The paper gave a long list of names of highly educated and even 'anglicized' Bengalis from Rammohun Roy on who had cherished the warmest sympathy for the mass of their countrymen and laboured strenuously for the amelioration of the latter's condition.

While we have tried to correct some of the wrong notions which have been current regarding English-educated Indians in the 19th century, we should ourselves not commit the mistake of overestimating their strength and altruism. English-educated Indians in the 19th century were, relatively speaking, a very small class, with only a limited influence in contemporary society. Not only did they have little influence in the rural areas, even their influence in the towns was severely limited, because they were often torn asunder by the divisions of caste, class, community, region, religion, and faction. Like any other class or group of men in history, they cared first and foremost for their own interests, despite their claims to speak and act on behalf of the entire people. And however large their number in absolute terms, those among them who took an active and sustained interest in politics were very few.

In 1802, the English judge and magistrate of Midnapore, H. Strachey, had remarked: '...the natives can hardly be said to be attached to [the British government]; for none of them understand it. No government ever stood more independent of public opinion. I never knew one native, who had even a remote idea of the political state of the country. I have no idea that the natives ever consult or converse on political subjects.'[15] However, in 1840 we find an Indian correspondent writing to the *Calcutta Courier*: 'An ordinary degree of observation will enable everyone to perceive that a strong desire for studying the political interests and welfare of the Indian community at large constitutes one of the prominent features of the Calcutta public. In private conversations as well as in the public prints of the day, we find for the most part the prevailing topic to be of such a character as is more or less concerned with politics. The enlightened Hindoo with his new-born ideas of freedom as inculcated in the works of a Hume, a Goldsmith, a Rollin, a Russell and other eminent historians, manifests a strong penchant for the political emancipation of his degraded countrymen....'[16] But in 1843 the visiting Scottish agitator and philanthropist, George Thompson, warned the budding patriots of Calcutta: 'For the work of agitation and petitioning, as carried on in England, you are not yet prepared.

You have no representative body, no *public*, in the English sense of the word. Beyond your own immediate neighbourhood, all is tame acquiescence, or sullen discontent, or interested connivance, or profound ignorance, or perfect helplessness.'[17] Within the next forty years or so sufficient modernization had taken place in India, especially as regards the spread of education, the growth of mass communications, increased urbanization and the rise of the new professional classes, to provide conditions for the creation of a national organization on the convention model. In 1885 the Indian National Congress came into being.

Agitation in the press and through public meetings, conferences, memorials and petitions had become a normal feature of Indian political life long before the Congress was established. The Congress only increased the tempo of Indian politics. There was more activity henceforth and on a wider front. There was also more unity of purpose and action. But the difficulties of continuous political agitation in the 19th century in a vast subcontinent like India, with its economic and educational backwardness, were almost insuperable. Moreover, the leaders of the early Congress had neither the means, nor perhaps the desire, to enlist the support of the masses. And when the British government frowned on some of their initial attempts in this direction, they were content to confine their agitation to the platform and the press.

Most educated Indians in the 19th century—and even later—knew no other modern foreign language but English. Their knowledge of foreign countries was through English. Most of the news which they got of the wide world came to them via England—through the English press, through Reuter or through their London-based correspondents. English thus became India's only window on the world. This was a fact of great consequence. The nascent modern Indian political thought was in a subtle but profound way influenced by the English. For example, the Indian admiration for the French revolutionary tradition was tempered by the English criticism of it, their knowledge of European history and politics was confined to what was available in the English language, and they looked on Russia for a long time through English spectacles. True, the sources of information available in English were varied, but the language through which Indians imbibed their ideas could not fail to colour their thoughts. True also, that England spoke in many voices, but it was the voice of English liberalism which appealed to Indians generally, and for all its liberalism it was basically English. Alike in their appreciation and criticism of men and events, Indians tended to follow the English. Not only did they absorb English standards and values, in their approach to problems, in their method of work and in their mode of expression, they, consciously or unconsciously, imitated Englishmen.

Indian leaders of political thought in the 19th century were men who devoted the best part of their lives to the study of English literature, who found solace in English poetry, and whose minds were nurtured on English history, law and political thought. They valued English political institutions as the acme of human genius and were inspired by what Rabindranath Tagore called 'the large-hearted liberalism of the nineteenth-century English politics'.[18] They desired to put into practice the principles which they had learnt and to imitate the model held out to them. Presiding over the thirteenth session of the Indian National Congress in 1897, C. Sankaran Nair remarked: 'Just look for a moment at the training we are receiving. From our earliest school-days the great English writers have been our classics. Englishmen have been our professors in colleges. English history is taught us in schools. The books we generally read are English books.... It is impossible under this training not to be penetrated with English ideas, not to acquire English conceptions of duty, of rights, of brotherhood.... Imbued with these ideas and principles, we naturally desire to acquire the full rights and to share the responsibilities of British citizenship.'[19]

The British Raj in India in the 19th century was a despotism, but it was a constitutional and legal despotism. Moreover, though it deprived the Indian people of political freedom, it gave them civil liberty—the freedom of speech and association. The British rulers of India were not only accustomed to modern politics at home—increasingly becoming more democratic—they also encouraged—both by precept and by example—their Indian subjects to believe that the latter could achieve their objectives—immediate or distant—by following the British model. In 1859 Dr Bhau Daji told a public meeting in Bombay, attended by many Englishmen: 'If we are today anxious for participation in the rights you claim by virtue of your birth, it is you Englishmen who have taught us to aspire after them.'[20] Speaking at the second session of the

Indian National Congress at Calcutta in 1886, Madan Mohan Malaviya remarked: 'It is not to the great British Government that we need demonstrate the utility, the expediency, the necessity of this great reform [the grant of representative institutions]. It might have been necessary to support our petition for this boon by such a demonstration were we governed by some despotic monarch, jealous of the duties, but ignorant and careless of the rights of subjects; but it is surely unnecessary to say one word in support of such a cause to the British Government, or the British Nation—to the descendants of those brave and great men who fought and died to obtain for themselves and preserve intact for their children those very institutions which, taught by their example, we now crave.... What is an Englishman without representative institutions? Why not an Englishman at all, a mere sham, a base imitation.... Representative institutions are as much a part of the true Briton as his language and his literature. Will any one tell me that Great Britain will, in cold blood, deny us, her free-born subjects, the first of these, when, by the gift of the two latter, she has qualified us to appreciate and incited us to desire it?'[21]

Political Ideas of English-Educated Indians in the Nineteenth Century

'What people call their principles', said Leslie Stephen, 'are really their pretexts for acting in the obviously convenient way.'[22] Because of their social origins, training and relative weakness, English-educated Indians in the 19th century took to the politics of 'prayer, petition and protest'. They realized that their number was small and their influence and resources were limited. They also realized that their interests (which they tended to identify with those of the entire population) for a long time to come would best be served by working through the British Raj, not against it. Discretion dictated the policy of liberalism and moderation (or what is currently described as 'competition and collaboration'). It was ably and eloquently enunciated by M.G. Ranade: 'Liberalism and Moderation will be [our] watchwords.... The spirit of Liberalism implies a freedom from race and creed prejudices and a steady devotion to all that seeks to do justice between man and man, giving to the rulers the loyalty that is due to the law they are bound to administer, but securing at the same time to the ruled the equality which is their right under the law. Moderation imposes the condition of never vainly aspiring after the impossible or after too remote ideals, but striving each day to take the next step in the order of natural growth by doing the work that lies nearest to our hands in a spirit of compromise and fairness. After all, political activities are chiefly of value not for the particular results achieved, but for the process of political education which is secured by exciting interest in public matters and promoting the self-respect and self-reliance of citizenship. This is no doubt a slow process, but all growth of new habits must be slow to be real.'[23]

Most English-educated Indians in the 19th century were inclined to admire England despite all its faults. To quote Ranade again: 'The British nation has its own faults and foibles, but there can be no question that in spite of these their national character has been formed by ages of struggle and self-discipline in a way which illustrates better than any other contemporary power the supremacy of what I have characterized as the reign of law. Just as in the individual the will when counselled and perfected by discipline and struggle becomes the law for the man who listens to it, so in the collective nation it is when the Sovereign's will is similarly counselled and perfected by the advice of the estates and the free expression of public opinion that it becomes the dominant power in the land to which every subordinate power has to yield obedience, and which it has to carry out ungrudgingly.... In the absence of such a discipline mere power and fortune have a tendency to make men feel giddy till oftentimes their very greatness helps to precipitate them into ruin. It is this moral principle which is the source of British greatness and its armour of protection. It is also the same moral element which inspires hope and confidence in the colonies and dependencies of Great Britain that whatever temporary perturbation may cloud the judgement the reign of law will assert itself in the end.'[24]

– When, however, the British tended to assert the doctrine of racial superiority and physical force, as, for example, most of them did in 1883 during the Ilbert Bill[25] crisis, they were solemnly warned: 'The aegis of British protection is an acknowledged necessity [for India], and none feel its need with greater emphasis than the leaders of native thought. But it is not as the representative of brute force, but of the order and genius of equal law, that we bow down to this supreme necessity. The argument of force, if it is resorted to as a justification for denying concessions in time, necessarily weakens itself for want of sanction. It cannot, therefore, be in the true interests of the Empire that the British rulers of the country should be allowed to isolate themselves in this fashion. The iron hand must be concealed under the soft glove, and the sword sheathed in the scabbard of wise policy.... There can be no question that a nation of 250 millions can never be permanently held down by sheer force, and sooner or later in God's Providence, and under the encouragement of British example and discipline, the people of this country must rise to the status of a self-governed community, and learn to control their own affairs in subordinate alliance with England. The transfer of power is inevitable, and the duty of statesmen is to graduate it in a way to make the transfer natural and easy, so as to keep up the continuity of national growth.'[26]

The attitude of English-educated Indians in the 19th century towards British rule was discerning and discriminating. Occasionally they even tried to turn its drawbacks to their advantage. In an interesting leading article entitled 'Why We Prefer British Rule to All Others', the *Indu Prakash* of Bombay wrote on 8 June 1885: 'British rule has given the land peace, organized an administration which acts like clock-work, and given security of life and property to its subjects and introduced good roads, railways and the telegraph.... Even the shortcomings of the British Government, grave as some of them are, partake, in a way, of the character of blessings.... The greatest claim of the British administration to our admiration and gratitude is that, with all its drawbacks, the spirit of progress is so inherent in it that those drawbacks may be said to carry the seeds of their own destruction. The rulers come from a country, where man did not advance suddenly or by fits and starts, but by slow and steady stages, which alone make progress permanent.... We have come in contact not only with a liberty-loving and progressive people, but with a nation who are the foes of fatality as much as we are blind followers of it.... It is a striking feature of the English character, however, that they unite to the sentimentality of the French the practical element of the German character. This feature shows itself in the liberal foresight and wisdom with which, soon after they conquered this country, they not only sent the schoolmaster abroad to educate and elevate the people, but admitted the right of the people of India to all places and political privileges. Selfishness has prompted many to shrink from even in theory and on paper laying down principles of government of such a liberal character. But it is said, "Yes, the English declared us free to hold all places and enjoy all privileges, but see how theory has differed from practice—how slow and reluctant they are to grant what they promised". Now, in answer to this it must be pointed out that, starting as we do with the advantage of liberal promises and pledges, the very slowness and reluctance with which they are granted, however disagreeable they may be, exercise on us an educating influence. We are no apologists at all for such slowness and reluctance, but if it has a darker side, it has a brighter one too. Heaven knows what would have become of us if our rulers had in a moment, without effort and trials on our part, given us everything. An advancing people like ours must not only advance by stages, but our best interests require that we must have difficulties and opposition to meet, for these serve to draw our attention to the shortcomings in us, and to accustom us to the privileges already acquired, while preparing us for the acquisition of new.... The reluctance and slowness keep us on the alert, bring us all together, and serve as instruments of political education, thus vivifying and educating us, and thereby accustoming us to the exercise of political rights. The progress that is made by us may be slow, but it is steady, and its greatest beauty is that it is made in the way in which all progress has been hitherto made by most nations, i.e. after repeated efforts and struggles, disappointments and oppositions.... There are defects in the administration, and some of them are grave enough. For instance, it is too costly; the people are disarmed and made to feel that they are a subject race; and from most of the highest appointments they are excluded. But what makes up for these defects is the feeling of confidence, inspired by past history, that British rule has in it the germs of solid and steady progress—that it is not only liberal and progressive, but the liberality and progress are pervaded by a spirit of conservatism, so essential to make progress steady—that it has never stood still and cannot stand still—that it may refuse a privilege for a time but it will not refuse it for ever. To put it shortly, the spirit of continuity, which is the most marked feature of that rule, enhances its popularity, in spite of its drawbacks.'[27]

Most English-educated Indians in the 19th century were not inclined to regard good government as a substitute for self-government or to tolerate British rule as anything else but a transition and a means to a higher end. In July 1883 the *Indu Prakash* wrote that those Indians who dreamt of the period when their country would be free and self-governing indulged in a speculation which was as wild as it was unprofitable, and that given a good and impartial rule, it did not matter whether that rule was foreign or native.[28] This elicited an immediate and angry rejoinder from one of its readers who wrote to the editor of the paper that the latter's remark had 'struck many of us here in the Deccan with much surprise' and added that the people of India were 'not such slavish creatures' as to accept the 'most untrue and unnatural dictum' that good government was preferable to self-government. He concluded by saying: 'All men are born free, but a people, who, at a given time and place, happens to possess some advantage in energy, organization, honor, etc. over other races, becomes, for the time being and only while the advantage lasts, a dominant and ruling race. The people of this country had their days of superiority and dominance, not many years since, and the torch of freedom, though it now glimmers before the dawn of superior light, is most certainly destined, under the rule of a people pre-eminent for the love of, and sympathy with, freedom, to revive and shed a glorious lustre over the land.'[29]

English-educated Indians in the 19th century, particularly those of the older generation, were full of admiration for British history and culture. They gratefully acknowledged the advantages derived by their country from the British connexion, though they were not unaware of its disadvantages. They frankly and loyally accepted British rule, because they were convinced that 'that rule alone could secure to the country the peace and order which were necessary for slowly evolving a nation out of the heterogeneous elements of which it was composed, and for ensuring to it a steady advance in different directions'.[30] They were even inclined to believe that their British rulers would prove to be their deliverers, and that slowly but surely they would admit Indians as equal sharers in their 'noble inheritance of freedom'. It was this gratitude for the past and hope for the future which made men like M.G. Ranade, S.N. Banerjea and P.M. Mehta speak of the British connexion as 'providential'.

English-educated Indians in the 19th century knew by heart the Charter Act of 1833,[31] the Queen's proclamation of 1858,[32] and all that Burke or Bright, Macaulay or Munro, Elphinstone or Malcolm had said about the purpose of British rule in India.[33] They almost shared the belief in England's avowed mission in India. They persuaded themselves to believe that the British people were essentially just, righteous and freedom-loving. Dadabhai Naoroji, the greatest figure in early Indian nationalism, was never tired of recalling how, at a time when Indians were too unenlightened even to ask for them, the statesmen of England had themselves declared that their policy in India was to be one of justice and equality, that the possession of India was a solemn trust with them, that the material and moral welfare of her people was the prime object of British rule, that Englishmen were not to form a governing caste in the country, and that Indians were to be helped to advance steadily to a position of equality, so that they might in due course acquire the capacity to govern themselves in accordance with the higher standards of the west. And his advice to his countrymen regarding their course of action was very simple: Remind the British government and the British people of their pledges and demand their fulfilment. Take your stand on British charters and proclamations and insist that the rights of British citizenship be granted to you. If the British bureaucracy in India refuses to listen to you, approach the British democracy in England. 'Nothing is more dear', he assured his people, 'to the heart of England—and I speak from actual knowledge—than India's welfare; and, if we only speak out loud enough and persistently enough, to reach that busy heart, we shall not speak in vain.'[34] To the people of Britain, he said: Indians are either 'British citizens or British helots'. Tell us frankly how you mean to treat us. Speak out 'with your English manliness' whether 'you really mean to fulfil the pledges given before the world, and in the name of God . . . or to get out of [them]'.[35]

English-educated Indians in the 19th century realized that their country still lacked some of the essential elements which constituted a nation, and the people did not yet have sufficient powers of coherence among themselves; therefore, a foreign rule like that of the British, which kept them together and at the same time assured them an efficient and moderately liberal government, must be looked upon not merely as a necessity, but as a beneficial necessity. They were convinced that there was no better alternative, indigenous or foreign, to British rule in India at that time, and that there was not likely to be any such alternative to British rule in India in the foreseeable future. Their patriotism therefore demanded that they should be loyal to the British Raj, for a sudden and premature termination of British rule was likely to be harmful to their own national interests. This very consideration imposed upon them the obligation of gradualism and constitutionalism. The *Kesari* of Poona, for example, wrote on 21 April 1885: 'We are thoroughly convinced that India cannot recover her national freedom in the real sense of the word independently of English protection, assistance and control. We are aware of the loss which we are at present suffering from British Government, yet we do not believe that our condition will be any better by the exchange of the British rule for that of any other nation. There is no other nation that we know of on the face of the earth which will govern a foreign country more liberally than the English, and since we are not in a position to gain our independence by fighting with the English or to preserve it when gained it is desirable that we should advance step by step by behaving in a conciliatory manner with the English.'[36]

It was natural of English-educated Indians in the 19th century, who had studied history and watched the progress of movements for national freedom and unity in various parts of the world, including the British Empire, to desire that their country, too, should become self-governing. But the Indian National Congress in its early years did not concern itself with the remote ideal of self-government. Whether it was due to the advice and influence of their English mentors or their own realism and timidity, early Congressmen contended themselves with demanding isolated reforms (though some of them could be very far-reaching in their consequences), such as the increased employment of Indians in the public services, the liberalization of the legislative councils, the separation of the executive from the judicial functions, the extension of trial by jury, the reduction in military expenditure, commissions for Indians in the army, etc. This does not, however, mean that the ideal of a self-governing India was not at the back of many minds. As we have already noted, early Indian nationalists were loyal because they were patriotic. Their faith in British justice, their avowals of loyalty to British rule and their fervid declarations about perpetuating it were inspired by their belief that their British rulers would train and enable them to govern themselves. Bhau Daji remarked in 1859. 'If it shall ever come to pass that by the advance of civilization in my country, it shall be her fitting task to undertake her own government, I have sufficient faith in the progress of humanity to believe, that England will come to recognize the fact, and generously disencumber herself of the gift of Empire, and will remain content with the glory of having educated my people into a nation of free men.'[37] In 1861 Lal Bihari Dey avowed his 'profound conviction' that Britain was 'consciously or unconsciously—preparing India for a higher and nobler state of national life' and added: 'We are loyal to the British Government *because* we aspire for national freedom.'[38] S. Rangachari said in 1864: 'Loyalty and Patriotism are not irreconcilable elements in a country like India. On the contrary, it is my firm belief that India's welfare depends upon the stability of British sway over her...[and] as soon as their wards are of age, they [the British] will be ready to rid themselves of their trust.'[39] 'I am loyal to the British Government,' said B.C. Pal in 1887, 'because with me loyalty to the British Government is identical with loyalty to my own people and my own country; because I believe that God has placed this Government over us for our salvation; because I know that without the help and tuition of this Government my people shall never be able to rise to their legitimate place in the commonwealth of civilized nations; because I am convinced that there is no other government on the face of the earth which so much favours the growth of infant nationalities, and under which the germs of popular Government can so vigorously grow as under the British Government.... I am loyal to the British Government, because I love self-government.'[40] C. Sankaran Nair emphasized the same point in 1897. Presiding over the Amraoti session of the Indian National Congress, he remarked: '... it should not be forgotten for a moment that the real link that binds us to England is the hope, the well-founded hope and belief, that with England's help we shall, and, under her guidance alone, we can attain national unity and national freedom.'[41] In his presidential address to the 1899 session of the Congress at Lucknow, R.C. Dutt observed:

'Educated India has practically identified itself with British rule, seeks to perpetuate British rule, is loyal to the British rule, as Lord Dufferin said, not through sentiment, but through the stronger motive of self-interest; because it is by a continuance of the British rule that educated India seeks to secure that large measure of self-government, that position among the modern nations of the earth, which it is our aim and endeavour to secure.'[42]

Though deep down in the heart of every Indian nationalist there was the fervent hope that his country would some day become self-governing, and individuals often gave expression to that hope, yet it was not until 1906 that the Congress as an organization explicitly committed itself to the objective of attaining self-government for India. The leaders of the early Congress were practical-minded enough to realize that India could not be fit for parliamentary self-government in their own lifetime. 'So far as I know,' A.O. Hume had written in 1888, 'no leading member of the National Congress thinks that for the next twenty years at any rate the country will require or be fit for anything more than the mixed Councils that have been advocated at the Congresses. But we, one and all, look forward to a time, say 50, say 70 years hence, when the Government of India will be precisely similar to that of the Dominion of Canada; when, as there, each province and presidency will have its local Parliament for provincial affairs, and the whole country will have its Dominion Parliament for national affairs, and when the only officials *sent out to India* from England will be the Viceroy and Governor-General. . . . To such a system we all look forward. . . . But the country is not nearly fit for all this yet. No one expects that a full Parliamentary system can possibly be introduced here under fifty years. . . .'[43] Convinced that their ultimate objective lay in the distant future and that it could only be achieved through the good will and co-operation of Englishmen, the leaders of the early Congress saw no need to encourage impatient idealism in their followers or to scare their rulers by raising the cry of self-government for India. Moreover, the rejection of the Irish Home Rule Bill by the British Parliament in June 1886—within a few months of the launching of the Congress movement—must have served its leaders as a warning against putting forward a similar demand for India. Nor were the long years of Tory dominance and jingo imperialism which followed in England the right time for the Congress to inscribe the ideal of self-government for India on its banner.

All that English-educated Indians in the 19th century hoped for in the immediate future was that the British Government in India would associate them more closely and extensively with itself in the tasks of administration and legislation, and that it would increasingly identify itself with Indian interests. They looked upon the Congress as 'the Council of the Nation', giving 'articulate voice to the constitutional opposition' in the country, whose functions 'must grow yearly till it deserves the full confidence of Government and persuades it to welcome the National Council by incorporating it into its system of administration'.[44]

While examining the political pronouncements of English-educated Indians in the 19th century, we should be careful to make due allowance for their rhetoric, for their contemporary style of speaking and writing, for the peculiar circumstances in which they were situated, and for the fact that most of their arguments were aimed at persuading their British masters to part with power. It has been fashionable for a long time to dismiss the leaders of political thought in India in the 19th century as fools or cowards. We claim to be wiser and braver than our ancestors. In a sense this is true; but only in a sense. Politics is the art of the possible. And the possible of the 1970s, or even of the 1920s, was not the possible of the 1890s. English-educated Indians in the 19th century had a fairly correct estimate of their situation and of what they could possibly say and do. They behaved as they did not because they were naive, credulous or cowardly, but because they were helpless. They were being ruled by the British and they tried to deal with them as best as they could. Two examples would suffice to illustrate the point I am trying to make. (i) Almost every schoolboy in India in the 19th century was familiar with the French revolutionary doctrine of the inherent and inalienable right of all men to be free, but the leaders of the early Congress thought it prudent and politic to claim self-government for Indians as a British constitutional right. (ii) When, in 1897, the British Socialist leader, H.M. Hyndman taunted Dadabhai Naoroji and his colleagues for their 'moderation' and told them that 'suave, moderate gentlemen don't get much attention',[45] Dadabhai Naoroji replied: 'All that you say is true, but Indians cannot do yet what you say. You should realize their position in every respect.... The Government are now openly taking up a Russian attitude, and we are helpless. The mass of the people yet do not understand the position. John Bull does not understand the bark. He only understands the bite, and we cannot do this.'[46]

The intellectual mentors of English-educated Indians in the 19th century were men like Edmund Burke, Jeremy Bentham, Adam Smith, Thomas Paine, John Stuart Mill, Auguste Comte, Henry Maine, Herbert Spencer, Giuseppe Mazzini, Richard Cobden, John Bright, Henry Fawcett, William Ewart Gladstone, and John Morley. True to their indigenous eclectic tradition, they borrowed from the west whatever they thought was good, sensible and useful in it and adapted it to their own needs and requirements. It would be wrong to regard them as mere imitators or blind followers of the west. For example, unlike some of their western mentors, most English-educated Indians in the 19th century did not subscribe to the free trade dogma *in toto*, advocated an active role for the state in educational, economic and social development, and tended to subordinate individual interest to communal welfare.

English-educated Indians in the 19th century deliberately chose the British constitutional model of political change. They were generous enough to give the British credit for many things which the latter did in India, such as the promotion of English education, the establishment of law, order, peace and security, the grant of civil liberties, the extension, however slow, of representative institutions, and the concession, at least in theory, of several other rights and privileges. But they were the most outspoken and relentless critics of the drawbacks of British rule in India. In their view, British rule had been economically an unmitigated disaster for India.[47] The steady drain of capital and resources from India to Britain was materially and morally debilitating. The British had ruined the Indian handicrafts. The almost total exclusion of Indians from higher employments in their own country was extremely injurious, unjust and unprecedented. The government demand on land was arbitrary, immoderate, uncertain and ruinous. British officials in India were arrogant, ignorant, exclusive and remote. The government expenditure on the higher services, both civil and military, was excessive. The British judicial system was exotic, incomprehensible, cumbersome and expensive. The principle of equality before the law was violated in cases involving Indians and Europeans. Having admitted Indians to the rights of British citizenship in theory, the British government was tardy in granting those rights to them in practice.

The Extremist Challenge

We have so far discussed what may be called the dominant political ideas of English-educated Indians in the 19th century. There were often minor voices of dissent and protest raised against them, but these were kept firmly in check. The British, by granting concessions to Indians before it was too late, tried to spike the guns of the extremists and to help the moderate-minded majority to remain in control of the situation. In this respect, British policy in India differed essentially from that in Ireland, where concessions had to be made to violence and extremism long after they had been denied to reason and moderation.

By the last decade of the 19th century, however, the climate of political opinion in India had begun to change. The number of English-educated Indians was fast increasing and job opportunities were not keeping pace with it. Repeated droughts and famines which took millions of lives and caused widespread misery, a devastating plague epidemic that raged for years, the economic hardships of the middle classes due to the rise in prices and increase in unemployment, and the high-handed methods of the British government (which were usually compared by the Indian press with those of the Tsarist Russian autocracy) in dealing with both rural and urban discontent—all served to transform radically the temper of English-educated Indians in the 1890s.

The Indian National Congress was the child of Gladstonian liberalism, but the first twenty years of its existence coincided with the ascendancy of the Tory party and the growth of jingo imperialism in Britain. Disappointed of the bureaucracy in India, the Congress had from its very inception tended to concentrate all its hopes on the democracy in Britain. The apathy of the latter, too, during this crucial early period, towards their very modest and reasonable demands, saddened and disillusioned those who had launched the movement with great hope and faith in the sense of justice and freedom of the British people. The younger nationalists began to develop a Faust-like mood.

Even in the later 1880s, criticism of Congress ideals, organization and methods of agitation was occasionally voiced in the Indian press, particularly in papers like the *Amrita Bazar Patrika*[48] of Calcutta and the *Kesari* and the *Marhatta*[49] of Poona, which tried to reflect lower middle class opinion, but in the 1890s it became more marked. For example, in 1893-4, in a series of articles published in the *Indu Prakash* of Bombay, entitled 'New Lamps for Old',[50] Aurobindo Ghose made a scathing attack on the Indian National Congress. He denounced its suppliant ways, accused its leaders of timidity, lack of vision and earnestness, and pronounced it to be an utter failure. 'The walls of Anglo-Indian Jericho', he wrote, 'stand yet without a breach, and the dark spectre of Penury draws her robe over the land in greater volume and with an ampler sweep.'[51] The Congress represented 'not the mass of the population, but a single and a very limited class'[52]—'our new middle class'—'journalists, barristers, doctors, officials, graduates and traders—who have grown up and are increasing with prurient rapidity under the aegis of the British rule'.[53] Aurobindo Ghose maintained that 'the Congress fails, because it has never been, and has made no honest endeavour to be, a popular body empowered by the fiat of the Indian people in its entirety'.[54] Instead of drawing on the revolutionary traditions of France, or even those of America, Ireland and Italy, the Congress had slavishly followed the English model, which was unsuited to India.[55] He summed up his formidable indictment of the Congress thus: 'I say, of the Congress, then, this,—that its aims are mistaken, that the spirit in which it proceeds towards their accomplishment is not the spirit of sincerity and wholeheartedness, and that the methods it has chosen are not the right methods, the leaders in whom it trusts, not the right sort of men to be leaders; in brief, that we are at present the blind led, if not by the blind, at any rate by the one-eyed.'[56] 'Our actual enemy', he insisted, 'is not any force exterior to ourselves, but our own crying weaknesses, our cowardice, our selfishness, our hypocrisy, our purblind sentimentalism. . . . Our appeal, the appeal of every high-souled and self-respecting nation, ought not to be to the opinion of the Anglo-Indians, no, nor yet to the British sense of justice, but to our own reviving sense of manhood, to our own sincere fellow-feeling . . . with the silent and suffering people of India.'[57] According to Aurobindo Ghose, 'our first and holiest duty' should be 'the elevation and enlightenment of the proletariate',[53] for the proletariate was 'the real key of the situation'.[59] 'Torpid he is and immobile; he is nothing of an actual force, but he is a very great potential force, and whoever succeeds in understanding and eliciting his strength, becomes by the very fact master of the future.'[60]

Aurobindo Ghose's fierce attack on the Congress in 1893-4, which foreshadowed the coming extremist challenge, was symptomatic of the rebellious feelings which were animating the younger generation in India. The latter soon found a leader in the formidable personality of Bal Gangadhar Tilak, with his emphasis on Hindu conservatism, mass appeal and direct action. The rise of radical nationalism in India in the 1890s was at once a conservative and a revolutionary phenomenon. It drew its inspiration, on the one hand, from the reaction towards Indian religion and Indian way of life, of which the chief exponents were Dayanand and Vivekanand. On the other hand, it tried to apply to the Indian situation methods of mass agitation and even terrorism borrowed from the west. The tide of western liberalism began to recede in India by the end of the nineteenth century. Men searched for the moral basis of nationalism and found it in native history, religion and institutions. The past became glorified and transfigured. Old gods and heroes were invoked to drive away alien rulers.

The failure of the older moderate leaders of the Congress to secure any substantial concessions from the British, encouraged younger men—first called 'radicals' but later known as 'Extremists'—to become increasingly critical of them, their ideals, and their methods of agitation and organization. The younger men were bitter against their elders at their inability to wrest concessions from the British government, and against their rulers for their attitude of indifference and hostility towards the demands of moderate men. They denounced the Congress as a mere four-day *tamasha*, organized by a few anglicized lawyers. They condemned its domination by an oligarchy. They hated its abject and academic tone. They accused its leaders of lacking in patriotism and of being interested mainly in the loaves and fishes of office. They wanted the Congress to become a mass organization, pursuing more self-reliant and vigorous methods of agitation, and clearly aiming at the freedom of the country. They demanded that the Congress should have a definite constitution and be more democratically controlled and conducted.

The controversy over ideals and methods within the Congress in the last decade of the 19th century was indicative of a deeper schism within the movement. It was essentially a conflict between palsied age and fiery youth, between an upper middle-class leadership and a lower middle-class following.

The forces of radical nationalism in India were to be aided in the first decade of the 20th century by the accidents of time and circumstance. The carrying out of the partition of Bengal by Lord Curzon in 1905, in spite of determined local protests, finally discredited the moderate methods of remonstrance and petition. It bred a spirit of resentment among the educated classes throughout India and brought them face to face with their rulers. The hopes aroused by the coming into power of a Liberal government in Britain towards the end of 1905 were disappointed when John Morley, the new secretary of state for India, declared the partition to be 'a settled fact'[61] and remarked that the transplantation of English institutions in India was 'a fantastic and ludicrous dream'.[62] The need for new and more determined methods of agitation came to be widely felt. Those who watched the triumphs of Japan, the revolutionary rumblings in Russia, the rise of the Sinn Fein movement in Ireland, the Egyptian struggle for freedom, the Young Turk revolt, the adoption of a constitution in Persia, the introduction of representative institutions in the Philippines, and the grant of responsible self-government to the Transvaal and the Orange River Colony could not but be filled with new-born aspirations for their country and prompted to more energetic action.

3

ALLAN OCTAVIAN HUME AND THE INDIAN NATIONAL CONGRESS

After talking about its long history, its adaptability and its political sophistication, an English writer on Indian history and politics remarked in 1973: 'Almost everything about the Congress is remarkable....'[1] The first and the most remarkable thing about the Indian National Congress is that it was founded by a foreigner and a member of the British Indian Civil Service. It provides probably the only instance in modern history of a nationalist party in a colonial territory organized and led for many years by a member of the ruling race. His name was Allan Octavian Hume.

I have been interested in Hume for many years now. For long I was interested in him because of his role in founding the Congress. Of late I have been busy examining his career as general secretary of the Congress from 1885 to 1906. This afternoon* I propose to tell you as briefly and as simply as I can about this remarkable man and his association with the Indian National Congress.

Herbert Butterfield once complained that he had known undergraduates who could easily find fault with the diplomacy of Bismarck, but who themselves were quite incapable of wheedling sixpence out of a college porter.[2] I have known many Indian intellectuals who have probably never given five minutes of their time or five rupees of their money to a public cause, but who dismiss Hume, who gave years of his life and spent thousands of pounds in India's cause, as a spy and an imperialist agent.

---

*A lecture delivered at the Nehru Memorial Museum and Library, New Delhi, on 18 February 1976.

If after listening to me you form a juster estimate of Hume I shall be happy.

Hume was a Scotsman. He was born in 1829. His father, Joseph Hume, had served in India. He was a jack of all trades. He came to India in 1797 as a doctor. He worked as a political officer and made money as a contractor. In ten years he earned £ 40,000 and returned to England in 1807. Joseph Hume purchased a seat in Parliament in 1812 and became the founder and leader of the Radical party. He remained an M.P. until his death in 1855. He used his money and influence to promote political and social reforms and to get jobs for his sons and nephews in India.

Allan Octavian Hume was a great admirer of his father, particularly of his radical politics. Hume studied medicine and even joined the navy for some time. But then he went to Haileybury—the college which trained British civilians for India—and at the age of twenty he arrived in Calcutta as a member of the Bengal Civil Service. The year was 1849 and Dalhousie was governor-general of India.

A year earlier—in 1848—there had been revolutions in many countries of Europe. Young Hume had shown a great deal of interest in these revolutions and in the Chartist movement at home. He even became a member of a revolutionary society.[3] This might have been one of the reasons why his father packed him off to India. Hume came to India as a member of the Bengal Civil Service, and he rose to be a secretary to the government of India. But he always remained a bit of a revolutionary—very unorthodox in his views and behaviour. He, however, hated violence. Freedom and progress through peace, order and brotherly love—this became his motto in India.[4]

Hume arrived in Calcutta in 1849 and stayed for some time with his cousin, James Hume. No sooner did he arrive in Calcutta than a 'white mutiny' broke out in that city. The Britons of Calcutta were up in arms against the government of India because the latter wanted that Britons and Indians should be equals before the law. Hume's cousin, James, was one of the few Britons who supported the government and the Indians, led by Ram Gopal Ghose.[5] So Hume had his first taste of a 'white mutiny' soon after his arrival in India in which his cousin sided with the Indians against the vast majority of his own countrymen. Hume was to play a far more remarkable role than did his cousin when another 'white mutiny' broke out in 1883 in connexion with the Ilbert Bill.

Hume was soon posted to the Etawah district in the North-Western Provinces, where he received his training in a police station, then as a tehsildar, and later as a sub-judge in a kutcherry. After his training was over he became assistant magistrate and collector at Etawah. Hume was a very energetic and popular official. He opened schools, orphanages and hospitals. He encouraged land redistribution and cotton cultivation. He even started a newspaper called the *People's Friend* in English, Hindi and Urdu. He was very friendly with the local zamindars, with whom he exchanged turbans.[6] Even the colonial bureaucracy had other tasks to perform besides collecting the taxes and maintaining law and order. But in May 1857, when Hume was joint magistrate and deputy collector in Etawah, came the mutiny. Indian troops at several stations turned against the British and they were joined in by the discontented elements in Indian society. The mutiny was soon converted into a rebellion in many parts of northern and central India.

Hume had several encounters with the rebels and distinguished himself by his courage and bravery (not his cruelty). For this he was later awarded the C.B. Hume's Indian friends helped him in many ways, both in fighting the rebels and in escaping death at their hands by getting away safely to Agra. Visiting India soon after the revolt, G.O. Trevelyan recorded the reputation which Hume had acquired for his conduct during the upheaval. He wrote in his book *The Competition Wallah*: 'Mr. Hume of Etawah, who was blamed by many for excess of leniency, but who so bore himself that no one could blame him for want of courage, distinguished himself by keeping down the number of executions in his district to seven, and by granting the culprits a fair trial. These he treated with fatherly tenderness, for he invented a patent drop for their benefit; so that men prayed—first, that they might be tried by Mr. Hume, and next, that, if found guilty, they might be hanged by him!'[7]

The revolt of 1857 was a traumatic experience for Hume in several ways: first, he had himself narrowly escaped death at the hands of the rebels, thanks to the help given by his Indian friends; and, second, he had seen, as he later put it, 'the whole grand apparatus of a highly civilized government shrivel up in a single month over a vast country, far larger and more populous than Great Britain, like some emblazoned scroll cast into a furnace'.[8] Throughout his later life Hume was haunted by the precariousness of British rule and the fear of another and more terrible revolt in India. And he bent all his energies to seeing to it (*a*) that there was no repetition of 1857; and (*b*) that Indians gained self-government without violence and bloodshed. But his experiences during the revolt did not embitter Hume in any way towards India or Indians—probably because his Indian friends had stood by him in his time of danger and distress and saved his life.

What did Hume look like in the prime of his life? If you have not seen his photograph, let me try to describe his features to you. He was tall and erect. He had a round face. His eyes were beady, squinting and alert. He had a protruding walrus moustache which engulfed his face and gave him a rather authoritative and pontifical air.

Hume was a great traveller, a keen hunter (though he later became a vegetarian), a botanist and an ornithologist. No subject was too high or too low to interest him: Sanskrit literature, tribal customs, cotton cultivation, colonization, hospitals, narcotics, occultism, and yoga. Unlike most British officials in India, Hume did not regard India as a 'land of exile'. He genuinely loved the country and its people. He had the quality of making friends with Indians, high or low, young or old, educated or uneducated. Hume wielded a facile pen. He wrote long minutes and he regularly contributed to the press. A collection of his known writings would fill several handsome volumes.

Hume remained collector of Etawah from 1850 to 1867. Then he became chief commissioner of customs from 1867 to 1869. This job enabled him to tour the whole country and know India as few Indians or Europeans knew it. In late 1870 Lord Mayo, the then viceroy, appointed Hume officiating home secretary in the government of India. The appointment of a N.-W.P. civilian in preference to Bengal civilians as home secretary was not liked by many Bengal civlians such as Ashley Eden and Rivers Thompson.[9] They became very jealous of Hume and later took revenge on him.

Hume worked as secretary in the home department only for a few months. But the 1870s were very difficult and anxious years for the British in India. There was a great deal of discontent in the country because of rising prices, increasing taxation, famines, agrarian disturbances, the Wahabis, and the Kukas. This further convinced Hume that the British Raj was tolerated, but not liked, by the Indian people, and that its roots were in water.

Knowing that Hume was keenly interested in agriculture, Mayo appointed him secretary in the department of agriculture, revenue and commerce. It was called the *et cetera* department. Hume remained in this office from 1871 to 1879. Hume was anxious to organize a genuine and efficient department of agriculture and he had some very sensible ideas about improving agriculture which he published in 1879 as a pamphlet called *Agricultural Reform in India*. But all his schemes were frustrated by the lack of finances and the hostility of his official colleagues.

Hume had many qualities which were recognized even by his enemies. He was intelligent, industrious, experienced, and a good organizer. He was energetic, self-reliant, original and far-sighted. He wrote well. He was courageous and devoted. He disliked humbug and red-tape. But like many men of talent, Hume was slightly eccentric and egoistical. He was a nonconformist. He was outspoken. He delighted in controversy. He used to say: 'What good was ever yet worked out without diversity of opinion.'[10] He was rather tactless in handling his colleagues and he could not suffer fools gladly. His fellow officials did not like him. They accused him of being arrogant, cantankerous, crotchety, petulant, unbearable, untruthful and generally lacking in official decorum. And ultimately Hume's fellow officials combined to get rid of him.

In February 1872 Lord Mayo, the viceroy, was murdered by a Wahabi. Five months earlier (in September 1871) the chief justice of Bengal had also been murdered by a Wahabi. Hume knew that there was a great deal of discontent in India because of all sorts of reasons, and that unless remedial steps were taken it was likely, sooner or later, to blow up into some terrible catastrophe.

When Northbrook became viceroy, Hume wrote him a letter on 1 August 1872 in which he frankly told him that the British were not loved in India and that they were ruling solely by virtue of their artillery and bayonets. 'A studied and invariable disregard, if not actual contempt for the opinions and feelings of our subjects, is at the present day the leading characteristic of our Government in every branch of the administration.... The end may not be yet; it is possible under God's guidance, whose instruments we are, that...the evil days will be tided over, and the people weaned from their anger with us, and as education spreads, somewhat to appreciate our measures, before their opportunity comes. But the danger is great and real and who can tell what the morrow will bring. You are driving a coach that is utterly top-heavy and the slightest jolt, a single stone under a single wheel will probably upset it...I am strongly convinced that the fate of the empire is trembling in the balance and that at any moment some tiny cloud may grow with inconceivable rapidity and spread over the length and breadth of the land a storm raining down anarchy and devastation.'[11]

Hume had serious differences of opinion with Northbrook and his successor, Lytton. His official enemies—Ashley Eden, Rivers Thompson, and the Strachey brothers—succeeded in poisoning the ears of Lytton and in 1879 the department of agriculture, revenue and commerce was abolished in order—as Lytton put it—to get rid of a very troublesome secretary. Hume was demoted and sent back to Allahabad as member of the board of revenue.[12] Little did Lytton realize what a great service he was doing to India.

Hume's demotion in 1879 had undoubtedly something to do with his later behaviour as a political agitator. For one thing, it cut short his official career and set him free to devote his time and energies to the cause of Indian nationalism. But it must be remembered that his radicalism, his sympathetic interest in India and her people, his dissatisfaction with British policies in India, and his obsession with the probability of another bloody revolt in India long predated that melancholy event.

Hume had always been a deeply religious man. His health was not very good. He suffered of stomach and chest complaints. He was unhappy because he had no son.[13]

Now his official career was ruined at the age of 50. As chance would have it, at this very time Colonel Henry S. Olcott and Madame Helena P. Blavatsky arrived in India and began propagating their new cult of Theosophy. Hume was attracted to Theosophy and its two remarkable exponents. What particularly appealed to Hume in Theosophy was its emphasis on eclecticism, i.e. its principal tenet regarding the essential unity of all religions and the universal brotherhood of man.[14]

While Hume was secretary to the government of India he had in the early 1870s purchased a house in Simla (in Jakko), called Rothney Castle. Here he kept his unique collection of birds and plants. In 1881 Hume sought premature retirement and instead of returning to Britain decided to settle in Simla.

In Rothney Castle, Simla, Hume lived with his wife and only daughter, attending to his birds and plants, practising occultism and entertaining guests. Madame Blavatsky and Colonel Olcott used to be regular visitors for a few years. It was in Rothney Castle that Madame Blavatsky performed her famous 'Brooch Miracle'.[15]

Sometimes a man's most active and creative phase in life begins after his retirement from service. So it was with Hume. He had always been an enthusiast. Whether it was botany or ornithology, vegetarianism or Theosophy, Hume did nothing half-heartedly. It was not long before his active brain found another cause to engage it.

On 8 June 1880 Lord Ripon relieved Lord Lytton as viceroy of India. This was probably the only time in British Indian history that the viceroyalty changed hands in Simla. Hume became very friendly with the new occupant of Peterhof, which was then the Viceregal Lodge. By temperament and training the two men were very different from each other. But they had three things in common: (a) a staunch faith in Gladstonian liberalism; (b) a strong spiritual quest; and (c) an ardent desire for the good of India.

Ripon was a radical and a socialist. He came out to India inspired by a sense of mission that he had been chosen by God to do some good to the people of India. Ripon was not only a deeply religious and God-fearing man, he was also a very far-sighted statesman. He had the intelligence to realize that a new spirit was abroad in India, and that the greatest problem facing the British administration in the country was how to deal with English-educated Indians. He felt that unless safe, constitutional and legitimate outlets were provided for the discharge of the growing Indian ferment, it was likely to run into dangerous channels. Ripon also sympathized with the aspirations of educated Indians and believed that British rule must prepare India for self-government.[16]

A nobler viceroy than Ripon never came to India. In order to enable you to judge for yourself what kind of man he was, I shall read out to you an extract from a private and confidential letter which he wrote on 9 January 1883 to his intimate radical friend, Thomas Hughes: '... my view of the work in which I am engaged is that I am laying the foundations upon which may hereafter be built a more complete system of self-government for India which may convert what is now a successful administration by foreigners into a government of the country by itself. If in one or two generations, nay even if in another century, we can accomplish that undertaking, and can render India self-governing upon just and equal principles, our work here will have been done, and it will matter little whether we remain to lead and guide the people whom we shall then have taught to rule themselves, or whether we withdraw, as guardians who lay down their trust, after having performed not unsuccessfully, the mighty task which, as I believe, God has given us to do in this land. These are visions doubtless of a distant future, and it may be that they will not be realized, but I have all my life believed that no great work can be accomplished unless the ideal of it which a man sets before him is the highest and noblest within his reach, and I could not labour with any heart even at laying the corner-stone of the fair edifice which rises before my eyes unless I were encouraged by the hope that what is now my dream may become a reality when I have long finished my time on earth, and that perhaps it may be given me, if I am not too unworthy, to look down hereafter on the completion of the task which I have now begun.'[17]

Ripon's liberal and pro-Indian measures, particularly his extension of local self-government and the so-called Ilbert Bill (which sought to remove judicial disqualifications based on race distinctions), aroused a great deal of opposition from the British in India and some of them even planned to kidnap the viceroy and deport him to England.

In May 1882 Hume, who had already retired from service and was living like a hermit in Simla, came out of his retirement and began acting as an intermediary between the viceroy and Indians. Ripon used him effectively for ascertaining and organizing Indian opinion in favour of his liberal policies and for telling Indians what he himself because of his official position could not tell them directly and publicly.

Educated Indians were so impressed with Ripon's sincerity and honesty of purpose and his desire to do all in his power for the good of India that they called him 'Mahatma' and 'Ripon the Righteous'. And when he left India in December 1884 Indians gave him a send-off which no other viceroy of India has ever got—not even Mountbatten. Hume played the leading role in organizing this farewell for Ripon.

Theosophy had already brought Hume into close contact with the leading Indians of his time. The events of Ripon's viceroyalty served to widen and deepen this contact.

The developments during Ripon's viceroyalty made it clear to Ripon and Hume that Indians must organize themselves better in order to protect and promote their interests. Indians themselves had already learnt this lesson (recent events had only served to underline it) and several attempts had been made during the last few years to bring about greater concert and co-operation among people in different parts of the country. But these attempts had not been very successful mainly for want of the right leadership. Now Hume provided this leadership.

By the early 1880s sufficient modernization had taken place in India, especially as regards the spread of education, the growth of mass communications, increased urbanization and the rise of the new professional classes, to provide conditions for the creation of a national organization. Some efforts in that direction were already being made. What was needed for these efforts to be crowned with success was 'the occurrence of political crises of systemic magnitude' and, since human institutions are the creation of men of flesh and blood and do not spring to life spontaneously, the emergence of the right leadership. Both these needs were fulfilled during Ripon's viceroyalty.

Hume was not the first person either to conceive the idea of an all-India political organization or to attempt to realize it, nor did he stand alone, but his were the authority, the energy and the organizing skill that accomplished the seemingly impossible. But we are anticipating events. Let us see how it was done.

While Ripon was still in India—in late 1884—Hume wrote to his Indian friends in various parts of the country, outlining his scheme for a national organization. Fortunately, we have one such letter in the possession of Shri S.B. Bhat of Dhulia. The letter was written by Hume on 16 November 1884 to S.H. Chiplonkar, secretary of the Poona Sarvajanik Sabha, which was then the leading political association in India. A few extracts from this letter will show clearly what Hume was aiming at.

'I am very sorry to learn that you did not get any letter embodying my ideas about "linking in". They were the result of a good deal of thought and though I have talked the matter over with a good many men I wrote to you first as the leading Sabha in India. I have not now the time to write the whole thing out again but this is of less consequence because I hope to talk the whole matter over with you next month. I may tell you in strict confidence that Lord Ripon has made a point of my coming down to meet him at Bombay. Though he knows Lord Dufferin well and though the latter's letters to him since his appointment seem to promise well for the National Cause, yet we cannot feel any surety as to the line he is likely to pursue until Lord Ripon has thoroughly discussed the situation with him.

'I propose to make a little private tour—having made the personal acquaintance of all the earnest men in Bombay and having discussed the situation with them—I propose to come to Poona and do the same to you. Then go on to Madras, Calcutta, Patna (perhaps Dacca), Benares, Allahabad, Agra, Delhi, Amritsar and Lahore—possibly also Lucknow and some other places. I want to make a practical effort towards that linking in which has now become a matter of vital importance to us....

'But as you know I am no notoriety-seeker—that I believe that all the best work is done in secret and silence, as is nature's work—and that I want to effect this journey without anyone but those leaders of thought with whom I deal, knowing anything about it....This trip will be rather troublesome to me because I daresay you know, since I became a regular Chela 3 years or more ago, I eat neither fish, flesh, fowl, eggs, onions, Masoor ki dal, etc. And it is difficult on railway journey to get pure food—and one meets with great impertinence simply because one's ways are different from those with whom one has unavoidably to come into contact.'[18]

Hume's 'linking in' project took him round the country from November 1884 to April 1885. He visited almost every province of India. On his return to Simla, in early May, he met Dufferin, who had succeeded Ripon as viceroy of India, and told him that he and his Indian friends were thinking of meeting in a congress at the end of the year in Poona.[19]

Before leaving India in December 1884 Ripon had already told Dufferin about Hume, his great knowledge of India and Indians, and advised Dufferin to keep in touch with Hume. Hume and

Dufferin met frequently. They wrote to each other regularly. At this time they were on friendly terms, though later differences cropped up (they were aggravated by jealous officials) and Dufferin turned against Hume.

When Hume told Dufferin about his plan of a congress to be held in Poona in December 1885, Dufferin approved of it, saying that it would furnish the government with something like an authoritative expression of the views and wishes of the educated and intelligent classes throughout India. But Dufferin advised Hume against two things. Hume's idea was that the governor of Bombay, Lord Reay, in whose province the congress was going to meet and who was reputed to be friendly to Indian aspirations, should preside over the gathering; and that the congress should be attended by both officials and non-officials. Dufferin advised Hume not to have Reay as chairman, and also not to invite officials to the congress, because both these things were likely to embarrass the persons concerned.[20]

Having won the approval of the viceroy, Hume issued a circular inviting his chosen friends and associates to the proposed conference in Poona. He then went to England to acquaint Ripon and other Liberal leaders with the progress of his plans and also to organize an Indian parliamentary party in London. He returned to India in the first week of December 1885.

The first Indian National Congress was to be held in Poona in the last week of December 1885. But fate deprived Poona of the honour of hosting the first Congress. An outbreak of cholera there forced the organizers to shift the venue to Bombay at the eleventh hour.

The first Congress met from 28 to 30 December 1885 in the hall of the Gokuldas Tejpal Sanskrit College, above Gowalia Tank, in Bombay. It was presided over by Hume's close Bengali friend, W.C. Bonnerjee. Most of the 70 odd delegates who came to attend it and met *in camera* did not even know each other personally in advance. But Hume knew all of them.

Without making himself unduly prominent, Hume dominated the first Congress and he continued doing so for many years. He brought to bear upon his self-imposed task the efficiency of a British civil servant, a tireless energy even in old age, his great organizing skill, and his unequalled knowledge and love of India.

Hume acted as general secretary of the Congress from the

very beginning. About a month before the Congress was to meet, Hume would go over to the town where the meeting was scheduled to be held, see to it that everything was properly organized—from the construction of the *pandal* to the arrangements for seating, boarding, lodging, and the drafting of resolutions. Though he seldom intervened in the public proceedings of the Congress, he stage-managed the whole show. After the Congress was over, he would return to Simla and write out the report of the session, with a long introduction.

As the chief executive head of the Congress, Hume looked after the correspondence, the publicity, the organization, and the finances of the party. The Congress kept him busy from year's end to year's end. In fact, Hume was for many years the only Congressman who devoted his whole time to political work. It was not until 1901 that we had an Indian doing the same. He was G.K. Gokhale, who resigned his job at the Fergusson College, Poona, and became a wholetime worker of the Congress.

Hume was the leader of the Congress from its establishment in 1885 until the early 1890s, when he left India, and he exercised over it what Ananda Charlu called a 'loving and lovable despotism'.[21] But he was by no means a dictator and the Congress had a mind of its own from the very start. For example, Hume was opposed to the permanent settlement of the land revenue in Bengal, but the Congress approved of it and wanted its extension to the other provinces of India. Again, in 1891 Hume suggested that because of financial difficulties the annual sessions of the Congress should be postponed for a couple of years, but the Congress openly defied him over this issue. Similarly, the vast majority of the Congress leaders did not approve of Hume's aggressive methods of agitation, his open support of the Age of Consent Bill in 1891 and some of his writings in 1892.

In his famous controversy in 1888 with Sir Auckland Colvin, then lieutenant-governor of the North-Western Provinces, Hume described the Congress as 'a safety-valve for the escape of great and growing forces, generated by our own action'.[22] This has been seized upon by certain historians as revealing the true character of the Congress and the real motive of Hume in establishing it—i.e. as an attempt to sidetrack or abort the revolutionary upsurge in India. Yes, Hume did think of the Congress as a safety-valve, as providing overt constitutional channels through which the surging tide of new ideas and aspirations in India may flow, 'not to ravage and destroy but to fertilize and regenerate'.[23] He had seen one revolt and he did not want to see another. But he did not think of the Congress merely as a safety-valve. In several of his private letters and public pronouncements he referred to the Congress as 'the national movement' and 'the national party' which was intended to weld India into a nation and to secure for it home rule or dominion status in about half a century.[24]

Hume believed that situated as India and Indians were in the late 19th and early 20th century, they could only take recourse to constitutional agitation—to what was later on dubbed as 'mendicant politics'. In January 1906 a young Indian resident in England, named S.R. Rana, wrote an angry letter to Sir William Wedderburn, whose name is imperishably associated with that of Hume in the Indian nationalist movement, criticizing Congress methods. Wedderburn sent that letter to Hume with the comment that it was a melancholy result of despotic rule that it produced Bhownagrees on the one hand and Krishnavarmas on the other. Hume's comment on this is significant. He wrote: 'If there were only 3 or 4 hundred thousand of them out of the 270 millions, ready to sacrifice their own interests—ready to fight—ready to die nobly in the cause—I would agree with him—but as there are only at most a dozen, who are ready to do even as much as Gokhale does—and not one who is ready to fight to the death—our line of proceeding is the only possible.'[25]

After his retirement from the Indian Civil Service in 1882 Hume had settled in Simla. He was not a healthy man. He was getting old. His only child—a daughter—got married. His wife died in 1891. He was very lonely. Hume developed serious differences with the government of India. Dufferin turned hostile and publicly criticized him in 1888. British officials hated him. In February 1892 he issued a secret circular to the members of the Congress party, talking about the growing poverty and discontent and the inevitability of an agrarian uprising in India, which the government considered to be seditious.[26] While the government of India thought of deporting him, angry Tory M.P.s demanded that he be tried and hanged as a traitor.

Hume also developed serious differences of opinion with his Indian colleagues, who felt that he was too impulsive and radical. He had already annoyed some of the orthodox Indian leaders by his enthusiastic support of the Age of Consent Bill in 1891. His circular of February 1892 and his introduction to the report of the 1891 Congress were disapproved of by many lead:ng Congressmen.[27]

Both Hume and his Indian colleagues began to realize that, though Hume had performed a unique and significant role in the early stages of the Congress, his leadership of the movement had serious drawbacks and limitations. His style and technique of agitation were rather unusual, and there were modes of social and political mobilization which he, being a foreigner, could not attempt. Because of all these and other developments Hume left India in 1892. He returned for the 1893 Congress at Lahore and finally departed from the country in March 1894. He never returned to India again. He died in 1912.

But even after Hume returned to England and settled there, he continued to work for the Congress. In fact, he remained general secretary of the Congress until 1906, when ill health forced him to give up the job. And he laboured for India along with Wedderburn and Naoroji in the British Committee of the Congress. He never accepted the presidency of the Congress and he scornfully rejected the proposal to erect a memorial to him in India.[28]

Hume occasionally sent messages to Congressmen. Their invariable burden was: Fight on; hammer on; do not lose faith; be united and self-reliant; be bold to say and do what you feel to be right in the interests of your country regardless of who blesses and who bans; fear nothing except being false to yourselves and your country; appreciate the good work of all who stand in any degree upon your platform—of all who, no matter what their race or creed or office, have the good of India's people at heart. Often he scolded Congressmen as a parent or headmaster would scold children. In 1903 when the Congress movement was in the doldrums and gloom and despair reigned in India, Hume issued a 'Call to Arms' for Indians, in which he said: 'You are, most of you, alas! it seems to me never more than half in earnest. You are not prepared for self-sacrifice, you lack mutual trust. You have indeed ever eagerly clamoured for and vainly clutched the Crown, but how many of you will touch the Cross with even your fingertips?'[29]

The last pen-portrait of Hume, a few months before his death in July 1912, is by the Bengali leader Bhupendranath Basu: 'In 1911 I was commissioned by my friends in Bengal to proceed to England in anticipation of the Royal visit to agitate for the reconsideration of the question of the partition of Bengal. Mr. Allan Hume was then in his eighty-fifth [sic] year. He was suffering from very, very bad health. For nearly 20 years, he and I had not met; but he travelled all the way from his home to meet me in London. In the committee room of the British Committee of the Congress he had caused to be assembled a large and distinguished gathering of members of Parliament. I went there unknown to them. There after 20 years I saw Mr. Hume and with the impulse and instinct of an Oriental I bowed my head to the ground and took the dust of his feet. Well, I saw tears rolling down his cheeks; he stretched his arms forward and embraced me on his bosom. Even now I feel that warm breath on my forehead and I feel the warm touch on my breast, and the members of the House of Commons who had not witnessed a scene like that stood surprised and moved at the bond of affection and reverence that bound me and Mr. Allan Hume.... When I was coming away, I went to pay my last respects to him at his house in Norwich. There also in the gathering gloom of the evening as I bade him good-bye I knew that we had no reasonable expectation of meeting on this side of life. I bade him good-bye in the simple style of an Indian and asked for his blessing. He said, "Bhupendra Nath, who am I and what, that I can give you a blessing! All that I can do is to ask Him who sees all hearts to give you His blessing and mine. I am old; you are also getting old. We may never meet"; and he said, "Bhupendra Nath good-bye. If for ever, then for ever." These are the last words that I heard from Mr. Hume before I left England.'[30]

Reconstructing the story of Hume's life is not an easy task. The papers of Hume—even those with the help of which Wedderburn wrote Hume's biography in 1913—are no longer available. A great deal of time and effort is required to collect and ascertain such simple facts as I have mentioned above. I have contented myself with describing what sort of man Hume was and how he worked for the Indian National Congress and for India. I have deliberately avoided the many controversies connected with the career of Hume. Before I close, allow me to read out to you a couple of Hume's poems and certain passages from his writings (see Appendices I-IV).

APPENDIX I

AWAKE

Sons of Ind, why sit ye idle,
Wait ye for some Deva's aid?
Buckle to, be up and doing!
Nations by themselves are made!

Are ye Serfs or are ye Freemen,
Ye that grovel in the shade?
In your own hands rest the issues!
By themselves are nations made!

Ye are taxed, what voice in spending
Have ye when the tax is paid?
Up! Protest! Right triumphs ever!
Nations by themselves are made!

What avail your wealth, your learning,
Empty titles, sordid trade?
True self-rule were worth them all!
Nations by themselves are made!

Are ye dazed, or are ye children,
Ye, that crouch, supine, afraid?
Will your childhood last for ever?
By themselves are nations made!

Ask no help from Heaven or Hell!
In yourselves alone seek aid!
He that wills, and dares, has all;
Nations by themselves are made!

Sons of Ind, be up and doing,
Let your course by none stayed;
Lo! the Dawn is in the East;
By themselves are nations made!

The Old Man's Hope
(Calcutta, 1886)

APPENDIX II

THE STAR IN THE EAST

Robed in mourning, crowned with ashes,
Night-enshrouded, India weeps,
Rolls the storm, the lightning flashes,
Still the nation heedless sleeps.

Has, she cries, this bitter tempest,
Has this cruel night no end,
Must pain ever rack this sad breast,
Will none save me, none befriend?

Once I reigned the Orient's empress
Ah! The glory of that past!—
Crowned with learning, science, gladness,
Woe is me! too bright to last.

Crownless, now, forlorn I'm weeping,
Dust and ashes all my meed,
Sluggard sons ignobly sleeping
In a slough of selfish greed.

Oh heaven! Are hope and justice dead,
Shall a new day waken never?
Ah children! shall your mother plead,
Plead vainly, thus, for ever?

Weep no more! A star is gleaming
In the pearling eastern skies,
And thy sons, long spell-bound dreaming,
Hear, at last, thy call ARISE!

Weep no more, my love, my glory,
Weep no more dear mother-land,
See thy children rally round thee
Heart to heart and hand in hand.

The Star in the East
(Calcutta, 1886)

APPENDIX III

HUME ON THE POVERTY OF INDIA

'As I move, silently and unnoticed, from one district and province to other districts and other provinces of this great Empire, amidst much that seems to me to be regretted, much that I cannot but think wrong, one feature of Indian life of the present day forces itself everywhere on my attention, with an intensity that overpowers and almost excludes all other sensations. Struggle against it as I will, and as I have for years now struggled, one gloomy shadow overclouds all my waking hours, one hateful spectre haunts all my dreams. Whatever I do, wherever I go one sorrowful fact stares me in the face and withers all the flowers of my life. I have endeavoured to drape it over with more pleasing and presentable facts, but the best of these, that I could procure, look only as little scraps of coloured rags, sparsely scattered here and there upon a vast and rugged mountain side. I have tried to forget, to ignore it, to live and float upon the surface, without looking down into or giving heed to the depths below; but all in vain. Year after year, the heartache has grown within me, till now at last, urged by a power stronger than myself, I feel that I must speak, and speak out. I have long hesitated to do this, for until recently I have been unable to see my way—unable to set before myself any distinct goal, any definite course of action offering any hopes of mitigating the misery that so oppresses me. But the time of doubt has passed. I see my way, my goal, the definite course of action clearly enough now . . .

'. . . at this moment there are fully fifty millions of your countrymen who are moaning hunger-stricken, for better times that *never* come, who with one single dirty rag about their loins, shiver even in this warm clime, in the chill evenings and raw mornings, who can never fill their own stomachs, who, worse still, have to see the one joy and crown of their lives, their little children, unfed, unclothed, to watch them, weakened by insufficient nourishment, fall innocent victims to the demons of disease that are ever prowlling through our famished population.

'Ah men! well-fed and happy! with, so to say, scarce a sorrow or a care (for what are your troubles to theirs?) do you at all realize the dull misery of these countless myriads? From their births to their deaths, how many rays of sunshine think you chequer their gloom-shrouded paths? Toil, toil, toil; hunger, hunger, hunger; sickness, suffering, sorrow, these alas! are the key-notes of their short and sad existence, and who can deny that for these fifty odd millions and more, it were better that they had never been born, better, almost, that stones were now tied around their necks, and that they were cast into the rivers and drowned!

'You, who are comparatively so well off ... *do* you, *can* you, picture to yourselves the hopeless sadness of these your unhappy brethren's hard and suffering lives? Do you feel for them? Are you men, or stones? I will not say animals, for all know how much many animals sympathize in the sufferings of their fellows; but are you stones? And if not, how is it that with this ocean of misery surging beneath your feet, you are all so smiling and comfortable? How is it that you are apparently making no single effort to remove this national calamity, and—in so far as you calmly tolerate it—disgrace?'

The Old Man's Hope
(Calcutta, 1886)

APPENDIX IV

HUME'S FAREWELL TO INDIA

Bombay, 18 March 1894

'This day I have to bid farewell not only to you, my friends, but to all the thousands of friends, spread over the length and breadth of this vast empire—friends with whom I have laboured in India's sacred cause for so many years. . . . It is not only Bombay that I am leaving, I fear, for ever, but that dear India in which, with brief sojourns in England . . . I have spent forty-five years of my life. . . . How can I forget the happy hours, the friendships, the love that India has given me, or how fail to remember that here sleep my own dearest? India is sacred to me not alone by that one pine-shrouded grave in the far distant hills, but scarcely less so by the memories of other dear friends and fellow-labourers, bright stars, too early lost alike to India and to me—Girija Bhusan Mookerjee, George Yule, Ajoodhia Nath, Telang, and others no less beloved, though less well known to fame—India that has become an integral and the best part of me, myself, my thoughts, my hopes—India and India's people, that, with all their faults and failings, I still so dearly love. And from all this, tomorrow, I am to wrench myself away—for ever. You can hardly, my friends, understand what the sadness of this parting is to me. . . . To you my going is but as one dim star dropping from your firmament, in which thousands of brighter luminaries still shine. But to the poor lost star it means the end of all things, and when I think of this final parting from you, from everything that for years has filled my heart, it seems as if all colour were fading out of life.

'I must confess that to me the present outlook promises ill for the speedy fruition of our most cherished hopes and aspirations. The great bulk of the leading politicians of both parties in England are in public life the veriest humbugs, talking like angels, but ready to do the devil's work, to sacrifice principle to party. . . . Taking them in the gross there is little to choose between the professional ministerial gangs of both parties. They are politically dishonest to the core. That anything like full justice will ever be done to India until our working men put forth in earnest the power now vested in them, and bring into office a real democratic ministry, I do not suppose and never for a moment have supposed. ... I wish India to be prepared for the re-entry of the Imperialists into power, and the consequent arrest for a time of all progress in the direction in which we long to travel; but when it comes be not disheartened—contain your souls in patience—work on steadily—organize—provide funds for the work in England—never relax your efforts ... and rest assured that this time of frost shall not endure for ever, but shall melt away before the rising sun of democracy.... The day of democracies is opening out. We may have to wait but we are on the winning side. The spirit of the age is behind you. If only you the people of India do your duty, India, our beloved India shall yet be free and happy. [Hume even prophesied the coming war in Europe and advised Indians to be on the side of the British in that calamity.]

'A great and honourable task lies before you. You have heard it said that,

"They would be free
Themselves must strike the blow."
but I say to you,
"They would be free
Must first deserve to be so."

Do you as yet so deserve? Lover as I am of India and India's children, I cannot answer this question as I would wish to. No, my friends, you, the people of India must raise your general level, physical, mental, moral, above the pitch at which it now stands, before you can either deserve to be or really call yourselves free.

'What have you to do? Perhaps you know this better than I do, but yet, as a father parting for ever from his children that he loves, and whose future he fears for, I will not shirk from trying to tell you some of the things which it seems to me that you must first and foremost do. I am an old man. I have lived my life amongst you and perhaps know as much of India as a whole as anyone living; but for all that I do not pretend to dogmatize—I only tell you what I who love you believe to be essential to your ultimate success. If in doing so I offend any of my strictly orthodox friends I shall deeply regret it; but I have to say truly what I honestly think and believe—the welfare of the nation is the highest law. I care not about orthodoxy or heterodoxy. . . . what I care for is that India should become free and happy and grow great and glorious. . . .

'First, you must have the sound body in which the sound mind may grow. . . . You must prevent the marriage of immature persons. . . .

'[Second,] you must educate the girls. . . . Believe me that a nation whose women are degraded to the position of mere ministers to man's pleasures, mere toys and household drudges, goes into the world's struggle with only one arm. . . . Raise your women and you will have raised incredibly the moral tone of the nation. . . .

'[Third,] a want of reliability—a want of a due conception of the sanctity of a promise—is one of your chief failings. Here—and I speak from painful experience—men promise, promise, promise— no doubt in all good faith; but when the time comes for performance, how often do they allow any trifle to intervene to prevent their redeeming their word. You cannot rely on your fellows as a body. There are naturally bright exceptions, men whose words are as their bonds; but taking Indians in the gross, you cannot tell whether when the time comes, they will do what they promise. . . .

'Then there is another point—a thing that has broken my heart time after time—and that is the internecine jealousy that every other active man seems to cherish towards every other active man who is working on the same side as himself. . . . This is a cancer eating into the very heart of your national greatness. Believe me, until the greater number of your workers are content to fight the battles of India solely for India's sake, careless who gets the credit, who reaps the fame, who wears the laurel, careless who is ranked first or last in the army of progress, by the world, but careful only that his country's cause prevails—there is little chance of that ultimate triumph, that glowing national revivication, which we all so earnestly long for. . . .

'I can find no adequate words to express my feelings, for the patience and unvarying kindness with which you have ever dealt with me. It is a great thing to be able to say, and say truly, after a residence of five and forty years that I have *never* yet met with unkindness or discourtesy from any Indian. Indians have their faults, but where kindness and courtesy are concerned, no people on the face of the earth can rival them.

'Farewell, dear friends, farewell. A little space and I shall have left you for ever—a failure—for I have not succeeded in securing for you any appreciable fraction of what I hoped to win for you—a sower of seed never destined to see the harvest—a planter of trees whose fruit I shall never taste—but yet not disheartened, because I know to a certainty that the land I have loved will surely some day win all I hoped for her, will some day reap that harvest and some day enjoy those blessed fruits. Then when those happier times come round, may I too be sometimes remembered, and may India's kindly sons accord me this epitaph, not graven in bronze or marble, but written in their loving hearts:

"He laboured zealously in India's cause,
And if he sometimes erred, he greatly loved us."

'Good-bye, once more, good-bye. And may the Divine blessing rest ever on you and yours, and upon the whole of this dear land of India and all her teeming children.'

Mr. A.O. Hume's Farewell to India
(London, 1894)

4

THE ORGANIZATION OF THE INDIAN NATIONAL CONGRESS, 1885-1920

Introductory

The beginning of associational activity—of the modern political kind—can be traced back in India to the thirties of the 19th century.[1] It followed the establishment of British rule in the country, the restoration of law and order, and the dissemination of western ideas of liberty, rights of subjects, public spirit and patriotism. It was aided by the spread of English education, which created a class throughout the country, possessing a common stock of ideas and aspirations; by the increasing influence of a free press; by the progress of railways, posts and telegraphs, which broke down internal barriers and facilitated union for a common purpose; and by the growing contact with Europe and its movements. By the beginning of the 1880s political or quasi-political associations existed in many important towns of India. The need for some sort of concert and co-ordination between the activities of these scattered associations had for long been felt and voiced. It was underlined by some developments in the viceroyalty of Lord Ripon (1880-4), especially his extension of local self-government and the Anglo-Indian opposition to his liberal, pro-Indian measures.

While it is easy to point to the general causes which led to the emergence of a national movement in India, the precise origins of the Indian National Congress are hard to ascertain. It is, however, generally believed that early in 1885 some leading public men in India decided to hold a 'conference' or 'convention' later in the year and that a retired British civil servant, A.O. Hume, son of the radical Joseph Hume, took the leading part in its organization. He travelled all over the country organizing, 'select committees' in important towns. He secured the acquiescence, if not the blessings, of the viceroy of the day, Lord Dufferin (1884-8), and then went over to England to sound leading Liberal politicians. The first session of the Congress at Bombay during the Christmas week of 1885 was a private gathering of friends (72 in all) who came as 'volunteers' and met for three days without any constitution or rules to guide them. In subsequent years attempts were made to give a representative character to the hundreds of delegates who came to attend the Congress, to evolve a procedure for conducting its meetings, and to organize its activities in India and in England.

The Reception Committee

The Indian National Congress was not originally the name of a party but of the annual gathering of leading Indian nationalists for three or four days during Christmas week in some important town of India. Every year they assembled in a different place—decided upon at their previous meeting—to deliberate upon the important questions of the day and to give some definite and authoritative expression to the public opinion of the country. Early in the year the town where the Congress was to meet organized a reception committee, consisting of leading citizens of the province. Until 1907, the reception committee was elected at a public meeting called for this purpose by the local standing Congress committee. The constitution adopted by the Congress in April 1908, however, laid down that the reception committee was to be organized by the provincial Congress committee of the province in which the Congress was to be held, and that it was to consist only of persons who subscribed in writing to the objects and rules of the Congress and paid a minimum contribution of Rs 25. The reception committee elected a chairman and created from among its members a small executive committee for the work of general supervision, and a series of sub-committees to look after the various arrangements for the Congress session. The reception committee was responsible for raising the necessary funds for the expenses of the Congress session as also the cost of preparing, printing, publishing and distributing the report of its proceedings. It raised money by way of voluntary contributions. Apparently because it shouldered such heavy financial and other responsibilities, and also because the success of the Congress depended largely on the local enthusiasm which it was able to evoke, the reception committee was given the right of electing the president of the Congress session in consultation with other provincial Congress committees and subject to the condition (unwritten before 1908) that the person elected president did not belong to the province in which the Congress was to be held. Until 1908 the reception committee was responsible for the preparation and circulation of the draft resolutions to be discussed at the forthcoming Congress as also for the proceedings of the Congress, but the constitution adopted in that year transferred these responsibilities to the general secretaries. Critics who dismissed the Congress session as a three-day *tamasha* (show) had but an imperfect idea of the spadework which the reception committee was required to do in order to ensure the success of the annual gathering.

The President

The president of the Congress was some prominent public man—Indian or British. No less than five Britons presided over the sessions of the Congress during the period under review:[2] George Yule (1888); Sir William Wedderburn (1889 and 1910); Alfred Webb (1894); Sir Henry Cotton (1904); and Mrs. Annie Besant (1917). The Congress deliberately chose Britons as presidents to prove its loyal, moderate and non-racial character. While choosing its Indian presidents the Congress—so long as it was controlled by the moderates—took care to exclude those who were known to be anti-British, whatever their popularity in the country, but it never chose a toady or a rich man—landlord or merchant—because he gave money to the Congress. Till 1917, when Mrs Besant asserted her right to function, as she was clearly entitled to, as president of the Congress all through the year, the Congress president remained in office only during the three or four days of the annual session. His address to the meeting was the principal event of the session. He controlled the proceedings of the session and also acted as chairman of the various committees appointed to discuss questions and report to the main body. As already noted, the president was elected by the reception committee. The election was formally ratified by the general assembly. In 1899, the choice of the president was delegated to the Indian Congress Committee—designed to be the central executive of the Congress—but the committee ceased to function in 1902 and the earlier practice was reverted to. It was reaffirmed in 1906 and again in 1908 and 1920. Until the beginning of the present century there used to be little competition or canvassing for the office of the president, but as groups and factions developed within the Congress the elections of the president became a contentious issue, an occasion for a trial of strength. In 1907, the choice of the president was the immediate cause of disorder and split at the Surat session. The constitution of 1908 laid down that the president was to be elected by the reception committee by a majority from among the names recommended by the provincial Congress committees, and in case it failed to do so, by the All-India Congress Committee. In either case the election was to be final, requiring no formal sanction by or in the Congress session. But the presidency of the Congress continued to be a subject of keen controversy and contest in the years which followed.

General Secretaries

The Congress owed its organization, if not, indeed, its inception, largely to the exertions of A.O. Hume. He brought to bear upon his self-imposed task the efficiency of an Indian civil servant, the experience of radical British politics which was almost in his blood, a tireless energy even in old age, and an unequalled knowledge and love of India. He remained honorary general secretary of the Congress from 1885 to 1906. As long as he stayed in India he was the virtual executive head of the Congress, exercising a 'loving and lovable despotism'[3] over Congressmen. He personally supervised all arrangements connected with the Congress sessions, maintained communications with Congress committees and leaders all over the country, looked after the finances of the Congress, drew up its reports, etc. This kept him busy from year's end to year's end. In fact, Hume was the only Congressman in India who devoted his whole time to political work until G.K. Gokhale followed his example in 1901. In 1889, when Hume was contemplating returning to England, an honorary joint general secretary was appointed to assist him and a sum of Rs 5,000 (increased to Rs 6,000 in 1890) was voted for his office and establishment. Even after Hume returned to England finally in 1892, he continued to remain nominally the general secretary of the

Congress—being elected annually to that office—until 1906, but much of the power and authority of the office passed to his Indian counterpart. As the honorary joint general secretary, being a busy professional man himself, could not find sufficient time for Congress work, the experiment of appointing a paid assistant secretary to help him was tried in 1899, but it was abandoned in 1902 due probably to lack of funds or to the fact that the particular person appointed to that office—Alfred Nundy—fell foul of the Congress leadership. In 1903, the Congress increased the number of honorary joint general secretaries to two. The constitution adopted by the Congress in 1908 provided for two (honorary) general secretaries; one more was added in 1917. The general secretaries[4] occupied a key position in the organization and were invariably persons of eminence and authority. The long predominance of Bombay in Congress politics was demonstrated by D.E. Wacha's remaining general secretary of the Congress continuously from 1895 to 1913.

Delegates

In order to give those who attended the Congress a representative character and to meet the accusation that they were self-styled leaders with no mandate from the people, the Congress made it obligatory in 1886 that the delegates should be elected at public meetings of citizens or by public associations. Full details about these meetings and the elected delegates were furnished to the reception committee and published in the report of the Congress. Attempts were made in later years to improve this rough and ready electoral system. The country was divided into circles and subdivisions for the election of delegates to the Congress and the number which each circle or sub-division could send was sought to be fixed. But the Congress in its early years had no regular membership or machinery for conducting these elections and virtually anyone who had the desire, the money and the time to go to the Congress session could get himself elected as a delegate. As the number of delegates to the Congress went on increasing, it was decided in 1889 to fix the maximum at 1,000—roughly 5 per million of the population—but the decision was not adhered to for long. The large number of delegates attending the Congress placed a severe strain on the resources of the reception committee. But the Congress had acquired the character of a grand annual demonstration and any substantial reduction of the number of delegates would have reflected adversely on its popularity, besides depriving it of its educative value and a great source of income. The limitation of the number of delegates would have also involved, by necessary implication, the fixing and formation of electorates on some basal principle—a work which was hopelessly beset with difficulties. The leaders of the early Congress, therefore, wisely refrained from interfering with the number of delegates who came to the Congress, with their qualifications and the mode of election. Attendance at the Congress varied from year to year.[5] Provinces remained unevenly represented, the majority of delegates being supplied by the province in which the Congress was held. When, however, the radical and the allegedly less responsible nationalists threatened to swamp the Congress, the right of public meetings to send delegates was done away with in 1908 and only recognized Congress committees and associations affiliated to them were allowed to send delegates. As this resulted in a sharp decline in the popularity of the Congress and became a source of grievance with the radical nationalists, the Congress relaxed the rule a bit in 1912 and again in 1915 and permitted public meetings held under the auspices or recognized associations to elect a limited number of delegates to the Congress session. But the constitution adopted by the Congress at Nagpur in 1920 re-introduced institutional electorates in a stricter form. Provincial Congress committees were made responsible for the election of delegates to the Congress and the number of delegates which each province could send was fixed at the rate of one for every 50 thousand of its population. The qualifications of electors and delegates were clearly laid down and the provincial Congress committees were required to frame definite rules for the election of delegates, having due regard to the return of women delegates and the representation of minorities, special interests or classes needing special attention.

In the beginning, the delegates to the Congress were treated as guests and were lodged and fed at the expense of the reception committee, but in 1891 it was decided that they should pay for their boarding, arrangements for which were still made by the reception committee. From 1888 onwards every delegate to the Congress was also required to pay a 'delegate fee' of Rs 10; it was raised to Rs 20 in 1902, but was again reduced to Rs 10 in

1912. The delegate fee, the cost of travelling—often thousands of miles—to the place where the Congress session was held and the fact that the proceedings of the Congress were, until 1920, conducted almost entirely in English, all ensured that the Congress was a body of educated respectable and well-to-do people.[6] Though the reception committee often enlisted the co-operation of the local students in making arrangements for the annual session, the Congress did not admit students as delegates.

The original idea of the founders of the Congress was that the delegates should stay together when the Congress was in session, so that they could come into close and intimate contact with each other, but as the number of delegates increased this did not always prove practicable—they had to be housed separately, often in different parts of the town, in groups, according to their region, religion or style of living. Though the great majority of the delegates to the Congress availed themselves of the modest community accommodation provided for them by the reception committee, quite a few Congress grandees preferred to stay away from their humbler brethren in hotels and bungalows specially hired for them for the season. The aristocracy of the Congress was thus socially—as it was in course of time politically—estranged from its rank and file. It was not until Gandhiji revived the original idea of the founders of the Congress and forced all delegates to stay together in the Congress camp—in simple huts—that Congressmen developed a real spirit of *camaraderie*.

In the early years of the Congress a few Eurasians and resident Britons attended its sessions, but they soon dropped out. Similarly, many big landlords, especially in northern India, who in the beginning co-operated with the Congress, stayed away from it due to official pressure or the anti-landlord attitude of leading Congressmen. The small Parsi element in the Congress exercised an influence out of proportion of its numbers, mainly because it had such able leaders as Dadabhai Naoroji, Pherozeshah Mehta and Dinshaw Wacha. A few eminent and intelligent Muslims from all parts of India joined the Congress during these years, but they were not really representative of their community, the bulk of which remained indifferent and even hostile to the Congress. The Congress strove hard to secure the co-operation of the Muslims. By a formal resolution in 1888, it assured them that it would not discuss any subject to which the Muslim delegates objected in a body, unanimously or near unanimously.[7] It scrupulously refrained from discussing religious or social questions. It provided for the due representation of the Muslims in its inner councils[8] and often allowed them to wield a greater influence over its deliberations than their numbers warranted. Numerous instances can be cited to prove how the Congress, in deference to the sentiments of the Muslims, acted against the wishes of its Hindu supporters and consistently tried to maintain its national and non-sectarian character.[9] But the Muslims as a community—for reasons which are well known and need not be mentioned here—remained aloof from the Congress and later developed a separate organization of their own. If the gulf between the Hindus and the Muslims in India remained unbridged, only a part—and a very small part—of the blame can be laid at the door of the early Congress. It is difficult to see what more it could have done, without being false to the law of its being; constituted as it was, it could easily have done less.

The Congress was, during the years under review, composed chiefly of English-educated lawyers and the smaller gentry, with a fair sprinkling of the commercial and professional classes. It was urban-based and its programme was ill designed to secure the support of the masses.

The Subjects Committee

The original intention of the founders of the Congress was to bring together once a year a few 'most earnest labourers in the cause of national progress', to discuss and decide upon the political operations to be undertaken during the ensuing year.[10] They did not anticipate that hundreds and thousands would begin to flock to the Congress session each year. Realizing that such a large and amorphous gathering was ill suited to serious deliberations, and also that there was some dissatisfaction in its ranks at the arbitrary manner in which a handful of self-constituted leaders disposed of its business, the Congress, at its Madras session in 1887, appointed a small representative committee of 35 to consider the many suggestions made for discussion and to draw up a programme of work. It was given a more formal character in 1888 and was called the 'subjects committee'. It consisted of about 100 members, elected each year by delegates of each province according to a fixed schedule. It met each day after the opening of the general session, reviewed the proceedings, discussed and drafted the resolutions to be taken up in the general session and selected the speakers on the resolutions. All real business of and debate in the Congress was gradually shifted to this body, which sat in private and came to wield great influence. The public sittings of the Congress were soon reduced to a merely formal passing of the resolutions agreed to in the subjects committee. It was an unwritten rule of the Congress not to take up for discussion any subject which was of a purely local character or which did not command the more or less unanimous agreement of all the provinces. Voting at the Congress was very often by provinces.

Annual Session

The last week of December every year used to be a period of unusual activity in India. Thousands of delegates and visitors flocked to the town where the Congress was to meet. As most towns in India had no big hall to accommodate them, a temporary building was constructed for this purpose at the cost of several thousand rupees. Even chairs had to be brought from other places. Elaborate arrangements were made for the boarding and lodging of delegates.

The Congress opened on the first day at 2 p.m. with the address of the chairman of the reception committee, welcoming the delegates and making a few general remarks about the political situation in the country and the work of the Congress. The name of the president-elect was then formally proposed, seconded and approved by the assembly. The president being formally installed, read out his long and rather verbose thesis on the outstanding problems facing the country. Following the presidential address, the names of members of the subjects committee—for which the elections had already taken place—were announced and the proceedings of the day were concluded.

Less than an hour after the president adjourned the meeting, the subjects committee would meet to settle the resolutions, the speakers and procedure for the next day.

The Congress re-assembled the next day at noon. The rules of business were first announced. Some time was spent on considering the annual reports of the various standing (later provincial) Congress committees, in making important announcements and in reading out messages of sympathy received from persons in India or abroad. The resolutions of the day were then proposed, seconded and supported by speakers chosen by the subjects committee. The president set the time-limit for speakers—usually ten minutes for the proposer and five for the other speakers. Any delegate had the right to move an amendment or propose a new resolution in the general session, but the introduction of new subjects was discouraged and the Congress generally adhered to the agenda laid down by the subjects committee.

The proceedings of the third and the fourth day were similar. The Congress concluded its sittings with a short speech by the president and three cheers for the Sovereign and a vote of thanks to the reception committee, the British Committee, etc. The Congress conducted its business in an orderly, peaceful and responsible manner. Incidents like those at Calcutta in 1906 and at Surat in 1907 were exceptions; hence the shock which they produced.

The annual session of the Congress was an expensive affair and suggestions were repeatedly made to discontinue it or to do away with its spectacular character. But the leaders of the Congress rightly judged that an annual congregation of representatives of many provinces and creeds at one place, for the advancement of a common purpose, was in itself a great advantage and worth all the expense and the inconvenience it involved. It broadened the outlook and widened the sympathies of all those who participated in it. It was a symbol of a nation in the making.

Finances

The expenditure incurred in holding the annual session of the Congress varied from year to year, depending largely upon the attendance at each session. From 1886 to 1914 it ranged between Rs 30,000 and Rs 60,000. From 1915 onwards, the number of delegates and visitors to the Congress sessions rose sharply with a corresponding rise in the expenditure. The total expenses of the session held at Amritsar (1919) amounted to over Rs 2 lakhs and of that held at Nagpur (1920) exceeded Rs 3 lakhs. Part of this expense was recovered from the delegates' and visitors' fees, but the practice of waiving fees restricted this income. The reception committee was responsible for raising funds. It appointed agents to collect money. Some provinces—for example, Madras—were more methodical in raising funds than others. Bengal, which had a large number of wealthy landholders, and Bombay, which had a flourishing business community, found it easier to raise money than the United Provinces or Panjab, which had no such advantages. Besides small sums collected from the general public, rich individual sympathizers—businessmen, landlords and princes—occasionally made substantial contributions. The reception committee had also to find money for the expenses of the general secretaries' establishment (about Rs 5-6,000) and those of the British Committee. In 1900, the Congress set up a permanent fund—invested in the names of seven trustees, one from each province—on which it could draw in emergency.

The Congress had also to spend a lot of money in England on its British Committee. The journal *India* alone cost about Rs 30,000 per annum. The activities of the British Committee cost another Rs 20,000. Theoretically, Rs 50-60,000 were annually voted for the British Committee, but this amount was seldom remitted in full. Hume, Wedderburn and Naoroji were always complaining that remittances from India were irregular and insufficient. Various methods were successively tried for raising money for the British Committee, such as by requiring the provinces to pay a fixed contribution, by guaranteeing subscribers to *India*, and by earmarking half the amount of the fees received by the reception committee from the delegates at each session. There was a growing reluctance in India to contribute towards the expenses of the British Committee due to the feeling that the British Committee had failed to achieve anything, that it was extravagant and inactive, and that its journal was not well conducted. In 1920, the British Committee was abolished.

The financial position of the Congress was never very sound. This imposed a serious restriction on its activities and there was considerable strain on the pecuniary resources of a comparatively few public-spirited men in the country. 'Those who can and ought to pay for the Congress', lamented the *Sudharak* in 1892, 'have not the will, while those whose heart is in the movement are, most of them, too poor to pay.'[11] The Congress failed to wrest any concessions from the government during the first 20 years or so of its existence, with the result that many of its early supporters began to fall off. Criticism of heavy Congress expenses increased. Proposals were even made to discontinue the Congress sessions. It is no mean tribute to the public spirit and patriotism of Indians that the Congress did not die for want of funds. Very few organizations in any part of the world would have continued for so long and at such a cost, without showing any tangible results.

Agitation in India

Agitation in the press and through public meetings, conferences, memorials and petitions had become a normal feature of Indian political life long before the Congress was established. After all, Indians had not been studying English history and politics for over half a century in vain. The Congress only increased the tempo of Indian politics. There was more activity henceforth and on a wider front; there was also more unity of purpose and action.

As a grand national demonstration, the annual session had immense propaganda value and this was the main reason why, in spite of its great cost and inconvenience, it was not discontinued. On a minor scale this grand performance was repeated in the provincial conferences, which began to be held in some of the provinces—generally during Easter—from 1888 onwards, and later in the district conferences. Another source of popular attraction was the industrial exhibition organized alongside the Congress since 1901.

The Congress had no newspaper of its own in India, but there were scores of English and vernacular newspapers—many of them owned by Congressmen—which constantly agitated the Congress cause. Next only in importance to the press as a vehicle of Congress propaganda, were the public meetings held frequently in different parts of the country. Congress leaders were in their best form on the platform and never missed an opportunity of delivering an oration. Agents—paid or unpaid—were occasionally sent round the districts to secure funds and supporters for the Congress. Reports of the proceedings of the annual sessions were regularly published and distributed in India and in England. Handbills and pamphlets were frequently issued and patriotic publishers like G.A. Natesan of Madras produced a mass of cheap Congress literature. The founders of the Congress deliberately followed the methods of agitation of the Anti-Corn Law League—even to the extent of issuing 'Tracts for the Times' and 'Congress Catechisms'.

But in its early years the Congress had no regular machinery of its own for continuous agitation throughout the year. It was

The Organization of the Indian National Congress, 1885-1920

still a ramshackle continental alliance, relying heavily on its constituents, the regional associations, to carry on its agitational work during the year, when it was itself in abeyance. The regional associations lacked funds and workers and their activity was at best spasmodic. The result was that, when the Congress dispersed after its three- or four-day meeting, not much was heard of it or of its work, except in the press. The difficulties of continuous political agitation in a vast subcontinent, economically and educationally backward, were almost insuperable. Moreover, the leaders of the Congress had neither the means, nor perhaps as yet the desire, to enlist the support of the masses. And when the government frowned on some of their early attempts in this direction, they were content to confine their agitation to the platform and the press. The *swadeshi* and boycott agitation which grew up in India during the years 1905-8 in connexion with the partition of Bengal, in a way, came in spite of the Congress and was not controlled by it. The same was true of the home rule movement during the war. It was Gandhi who made the Congress a formidable instrument for marshalling public opinion and the execution of policy.

Agitation in England

The early leaders of the Congress attached more importance to their work in England than to that in India. They believed that John Bull at home was better than John Bull overseas and that the real impulse for reform would have to come from Parliament. Long before the Congress was established, Indians had learnt to influence the British public. Paid agents were appointed in England, contacts with friendly societies and M.P.s were established, and attempts were occasionally made to influence the English electorate. The Congress took up this work in a more regular and systematic fashion. In 1887, Naoroji began to act as the agent of the Congress in England; in 1888, he was joined by W.C. Bonnerjee and Eardley Norton and the co-operation of Charles Bradlaugh was secured. In the same year, an Indian Political Agency was established at 25, Craven Street, Strand, London, under William Digby to carry on agitation in England. In 1889, it was transformed into the British Committee of the Indian National Congress, with Wedderburn as chairman, Digby as secretary, and a few radical friends of India as members. The

British Committee published a journal (*India*) to place before the British public the Congress view of Indian affairs. At first it came out irregularly, but in 1892 it became a monthly and in 1898 a weekly. It was supplied free to M.P.s, journalists, political associations and clubs, but few cared even to glance through its contents. The Committee also arranged meetings, addresses and interviews. It briefed M.P.s on Indian questions and invited them to political breakfasts and dinners. Encouraged by the Committee, the Congress repeatedly discussed the proposal of holding one of its sessions in England, but the cost of such a venture was prohibitive and the Congress had to content itself with sending an occasional delegation to England.

The Congress was the child of Gladstonian liberalism and relied mainly on the Liberal party for the fulfilment of its demands. The eclipse of that party in England during the first twenty years of the life of the Congress was the greatest single set-back which the Congress suffered. Congressmen repeatedly tried to enter Parliament and to get their English friends elected thereto, but without much success. Only in 1892, did a Congressman—Naoroji—manage to enter Parliament. Taking advantage, however, of the presence of many Liberal sympathizers with India in Parliament, an Indian Parliamentary Committee was organized in 1893, which succeeded in carrying through a resolution in the House of Commons, recommending the holding of simultaneous examinations for the Indian Civil Service in India and in England, and to wring from the government a commission on Indian finance. The Indian Parliamentary Committee remained dormant for ten years, following the Conservative victory at the election of 1895. It was revived in 1906, when the Liberals returned to power, and did some useful work.

It is difficult to measure the success achieved by the Congress agitation in England. British friends of the Congress, especially Hume and Wedderburn, were inclined to think that 'a frontal attack' upon the bureaucracy in India was hopeless and that more could be achieved by 'a flanking movement' in England.[12] A good many years of expensive agitation in England, however, convinced many an Indian nationalist that the ordinary Englishman was too busy to care about India and that nothing but 'a frontal attack' could disturb his complacency. The result was an Indian version of Sinn Fein and the bomb.

The British Committee was periodically torn by dissensions. It imposed a heavy financial burden on the Congress without being able to show corresponding results. But as long as Moderates retained control of the Congress they continued to support the British Committee because of their faith in the efficacy of agitation in England and as a matter of personal loyalty to Hume and Wedderburn. After the death of Hume in 1912 and of Wedderburn in 1918, the Committee ceased to inspire confidence in India. Serious differences developed between the British Committee and the Congress under Extremists, Especially over the Montagu-Chelmsford reforms, and it was abolished in 1920.

Congress Constitution

The Congress was launched with a few 'select committees' in about a dozen important centres in India and a general secretary, and it was intended to give it a regular, written constitution at its very first meeting in Bombay in December 1885. But fourteen years were to elapse before the intention was even partly realized. The question was repeatedly discussed during the intervening years; committees were appointed, draft constitutions were prepared and circulated, but no final decision was reached until 1899. The main reason often advanced for this delay was that the Congress was too young for a formal constitution and that some of the oldest parliamentary bodies had functioned without a constitution. The real reasons probably were the unwillingness of some of the older, well-established local associations, for example, the British Indian Association of Calcutta,[13] to merge their identity in the Congress, and, more importantly, the fear of the leaders who founded the Congress that the constitution might not work well in practice and thereby further expose the weaknesses of the organization, or that it might result in their losing their control over it. The constitution which the Congress adopted in 1899, in response to mounting criticism of its organization and methods of work, defined its object as being 'to promote by constitutional means the interests and the well-being of the people of the Indian Empire',[14] and provided an organizational framework at three levels:

(*i*) An Indian Congress Committee of about 45 elected members from the various provinces, with an honorary secretary and a paid assistant secretary, which was to meet at least three times a year and was empowered to nominate the president, draft resolutions, make rules for the election of delegates, and deal with 'all other business in connection with the Congress'.

(*ii*) Provincial Congress committees, which were to carry on 'the work of political education, on lines of general appreciation of British rule and of constitutional action for the removal of its defects, throughout the year, by organizing standing Congress committees, holding Provincial conferences, and by such other means as they deem proper, in consultation with the Indian Congress Committee, for furthering the objects of the Congress'.

(*iii*) Standing Congress committees in important towns, whose functions were not defined and which were in theory already in existence.[15]

The most important feature of the 1899 constitution was the provision for an elected committee (the Indian Congress Committee) to control the Congress. It was intended to end the virtual monopoly of the Congress by an oligarchy and it was for this reason that the oligarchy killed it unceremoniously in 1902. If the fear that the Congress organization might be captured by the radicals persuaded the moderate leaders to delay giving it a constitution until 1899 and to subvert the 1899 constitution in 1902, it was the same fear that prompted them to impose a full-blown constitution on the Congress in 1908.

For the first 30 years of its existence the Congress was controlled by what may be called 'the centre party'—by men belonging to the upper middle class who were highly educated and westernized, who stood for social reform and representative government, to be achieved by strictly constitutional and legal means, and who had firm faith in the liberal instincts of the British people. These 'loyal patriots' organized the Congress more as a political pressure group than as a popular movement. But the mass of Congress sympathizers consisted of the lower middle classes, who had neither the bank balance nor the liberal education which makes men moderates.

While most of the top leaders of the Congress were ardent social reformers, they realized the great diversity in the country in social matters and the consequent difficulty of a consensus for any practical purpose. The aim of the Congress was to unite the country, and to take up social questions would have meant division. They decided, therefore, not to discuss social questions on the Congress platform and instead organized a separate Social Conference which met in the Congress pavilion after the Congress sessions were over. The activities of the social reformers were not to the taste of conservative Congressmen. In 1891, when some leading social reformers, who were also Congressmen, invited government legislation to raise the age of consent in India, the conservatives threatened to boycott the Congress and organize a separate 'Peoples' Congress'. Fortunately, a split was averted, but not without creating deep personal animosities and distrust of the westernized Congress leaders.

The failure of the older moderate leaders to secure any substantial concessions from the authorities, encouraged younger men— the so-called Extremists—to become increasingly critical of them and their methods of agitation. The older leaders, who came to be known as Moderates, were convinced that there was no alternative to British rule in India just then and there would not be one for a long time to come. They, therefore, wanted to work for the advancement of their country in co-operation with the alien rulers. They stood for gradual, ordered and all-round progress. They demanded isolated reforms and the redress of acknowledged grievances—extension of the representative element in the legislative councils, increased employment of Indians in the public services, separation of the executive and judicial functions, reduction of military expenditure, commissions for Indians in the army, etc. They had faith in British justice and liberality and were wedded to strict constitutionalism. The younger men wanted the political kingdom first. They denounced their elders' method of work by way of 'prayers, petitions and protests' as 'mendicancy' and their faith in British benevolence as a delusion. The Congress was tame and timid. The younger men wanted to inject some fibre into it.

The rise of radical nationalism in India, which became marked in the mid-nineties, was at once a conservative and a revolutionary phenomenon. It drew its inspiration, on the one hand, from Indian religions and the Indian way of life; on the other hand, it tried to apply to the Indian situation western methods of mass agitation and even terrorism.

The controversy over ideals and methods within the Congress was but a symptom of the deeper schism within the movement. It was essentially a conflict between palsied age and fiery youth, between an upper middle-class leadership and a lower middle-class following. Extremists were dissatisfied with the Congress as a four-day pageant, organized by a few English-educated barristers. They hated its abject, academic tone. They wanted the Congress to become a mass organization, pursuing more self-reliant and vigorous methods of agitation. And their demand for new and more determined methods of work was related to their desire for a more democratic control of the Congress.

Under pressure from Extremists, the Congress leadership adopted in 1905-6 a sterner tone in making its demands, revived the Indian Congress Committee and declared self-government within the British Empire to be the goal of its endeavours. But there was a point beyond which the Moderate leaders of the Congress were not prepared to go. They could not tolerate disloyalty to the British Raj and a resort to illegal and violent methods of agitation. Therefore, when some Extremists began to talk of *swaraj* outside the British Empire and to advocate 'boycott' and 'passive resistance', the leaders decided to bridle the youthful firebrands or, in case they proved recalcitrant, to throw them out of the Congress. The result was a split in the Congress, following disorderly scenes at the Surat session in December 1907, and the adoption of a rigid constitution in 1908.

The 1908 constitution was an elaborate and exhaustive document which, despite numerous changes in later years, has retained its basic character to this day. It laid down that the objects of the Indian National Congress were 'the attainment by the people of India of a system of government similar to that enjoyed by the self-governing Members of the British Empire and participation by them in the rights and responsibilities of the Empire on equal terms with those Members' and that these objects were 'to be achieved by constitutional means by bringing about a steady reform of the existing system of administration and by promoting national unity, fostering public spirit and developing and organizing the intellectual, moral, economic and industrial resources of the country.[11] Every delegate of the Congress was required to express in writing his acceptance of this 'creed' of the Congress. The constitution provided for the creation of an All-India Congress Committee, composed of about 100 elected representatives, which was 'to carry on the work and propaganda of the Congress' and was empowered 'to deal with all such matters of great importance or urgency as may require to be disposed of in the name of and for the purpose of the Congress'.[17] Provision was also made for the creation of Congress committees in the provinces, districts and sub-divisions, and the qualifications for the membership of these committees were specified. The constitution tightened discipline within the Congress and regularized its procedure. The right of public meetings to send delegates to the Congress was withdrawn and only Congress committees and associations recognized by or affiliated to them were permitted to elect delegates to the Congress. Detailed rules were made for the conduct and regulation of the annual meetings of the Congress. The Congress still did not have a formal membership and was far from being a concrete political party. But it had now at least a regular, well-defined organization of its own at various levels. The 1908 constitution tried to ensure that those whom Moderates regarded as 'irresponsible', 'unscrupulous' and 'frankly anti-British' elements would find no place in the Congress. But what the Congress gained in respectability, it lost in popularity. In its anxiety to remain a loyal and moderate organization, it cut itself away from the rising generation of Indian nationalists. It won the recognition of the alien government, but was abandoned by its own people.

Moderates against Extremists

This rigid and over-elaborate constitution did not work well in practice. The average Moderate politician was not only a busy professional man who had little time for the work of the Congress, he was also an apathetic man. The provincial and district Congress committees led a dead-and-alive existence. Their membership was small. The only sign of activity which they showed was to meet once a year in December to elect delegates to the forthcoming session of the Congress. The earlier method of electing delegates to the Congress at public meetings, however faulty and open to objection on other grounds, at least gave the masses some sense of participation in the work of the Congress and contributed to their political education. The new system, by which half a dozen men met in solemn conclave and elected themselves and their friends—often many times their own number—as delegates, made a mockery of the Congress electoral system. As Gokhale admitted: 'For this ... [the Congress electoral system] to work successfully it was necessary that the Provincial Congress Committees all over the country should take steps to revive District and Taluqa

Congress Committees and establish them where they did not exist and get them all by constant vigilance and touch, to take a living interest in the Congress. Unfortunately this was not done except in two provinces—Madras and U.P.—and even there the Committees collapsed after a time. And by the 1910 Congress session in Allahabad it became obvious that the scheme of the constitution, as a means of pushing on the Congress organization, had totally failed and that its only utility—real in the beginning, doubtful later on—was to keep those who had seceded from the Congress in 1907, out of that body.'[18]

Not only did Extremists stand aloof from the Congress, the interest of the public in its proceedings visibly declined. Attendance at Congress sessions fell sharply. The soul had gone out of the Congress. In its desire to become a party, the Congress movement had degenerated into a political pressure group, waiting upon the frowns and smiles of the British officials. 'The Congress', wrote B.N. Basu, a Moderate leader from Bengal, 'is a decadent movement and badly wants life: the question is, how is the Congress to be brought into contact with the living life of the country?'[19]

Alive to these developments and to the growing clamour of the press and the public for a united Congress, some of the more sensitive and sincere Congressmen themselves began urging a modification of the constitution of 1908. The result was that the 1912 session at Bankipur (Bihar) lowered the delegate fee from Rs 20 to Rs 10 and allowed public meetings to be held under the auspices of the Congress committees and other recognized associations for electing persons, otherwise qualified, as delegates to the Congress.

These modifications, however, failed either to revive the waning popularity of the Congress or to conciliate Extremists. The vast majority of the latter had by now given up their objection to the Congress creed, but they insisted—more as a matter of self-respect than anything else—that they should not be forced to enter the Congress through the electorates of their opponents. They demanded that all public associations, which professed to aim at self-government for India within the British Empire to be achieved by constitutional means, should be automatically affiliated to the Congress, instead of being required to seek affiliation formally, and that the right of public meetings to elect delegates to the Congress, withdrawn in 1908, should be restored. A long debate ensued over the issue of allowing public meetings to elect delegates to the Congress and it underlined the different approaches of Moderates and Extremists towards the character and purpose of the Congress. Moderates looked upon the Congress as a political party, composed exclusively of men who subscribed to its basic creed, and having an organizational framework of its own. Even those Moderates who favoured a relaxation of the 1908 constitution in order to bring back the seceders wanted the latter to give an assurance that they wished 'to come back to co-operate with us in carrying out the present programme of the Congress by present methods' and that they would 'not seek to overthrow the present programme and substitute other methods for present methods'.[20] Moderates feared the energy and activity of Extremists and the latter's numerical preponderance in the country. They knew that to allow public meetings of all sorts to send delegates to the Congress would mean the swamping of the Congress by Extremists, who would soon proceed to overthrow the present leadership and programme of the organization. They also feared that a *rapprochement* with Extremists might result in their forfeiting the goodwill and sympathy of the rulers which they had only recently secured. Extremists wanted the Congress to retain its character as a national movement. They looked upon the Congress as an unofficial parliament of India, representative of all the different views and interests in the country. They were eager to re-enter the Congress for the simple reason that outside the Congress they were in a political wilderness. And it was a dangerous wilderness, for the authorities could easily strike them down. Most of their leaders were already in jail or in exile and their attempt to organize a separate 'Congress' of their own in 1908 had been frustrated by the government. But, while eager to return to the Congress fold and willing to subscribe to its ideal, most Extremists had no faith in the Congress programme or its methods of work. They did not wish to merge their identity with Moderates or to give up their principles. They, therefore, insisted on retaining their separate electorates and their freedom of action on re-entering the Congress.

The shrewder among the Moderate leaders realized that a reconciliation with Extremists on the latter's terms would mean a return to the state of things which prevailed before the split at Surat. A united Congress would either mean the end of the Congress or its capture by Extremists. They, therefore, foiled the attempt of Extremists and their sympathizers within the Congress to amend the 1908 constitution at the Madras session in December 1914. Extremists replied by turning the country against the Moderate leaders. They were aided in their task by the release of their leader, B.G. Tilak, the ferment created by the war and the deaths of Gokhale and Pherozeshah Mehta, the two most outstanding leaders of Moderates, in 1915. Under pressure from their own rank and file and outside public opinion in the country, the Moderate Congress leaders reluctantly yielded to an amendment of the constitution in 1915, by which any association of at least two years' standing, which accepted the 'creed' of the Congress and made it a condition for membership, was allowed to convene a public meeting and elect up to 15 delegates to the Congress. Some of the more militant Extremists were not satisfied with this rather grudging concession, but Tilak and his more realistic colleagues decided to rejoin the Congress, 'by taking advantage of the partial opening made for us and then strive to open the door full and wide'.[21] Having won the first round, Extremists embarked on a vigorous campaign of political agitation by organizing Home Rule Leagues (with the single object of securing *swaraj*), mass meetings and lecture tours, and by enlisting 'volunteers' and distributing political literature.

The reunited Congress met in a historic and joyous session at Lucknow towards the end of December 1916. For the first time in nine years, Extremists sat beside Moderates. The Congress also reached agreement with the Muslim League on a joint scheme of political reforms. It was, however, a reunification without reconciliation. Differences about the pace and method of political advance, which were quite fundamental and over which the Congress had split at Surat in 1907, continued to divide the two sections of Indian nationalists. Personal antipathies between the leaders of the two sections were bitter and deep-rooted. Between the old Moderate leaders and the new emerging class of Indian politicians—between 'the Yesterdays and the Tomorrows', as Mrs Besant aptly described them,[22]—there was the difference of a generation or more which could not be bridged. A period of uneasy truce followed, marked by a keen struggle for power. Though Extremists preponderated at the Lucknow Congress in December 1916, Moderates managed to get their nominee elected as president and to dominate the inner councils of the organization. But their position was difficult and they had repeatedly to use the threat of secession in order to have their way. Differences somehow patched up at Lucknow came into the open the next year. In the elections to the various Congress committees and offices, Extremists made a clean sweep of the 'old stagers'. Moderates realized that the machinery of the Congress had been captured by Extremists. Many of them were driven out of their positions of authority and influence within the organization, while those who had managed to survive the iconoclastic zeal of their opponents found the pace too hot for them. They began to think of withdrawing from the Congress and forming a separate organization of their own. Their experience of the 1917 session at Calcutta, presided over by Mrs Besant, confirmed them in their resolve. The publication of the Montagu-Chelmsford reform proposals in July 1918 provided Moderates with the necessary opportunity and excuse for seceding from the Congress. While the Congress looked the gift-horse of dyarchy rather closely in the mouth, Moderates prepared to ride it. They entered into a sort of compact with the authorities and stayed away from the special session held at Bombay in August 1918. In November 1918 they organized a separate Moderates' Conference.

'The new generation that is being prepared in political life', a political commentator had written in 1916, 'does not wholly like the old Moderate party, neither does it like the old Nationalist [i.e. Extremist] party in all its aspects. This is a fact which can be observed by anyone who looks at things closely.'[23] This was very true. The old Moderate party had served its purpose and its programme stood discredited. The old Extremist party did not inspire much confidence either and its programme of the bomb and the boycott, of which the country had had some taste earlier, was wholly negative. Young nationalist India needed a new leadership and a new programme of action. These were provided to it by Gandhi in 1920.

With the coming of Gandhi and the launching of the non-violent non-co-operation movement, the Congress entered the era of mass politics. The Nagpur session in December 1920 recast the constitution of the Congress. The object of the Congress was redefined as 'the attainment of Swarajya by the people of India by all legitimate and peaceful means'.[24] The question of India's membership of the British Empire was left open. The number of delegates to the Congress session was fixed in the proportion of one to fifty thousand of the population and provincial allotments were accordingly made. The country was divided into twenty-one 'provinces' on a linguistic basis, each headed by a provincial Congress committee. The 'provinces', in turn, were sub-divided into districts, taluqas or tehsils, towns and villages, each lower body electing representatives to the committee immediately above it and ultimately to the All-India Congress Committee, the highest executive organ of the party. The All-India Congress Committee was to consist of about 300 members and conduct all Congress business between the annual sessions. It was also to function as the subjects committee for the Congress session. The All-India Congress Committee was to appoint a Working Committee, consisting of the president, the general secretaries, the treasurers and 9 other members, which was to 'perform such functions as may be delegated to it from time to time by the All-India Congress Committee'.[25] It became in fact the real decision-making organ of the Congress. The primary membership of the Congress was thrown open to all persons over the age of 21 who expressed in writing their acceptance of the object and methods of the Congress and paid an annual subscription of 4 annas.

With a new leader, a new ideal, a new constitution and a new organization capable of penetrating to the grass roots, the Congress prepared for *satyagraha*—a new method of political action, which was revolutionary without ceasing to be constitutional.

5

THE OBJECTIVES AND METHODS OF THE INDIAN NATIONAL CONGRESS, 1885-1920

It was natural of English-educated Indians in the nineteenth century, who studied history and watched the progress of movements for national freedom and unity in various parts of the world, including the British Empire, to desire that their country, too, should become self-governing. Long before the Indian National Congress was founded the British Indian Association of Bengal had petitioned Parliament in 1852 'that the legislature of British India be placed on the footing of those enjoyed by most of the Colonies of Her Majesty'.[1] Speaking in London in 1867, W.C. Bonnerjee had demanded a 'Representative and Responsible Government for India'.[2] In 1870 the *Amrita Bazar Patrika* had raised the cry of 'A Parliament for India'.[3] In 1874 Kristodas Pal had written in the *Hindoo Patriot*: 'Our attention should... be directed to Home Rule for India.... If the Canadas could have a Parliament, if such small and little advanced Colonies as Prince Edward Island, Newfoundland, New South Wales, New Zealand, St. Christopher's Island and Barbadoes could have elected Councils, surely British India has a fair claim to similar representation. If taxation and representation go hand in hand in all British Colonies, why should this principle be ignored in British India... Home Rule for India ought to be our cry, and it ought to be based upon the same constitutional basis that is recognized in the Colonies.'[4] In 1880 Surendranath Banerjea had remarked: 'The question of representative government looms in the not-far-off distance. Educated India is beginning to feel that the time has come when some measure of self-government must be conceded to the people of this country. Canada governs itself. Australia governs itself. And surely it is anomalous that the grandest dependency of England should continue to be governed upon wholly different principles.'[5] Ripon's extension of local self-government in India in 1883 was hailed by politically-alert Indians as the first step on the road to national self-government. In the same year the *Quarterly Journal of the Poona Sarvajanik Sabha* had written: 'There can be no question that a nation of 250 millions can never be permanently held down by sheer force, and sooner or later in God's Providence, and under the encouragement of British example and discipline, the people of this country must rise to the status of a self-governing community, and learn to control their own affairs in subordinate alliance with England. The transfer of power is inevitable, and the duty of statesmen is to graduate it in a way to make the transfer natural and easy, so as to keep up the continuity of national growth.'[6]

Both the direct and the indirect objects of the Indian National Congress were clearly, though briefly, stated in the circular issued in March 1885 which proposed the convening of the first 'Conference of the Indian National Union' in the following December. The circular said: 'The direct objects of the Conference will be: (1) to enable all the most earnest labourers in the cause of national progress to become personally known to each other; (2) to discuss and decide upon the political operations to be undertaken during the ensuing year. Indirectly this Conference will form the germ of a Native Parliament and, if properly conducted, will constitute in a few years an unanswerable reply to the assertion that India is still wholly unfit for any form of representative institutions.'[7]

As president of the first session of the Indian National Congress held at Bombay in December 1885, W.C. Bonnerjee remarked that 'the objects of the Congress could for the most part be classed under the following heads:

'(*a*) The promotion of personal intimacy and friendship amongst all the more earnest workers in our country's cause in all parts of the Empire.

'(*b*) The eradication by direct friendly intercourse of all possible race, creed, or provincial prejudices amongst all lovers of our country, and the fuller development and consolidation of those sentiments of national unity that had their origin in their beloved Lord Ripon's ever memorable reign.

'(c) The authoritative record, after this has been carefully elicited by the fullest discussion, of the matured opinions of the educated classes in India on some of the more important and pressing of the [political and] social questions of the day.

'(d) The determination of the lines upon and methods by which during the next twelve months it is desirable for native politicians to labour in the public interests.'[8]

Speaking on the resolution for the reform of the legislative councils in India at the first session of the Congress in 1885, one of the leaders of the movement, Dadabhai Naoroji, insisted that the ultimate objects of the Congress should be 'clearly and boldly' declared. 'I may here remark,' he said, 'that the chief work of this first National Congress of India is to enunciate clearly and boldly our highest and ultimate wishes. Whether we get them or not immediately, let our rulers know what our highest aspirations are. And if we are true to ourselves the work of each delegate present here will be to make the part of India where he happens to live devote itself earnestly to carrying out the objects resolved upon at this Congress with all due deliberation. If, then, we lay down clearly that we desire to have the actual government of India transferred from England to India under the simple controlling power of the Secretary of State, and of Parliament, through its Standing Committee, and that we further desire that all taxation and legislation shall be imposed here by representative Councils, we say what we are aiming at.'[9]

But the first Congress refused to do what Naoroji wanted it to do and obviously contented itself with the general statement of its objects made by its president, W.C. Bonnerjee. With slight modifications these objects were publicly reiterated by A.O. Hume in 1887 and 1888. In his Introduction to the *Report of the Third Indian National Congress*, 1887, he said that 'the objects of the National Movement, of which the Congress is one, and at the moment, the most prominent and tangible outcome, are threefold: the fusion into one national whole of all the different and, till recently, discordant elements that constitute the population of India; the gradual regeneration along all lines, mental, moral, social, and political, of the nation thus evolved; and the consolidation of the union between England and India by securing the modification of such of its conditions as may be unjust or injurious to the latter country'.[10] These objects were further amplified in the same Introduction as follows: 'The Congress was intended to bring face to face, and make thoroughly known to each other, all the men of light and leading of all portions of the empire. Thus far, there had been much correspondence, and, here and there, a single leader from one province, on his way to Europe or in the course of travel, found his way to the capital of another province, and there made the acquaintance of some of its leaders. But it was now intended to bring all such yearly together and establish the closer bonds of personal friendship between the most earnest and eminent labourers in the work of India's political regeneration.

'Of course, it was not overlooked that in this way would also be brought together men equally, or even more, interested in other branches of the national regeneration; and that these would equally profit indirectly from these gatherings; and that in conjunction with, though distinct from them, conferences, of groups of co-religionists or co-workers in the same branches thus met together, would be held, and some advance thus secured in all directions. But the primary and avowed objects are political, in the broadest sense of the word, and with these only, and not with the incidental advantages it brought in its train to other branches of the work, is it now proposed to deal.

'Further, the Congress was intended to enable all interested in public questions to supplement their knowledge and correct their views in the light of the information possessed, and the opinions held, by others equally interested.

'It was intended to eliminate provincial jealousies, prejudices, and misconceptions, by close personal intercourse, not only from the minds of the members of the Congress itself but from those of the leading inhabitants, and, so far as might be, the people generally, of all the presidencies and provinces, in each of which it was arranged that the Congress should in turn assemble.

'It was intended to exorcise sectarian and class antipathies by associating in one common work, for the common good, leading professors of all creeds and leading members of all sects and classes.

'It was intended—as no such gatherings could be accomplished, except at considerable cost in money, time, and personal convenience, not only to the members of the party in the province in which the assemblage took place, who were to act as hosts, but to all the members of the Congress delegated from other provinces, who had from one to two thousand miles to travel—to habituate all to personal sacrifices for the common good.

'It was intended, by concentrating the most strenuous efforts on great national questions and diminishing the absorption in local or purely selfish interests, to foster a wider altruism and a more genuine public spirit.

'It was intended to educate all who took part in it, not merely in the arts of public-speaking and debate, developing the faculty of thinking out clearly opinions and expressing them lucidly to others, not merely in habits of accuracy and research, but in the practice of self-control, moderation, and a willingness to give and take; to educate them, in fact, into what, but for the miserable displays of recent times, might fitly have been termed a genuine Parliamentary frame of mind.

'It was intended to familiarise the country with the methods and working of Representative Institutions on a large scale, and, thus, as this familiarity grew, to demonstrate to the Government and People of England that India was already ripe for some measure of those Institutions to which the entire intelligence of the country so earnestly aspires.

'It was intended to unify public opinion by the interfusion of the views held by all classes in all the various provinces, and, eliminating matters sectional and provincial, to arrive at definite and unanimous conclusions on all truly national questions, and to press these conclusions on the Government, not in the spirit of an Opposition but rather as *amici curiae*.

'It was intended to widen the basis of the National Party, the party of Progress and Order, the British Party in the truest sense of the word, until it became absolutely co-extensive with the entire population of the Empire, not solely by the awakening of the masses that follows in each province its assemblage there, but by the missionary labours of all the members of the Congress throughout the year, who, in and near their homes, as Standing Congress Committees and Sub-Committees, by lectures, public meetings, and the distribution of tens of thousands of simple tracts in the local vernaculars, were expected to spread from mind to mind an elementary knowledge of the burning political questions of the day and, generally, of the rights and duties of all good citizens of a civilized State.'[11]

Though the Congress avoided committing itself officially to any definite ideal in its early years, we have evidence to suggest that its ultimate aim from the very beginning was to secure home rule or colonial self-government for India. In a private letter to Dadabhai Naoroji, dated 12 December 1887, Hume wrote that 'though we do not thus designate them—and do not aim at any such radical separation—even in a pretty distant future—as do the Irish—after all our efforts are directed towards Home Rule for India'.[12] Writing to the editor of the Allahabad *Morning Post* on 17 May 1888, Hume said: 'So far as I know, no leading member of the National Congress thinks that for the next twenty years at any rate the country will require or be fit for anything more than the mixed Councils that have been advocated at the Congresses. But we, one and all, look forward to a time, say 50, say 70 years hence, when the Government of India will be precisely similar to that of the Dominion of Canada; when, as there, each province and presidency will have its local Parliament for provincial affairs, and the whole country will have its Dominion Parliament for national affairs, and when the only officials *sent out to India* from England will be the Viceroy and Governor-General.... To such a system we all look forward.... But the country is not nearly fit for all this yet. No one expects that a full Parliamentary system can possibly be introduced here under fifty years....'[13]

That the Congress was not to remain satisfied for all time to come with self-government in the internal affairs of India, but would also some day try to control the foreign affairs of the country, was made clear by Hume in his famous letter of 13 October 1888 to Auckland Colvin, wherein he wrote: '...our Congress, though in its infancy, *is* destined to be a Hercules, and true to its prototype, it now, in its infancy, aims only at reforming the internal administration, the nation's domestic affairs, though doubtless, as the years roll on and the reformed and expanded Legislatures it contends for, broaden into Parliaments, it will, in its maturity, cleanse and thoroughly purge the Augean stable of our Foreign Policy.'[14]

The leaders of the early Congress realized that their country still lacked some of the essential elements which constituted a nation, and the people did not yet have sufficient powers of coherence among themselves; therefore, a foreign rule like that of the British, which kept them together and at the same time assured them an efficient and moderately liberal government, must be looked upon not merely as a necessity, but as a beneficial necessity. They were convinced that there was no better alternative, indigenous or foreign, to British rule in India at that time, and that there was not likely to be any such alternative to British rule in India in the foreseeable future. Their patriotism therefore demanded that they should loyally accept the British Raj as a fact, for a sudden and premature termination of that Raj was likely to be harmful to their own national interests. Early Congressmen openly avowed their belief that they were loyal because they were patriotic. Even their faith in British justice and their fervid declarations about perpetuating the Raj were inspired by their faith and hope that their British rulers would train and enable them to govern themselves. 'I am loyal to the British Government,' said B.C. Pal in 1887, 'because with me loyalty to the British Government is identical with loyalty to my own country; because I believe that God has placed this Government over us for our salvation; because I know that without the help and tuition of this Government my people shall never be able to rise to their legitimate place in the commonwealth of civilized nations; because I am convinced that there is no other government on the face of the earth which so much favours the growth of infant nationalities, and under which the germs of popular Government can so vigorously grow as under the British Government....I am loyal to the British Government, because I love self-government.'[15] M.M. Ghose remarked in 1890: 'To my mind, our allegiance to the British Government is based, not only on the feeling of gratitude which the benefits conferred upon us must evoke in our hearts, but also upon the highest grounds of expediency; for every sane man in India, who is capable of thinking, must feel that any change of Government at the present time would be the greatest calamity that could befall the people of this country. That we should have been better pleased if we could have governed ourselves as well as we are governed by England, is a sentiment which we need not in the least shrink from avowing, because not only is such a feeling natural, but it is perfectly consistent to my mind with true loyalty to England.'[16] C. Sankaran Nair emphasized the same point in 1897. Presiding over the Amraoti session of the Indian National Congress, he said: '...it should not be forgotten for a moment that the real link that binds us to England is the hope, the well-founded hope and belief, that with England's help we shall, and, under her guidance alone, we can attain national unity and national freedom.'[17] In his presidential address to the 1899 session of the Congress at Lucknow, R.C. Dutt observed: 'Educated India has practically identified itself with British rule, seeks to perpetuate British rule, is loyal to British rule, as Lord Dufferin said, not through sentiment, but through the stronger motive of self-interest; because it is by a continuance of the British rule that educated India seeks to secure that larger measure of self-government, that position among the modern nations of the earth, which it is our aim and endeavour to secure.'[18]

The progress of self-government in the colonies, more than anything else, gave Congressmen cause for hope and confidence. Will England refuse to her brown subjects what she gave to her white ones? Surendranath Banerjea remarked in 1895 that England was 'the august mother of free nations' and appealed to her 'gradually to change the character of her rule in India, to liberalize it, to shift its foundations, to adapt it to the newly-developed environments of the country and the people, so that, in the fullness of time, India may find its place in the great confederacy of free States, English in their origin, English in their character, English in their institutions, rejoicing in their permanent and indissoluble union with England, a glory to the mother-country, and an honour to the human race'.[19]

Though deep down in the heart of every Indian nationalist there was the fervent aspiration that his country would some day become self-governing and individual Congressmen often gave expression to that aspiration, yet for many a long year after its inception, the Congress as an organization did not explicitly commit itself to the objective of attaining self-government for India. Even as late as 1899, when the Congress gave to itself a written constitution for the first time, it did not consider it worth while to declare in set terms what its ultimate aim was. The constitution adopted in 1899 merely said: 'The object of the Indian National Congress shall be to promote by constitutional means the interests and the well-being of the people of the Indian Empire.'[20] The leaders of the early Congress were practical-minded enough to realize that India could not be fit for parliamentary self-government in their own lifetime. Convinced that their ultimate objective lay in the distant future and that it could only be achieved through the good will and co-operation of Englishmen, the leaders of the early Congress saw no need to encourage impatient idealism in their followers or to scare their rulers by raising the cry of self-government for India. It is not improbable that Congressmen would have immediately inscribed home rule on their banner if Gladstone had succeeded in his efforts to grant home rule to Ireland in 1886 or 1893, for they were intelligent enough to realize that whatever was given to Ireland would have to be, sooner or later, given to India also. But the defeat of Gladstone's efforts (the first Irish Home Rule Bill in 1886 was rejected by the House of Commons; the second in 1893 passed the Commons but was thrown out by the Lords), was a terrible disappointment to Congressmen in India. It warned them against the folly of asking for India something which had only recently been denied to Ireland or of even using a phrase which had become suspect in the eyes of most members of the ruling race. Nor were the long years of Tory dominance and jingo imperialism which followed in England the right time for the Congress to formally adopt the ideal of self-government for India.

By 1904, however, the situation had begun to change. The fever of jingoism had abated in England and there were signs of a Liberal revival. Indian nationalists could now expect to get a better hearing in England. The victories of Japan over Russia had aroused new hopes and aspirations throughout Asia. The avowed policy of the United States of America to prepare the Filipinos for self-government and that of Britain to grant representative government to its erstwhile enemies, the Boers, in South Africa were jealously noted by the Indians. Twenty years of almost fruitless agitation had demoralized the Congress. Its policy of loyalty, moderation and reasonableness had obviously not paid off. The need for an ennobling ideal and more vigorous methods of agitation was being widely discussed in India. It was at this time that William Digby and Dadabhai Naoroji advised the Congress to unfurl the banner of self-government for India. Speaking before the London India Society on 1 June 1904, Digby referred to the new Asia being called into existence by the marvellous achievements of Japan, to the noble policy being pursued by the United States of America in the Philippines and to the inability of the average Englishman to appreciate the numerous individual and local grievances voiced by the Congress, and he suggested that the forthcoming session of the Congress at Bombay 'should concentrate on one subject only'—'the need for Indian self-government'.[21] Naoroji, who followed Digby, spoke in a similar vein. He emphasized that there was only 'one remedy for the present dishonourable, hypocritical, and destructive system' of British rule in India and that was 'self-government under British paramountcy'. 'When this fundamental remedy would be accomplished', he remarked, 'every other evil or defect of the present system—all material and moral evils and administrative defects—would right themselves.' He revealed how at the very first Congress in 1885 he had indicated 'this great and absolute necessity of the situation as the chief object and mission of the Congress' and remarked that 'it was high time—as matters had gone from bad to worse under such rulers as Lord George Hamilton and Lord Curzon—that Indians took up this demand as the front and foreground of their work'.[22]

The suggestion of Digby and Naoroji was at once approved of by the nationalist press in India and in December 1904 the president of the Bombay session of the Indian National Congress, Sir Henry Cotton, acting probably upon their suggestion, declared self-government within the British Empire to be the objective of the Indian people. 'The ideal of the Indian patriot', remarked Cotton on the occasion, 'is the establishment of a federation of free and separate States, the United States of India, placed on a fraternal footing with the self-governing Colonies ... under the aegis of Great Britain.'[23]

There was nothing new or revolutionary about this ideal, but it had never before been put forward in such unmistakable terms from the Congress platform. And in the circumstances of the time it acquired a peculiar significance and was immediately taken up by others. G.K. Gokhale incorporated the ideal of colonial self-government in the preamble to the rules of his Servants of India Society founded in June 1905.[24] In the autumn of 1905, while on a visit to England, he advanced it from numerous platforms as the ultimate goal of the educated classes in India.[25] In his message to the Indian people in November 1905, Naoroji re-emphasized 'the absolute necessity of freedom and self-government like that of the Colonies' as the only remedy for India's woes and

The Objectives and Methods of the Indian National Congress

wrongs.[26] Presiding over the 1905 session of the Congress at Banaras, Gokhale declared: 'The goal of the Congress is that India should be governed in the interests of the Indians themselves, and that in course of time a form of Government should be attained in this country similar to what exists in the self-governing Colonies of the British Empire.'[27] In an interview with John Morley, 1 August 1906, Gokhale acquainted the new Liberal secretary of state for India, with the ultimate hope and design of the Congress—'India to be on the footing of a self-governing colony'—and was met with the rejoinder that 'for many a day to come—long beyond the span of time that may be left to me—this was a mere dream'.[28] But Gokhale could not afford to be discouraged. Curzon had raised a storm in India by his words and deeds. He had bred a spirit of resentment among the educated classes throughout the country and brought them face to face with their rulers. As a combative response to his partition of Bengal, a boycott movement had been launched in that province. A new school of thought had developed within the Congress which began to preach the ideal of 'absolute autonomy' and 'freedom' from British rule. A 'new patriotism' had grown up as opposed to the 'old', 'loyal patriotism' of the founders of the Congress. The rebels within the Congress, led by men like Bal Gangadhar Tilak, Aurobindo Ghose, Bipin Chandra Pal and Lajpat Rai, styled themselves the 'New Party' in order to distinguish themselves from the old organization. They called themselves 'Nationalists' as opposed to the old loyalist Congressmen. Their critics nicknamed them 'Extremists'.

The elder nationalists, we shall henceforth call them Moderates, had tended to regard British rule as a beneficial necessity. Extremists believed that any foreign rule, however just and benevolent, was a curse. For Moderates, loyalty was synonymous with patriotism. Extremists thought that loyalty to British rule was incompatible with patriotism. Moderates had faith in the liberality and sense of justice of the British people. Extremists dismissed this faith of elder Congressmen in British justice and liberality as a snare and a delusion. Philanthropy, they said, had no place in politics; and appeals to the good feelings of rulers were vain. Moderates had been anxious to keep down the racial element in their political agitation. Extremists did not hesitate to foster racial antagonism.

The Congress had so far devoted itself to demanding isolated reforms and the redress of particular grievances. Extremists did not believe in these palliatives and tinkerings. They demanded a radical change in the system of government itself—'the substitution for the autocratic bureaucracy, which at the present misgoverns us, of a free and democratic system of Government and the entire removal of foreign control in order to make way for perfect national liberty'.[29] The older Congressmen believed that the continuance of British rule was the indispensable condition of India's progress and prosperity. Extremists argued that political freedom was the essential preliminary to all national progress. As Aurobindo Ghose put it: 'Political freedom is the life-breath of a nation; to attempt social reform, educational reform, industrial expansion, the moral improvement of the race without aiming first and foremost at political freedom, is the very height of ignorance and futility.'[30]

Extremists were eager to foreshorten history. England had hitherto been the model for the politically-minded classes in India. Their teachers had been English books and English politicians. They could not conceive of a truly popular and democratic government in India except by a process of gradual and slow evolution, of progress broadening from precedent to precedent. Extremists dismissed the English model as unsuited to India. How could the experience of an independent nation, they asked, be a valid guide to a subject people? They appealed instead to the revolutionary traditions of France, America, Italy and Ireland. Constitutional agitation, they said, in a country where there was no constitution and the people had no control over the administration, was futile. Borrowing the methods of the Irish Sinn Fein,[31] they preached the need for organized passive resistance and self-reliance. The British government in India was, they argued, based upon the help of the few and the acquiescence of the many. It was *maya*, a hypontic illusion, which had to be destroyed. They hoped to make the administration impossible by an organized refusal to do anything which might help the rulers. They advocated a boycott of British goods, government-controlled schools and colleges, law courts, and executive authority in general. Along with this boycott, a campaign of self-development was to be launched aimed at the promotion of *swadeshi* (indigenous) goods, national education, arbitration courts and the organization of public life independent of the government—building up from the villages to a central national polity. For the time being their movement was to be confined to abstention from any co-operation with the government, but if the latter did not pay any heed to their demands, recourse was to be taken to such measures as the non-payment of taxes. They were to begin with the principle of 'no control, no assistance', but when they had developed strength and a parallel government of their own, they could present an ultimatum to their alien rulers. Extremists hoped to achieve their objectives by peaceful and legal methods, but they did not rule out the possibility of resistance to 'unjust laws', or of resorting to force in self-defence, for after all, as they said, boycott was war.

With such ideas and such a programme, it was but natural that the New Party should have fallen foul of the Congress ideal of self-government for India on the colonial model. Aurobindo Ghose wrote in 1907: 'The Congress has contended itself with demanding self-government as it exists in the Colonies. We of the new school would not pitch our ideal one inch lower than absolute Swaraj—self-government as it exists in the United Kingdom. We believe that no smaller ideal can inspire national revival or nerve the people of India for the fierce, stubborn and formidable struggle by which alone they can again become a nation. We believe that this newly awakened people, when it has gathered its strength together, neither can nor ought to consent to any relations with England less than that of equals in a confederacy. To be content with the relations of master and servant or superior and subordinate, would be a mean and pitiful aspiration unworthy of manhood; to strive for anything less than a strong and glorious freedom would be to insult the greatness of our past and the magnificent possibilities of our future.'[32] It is noteworthy that Aurobindo Ghose and his associates were not opposed to having friendly relations with Great Britain on a footing of equality. In fact, the new religion of patriotism which they preached was permeated with a vague universal ideal of the ultimate unity of mankind. But they insisted that the nation must realize its destiny to the full—unhampered in the least degree by foreign control. If India was to retain her individuality, said Aurobindo Ghose, as a political and cultural unit and fulfil her mission in the world, she could not do so 'overshadowed by a foreign power and a foreign civilization'.[33] 'The world needs India', he wrote, 'and needs her free. . . . She must live her own life and not the life of a part or subordinate in a foreign Empire.'[34] To Aurobindo Ghose the ideal of colonial self-government for India was 'the very negation of patriotism' and a 'political monstrosity'.[35] He, instead, propagated the ideal of 'absolute autonomy' and 'unqualified Swaraj'.

One of Aurobindo Ghose's closest political associates, B.C. Pal, discussed at length the impracticability and impossibility of 'self-government under British paramountcy' for India in his famous speeches at Madras in May 1907.[36] If Britain controlled Indian foreign policy, he said, she could not do so without controlling India's armed forces and this would entail control of the purse, which would be a negation of India's right of self-taxation and self-government. The argument that Britain protected her colonies without demanding the expenses thereof and could treat India similarly was, in his view, invalid, for the colonies stood on a different footing. They were white and inhabited by the kith and kin of the British people. They received Britain's surplus population and her help in developing their resources. Britain was interested in their safety and well-being both for their sakes and her own. What Britain did for her colonies, Pal argued, she would not do for India. He then tried to prove how self-government within the British Empire would either be no self-government for India or no real overlordship for Britain. Indians would not be satisfied with 'a shadow of self-government' nor would Britain be satisfied with 'a shadowy overlordship'.[37] If India became self-governing like the colonies, he said, she would impose protective tariffs in order to encourage her industries and do away with the privileges enjoyed by British capital in the country at present, and this would never be tolerated by Britain. Moreover, if a country as large and populous as India obtained self-government, 'the British Empire would cease to be British', for India would soon become 'the predominant partner in this imperial firm'.[38] Pal, therefore, believed that Britain would herself prefer to have a self-governing India as an ally, like Japan, rather than as a partner in the Empire.

This frank and open repudiation of the ideal of colonial self-government for India by Aurobindo Ghose and B.C. Pal was not much to the taste of the acknowledged leader of Extremists, Tilak, who, for all his active and militant politics, was a great realist. He wrote in his paper, the *Kesari*, early in 1907 that self-government on the colonial model sufficed for him as an ideal to work for.[39] His difference with Moderates, he repeatedly pointed out, was not with regard to the objective but only with regard to the methods of agitation to be pursued by the Congress. The young, impatient idealists in India, who looked up to Tilak as 'the one possible leader for a revolutionary party',[40] were disappointed to discover in their hero an old-world politician, cautious and conservative, who would not inscribe an academic and dangerous ideal on his banner.

While Moderates demanded self-government as the right of Indians as British citizens, Extremists were inclined to take their stand on the French revolutionary doctrine that freedom was their birthright as human beings. While Moderates believed in appealing to the reason and generosity of their rulers, Extremists tried to appeal to their fears. While Moderates believed in borrowing wholesale from the west, Extremists were anxious that India should retain her individuality. Moderates and Extremists also differed on the question of the character of the Indian National Congress. Moderates wanted the Congres to remain an elitist organization. Extremists were out to wrest control of the Congress and turn it into a mass organization.

Generally speaking, Moderates were upper middle-class men, elderly, well-to-do liberally educated, anglicized, secular in outlook, conservative in political matters, influenced by British constitutionalism, apathetic and cautious. In the same manner, Extremists may be described as lower middle-class men, younger, in age, not very well-to-do, not so liberally educated, less anglicized, less secular in outlook, radical in political matters, influenced by European revolutionary ideas, energetic and bold. In 1913 Edwyn Bevan tried to distinguish between Moderates and Extremists in India by using the metaphor of a man unable to swim, who was upheld and grasped in deep water by a strong swimmer. 'The swimmer says, "If I let you go, you will only sink". The man, if he is a Moderate, replies, "Yes, I want you to go on holding me, but I don't want you to hold me so *tight*", whereas the Extremist says, "I know I shall go under and have a horrible time of choking and distress, but that is the only way in which I can learn to swim".'[41] Bevan also tried to point out that Extremists had got splendidly one great truth—that emancipation was something much wider and deeper than politics, that it was a matter of building up a national character, of renewing all departments of life. Extremists, he added, had turned away from the rationalism and secularism of Moderates to old religious and cultural traditions. They believed that India would gain little if she only shook off the alien government and did not get back her soul. They had a genuine religious craving for something larger and richer than narrow rationalism. This aspect of Extremism in India seemed to Bevan in many ways like the Romantic movement which marked the early part of the nineteenth century in Europe and which was a recoil from the eighteenth-century rationalism and enlightenment. It was in part the outbreak of the human spirit from an imprisonment which cut it off from the wide-stretching fields of its inheritance.[42]

The rapid growth of the New Party alarmed Moderates. It threatened to destroy them, the Congress, and the reforms which they expected the Liberal government in Britain to introduce in India. Already in the summer of 1906 Morley, the secretary of state for India, had assured Gokhale that the British government was in earnest to make an effective move in the direction of 'reasonable reforms' in India and warned him that the surest way to spoil their chances was 'the perversity and unreason' of his friends and their 'clamour for the impossible'.[43] Would the old leaders of the Congress throw overboard their rebellious followers and thus save the Congress and the reforms? *The Times* in a special article, 16 October 1906, frankly recommended such a course of action. It suggested to Moderates 'a public repudiation' of Extremists both as a matter of public honesty, for men holding such divergent views as Gokhale and Tilak should not continue the pretence of working together, and in order to strengthen their own position. 'If the idea of separation from England were explicitly disavowed and condemned' and Extremists formally repudiated, the writer of the special article in *The Times* said, the Congress would secure the support of Englishmen and Muslims who sympathized with its aspirations for moderate progress; it would be able to exert greater influence upon public affairs and 'the bulk of the other reforms demanded by the Congress would probably be realized'.[44]

Moderates still hesitated to take such a course. They were anxious to avoid an open split in the Congress and thereby weaken it. Nor were they without hope of winning over Extremists by means of persuasion. In order to counteract the election of Tilak as president of the 1906 Congress, for which some Extremists, notably from Bengal, were working and which would have been a signal that the Congress had been captured by the radicals, Moderate leaders persuaded Dadabhai Naoroji to come over from England in order to preside over the 1906 session of the organization to be held in Calcutta. The great personal influence of 'the Grand Old Man of India' sufficed to maintain the unity of the Congress for some time, but it was not without making large concessions to the wishes of Extr mists.

There was a curious mingling of old ways and new at the 1906 session of the Congress. Naoroji proclaimed the Congress ideal to be 'Self-government or *Swaraj* like that of the United Kingdom or the Colonies'.[45] The ideal of *swaraj* emerged as the one main and comprehensive object. Naoroji demanded it as the birthright of Indians as British citizens. 'I say we are British citizens and are entitled to and claim all British citizens' rights. . . . This birthright to be "free" or to have freedom is our right from the very beginning of our connection with England when we came under the British flag. When Bombay was acquired as the very first territorial possession, the government of the day in the very first grant of territorial rights to the East India Company [24 March 1669] declared thus: "And it is declared that all persons being His Majesty's subjects inhabiting within the said Island and their children and their posterity born within the limits thereof shall be declared free denizens and natural subjects as if living and born in England".'[46] This declaration of the rights of Indians as British citizens, Naoroji added, had been reinforced by latter-day pledges, chief among which was the Queen's proclamation of 1858 which read: 'We hold ourselves bound to the natives of our Indian territories by the same obligations of duty which bind us to all our other subjects, and these obligations, by the blessing of Almighty God, we shall faithfully and conscientiously fulfil.'[47] Naoroji was basing his claim on documents which had no legal validity, but what is significant is the fact that he claimed a British constitutional right instead of appealing to the French revolutionary doctrine of the inherent and inalienable right of all men to be free.[48]

By a formal resolution the Calcutta Congress expressed its opinion 'that the system of Government obtaining in the self-governing British Colonies should be extended to India' and urged the immediate adoption of certain reforms as 'steps leading to it'.[49]

Soon after the Calcutta session of the Congress Gokhale undertook a tour of northern India in order to combat the influence of the dangerous doctrines preached by Extremists. In a speech at Allahabad on 4 February 1907, he stated frankly and fully the creed of Moderates. He recognized, he said on the occasion, no limits to his aspirations for his motherland. He wanted his people to rise to the full stature of their manhood and be in their country what other people were in theirs. He aspired to see his country take her proper place among the great nations of the world. But he felt convinced that the whole of this aspiration, in its essence and in its reality, could be realized within the British Empire. 'The cases of the French in Canada and the Boers in South Africa showed', Gokhale remarked, 'that there was room in the Empire for a self-respecting India.' It was not a question, he said, 'of what was theoretically perfect, but of what was practically attainable'. While working for the achievement of self-government within the British Empire, they were trying to advance along lines which were well understood and which involved 'a minimum of disturbance of existing ideas'. They would have in such an advance the sympathy and support of much that was high-minded, freedom-loving and honourable in England. Gokhale asserted that, despite occasional lapses and reactions, 'the genius of the British people, as revealed in history, on the whole, made for political freedom, for constitutional liberty', and that it would be folly and madness on the part of Indians to throw away this great asset in the struggle that lay before them. He deprecated the cry that constitutional agitation had failed while they had not yet exhausted a thousandth part of its possibilities. While he recognized that nine-tenths of their work had to be done by them in India, Gokhale insisted on keeping in touch with 'British democracy', for it could be of valuable assistance to them in checking official retrogression and in promoting nation-building. He condemned the doctrine of passive resistance and all-round boycott preached by Extremists not only because he thought it to be impracticable and injurious, but also because he saw in it an 'attempt to shift the foundations of their public life'. He pointed out that nation-building was nowhere an easy task and that in India it was beset with difficulties which were truly formidable. He warned his countrymen of the long and weary struggle that lay before them and of the dangers of undue impatience. Gokhale concluded on a note which, for all its wisdom and sincerity, showed that Moderates were fighting a losing battle. 'Let us not forget', he said, 'that we are at a stage of the country's progress when our achievements are bound to be small, and our disappointments frequent and trying.... It will, no doubt, be given to our countrymen of future generations to serve India by their successes; we, of the present generation, must be content to serve her mainly by our failures.'[50]

But the young were impatient, heedless of obstacles, and careless as to methods. They were no longer in a mood to serve India by their failures. Their attacks on the Moderate leaders and the authorities grew increasingly bitter and strident. Moderates judged correctly that the Extremist heresy was not yet widespread. They decided to coerce Extremists into submission or to eject them out of the Congress. They shifted the venue of the forthcoming session of the Congress in December 1907 from Nagpur, where it was likely to be flooded with the followers of Tilak, to Surat, which was Pherozeshah Mehta's pocket borough. They managed to get a Moderate Bengali, Rashbehari Ghose, elected as president of the session. And finally, to force a few Extremists who had openly preached the doctrine of complete independence and all-round boycott, out of the Congress, they decided to impose a new constitution on the organization which required every delegate to the Congress session to subscribe to the ideal of self-government similar to that enjoyed by the self-governing members of the British Empire, to be attained by strictly constitutional means.

Amidst all the dust and din of the controversy about the Surat split—the clash of personalities, the charges and countercharges of irregularities and backslidings, of obduracy and responsibility for hurling the 'Mahratta shoe'—it is easy to discern two points of cardinal importance which divided the two sections in the Congress. Some of the Extremists, led by Aurobindo Ghose, already stood committed to the ideal of absolute autonomy and complete self-government. The attempt to confine the membership of the Congress only to those who definitely and openly subscribed to the ideal of self-government within the British Empire was interpreted by them as a clever move designed to eliminate them from the organization. The second major difference was over the methods. The Congress at its Calcutta session in 1906 had given its approval to the campaign for the boycott of British goods as a temporary measure intended to put pressure on the British government and draw its attention to the grievance about the partition of Bengal. Extremists interpreted boycott in the widest possible sense. To them it was complete Irish Sinn Fein—a boycott not only of British goods, but of everything connected with the British administration in India. To yield to Extremists on these two points—the creed and the methods—would have meant handing over the Congress to them. If the Congress were to remain a loyal, moderate and respectable organization, it could not shelter under its wings those who stood for 'absolute Swaraj' outside the British Empire and preached non-co-operation with the government. The Congress had so far endeavoured to work for national advance in association with the British rulers. It was convinced that there was no alternative to the British Raj in India except chaos. Though disappointed of the British bureaucracy, it still retained its faith in the British democracy. Moderates felt that Extremists were not only challenging the very bases of older thought and belief, but endangering national progress itself. They decided, therefore, either to bridle Extremists, or, if they proved recalcitrant, to disown them. Some youthful Extremists, headed by Aurobindo Ghose, decided to wreck the organization instead of being driven out of it.[51] The result was the Surat episode.

The Congress did not, however, dissolve in chaos at Surat. Soon after the disorderly scenes of the second day of the session, 27 December 1907, the older Moderate leaders, P.M. Mehta, D.E. Wacha, G. K. Gokhale, R.B. Ghose, V. K. Iyer, M. M. Malaviya and others, met in private and drew up a notice calling a National Convention to meet the next day, 28 December, of all those delegates who subscribed to the ideal of self-government for India on the colonial model and its attainment by strictly constitutional means. Over 900 delegates, out of the 1,600 who had come to Surat, attended the Convention, which appointed a committee to draw up a constitution for the Congress.[52] This 'Convention Committee' met at Allahabad on 18-19 April 1908 and framed a constitution for the Congress, as also a set of rules for the conduct of its meetings. Article I of the new constitution enunciated the

The Objectives and Methods of the Indian National Congress

creed of the Congress. It read: 'The Objects of the Indian National Congress are the attainment by the people of India of a system of government similar to that enjoyed by the self-governing Members of the British Empire, and a participation by them in the rights and responsibilities of the Empire on equal terms with those Members. These Objects are to be achieved by constitutional means by bringing about a steady reform of the existing system of administration and by promoting national unity, fostering public spirit and developing and organizing the intellectual, moral, economic and industrial resources of the country.'[53] Article II required every delegate to the Congress to express in writing his acceptance of this creed.[54]

The *Bande Mataram*, the organ of Bengali Extremists, in its issue of 23 April 1908, accused the Convention of having betrayed 'the mandate of the country and the future of their people'. It condemned Moderates as 'advocates of contradiction', 'servants of the alien bureaucrat disguised as patriots', 'foes of Indian independence', timid men who had 'refused to serve the Mother with an undivided heart' and 'placed the alien on the throne of her future and dared to think that she would accept a left hand and inferior chair at the side of his seat of empire'.[55] Again, on 3 May 1908, it denounced the ideal adopted by the Convention as a denial of India's birthright, her individuality, her past and her independent future, an attempt to maintain India in 'the position of a subordinate satellite in a foreign system'.[56]

Though Moderates succeeded in driving out Extremists and in retaining their hold over the Congress for a few more years, they knew that a large part of the country's politically-minded population sympathized with Extremists. As Gokhale wrote to Mrs Besant in January 1915: 'The two parties are not evenly matched. There is naturally a great volume of anti-foreign feeling—expressed or unexpressed—in the country and it loads the scales heavily on Tilak's side. We have to ask our countrymen to be reconciled to foreign domination—even though it be a transitional arrangement—and our propaganda has to rest on one of its sides on some measure of faith in the sense of justice of British democracy. Tilak has no difficulty in ridiculing the latter as "mendicancy" and denouncing the former as pusillanimous and unpatriotic cringing to the authorities. The number of men who can form a sound political judgement in the country is not large. But you can find any number of unthinking men, filled with an honest but vague longing for the emancipation of the country, ready to follow any plausible leaders, whom, in their heart of hearts, they believe to be wholly "against the foreigner". It was with the help of such a following that Tilak captured the Poona Sarvajanik Sabha, the work of Ranade's hands—and destroyed its usefulness in less than twelve months (the Government placing it under a ban owing to its excesses). It was with the help of such a following that he nearly wrecked the Congress at Poona in 1895. And finally it was with the help of such a following that he actually wrecked the Congress at Surat in 1907.'[57]

The *Indian Social Reformer*, 5 May 1907, however, asserted that the main reason why Extremist fancies were gaining ground more rapidly among the younger generation of Indians than the weighty counsels of Moderates was that the Moderate programme made 'little or no demand for sacrifice from its advocates and supporters'. The paper added: 'Ease does not possess for the human mind any fascination whatever. It is comfortable, but the minds which rest in the comfortable belong to faded natures lacking in sensibility....Bravery attracts humanity, even if it is limited to words....Why do the wise, sensible, moderate utterances of our leaders fall comparatively flat on younger minds? Because they do not make any demand on chivalry and the burning instinct of self-sacrifice in youthful natures. The Moderate programme is too comfortable to fascinate fresh and energetic natures.'[58]

The ouster of Extremists from the Congress had an extremely debilitating effect on the organization. Energy, activity and fighting quality were not the strong points of Moderates. And though they came to be increasingly patronized by the British government, they were steadily rejected by their own people. They controlled an organization from which the spirit had departed. Moderates were on the horns of a dilemma: the Congress could only be revitalized by getting back Extremists; but getting back Extremists meant handing over the control of the organization to them. Extremists tried to turn the people against the Moderate caucus. They raised the slogan of unity and democracy within the organization. They were aided in their efforts, during 1914-16, by the release of Tilak from jail, the coming of the First World War, the deaths of Gokhale and Mehta, the two most able and influential Moderate leaders, and Mrs Annie Besant's campaign for home

The Objectives and Methods of the Indian National Congress 113

rule and a united national movement in India.

Under the pressure of events abroad and of public opinion in India, Extremists were allowed to re-enter the Congress in 1916 and before the year was out the Muslim League had signed a pact at Lucknow with its old antagonist. The Home Rule Leagues of Besant and Tilak daily gained fresh converts. Though they gave India no new doctrine, the Home Rule Leagues did provide the country with a powerful slogan and a widespread organization for effective agitation. The rapid success of the home rule movement in India forced the British to resort to their old and familiar policy of 'rallying the moderates'. This did not prove to be very difficult. The Congress Moderates, in particular, were themselves willing to be rallied. They were feeling very uneasy within the Congress, where Extremists were busy displacing them from their positions of authority and influence within the organization, or making the pace too hot for those who managed to survive their iconoclastic fervour. The publication of the Montagu-Chelmsford Report in July 1918 provided many Moderates with an occasion and an excuse to leave the Congress and to organize, in November 1918, a separate Moderates' Conference of their own. But the aftermath of the war, scarcity, high prices, a devastating influenza epidemic, Muslim uneasiness about Turkey and the Khilafat, and the slow process of law-making at Westminster were hardly calculated to promote the influence of Moderates in India. The passage of the ill-timed Rowlatt Act, despite protests by Moderates, exposed their position and shook their prestige. And then, in 1919, came the Amritsar massacre which put the Montagu-Chelmsford reforms and Moderates into the dark shade from which they could never recover.

The Nagpur session of the Congress in December 1920 was the largest so far held. The *petit bourgeois* mass flooded the gathering. The leaders would have gladly moved at a slower pace, but the crowd had taken the reins in their hands and drove the former. At this session the Congress broke definitely and decisively with Moderates. The object of the Congress was redefined as 'the attainment of Swarajya by the people of India by all legitimate and peaceful means'.[59] The question of India's membership of the British Commonwealth was left open. But it was not yet a complete victory for the young radicals. As one of them commented later: 'Regarding both the goal and the means, the decision of the Nagpur

Congress represented the golden mean between the views of the Right-Wingers like Pandit Malaviya and Mr. Jinnah and the youthful Left-Wingers who swamped the Congress for the first time in 1920. The latter desired the goal of the Congress to be complete independence to be attained by all possible means. It was Mr. Gandhi, however, who by virtue of his tremendous influence and popularity was able to keep the Left-Wingers at bay.'[60]

6

THE MORLEY-MINTO REFORMS

The Indian National Congress was the child of Gladstonian liberalism, but the first twenty years of its existence[1] coincided with the ascendancy of the Conservative party and the growth of jingo imperialism in England. Disappointed of the bureaucracy in India, the Congress had from its very inception concentrated all its hopes on the democracy in Great Britain. The apathy of the latter, too, during this crucial early period, towards their very modest and reasonable demands,[2] saddened and disillusioned those who had launched the movement with great hope and faith in the sense of justice and freedom of the British people. The younger nationalists began to develop a Faust-like mood. They judged the limited objectives of the older Congressmen to be unsatisfactory and their methods of prayer and petition, futile and unbecoming. A new school grew up within the Congress which demanded self-government and advocated more self-reliant and vigorous methods for its achievement.

Various events combined to make the year 1905 a turning-point in Indian politics. Lord Curzon's policies, especially his partition of Bengal, aroused a great deal of resentment and gave rise to the *swadeshi*-cum-boycott movement. The victory of Japan over Russia in 1905 and the revolutionary stirrings in some parts of Europe and Asia encouraged radical agitation in India. In November 1905 Lord Minto succeeded Lord Curzon as the governor-general of India and in December of the same year a Liberal ministry came into office in Great Britain. Indian nationalists, who had come to regard the long years of Conservative dominance in England as a period of reaction, hailed with delight the coming into power of a Liberal government and the overwhelming majority it gained in the subsequent election of January 1906. The appointment of Morley, the great Radical, anti-imperialist and Home Ruler, to the India Office gave them cause for added optimism. Moderate Congress leaders, such as G.K. Gokhale and R.C. Dutt, hastened to England to acquaint the new secretary of state with their hopes and fears.

Had the partition of Bengal been modified and the reforms granted in 1906 or 1907, they would have gone a long way towards removing discontent in India and restoring confidence in British statesmanship. Both Minto and Morley agreed that the partition had been 'a sad mistake'[3]—ill-conceived and ill-managed—but Minto warned Morley against encouraging the impression in India that a change in government at home was likely to bring about the reversal of earlier decisions,[4] and that 'the faintest sign of withdrawal on our part would be construed as weakness—it would poison our whole rule here'.[5] In spite of his public declaration to the contrary, Morley never in fact considered partition to be 'a settled fact',[6] but he could not get a favourable opportunity of undoing it during his time of responsibility. The unfortunate delay in inaugurating the reforms, for which the government of India were mainly responsible, made matters worse. The disappointed Bengali agitators, incensed at Morley's remarks that the partition was 'a settled fact' and that the government of India was ever to remain 'personal and almost absolute',[7] intensified their passive resistance campaign. Moderates lost face and Extremism grew. At Surat in December 1907 the Congress was split and in April 1908 the bomb made its appearance on the Indian political scene. Other causes which contributed towards the growth of the so-called Indian unrest were a devastating plauge epidemic which had been raging unabated since 1897; the economic hardships of the middle classes due to the rise in prices and increase in unemployment; the agrarian grievances, especially in Panjab; and the policy of severe and indiscriminate repression adopted by certain panicky provincial governments.

It requires much knowledge and uncommon sympathy in alien rulers to understand the true nature and significance of a growing nationalism in a subject people. Neither Morley nor Minto had such knowledge and sympathy. They were primarily concerned with the agitation in India in so far as it seemed to threaten the security and stability of the British Raj. They had no ideas about, nor any desire of, guiding the nationalist movement in India towards what might be called its inevitable destiny. Indian unrest appeared to them to be more an evidence of original sin than a sign of grace.

Minto recognized that a new spirit was abroad in India, but he proposed to meet it by encouraging and strengthening the more conservative and loyal elements in Indian society as 'a possible counterpoise to Congress aims'.[8] Being the man on the spot and pressed by immediate anxieties, he was naturally more inclined to emphasize the subversive and disloyal character of the Congress movement. He often complained to Morley that the Congress agitation received mistaken sympathy and exaggerated importance at home and was aided by questions in the House of Commons. He considered the House of Commons to be 'perhaps the greatest danger to the continuance of our rule in the country'.[9] Minto was a man with a wide outlook and fairly liberal sympathies, but he was convinced that India was held by the sword and, therefore, too often prompted to underline the virtues of the strong hand. He even demanded that the government of India should be 'given a free hand to rule the country'.[10] Minto, however, did not fail to realize that the growth of education and political consciousness had created aspirations in India which it was difficult to ignore, and the urgent necessity of associating Indians with 'an administration which our military strength alone guarantee[d]'.[11]

Morley was nearing his seventieth year when he came to the India Office. He was, to quote his own words, 'as cautious a Whig as any Elliott, Russell or Grey, that was ever born',[12] and had 'no ambition to take part in any grand revolution'[13] during his time of responsibility. He was, however, determined to adjust the machinery of Indian government to meet the requirements of the changed circumstances in India and growing democratic opinion at home. The initiative, the guiding inspiration, and the driving force in the reforms were primarily his. He also did much to improve and enlarge upon the original scheme of reforms proposed by the government of India in March 1907.[14] His industry, earnestness and skill in the cause of Indian reforms were remarkable. The philosophic Liberal and the wise man of action peep out of every page in Morley's correspondence with Minto.

But, though it is possible to collect material for a complete manual on the arts of civil government from Morley's weekly letters to Minto, Morley had no more coherent and steadily developing plan of action *vis-a-vis* the growing nationalist movement in India than Minto. The vastness and complexities of the Indian problem defied the imagination of even the paragon Liberal. Or, perhaps, the pharmacopeia of nineteenth-century British liberalism had no remedy for the ills of twentieth-century India.

In Morley's view it was not the democracy in England but the cast-iron bureaucracy in India, with its outmoded ideas and methods, which was the real menace to the Empire. With the object-lesson of the Russian revolution of 1905 before him, Morley was unrelenting in his belief that the British Demos must keep a strict watch over the 'Tchinovniks'[15] in India.[16] He also hoped that the reformed legislative councils would serve the bureaucracy in India as a whetstone. Morley was convinced that conciliation, not repression, was the right policy to be pursued in India. 'Reforms', he wrote to Minto, 'may not save the Raj, but if they don't, nothing else will.'[17] The fundamental difference between the outlook of a Liberal statesman and that of a soldier-administrator is nowhere so clearly revealed as in the reply which Minto made to the above remark. 'You say', Minto wrote back, 'that the reforms may not "save the Raj"; they certainly will not, though if they are thoughtfully introduced they may help to render its administration happy. But when you say that "if reforms do not save the Raj, nothing else will" I am afraid I must disagree. The Raj will not disappear in India as long as the British race remains what it is, because we shall fight for the Raj as hard as we have ever fought, if it comes to fighting, and we shall win as we have always won.'[18]

While Morley and Minto differed widely in their political training, experience and general outlook, they were agreed on certain essentials of Indian policy. (The reforms of 1909 were the result not of their differences, but of the broad area of agreement that existed between them.) They were both convinced that the safety and welfare of India depended on the permanence of the British administration, that the government of India was always to remain autocratic, and that the sovereignty must be vested in British hands and could not be delegated to any kind of representative assembly in India. Besides being incompatible with

The Morley-Minto Reforms

British supremacy, representative government was wholly unsuited to Indian conditions. The only representation for which the country was fitted was only by classes and communities, and that, too, to a very limited extent. What they aimed at was, in the main, a 'scheme of administrative improvement',[19] calculated to enlist the support of the moderate elements in Indian society and thereby 'strengthen English government, and place it in a better position both for doing its work and for defending what it [did]'.[20] The government of India stood exposed, isolated and ignorant. As Morley put it: 'We don't know the minds of the Natives, and the Natives don't know what is in our minds. How to find some sort of a bridge? That's the question.'[21] The reforms were intended to provide this bridge.

The two main features of the Morley-Minto reforms were (*i*) the admission of two Indians to the council of the secretary of state and one each to the executive councils of the governor-general and the governors; and (*ii*) the expansion and liberalization of the legislative councils. The first was a gesture intended to give concrete proof that the government meant honestly to fulfil the promises contained in the Charter Act of 1833 and the Queen's proclamation of 1858, that race was to be no disqualification to high office in the state. The appointment of an Indian to the executive council of the governor-general was the most important and controversial issue. Morley considered it to be 'the cheapest concession'[22] that could be made, for it would leave the absolutism of British executive authority unimpaired. He wrote to the viceroy: 'He [the Indian member] would tell you how things strike that queer article the Native mind.'[23] And Minto remarked: 'This is exactly the information we want.'[24] While the secretary of state and the viceroy were convinced of the usefulness of admitting an Indian to the governor-general's executive council, a veritable storm raged over it for about two years. Every member of Minto's executive council, except one, was opposed to the proposal. Morley's council was equally hostile. The local governments in India expressed disapproval. The ex-viceroys, Curzon, Lansdowne, Elgin, and even Ripon, pronounced against it. The English press was universally opposed. Most Conservatives frankly detested the idea, and even many Liberals were dubious. Competent observers like Alfred Lyall and Valentine Chirol advised against the step. The Prince of Wales did not conceal his dislike and the King-Emperor administered an earnest remonstrance. The British community in India talked of organizing for self-defence. Morley and Minto feared a recrudescence of the clamour of the Ilbert Bill days and at times well-nigh decided to abandon the idea. Morley admitted later on that had parliamentary legislation been necessary for the appointment, the bill would have been lost in the Lords. The Lords took their revenge none the less by vetoing a clause in Indian Councils Bill of 1909 providing for executive councils to the lieutenant-governors. All this may give us some idea of the forces against which Morley and Minto had to contend.

The Indian Councils Act of 1909 was in the main an extension of the Act of 1892. It increased the number of Indians in the provincial legislative councils and gave the latter non-official (nominated+elected) majorities.[25] The central legislative council also received an addition of Indian members, but here an official majority was retained.[26] The principle of election, implicit in the Act of 1892, was now frankly recognized. The councils were allowed more time to discuss the budget, to move resolutions and call for a division. The right of interpellation was extended and members could ask supplementary questions. Morley and Minto, however, stoutly repudiated the suggestion that these enlarged councils were intended to pave the way for anything resembling parliamentary institutions.[27] The councils being already in existence, they attempted to make representation thereon more real and living with a view to making them better vehicles of expressing the opinions of the differing classes and communities in India, and affording the government 'additional opportunities both of becoming acquainted with the drift of public opinion and of explaining their own actions'.[28] They were not to control the administration but only to advise it. As Morley wrote, they were to enable 'the Government the better to realize the wants, and sentiments, of the governed, and on the other hand to give the governed a better chance of understanding, as occasion arises, the case for the Government against the misrepresentations of ignorance and malice'.[29] The elections were indirect, except in the case of the Muslims and the landlords; the electorate was indefinite and severely restricted.[30] The non-official majorities in the provincial legislative councils were unreal, and an attempt was made to counteract the influence of the advanced political classes by special electorates created and weighted in favour of the Muslims and the landed gentry.

Morley and Minto often gave expression to their vague disquiet about the future of the British Raj in India. 'The question is the Future',[31] they repeatedly told each other; but the question was posed only to be dismissed as unreal. 'I lay down as an "axiom",' wrote Minto in June 1909, 'that our considerations as to the future must be based on the recognition of our bounden duty to secure British administration in India and the welfare of the populations over whom we rule. As far as we can look ahead the existence of India must depend upon British supremacy.'[32] Proceeding on this 'axiom', it was but natural that Morley and Minto should have refused to give serious thought to the pregnant issue, 'Whither?'. They dismissed the ideal of self-government for India on the colonial model, entertained by the vast majority of Indian nationalists at the time, as 'a mere dream'[33] and 'an impossibility'.[34] They could not conceive of the government of India as anything but a benevolent despotism or a constitutional autocracy. Without concerning themselves with the distant scene, Morley and Minto set out to 'hatch some plan and policy for half a generation'.[35] Morley wrote to Minto: 'Do you know something said by Deak, the Hungarian statesman? "I can answer for today, I can pretty well for tomorrow, the day after tomorrow I leave to Providence." So do I.'[36] Parliament was equally disinclined to lift the veil of the future.[37] But 'the day after tomorrow' dawned sooner than expected—hastened by the reforms themselves and the war—and those who had to attend to its tasks accused the authors of the 1909 reforms of lack of faith and foresight.

Early in 1906 Morley had warned Gokhale, the leader of the Moderate section of the Congress, that if he and his friends attempted to belittle the reforms he contemplated to inaugurate, its only effect would be 'to set the clock back'.[38] Gokhale and other Moderates tried their best to create an atmosphere favourable to the reception of the reforms in India and in the attempt even split the Congress. When the reform proposals were announced towards the end of 1908, Moderates deliberately avoided voicing their dissatisfaction with them. They did so for two main reasons: first, because they knew that in Morley they had their best friend whom it would be impolitic to annoy; and, second, because they feared that any criticism of the reform proposals would give a handle to the Extremist agitators in India. Old friends of the Congress in England, men like Hume and Wedderburn, also advised acceptance with gratitude. This the Congress formally did at its annual session in December 1908. But the Congress could not conceal its disappointment and grief when the rules and regulations framed under the Act were announced towards the end of 1909. It condemned the separate electorates created for the Muslims as designed to aggravate communal differences. It considered the franchise to be illiberal and rooted in the distrust of the educated classes. It regretted that the non-official majorities in the provincial legislative councils had been rendered illusory by the system of nomination, that provinces like Panjab and U.P. had been denied executive councils, and that the Central Provinces had not been given even a legislative council. But, while disapproving of these illiberal regulations and urging modifications, the Congress gratefully accepted the reforms as a fairly liberal measure. Strange though it may seem, Indian nationalists welcomed the reforms for the very reason which Morley and Minto had so emphatically and repeatedly disavowed. They interpreted them as an advance towards parliamentary government. The Muslims had every reason to feel satisfied with the regulations,— they had not been generally very enthusiastic about the reforms— for they provided them with separate electorates, a comparatively liberal franchise and weightage in representation. The voice of Extremism was not much heard. Most of the Extremist leaders were in jails and their papers had been suppressed.

The feeling of dissatisfaction that developed with the actual working of the reforms was described by M.A. Jinnah before the Joint Select Committee in 1919. He entered, he said, the central legislative council in 1909 solely with the idea of making the best possible use of the opportunities offered by the reforms, but soon discovered that he was useless there. They were told that they were influencing the government, but he found that the government was not easily influenced. He, therefore, did not stand for the second election. When after a lapse of three years he again went to the council he found no improvement in the situation and felt extremely dejected. It was, he remarked, 'a very dispiriting, disheartening, slow process'.[39] Even in official circles in India it was realized 'as early as 1912-13 that the system of administration, resulting from the Morley-Minto reforms—especially in relation to the constitution of the legislative councils in the Provinces, would require amplification and development very shortly'.[40] Pleading for the removal of official majorities in the provincial councils, Morley had remarked in Parliament that they tended 'to weaken, even deaden the sense of trust and responsibility in the non-official members of the Councils', and throw them into 'an attitude of peevish, sulky, permanent opposition'.[41] But while the Act abolished the official majority, the regulations framed under it maintained it in another form. The evil to which Morley referred was not lessened but in fact aggravated by the reforms of 1909, for while the latter extended the opportunities for criticism they did little to train Indian leaders in habits of political responsibility.

If India was comparatively quiet during the subsequent few years and loyally and enthusiastically went to war in 1914, much was due to the Morley-Minto reforms, but far more to the policy of trust and conciliation adopted by Lord Hardinge, who succeeded Lord Minto in November 1910. Morley chose Hardinge in preference to Kitchener despite the tremendous pressure brought to bear on him on behalf of the latter; and we cannot but agree that his instinct was sound. Morley did a greater favour to India when early in 1910 he selected another Cambridgeman, E.S. Montagu, to be his under-secretary. Montagu understood and sympathized with the aspirations of Indian nationalists. He had faith in parliamentary institutions and the Commonwealth ideal. When opportunity came to him in 1917, Montagu courageously launched India on the path of democratic self-government within the Empire. India has reason to feel grateful to Morley more for the men than for the reforms he introduced.

7

THE HOME RULE MOVEMENT IN INDIA

Introductory

Probably no country in the world has exercised greater influence on the course of Indian nationalism, both as an example and as a warning, than Ireland. Educated Indians became interested in Ireland early in the nineteenth century. The sufferings of Ireland and her heroic struggle against heavy odds to preserve her religion, culture and nationality struck a responsive chord in the hearts of Indian patriots.[1] The latter also recalled with admiration and gratitude Edmund Burke's role in the impeachment of Warren Hastings and Daniel O'Connell's espousal of the cause of India.[2] They disliked Irish extremism, but were inclined to blame it more on the British than on the Irish. They regarded O'Connell's Catholic Association not only as a model of political organization, but also as a shining example of the success of constitutional agitation.[3] Conscious of the similarities between Ireland and their own country, they avidly followed developments in the Emerald Isle. They were greatly influenced by the emergence of the Irish home rule movement (under the leadership of Isaac Butt) and the formation of the Irish parliamentary party in the 1870s. In the 1870s and 1880s attempts were made to form an alliance between Indian and Irish nationalists, but they did not achieve much success.[4] Irish nationalists did not have the same interest in India as Indian nationalists had in Ireland. The former did not think that Indians could either teach them anything or be of any material help to them. Moreover, they were afraid that their cause might be compromised in the eyes of the British people if they allied themselves with Indian nationalists. Some Indian nationalists also were afraid that their cause might suffer if they joined hands with Irish nationalists. Unfortunately, the common rulers of Ireland and India, the British, never appreciated this concern of the Irish and Indian nationalists for their susceptibilities!

Like Irish nationalists, Indian nationalists tried to influence the British electorate and to form a party in the British Parliament, though they achieved far less success in both these matters than did their Irish counterparts. It is not improbable that Indian nationalists would have immediately inscribed home rule on their banner if Gladstone had succeeded in his efforts to grant home rule to Ireland in 1886 or 1893, for they were intelligent enough to realize that whatever was given to Ireland would have to be given to India sooner or later. But the defeat of Gladstone's efforts (the first Irish Home Rule Bill in 1886 was rejected by the House of Commons; the second in 1893 passed the Commons but was thrown out by the Lords) was a terrible disappointment to Indian nationalists. It warned them against the folly of asking for India something which had only recently been denied to Ireland or of even using a phrase which had become suspect in the eyes of most members of the ruling race. This was one of the main reasons why the early Indian nationalists did not consider it worth while for a very long time to declare in set terms what their ultimate aim was. And finally, when at the turn of the century they found it necessary to do so, they instead opted for 'a system of government similar to that enjoyed by the self-governing Members of the British Empire'[5] or what was more familiarly known as 'self-government on the colonial model'. There were, however, some Indian nationalists, particularly of Extremist persuasion, who disliked the ideal of 'self-government on the colonial model' as being something much less than complete independence. There were others who felt that the model was not suited to India as India was not, strictly speaking, a British colony.

Developments in Ireland continued to influence the course of Indian nationalism. The Irish Sinn Fein movement had a profound impact on the nationalist movement in India from 1905 onwards, particularly on the radical section which came to be known as Extremists. Early in the twentieth century the demand for home rule was again raised in Ireland by moderate, constitutional nationalists, led by John Redmond. Redmond succeeded in uniting the Irish parliamentary party under his leadership almost as effectively as C.S. Parnell had done in the 1880s and forced the Asquith government to attend to the Irish question. Redmond was not a separationist. 'Our demand for Home Rule', he insisted, 'does not mean that we want to break up the British Empire. We are entirely loyal to the Empire as such, and we desire to strengthen the Imperial bonds through a liberal system of government.'[6] In May 1912 an Irish Home Rule Bill was passed by the British House of Commons. It provided for an Irish House of Commons of 164 and an Irish Senate of 40, with a separate Irish executive, but retained 42 seats for Irish members in the British House of Commons. The Bill aroused fierce opposition in Northern Ireland and the Lords threw it out in January 1913. Under the terms of the Parliament Act the delaying powers of the Lords could prevent the Bill becoming law only until 1914. In September 1914 the Irish Home Rule Act finally received the royal assent. Its operation was, however, postponed until the end of the war by the simultaneous passage of a Suspensory Act.

The grant of home rule to Ireland, with its emphasis on internal self-government and the maintenance of the union, made home rule a respectable phrase. It was probably no accident that it was a British woman of Irish extraction who had settled in India—Mrs Annie Besant—who first perceived the political potential of the demand for home rule for India. But before we go on to discuss the role of Mrs Besant in the home rule agitation in India, we must take stock of the political situation in the country in the years immediately preceding the outbreak of the First World War in August 1914.

India and the First World War

Political life in India between the inauguration of the Morley-Minto reforms in 1909 and the outbreak of the war in 1914 was rather dull. The nationalist movement had been weakened by disagreements over goals and methods, by the split in the Congress, by British repression, by the political inactivity of many sections and regions, and by the lack of co-ordination of those regions and sections which showed some signs of activity. The Congress had passed into the hands of Moderates. It had become a respectable organization and had won some recognition of the alien government, but it had ceased to be representative and lost the affections of the Indian people. Extremists stood aloof from it. Voluntary exile or imprisonment had deprived them of effective leadership. They had neither the will, nor perhaps the means, to form a separate organization of their own. They were in fact anxious to return to the Congress fold, but were unwilling to do so on the terms which Moderate leaders tried to impose on them. B.G. Tilak was released from prison in May 1914. He was now a far more cautious man than before. Lord Hardinge, who succeeded Lord Minto as viceroy in 1910, had tried the policy of conciliation and he had succeeded where many of his more illustrious predecessors had failed. The revocation of the partition of Bengal had healed a running sore. But the politically-conscious sections in India, in whose mentality the Extremist agitation of 1904-8 had worked a lasting change, were disappointed with the inactivity of the Congress and were anxious that the Congress should become united and active again.

The war gave rise to a strange sort of double patriotism in India, somewhat similar to that in the white dominions. It evoked loyalty to Great Britain and heightened the sense of imperial unity, but it had an even more pronounced effect in developing a strong national consciousness. At first the twin sentiments of imperialism and nationalism went happily together, but as the war became prolonged the nationalist feeling asserted itself as the stronger, more confident and more articulate.

Mrs Annie Besant had dabbled in turn in Free Thought, Radicalism, and Theosophy. She came to India in 1893 to join the work of the Theosophical Society. She had a commanding personality and was an eloquent orator. She was 67 years old in 1914 when she joined the Indian National Congress and began taking an active interest in politics. On 2 January 1914 she started a weekly paper *Commonweal* from Adyar (Madras) and on 14 July a daily called *New India*. Her main objectives were to stir the Congress into activity, particularly by bringing about a union between Moderates and Extremists; to popularize the doctrine of self-government; and to promote friendship between Britain and India. Mrs Besant gave India no new political doctrine, but she did supply her with a new political slogan. She herself explained why she chose the new slogan of 'Home Rule': 'I used the words "Home Rule" instead of self-government. The first is shorter: self-government is four syllables and Home Rule only two. For a popular cry a short name is better than a long one. Moreover, it was a more explicit phrase, because self-government might mean independence, and so, to show that you did not mean a break between Great Britain and India, it was necessary to add "within the Empire", and so you have a great mouthful "self-government within the Empire on colonial lines". I prefer to call it Home Rule. The advantage is that it is a cry for freedom without separation.'[7] In a lecture at Poona on 24 September 1916 N.C. Kelkar explained why the term home rule had been chosen by Indian nationalists to express their ultimate ideal. He referred to the fact how early Irish nationalists, considering the union with Britain to be a great wrong, had demanded its repeal and how Isaac Butt had hit upon the phrase home rule, which 'reconciled freedom with no separation'. He quoted the words of Butt himself that home rule 'cut asunder a chain of slavery and allowed independence without provoking separation', and that it 'neither reversed the past nor compromised the future'. 'In India too', he added, 'the term Home Rule serves a useful purpose. For while it excludes the policy of separation ... it elevates to the proper pedestal the policy of India being governed for Indians and by Indians....' The ideal of home rule had been adopted in India, he added, because it 'briefly and beautifully expressed the subject matter of the claim for self-government within the Empire'; it was familiar to the English ear and saved them from all the imaginary terrors which the *swadeshi* word *swarajya* was likely to conjure up in their minds.[8]

Mrs Annie Besant was encouraged to try for a reunion of Moderates and Extremists by a statement made by Tilak soon after the outbreak of the war in which he said, among other things, that he and his followers were 'trying in India, as the Irish Home Rulers have been doing in Ireland, for a reform of the system of administration and not for the overthrow of Government'.[9] She travelled to Poona in early December 1914 and had talks with Gokhale and Tilak. Her efforts to bring about a reunion of Moderates and Extremists were, however, frustrated for the time being by the fear of Moderate leaders, notably Pherozeshah Mehta, that a united Congress would be dominated by Extremists.[10] The attitude of Moderate leaders compelled Mrs Besant and Tilak to think in terms of organizing Home Rule Leagues in order to bring pressure to bear on the former to re-admit Extremists and to intensify the Indian demand for internal self-government.

On 25 September 1915 Mrs Besant announced her decision to start a Home Rule League with the single objective of securing 'Home Rule for India'.[11] She envisaged a network of branches of the League to carry on agitation throughout the country. The League was to be an auxiliary to the Congress. She arranged to hold a conference in Bombay at the end of December 1915, concurrently with the annual session of the Congress, before launching the League. She hoped to obtain the support of at least some Congress leaders for her project.

Though Gokhale and Mehta had died before the Congress assembled at Bombay in late December 1915, the remaining Moderate leaders outmanoeuvred Mrs Besant and frustrated her attempt to get the Congress committed to home rule. But her efforts were not entirely in vain. The Bombay Congress passed a resolution allowing any association of at least two years' standing, which accepted the first article of the Congress constitution and made it a condition for membership, to convene a public meeting and elect up to fifteen delegates to the annual session of the Congress.[12] This partially opened the door for Extremists to re-enter the Congress. The Bombay Congress also instructed the All-India Congress Committee to draw up by 1 September 1916 a scheme of reforms demanding popular control over the executive.[13] Moderate leaders had hoped to subvert Mrs Besant's programme by first appropriating it to the Congress and then allowing it to drop. Mrs Besant saw through the game of Moderate leaders and announced that if the Congress failed to frame a scheme of self-government for India by 1 September 1916 she would be forced to launch her League even without their blessings.

The Home Rule Leagues

While Mrs Besant felt bound by her pledge to Moderate leaders, Tilak was under no such constraint. In late April 1916 he called a conference of Extremists from Maharashtra, the Central Provinces and Berar at Belgaum. The conference took two important decisions: that Extremists should re-enter the Congress; and that an Indian Home Rule League should be organized in order 'to attain Home Rule or Self-Government for India within the British Empire by all constitutional means' and 'to educate and organize public opinion in the country towards the attainment of the same'.[14]

The All-India Congress Committee having failed to produce the scheme of reforms by 1 September 1916, Mrs Besant launched her All-India Home Rule League (later called the National Home Rule League) on 3 September 1916.[15]

The two Home Rule Leagues tried to establish branches and very soon almost every major town in India was covered. They initiated an intensive campaign of propaganda through the press, public meetings and lectures, and the distribution of handbills and pamphlets. They had regular members. Though they worked in co-operation, they retained their separate organization. While Tilak's Home Rule League confined its operations to Maharashtra and Karnataka where it had an assured following, Mrs Besant's League worked in the rest of the country. The Home Rulers (as members of the Home Rule Leagues were called) assembled in large numbers at the Lucknow Congress in late December 1916 which marked the re-entry of Extremists into the Congress and the *rapprochement* between the Congress and the League.

The Home Rulers demanded self-government for India while retaining the British connexion. They wanted that the management of their country, its internal affairs, should be in their hands, such as the dominions had, or what had recently been admitted in the case of Ireland. Though they demanded home rule as the birthright of the Indian people, the Home Rulers were emphatic in their assertion that they did not repudiate the sovereignty of the Emperor or the rule of the British people. As Tilak observed: 'It is an undisputed fact that we should secure our own good under the rule of the English people themselves, under the supervision of the English nation, with the help of the English nation, through their sympathy, through their anxious care and through those high sentiments which they possessed.'[16] He compared the Emperor and the English government to the *Brahma*—the invisible, the absolute without attributes and form—and the bureaucracy in India to the *Maya*—the visible and the changeable. Home rule, he said, did not affect the Emperor and the English sovereignty 'the invisible government'; it only affected 'the visible government', the administration in India. Indians wanted the Emperor and the English government, but desired that the administration in India should be entrusted to them. 'From the Emperor's point of view there is neither anarchy, nor want of loyalty, nor sedition in this,' he added.[17] In another speech at Ahmednagar on 31 May 1916 he said: 'We want the rule of the English which is over us. But we do not want these intervening middlemen.'[18] The middlemen, according to him, were the members of the British bureaucracy in India. He compared them to the priests of the deity and remarked that they wanted the deity, that is the Emperor, but not those priests. 'We say, appoint other priests from amongst us.'[19] Nor was Tilak in favour of complete home rule at once. All that he wanted was 'a real beginning' and the goal to be reached within a fixed period of time.[20] 'Hope', he said, quoting the *Mahabharata*, 'should be made dependent upon time.'[21]

The Home Rulers only claimed a right to control the internal administration of their country. Defence, foreign affairs and other external and imperial matters they were content to leave in the hands of Great Britain or any other imperial organization which might be set up after the war.[22] But they demanded for India a position of equality with the dominions in the intra-imperial sphere. 'The true Home Ruler', B.C. Pal remarked, 'is above all else a Unionist and Imperialist, in the highest and truest sense of these terms. He is what the late W.T. Stead described ... "a Nationalist Imperialist".'[23] There was a good deal of talk during the war of imperial reorganization which would enable the dominions to share with Great Britain the burden of governing the Empire. This provided the Home Rulers with another argument for an early grant of self-government to India. Home rule, it came to be asserted, was the remedy not only for all the ills of the country, but also an urgent necessity in order that India might avoid the more galling and irksome burden of domination by the colonials.

The Home Rule Leagues appealed not only to western-educated Indians but also to mass groups and they presented a formidable challenge to British authorities. In the words of an official report from Madras, dated 18 December 1916: 'While Mrs Besant and her lieutenants pay particular attention to the student class, there are indications of the initiation of a special campaign for village work based mainly on the distribution of vernacular pamphlets and the itineration of Home Rule preachers. Hitherto the district reports have for the most part pictured the Home Rule movement as confined to younger vakils and students in central towns. But in the report from the Guntur district for the past fortnight the Collector lays stress upon the activities of the League in the delta villages of the Tesali taluk. *New India*, he writes, owing to its cheapness, has a very wide circulation in rural areas generally and the fact, in his opinion, is giving the Home Rule movement a marked impetus among English-knowing people of all classes; the paper has a specially large circulation in the lower ranks of Government service.'[24] The home member of the government of India wrote on 17 January 1917: 'The position is one of great difficulty. Moderate leaders can command no support among the vocal classes who are being led at the heels of Tilak and Besant.'[25]

In March 1917 the government of India issued a circular letter to the local governments outlining the policy to be pursued with regard to the home rule movement. In cases where the law had been transgressed, prosecutions were to be launched without any hesitation. Students were to be prohibited from attending meetings where home rule was likely to be discussed. 'It is scarcely necessary to state that neither the reforms recommended by the Government of India, nor any reforms which His Majesty's Government are likely to approve, can bear resemblance to the extravagant demands for the grant of early Home Rule to India which the agitators presented to their deluded audiences. It is evident, therefore, that the wider the hopes that are excited by the Home Rule organizations, the greater will be the disappointment and the more violent the protests when the actual reforms that may be approved by His Majesty's Government come in due course to be promulgated.' The letter advised the local governments: 'In these circumstances, it is most important that the several Local Governments should take steps to check these extravagant expectations which have been engendered by the Home Rule agitators. It seemed desirable that the Local Governments should, through their experienced officers, point out to all Indians who are likely to listen to reason that any thought of early Home Rule should be put entirely out of mind. They should warn all men of light and leading and all those who have hereditary influence over the people at large to dissociate themselves from the Home Rule campaign as it is at present being conducted.'[26]

In apprising the secretary of state for India, the viceroy suggested to him the need for a declaration of British policy. 'Mrs. Besant, Tilak and others', he wrote, 'are fomenting with great vigour the agitation for immediate Home Rule, and in the absence of any definite announcement by the Government of India as to their policy in the matter, it is attracting many of those who hitherto have held less advanced views. The agitation is having a mischievous effect on public feeling throughout the country. Consistent and malicious attacks on the system and method of present administration are aggravating the danger.'[27] The British government's promise of advance towards responsible government in India, contained in the famous Montagu announcement of 20 August 1917, was very largely the result of the home rule agitation.

In July 1916 Tilak had been tried for making speeches demanding home rule for India. He was ordered to furnish a personal bond of Rs 20,000 and two sureties of Rs 10,000 each and to be of good behaviour for a period of one year. But the Bombay High Court set aside the order against Tilak. About the same time a security of Rs 2,000 was demanded of *New India*. This security was forfeited on 28 August 1916 and a new security of Rs 10,000 was demanded. Mrs Besant appealed to the Madras High Court against the orders of the local government, but her appeal was rejected. In June 1917 the government of Madras interned Mrs Besant, together with her colleagues G. S. Arundale and B. P. Wadia. This was the signal for a countrywide outcry. Instead of crushing the movement, as the government had obviously hoped, the internment of Mrs Besant and her colleagues provided a powerful impetus to it. Many leading Indians, including Moderates, who had so far held aloof from her Home Rule League, now joined it and its membership doubled. The government's action was condemned by all sections of Indian public opinion. The younger men sought guidance from Tilak and Gandhi for a campaign of passive resistance. Montagu's announcement of August 1917 and the release of Mrs Besant in September lowered the political temperature in India a little.

Mrs Besant's popularity was at its height in India in 1917. It seemed as if she had the national movement at her feet. She was elected president of the Congress session in Calcutta at the end of 1917. But during 1918 she isolated herself from several groups which she had helped in bringing together and lost all claims to leadership of the Indian national movement. Mrs Besant had in 1917 favoured a programme of passive resistance against the government. In 1918 she renewed suggestions for passive resistance. But she soon realized that she was playing with fire and withdrew her suggestions. Indeed throughout 1918 she blew hot and cold on the question of opposing the government, thereby alienating the Home Rulers who had hitherto looked to her for leadership. When the Montagu-Chelmsford reform proposals were announced in July 1918, Besant denounced them as 'unworthy to be offered by England or to be accepted by India,' but later she became their supporter.[28] It was to Gandhi that many Home Rulers turned for a plan of action. Gandhi not only inherited the mantle which Mrs Besant refused to don, he also found the network of branches established by the Home Rule Leagues as valuable links for the communication of his plans to various parts of the country. The Home Rule Leagues thus provided 'an important grid of connexions for relaying Gandhi's message and arousing support for his proposals'.[29]

The Significance of the Home Rule Movement

The Home Rule Leagues created a significant impact on the national movement in India. For the first time—in 1916-18—agitation had been aroused on a nation-wide scale and a network of political committees covered much of India. They provided the country with a simple and forceful demand. They imparted a sense of impatience to the national movement as a whole. They introduced a new style of political agitation in India and mobilized the support of new regions and sections of the population. As Dr Judith M. Brown rightly observes: 'The Home Rule Leagues began in halting fashion what Gandhi was later to do boldly and with far greater success. They formulated techniques which he developed, and began to till the ground in areas where he was to reap a great harvest of support. Their activities were a hint that there might soon be an end to the politics of studied limitation. Some of the politicians at least had realized that if they were to succeed in gaining the raj's consent to anything beyond the very limited demands they had so far made they would have to expand their range of support, and in order to do so they would have to evolve a new political style.'[30]

8

GANDHI AND THE INDIAN NATIONAL MOVEMENT

The first biography of Gandhi was written by an Englishman, the Reverend Joseph J. Doke. It was published in late 1909 and bore the significant title, *M.K. Gandhi: An Indian Patriot in South Africa*.[1] Gandhi's patriotic sentiments were markedly reinforced by his long stay abroad. He spent about three years—from October 1888 to June 1891—as a student in England, and, then, he was in South Africa—almost continuously—from 1893 to 1914. It was as 'an exile'[2] that he discovered not only his 'vocation in life',[3] but also his country and culture. Distance lent enchantment to the view. Even after he returned to India for good and tried hard to identify himself completely with the land of his birth, Gandhi never ceased to idealize it or to look upon it with the eyes of a stranger.

Before going out to South Africa as a solicitor in 1893, Gandhi had evinced little interest in politics and he was scarcely known beyond the narrow circle of his friends and relatives. When, however, he finally returned from South Africa to India—via England —on 9 January 1915, he was widely known in three continents not only as a saint, but also as a patriot and public man. It is generally—and rightly—believed that Gandhi learnt his politics in South Africa. We should, therefore, begin by trying to know precisely what politics Gandhi learnt in South Africa.

To a large extent Gandhi's behaviour in South Africa was determined by his own early training and the peculiar situation of the Indians in that part of the world. Taking the Indian National Congress as his model, Gandhi established the Natal Indian Congress in 1894 and resorted to the usual methods of English constitutional agitation by way of 'prayer, petition and protest'. He declared that he regarded the British connexion with India as providential[4] and that the Indians were 'proud to be under the British Crown, because they think that England will prove India's deliverer'.[5] He avowed his faith in the 'British love of justice and fair play'.[6] He took his stand on the rock of the British constitution.[7] He invoked the principles of equality before the law, of the rights of British citizens, and of humanity. Racial discrimination was 'un-British',[8] unconstitutional, and harmful to the best interests of the British Empire. Disappointed of the white colonists in South Africa, Gandhi appealed to the people and government of Great Britain. In close imitation of the British Committee of the Indian National Congress, the South Africa British Indian Committee was formed in late 1906 for active and sustained efforts in this regard.

During his South African phase Gandhi was like most English-educated Indians of his generation a loyal and moderate nationalist. He had a romantic veneration for the British constitution, especially because it recognized the principles of individual freedom and racial equality. He was 'a lover of the British Empire'.[9] Like G.K. Gokhale, who was his beau ideal and political *'guru'*, Gandhi believed that Indians could rise to their full stature within and with the help of the British Empire. He wanted his countrymen to qualify for equal partnership in the Empire by loyal service and sacrifice. He himself served with distinction on the side of the English in the Boer War and the Zulu Rebellion. In his booklet *Hind Swaraj*, published in 1909, Gandhi supported the ideals and methods of Moderate Congressmen in India and denounced those of Extremists. Though extremely critical of many aspects of western civilization, Gandhi genuinely loved the English people and admired the outstanding qualities of their character.

Gandhi had a fairly good knowledge of British history and he had a deep understanding of British character and the British constitution. He seems to have clearly grasped the truth contained in C.P. Lucas's epigrammatic remark that 'British colonial policy may be summed up as an attempt to harmonise what ought to be done with what has been said'.[10] He knew that no British statesman could tell Indians what President Kruger had told an Indian deputation in 1896: 'You are the descendants of Ishmael and therefore from your very birth bound to slave for the descendants of Esau. As the descendants of Esau we cannot admit you to rights placing you on an equality with ourselves. You must rest content with what rights we grant to you.'[11] He also knew that the British were bound by their charters and proclamations, that they were prisoners of their ideals and even the 'fictions' of their constitution.[12] As Thiers in France had tried to keep the Bourbons tied to their charter, so Gandhi in South Africa tried to keep the British tied to their constitution. Racial equality was one of 'the fundamental principles of the British Constitution'.[13] South Africa was a part of the British Empire. The Indians living in any part of the British Empire were entitled to all the rights and privileges of British citizenship. The British could not, without being false to their own proclaimed ideals, repudiate the principle of racial equality. This was the great truth on which Gandhi insisted in South Africa. Though in later years Gandhi gave all sorts of wider and deeper meanings to his conception of *satyagraha* (literally, insistence on truth), it was originally and essentially an insistence on the truth enshrined in the British constitution.

Satyagraha was not only an appeal to the British constitution, it was also an appeal to the British conscience. In 1908 Gandhi defined it as 'self-imposed suffering of an acute type, intended to prove the justice of the cause, and thus bring conviction home to the minds of the Colonists'.[14] It was based upon a deep understanding of British history and character. In a petition of the British Indian Association of the Transvaal, dated 9 September 1908 and drafted by Gandhi, we read the following on *satyagraha*: 'The petitioning Association have learnt from experience that, within the British Empire, at any rate, subjects of the King-Emperor get redress of grievances only when they show that they are ready and willing to suffer for the sake of obtaining relief.'[15] In October 1909 Gandhi advised his countrymen in South Africa to emulate the Suffragettes' 'capacity for suffering', and added: 'We may also observe that the British will not concede any rights even to the women in their country without putting them to the test.'[16] Many years later Gandhi told C.F. Andrews: 'An Englishman never respects you till you stand up to him. Then he begins to like you. He is afraid of nothing physical; but he is mortally afraid of his own conscience, if ever you appeal to it and show him to be in the wrong. He does not like to be rebuked for wrong-doing at first; but he will think over it, and it will get hold of him and hurt him till he does something to put it right.'[17] Though Gandhi claimed that his weapon of *satyagraha* was capable of being used against any antagonist anywhere, he knew that the British were, of all people, peculiarly vulnerable to it. As early as 1904 he had written: 'Earnestness commands success anywhere. It does so much more in the British Dominions. If the British machinery is slow to move, the genius of the nation being conservative, it is also quick to perceive and recognise earnestness and unity.'[18] Again, on 9 March 1907 he wrote: 'In keeping with British traditions it has first to be shown that people who make demands are prepared to die for them. It is not enough to go on making verbal demands. The British follow this rule in their own country and that is how they endure.'[19]

Satyagraha was not added to the repertoire of Gandhi's methods of agitation in South Africa until 1907. Its adoption represented a particular phase in Gandhi's mental evolution which was induced by his increasing interest in religions and his study of writers like Leo Tolstoy, John Ruskin and Henry David Thoreau.[20] It was dictated by the needs of the situation in South Africa. As Gandhi himself admitted, *satyagraha* was 'undertaken after the methods of petitioning, etc., had been exhausted, and in order to draw public attention to a grievance that was keenly felt and resented by the [Indian] community'.[21] But it was not entirely uninfluenced by developments outside South Africa, notably those in Ireland, England and India.[22] Gandhi was a keen observer of events and movements in foreign lands. He saw the struggle of the Indians in South Africa not as an isolated venture, but as part of a wider, international movement.

Gandhi was particularly anxious to relate the struggle of the Indians in South Africa with the national movement in India. From very early on he kept the leaders of the Indian national movement—in India or in Britain—regularly and fully briefed about the progress of the struggle in South Africa and sought their aid. Similarly, he kept the Indians in South Africa well informed about developments in India and exhorted them to 'march boldly with the progressive current which is ... impelling the Indian nation onward to its goal'.[23]

Gandhi was at pains to emphasize that the Indians in South Africa were fighting not so much to preserve their own rights and interests as to protect the honour of their motherland and their self-respect as Indians, that they were engaged in a struggle which was 'righteous, godly and national'.[24] In a message to the members of his community from Volksrust Gaol on 13 October 1908, he wrote: 'All of us are Indians, and are fighting for India. Those who do not realise this are not servants but enemies of the motherland.'[25] Writing from London in early September 1909 for the *Indian Opinion*, he remarked that 'we have been fighting not for [the admission of] a particular number [of educated men], but for India's honour'.[26] In a letter to G.A. Natesan of Madras, who had asked him to send a message for the forthcoming session of the Congress at Lahore, Gandhi wrote in late 1909: 'I hope our countrymen throughout India realise that it [the struggle that is going on in the Transvaal] is national in its aim in that it has been undertaken to save India's honour.'[27] Gandhi even invited G.K. Gokhale, one of the most prominent leaders of the moderate nationalists in India, to come and join him in his struggle in South Africa, saying: 'I venture to suggest that you should come to the Transvaal and join us. I claim that the Transvaal struggle is national in every sense of the term. It deserves the highest encouragement. I have considered it to be the greatest struggle of modern times. That it will succeed in the end I have not the slightest doubt. But an early success will break up the violence movement in India.'[28]

Realizing what Gandhi called 'the national importance of the struggle'[29] waged by their countrymen in South Africa, nationalists in India tried to support it in all sorts of ways. The Indian National Congress discussed the subject year after year. The Indian press was full of it. Even substantial financial assistance was forthcoming from India. But in the long run the Indian struggle in South Africa did far more to promote the cause of the national movement in India than Indian nationalists did to promote the cause of their countrymen in South Africa.

Probably no other issue in the first fourteen years of the twentieth century so deeply and widely affected India as did that of the treatment of Indians in South Africa. This was so both because of the nature of the problem and because of the manner in which Gandhi agitated it. As Thakurdas Khemchand remarked at the Karachi session of the Indian National Congress in 1913: 'Never before in the history of this country have the hearts of the people been so much excited and overwhelmed with grief as they have been today in connection with the present Indian calamity in South Africa. The indignation created throughout the country is not confined to the enlightened men who read newspapers and follow the current of events in the different parts of the world. It is shared by the educated and the uneducated alike. It has spread to the school-going world and what is most striking is that it has penetrated into the zenana. It is indeed very interesting to see some of our womenfolk bursting into tears of touching sympathy on being told the tale of misery and oppression of their sisters in a far-off land, how they are being mercilessly treated as concubines and subjected to all sorts of indignities and degradation which the human mind cannot possibly conceive. The ennobling acts of heroism and chivalry of that selfless saint of the twentieth century, that paragon of purity, that soul of sanctity, Mr. Gandhi, have stirred the heart of India to its very depths.... It is undoubtedly a very happy sign of the times to see men, women and children of all races and religions combining themselves into one harmonious whole to offer a united and determined opposition to the most inhuman ordinance of the South African Government in order to save the honour and prestige of their motherland.'[30]

As early as 1909 Gandhi was reported to have remarked that 'it was in South Africa that the Indian nation was being formed. A nation ... could come into being only when people made sacrifices for the sake of freedom. Moreover, the Hindu-Muslim problem just did not arise in South Africa.'[31] The same point had been made in December 1908 by a correspondent of the Anglo-Indian *Times of India* who wrote that it was not sufficiently realized in England how the question of the Indians in South Africa had come to the forefront in the last few years and added: 'Many people believe that the real Indian nation is being hammered out in South Africa.'[32]

Two of Gandhi's major achievements in South Africa were (*i*) to have united all sections of the Indian community in that country in their struggle against racial discrimination, and (*ii*) to have conducted that struggle in a non-violent manner. Gandhi became increasingly convinced that both these achievements could be models for the Indians to follow in India. Writing to G.A. Natesan in late 1909 he insisted that 'for the many ills we suffer from in India passive resistance is an infallible panacea. It is worthy of careful study, and I am sure it will be found that it is the only weapon that is suited to the genius of our people and our land, which is the nursery of the most ancient religions and has very little to learn from modern civilization—a civilization based on violence of the blackest type, largely a negation of the Divine in man, and which is rushing headlong to its own ruin.'[33] At about the same time he wrote to Tolstoy that 'this struggle of the Indians in South Africa . . . is highly likely to serve as an example to the millions in India and to people in other parts of the world, who may be downtrodden, and will certainly go a great way towards breaking up the party of violence, at least in India'.[34]

The greatest gift of the Indian struggle in South Africa to the Indian national movement was Gandhi himself. Gandhi found the unusually complex and confused situation in South Africa in the late nineteenth and early twentieth century extremely favourably to discovering and developing his great qualities of leadership and organization. The only leading figure in Indian politics whom Gandhi knew intimately before 1915 was Gokhale. He first met Gokhale in 1896. He stayed with him for about a month in Calcutta in 1901-2. He corresponded with him more or less regularly. He was actively associated with him during the latter's visit to South Africa in 1912. It is generally well known how Gandhi admired Gokhale and acclaimed him his political *'guru'*. What is not so generally well known is how early on Gokhale recognized the great talents of his self-proclaimed disciple and marked him out as a leader of men.

At a public meeting held in Albert Hall, Calcutta, on 19 January 1902, Gokhale, while introducing Gandhi to the gathering, recalled his first encounter with him in 1896 and how he was impressed 'by his ability, earnestness and tact, and also by his manner, at once so gentle and yet so firm'. Since then he had followed his career 'with the deepest interest and admiration, having studied every utterance of his and watched every movement in which he had any share', and he could say without hesitation that 'Mr. Gandhi was made of the stuff of which heroes were made'. What he most admired in Gandhi, Gokhale went on to say, was 'his moral worth'. In spite of all the bad treatment that he had received at the hands of the whites in South Africa, there was not a trace of bitterness in Gandhi. He had proved that the fiercest opposition could be overcome and the bitterest misunderstanding removed, if only they were true to themselves and worked in an earnest, selfless, straightforward manner, and did not return insult for insult, abuse for abuse. In Gokhale's view, Gandhi had set an example of how to work for India. 'If Mr. Gandhi settled in this country,' Gokhale added, 'it was the duty of all earnest workers to place him where he deserved to be, at their head.'[35] Speaking at the 1909 Congress at Lahore, Gokhale remarked: 'Fellow-delegates, after the immortal part which Mr. Gandhi has played in this [South African] affair, I must say it will not be possible for any Indian, at any time, here or in any other assembly of Indians, to mention his name without deep emotion and pride. (Here the huge gathering rose to its feet and accorded three hearty and most enthusiastic cheers for Mr. Gandhi.) Gentlemen, it is one of the privileges of my life that I know Mr. Gandhi intimately; and I can tell you that a purer, a nobler, a braver and a more exalted spirit has never moved on this earth. Mr. Gandhi is one of those men who, living an austerely simple life themselves and devoted to all the highest principles of love to their fellow beings and to truth and justice, touch the eyes of their weaker brethren as with magic and give them a new vision. He is a man who may be well described as a man among men, a hero amongst heroes, a patriot amongst patriots, and we may well say that in him Indian humanity at the present time has really reached its high watermark.'[36]

Before Gandhi finally returned to India in early 1915, his friends and admirers wondered what role he would play in the public life of his native land. For example, on 27 December 1914 we find C.F. Andrews writing to Gokhale, who had been mainly responsible for persuading Gandhi to return to India, as follows: 'I have been thinking a great deal about what Mr. Gandhi will do on his return. Perhaps it is no use thinking, as he is bound to take his own course, whatever it may be. He is not one who can be bound. I do feel positive about one thing, that he could not for long work in with the general work of the Servants of India [Society]. He might take up some special sphere, such as work among the depressed classes but he would need to be quite independent.... He will want of course to go home for some time first and settle all things there.... I believe he will not wish to take up public work of any kind for some time. He told me very definitely that he wished to have a time of retirement and rest.'[37]

In the event, Andrews's assessment of Gandhi proved to be remarkably correct. Gandhi had a mind of his own and he was not a person to play second fiddle to any Indian leader. As Gandhi himself wrote a few years later: '...at my time of life and with views firmly formed on several matters I could only join an organization to affect its policy and not be affected by it.'[38]

Gokhale wanted Gandhi to join his Servants of India Society. But most other members of the Society rightly feared that if Gandhi were admitted to the Society he would soon try to capture it and mould it nearer to his heart's desire. They, therefore, vetoed Gandhi's entry into it.[39] Gandhi was not particularly enamoured of the Servants of India Society[40] and he must have felt immensely relieved at being kept out of it. Gokhale's death on 19 February 1915 made Gandhi feel extremely sad and lonely, but it gave him greater freedom of action and allowed him to pursue his own chosen path in India.

What was the path which Gandhi had chosen to pursue in India? Shortly before leaving South Africa in July 1914, Gandhi wrote that 'one of the reasons for my departure to India is still further to realise, as I already do in part, my own imperfection as a Passive Resister, and then to try to perfect myself, for I believe that it is in India that the nearest approach to perfection is most possible'.[41] In his autobiography he said: 'I wanted to acquaint India with the method I had tried in South Africa, and I desired to test in India the extent to which its application might be possible.'[42] There can thus be no doubt that Gandhi returned to India in 1915 determined to try there the lessons he had learnt in South Africa, particularly to experiment there on a larger scale with the technique of *satyagraha* which he had discovered in that country. But beyond this general determination everything about him was uncertain. As he finally set sail for India from England, Gandhi himself wrote: 'I have been so often prevented from reaching India that it seems hardly real that I am sitting in a ship bound for India. And having reached that what shall I do with myself? However, "Lead Kindly Light, amid the encircling gloom, lead Thou me on." That thought is my solace....'[43]

Before we go on to discuss Gandhi's career in India from 1915 onwards, it would be worth our while to recapitulate the lessons which he had obviously learnt during his long residence in South Africa and which he came determined to apply to the Indian situation. Some of these lessons were as follows.

Generally speaking, 'the British Government's intentions are fair and . . . it desires to do justice. . . . It takes time, but in the end the thing intended comes to pass (if it is reasonable). It is not that it takes time for Indians alone to get justice. Consider Ireland's example; British nature is like that. It is . . . our duty to bear this in mind and labour on. If we . . . go on working with single-mindedness, we shall certainly attain our objective, because we ask for justice, not favour.'[44]

'They [the British] are a brave and considerate people, and on the whole honest. Blind where self-interest is concerned, they give unstinted admiration for bravery wherever found. . . . If . . . [public] spirit grows, the British may grant our demands even without a fight, and may leave India if we want them to do so. The British Colonies are what they are, not because the people there are white but because they are brave and would take offence if their rights were not granted.'[45]

'Strength and justice [are] dear to the British people. Under British rule, justice is often not to be had without some show of strength, whether of the pen, of the sword, or of money. For our part we are to use the strength that comes from unity and truth. That is to say, our bondage in India can cease this day, if all the people unite in their demands and are ready to suffer any hardships that may befall them.'[46]

Earnestness, perseverance, unity and a willingness to sacrifice and suffer are essential for the success of any cause in any part of the world; they are particularly so in the British Empire. But while the British test the determination and strength of their adversary to the uttermost, they seldom carry matters to the breaking-point.

'It is the [proclaimed] mission of the English race, even where there are subject races, to raise them to equality with themselves, to give them free institutions and make them absolutely free men.'[47] It is not easy for the British to go back on their publicly and repeatedly avowed intention. Any agitation on the part of subject peoples in the British Empire to gain their rights and privileges should aim at persuading and pressurizing the British people to redeem their pledges and to put into practice what they have already promised in theory.

No government can afford to flout the opinion of its people for long,[48] least of all the British government, for it is extremely sensitive to public opinion. If ever the people inhabiting any part of the British Empire feel that their government is in the wrong, all that they have to do to set it right is to let it know their views and feelings in a clear and determined manner, if necessary through civil disobedience, non-co-operation and *satyagraha*.

The subjects of the British Empire enjoy many more civil liberties and they have greater scope for the practice of civil disobedience, non-co-operation and *satyagraha*, without being branded and shot as rebels, than the subjects of any other empire in the world, both past and present.[49]

Violence is an evil and must be avoided at all costs. *Satyagraha* is not merely a means of aborting violence, it is an infallible remedy which can 'well be adopted by every oppressed people, by every oppressed individual, as being a more reliable and more honourable instrument for securing the redress of wrongs than any which has heretofore been adopted'.[50] *Satyagraha* is twice-blessed. It blesses him who practises it and also him against whom it is practised.

It is possible to unite persons belonging to different classes, creeds and communities in a common struggle against injustice and oppression. *Satyagraha* is the most effective means of forging such a unity, for to undergo suffering is a stronger bond of union than to inflict suffering on others.

If Indians are united they do not need the sword to free themselves from bondage. But if they are not united, the mere possession of the sword is not likely to be of any help to them, for 'the methods we imagine we would use only against the foreigners will be used against ourselves'.[51] In fact, the sword in India is more likely to be used for fratricidal purposes than for getting rid of the British.

In his later life Gandhi really unlearnt very few of the lessons which he had learnt in South Africa. But after his return to India Gandhi did learn some new lessons. Of these the following two deserve prominent mention here.

While in South Africa, Gandhi was not entirely unfamiliar with the darker aspects of British rule in India, having read, among other things, the writings of Dadabhai Naoroji[52] and William Digby[53] early in his life, but he had tended to ascribe them to 'modern civilization,'[54] to regard them as being 'more the fault of individual British officials than of the British system',[55] and even to think that they were outweighed by its brighter aspects.[56] Within a few years of his return to India, however, Gandhi began to appreciate more fully what he described as the 'Satanic'[57] character of British rule in his country.

The second important lesson which Gandhi learnt after his return to India related to the idea of non-co-operation. Like most of Gandhi's discoveries, it was not entirely new. For example, in his well-publicized lectures delivered at Cambridge in the early 1880s, J.R. Seeley had remarked: 'Now if a feeling of a common nationality began to exist there [in India] only feebly, if, without inspiring any active desire to drive out the foreigner, it only created a notion that it was shameful to assist him in maintaining his dominion, from that day almost our Empire would cease to exist. . . . For it is a condition of our Indian Empire that it should be held without any great effort. As it was acquired without much effort on the part of the English state, it must be retained in the same way. . . . The moment India began really to show herself what we so idly imagine her to be, a conquered nation, that moment we should recognise perforce the impossibility of retaining her.'[58] Gandhi was familiar with the views of Seeley[59] and we find references to and echoes of them in his own writings. For example, he wrote in *Hind Swaraj* in 1909: 'The English have not taken India; we have given it to them. They are not in India because of their strength, but because we keep them. . . . The causes that gave them India enable them to retain it. Some Englishmen state that they took and they hold India by the sword. Both these statements are wrong. The sword is entirely useless for holding India. We alone keep them.'[60] But it was not until after he had returned to India that Gandhi realized the extent to which the British Raj was based upon Indian co-operation and acquiescence and drew the inescapable conclusion that the easiest and surest way for his countrymen of gaining their liberation was to learn to say 'no' and to non-co-operate with the Raj. As *satyagraha* was dictated by the peculiar and immediate situation of the Indians in South Africa, so was *asahayoga* (non-co-operation) dictated by the peculiar and immediate situation of the Indians in India.

Gokhale was, as we have already noted, full of admiration for Gandhi, but he did not share all his views on the Indian situation.[61] In fact, Gokhale thought that, having lived outside India for such a long time, Gandhi had lost touch with Indian reality. He, therefore, advised Gandhi—even before the latter left South Africa in July 1914—that for one year after his return to India he should abstain from expressing his views on any Indian problem except that of the Indians in South Africa, and travel extensively round the country in order to familiarize himself more intimately with its people and their problems.[62] This proved to be a blessing in disguise for Gandhi. The political situation in India in 1915-16 was extremely fluid and tricky. Gandhi's 'compact of silence'[63] with Gokhale saved him from committing himself prematurely and irrevocably on any point or to any party at a very critical stage in Indian politics. On the other hand, his extensive travels up and down the country[64] enabled him to know his countrymen and to be known by them unlike any other Indian politician of his day.

India might have become, as Gokhale had reminded Gandhi shortly before the latter's return home, 'a strange land to him',[65] but Gandhi was no stranger to India. For many years past the people of India had been watching with intense interest and admiration the heroic struggle that he had been waging in South Africa, and his name had become a household word in India. He had narrowly escaped being the president of the 1911 session of the Congress at Calcutta.[66] When, therefore, after his latest triumph in South Africa, Gandhi finally returned to India in January 1915, he came trailing clouds of glory. For long he had represented to his countrymen in India the devotion to something afar from the sphere of their sorrow, and his return to his native land had been ardently desired and awaited.[67] He received a hero's welcome on his return home and there were great expectations of him in all quarters.

In February 1915—a month after his arrival in India—Gandhi was asked by C.F. Andrews: 'Do you think that a time will come for Satyagraha in India? And if so, have you any idea when it will come?' To these questions Gandhi replied as follows: 'It is difficult to say. For one year I am to do nothing. For Gokhale took from me a promise that I should travel in India for gaining experience, and express no opinion on public questions until I have finished the period of probation. Even after the year is over, I will be in no hurry to speak and pronounce opinions. And so I do not suppose there will be any occasion for Satyagraha for five years or so.'[68] It is clear that Gandhi's prognostication was based more on his personal circumstances than on any objective assessment of the political situation in India. The occasion for *satyagraha* came sooner than even Gandhi had expected. Champaran, Ahmedabad and Kheda in 1917-18 were mere preparations for the *satyagraha* against the Rowlatt Act[69] in 1919 and for the far more ambitious campaign of 1920-2.

On his return to India in 1915 Gandhi was inclined to work for the welfare of his country—as far as possible—in co-operation with the British Raj. This was due to his training and experience in South Africa, of which mention has already been made, particularly his latest success there, embodied in the Gandhi-Smuts agreement of 1914, which seemed to confirm the validity and efficacy of most of Gandhi's beliefs and practices. Gandhi was also encouraged to do so by the outbreak of the First World War, by the obviously courteous and sympathetic manner in which he was treated by the highest British officials both in England and in India, and by his loudly-proclaimed discipleship of Gokhale. Gandhi preached 'absolutely unconditional and whole-hearted co-operation with the Government on the part of educated India' in the war effort and emphasized what he considered to be the elementary truth that if the British Empire perished, with it would also perish their cherished political aspirations for their own country.[70] He disappointed Mrs Besant in 1915 when he refused to join her in launching a home rule movement in India. He told her in so many words that he did not share her distrust of the English people and would do nothing which might embarrass them during the war.[71] He would have liked his countrymen to 'withdraw all the Congress resolutions, and not whisper "Home Rule" or "Responsible Government" during the pendency of the war'.[72] The secretary of state, E.S. Montagu, while in India in 1917, noted in his *Diary* after an interview with him: '[Gandhi] does not understand details of schemes. He wants the millions of India to leap to the assistance of the British throne.'[73] Busy recruiting soldiers for the war, Gandhi wrote to the then viceroy, Lord Chelmsford, in April 1918 that he loved the English nation and wished 'to evoke in every Indian the loyalty of the Englishman [towards the Empire]'.⁷⁴ To M.A. Jinnah, who was then engaged, along with Besant and B.G. Tilak, in popularizing the gospel of home rule for India, Gandhi wrote on 4 July 1918: 'Seek ye first the Recruiting Office and everything will be added unto you.'⁷⁵ The not entirely unsympathetic reaction of most British officials to his *satyagraha* campaigns in Champaran and Kheda confirmed Gandhi in his belief that his tactics were right and that he could even win 'swaraj through its [British government's] co-operation'.⁷⁶ In fact, it would not be an exaggeration to say that during 1915-18 Gandhi, with his 'strong, and probably peculiar, views'⁷⁷ on many Indian questions, was more 'at war with [Indian] leaders'⁷⁸ than with the British government in India. As he himself sadly admitted in August 1918: 'I hold views which are acceptable to neither party.... I know that the Extremists do not agree with me and I hardly think the Moderates go as far as I go.... I must therefore bide my time patiently and plough my own solitary furrow.'⁷⁹ Surprisingly, both the press and secret police reports⁸⁰ testified to the fact that Gandhi's stock with the Indian people was constantly rising. And Gandhi himself knew that his 'star [was] in the ascendant'.⁸¹

Gandhi was surprised and pained at the 'flouting of the unanimous voice'⁸² of the politically-conscious Indians by the British government in India in the matter of the Rowlatt legislation. He considered it 'to be an unmistakable symptom of a deep-seated disease in the governing body' which needed 'to be drastically treated' ⁸³ and he organized against it his first major country-wide *satyagraha* campaign in the spring of 1919. Though the apparent and immediate purpose of this *satyagraha* was to make the government see the error of its ways ⁸⁴ Gandhi was fully aware of its deeper and long-term significance. Writing to Rabindranath Tagore on 5 April 1919, Gandhi described it as 'the national struggle which, though in form it is only directed against a single piece of legislation, is in reality a struggle for liberty worthy of a self-respecting nation'.⁸⁵ Like most of his countrymen, Gandhi was deeply shocked and hurt by the cold-blooded murder of hundreds of unarmed civilians by General Dyer at Amritsar on 13 April 1919. Gandhi was also deeply disturbed by the manner in which the British government had gone back on its wartime promises to the Indian Muslims regarding the future of Turkey and the Khilafat, and it was in this connexion that he first propounded the idea of non-violent non-co-operation in late November 1919.[86]

However, in spite of the ill-conceived Rowlatt Act, the unfortunate Amritsar massacre and the apparent breach of faith by the British government in regard to Turkey, Gandhi pleaded with his people to work the Montagu-Chelmsford reforms of 1919 in a spirit of genuine co-operation and goodwill. 'The Reforms Act', he wrote, 'coupled with the Proclamation is an earnest of the intention of the British people to do justice to India.'[87] He advised his countrymen not to subject the reforms to carping criticism but to settle down quietly to work so as to make them a thorough success and thereby qualify for further advance. At the Amritsar session of the Indian National Congress, held towards the end of December 1919, the latter-day apostle of non-co-operation would not even brook the idea of grudging acceptance or Irish obstructionism which Tilak and C.R. Das contemplated practising in the legislative councils. 'I shall challenge that position,' he remarked, 'and I shall go across from one end of India to the other and say we shall fail in our culture, we shall fall from our position...if we do not respond to the hand that has been extended to us.'[88] Gandhi also made the Congress pass a resolution condemning the excesses committed by the Indian mobs in Panjab and Gujarat.[89]

It was the events of the next few months which turned the great loyalist and co-operator into a rebel and a non-co-operator.[90] The terms of the Treaty of Sevres[91] with Turkey, published in May 1920, were considered by most Indians to be a breach of the pledges given earlier by British statesmen. The report of the Hunter Committee[92] appeared to them as an attempt to whitewash the culprits in the Amritsar massacre. The manner in which Dyer's action was acclaimed by the general body of Britons in India and their friends in the United Kingdom filled Indians with pain and indignation. Gandhi pleaded with the authorities to put themselves morally right with the Indian people, but the latter failed to appreciate the moral aspect of the issues involved until it was too late. Gandhi became convinced that 'the present representatives of the Empire' had become 'dishonest and unscrupulous', that they had no real regard for the wishes of the Indian people and counted the honour of India as of little consequence.[93] To an enraged and aggrieved people he suggested the way of non-violent non-co-operation in order to enforce the national will and to secure the redress of the Khilafat and Panjab wrongs. The non-co-operation movement was launched on 1 August 1920. A special session of the Congress, held at Calcutta in September 1920, approved of and adopted Gandhi's programme and affirmed that 'the only effectual means to vindicate national honour and prevent a repetition of similar wrongs in future is the establishment of swaraj'.[94] At its annual session, held at Nagpur in December 1920, the Congress reaffirmed its adherence to Gandhi's leadership and programme with a vastly increased majority.[95]

On 19 March 1915—about two months after Gandhi's return to India and a month after Gokhale's death—Besant's *New India* had noted that it was being suggested in certain quarters that Gandhi should have been president of the Servants of India Society and made it truly national. The paper had dismissed the suggestion as being 'sentimental and impracticable' and added: 'It is as though we said: "The Archbishop of Canterbury is a saint; he should be placed at the head of the Bank of England." Gandhi is not a politician.'[96] Within five years of this remark having been made, Gandhi had placed himself at the head of the largest and most influential political organization in India; he had displaced prominent leaders like Besant from their high pedestals and become the supreme commander of the Indian national movement. How did the Mahatma perform this miracle? Both contemporary observers and latter-day researchers have tried to unravel the mystery of this remarkable development in Indian politics. All that we can do here is to indicate briefly some of their more important conclusions.

Gandhi had had no political past in India. He had made himself and earned his reputation in a foreign land. He belonged to no particular group or faction in Indian politics. He was neither a Moderate nor an Extremist. Of all Indian politicians of the time, he had the best claim to be regarded as a national, all-India leader, though he was firmly anchored in his native Gujarat. Gandhi returned to India with an unsullied and unsurpassed reputation, and, despite his strange manners and peculiar views (or was it because of them?), he managed not only to preserve that reputation, but also to enhance it by taking up popular causes, such as those concerning the peasants and workers, the third-class railway passengers and untouchables, *swadeshi* and the vernaculars. Unlike most Indian political leaders of his day, Gandhi had the experience of having worked—while in South Africa—with all sections of the Indian community. Gandhi was a strange mixture of the Victorian liberal, Indian patriot, philosophical anarchist and simple-lifer. He was a curious combination of the saint and the statesman, of the traditional and the modern, of the conservative and the radical, of the nationalist and the universalist, of the realist and the visionary. He was all things to all men. His many-faceted programme appealed to almost every section of the Indian people. Gandhi was a great organizer. He was a superb judge and leader of men. His simplicity, earnestness and directness made a ready appeal to the masses. While others merely talked, Gandhi acted. Unlike many other contemporary Indian leaders, he had the courage of his convictions. Moreover, he had succeeded where others had failed. To a disillusioned and despairing generation in India which had lost faith both in the old Moderatism and in the old Extremism, Gandhi brought a new message of faith and hope by offering them a new ideology and a new programme of action which were revolutionary without ceasing to be constitutional. Gandhi's rise to power in Indian politics was also aided by the accidents of time and circumstance, such as the deaths of old, established leaders like Gokhale, Mehta and Tilak, the First World War and its aftermath, and the British bungling over the Rowlatt legislation, the Amritsar massacre, the question of the Khilafat and the reforms of 1919. But, with the advantage of hindsight, we are almost inclined to say: 'Such a man was wanted and such a man was found.'

Jawaharlal Nehru thus recalled more than twenty years later the sense of relief and exhilaration which he and many of his contemporaries in India felt at the emergence of Gandhi as the supreme leader of the Indian national movement: 'And then Gandhi came. He was like a powerful current of fresh air that made us stretch ourselves and take deep breaths; like a beam of light that pierced the darkness and removed the scales from our eyes; like a whirlwind that upset many things, but most of all the working of people's minds. He did not descend from the top; he seemed to emerge from the millions of India, speaking their language and incessantly drawing attention to them and their appalling condition. Get off the backs of these peasants and workers, he told us, all you who live by their exploitation;

get rid of the system that produces this poverty and misery. Political freedom took new shape then and acquired a new content. Much that he said we only partially accepted or sometimes did not accept at all. But all this was secondary. The essence of his teaching was fearlessness and truth, and action allied to these, always keeping the welfare of the masses in view.'[97]

From 1920 to 1947 Gandhi dominated the Indian national movement—directly or indirectly—in a manner that has few parallels in the history of the world. The story of his multifarious activities during this period is fairly well known and need not be repeated here. Instead, let us address ourselves to the more important task of answering the question: 'What did Gandhi contribute to the Indian national movement?'

Gandhi made the Indian national movement more truly Indian and national than it had so far been. He provided it with a firmer and larger indigenous base—both ideological and organizational. Gandhi brought into bolder relief the idea which Extremists like Tilak and Aurobindo Ghose had already perceived that national freedom meant something wider and deeper than emancipation from a foreign yoke, that it was a matter of preserving national culture, of building up a national character, of developing internal strength, and of renewing all departments of life. He emphasized that India would gain little if she only shook off the alien government and did not get back her soul. Every nation represents an ideal, a principle, a spirit. India must discover herself and what she stood for. She should be herself and stop imitating the west. Hence his great preoccupation with Indian cultural, literary and religious traditions. Hence also his insistence on *swadeshi* and *satyagraha*.

Gandhi converted the Indian national movement into a genuine mass movement. He carried politics from the drawing-rooms and council chambers to the streets and fields. He was a great mobilizer. By his personal charisma, by his remarkable capacity for mediating between various groups and forces, by his skilful use of popular myths and symbols, and by his reinterpretation of tradition for modernist purposes, Gandhi drew into the national movement those sections of the Indian population, such as the peasants, workers, untouchables and women, which had hitherto remained virtually untouched by it. As Rajni Kothari rightly says: 'He [Gandhi] realized clearly what few before him did, that the urbanized middle class alone did not provide a sufficient basis for national awakening. The task was to penetrate the masses, to arouse them from their state of apathy and isolation, to provide them with self-confidence and a positive elan in place of both the defensive postures of the moderates and the inferiority complex of the "anti-Western" radicals, and to confront the authorities with proof that they were dealing not with a small group of agitators, but with tens of thousands of people organized and disciplined into a great movement, drawn from all over the country.'[98]

Gandhi was a great organizer and builder. He transformed the character of the Congress by giving it a new direction, a new constitution, a new organizational structure, a new technique of agitation, a new leadership, and a new programme of action. Under Gandhi's stewardship the Congress became a formidable instrument for marshalling public opinion and the execution of policy. It moved out from the larger towns into the smaller towns and the villages. In *satyagraha* and *asahayoga* the Congress evolved a technique of agitation which was not only best suited to the genius and circumstances of the Indian people, but was also most effective against their British rulers. Gandhi provided the Congress with a comprehensive programme of 'constructive work' which kept it in good trim, especially during what may be called the slack season—in the routs following the great rallies. Though even under Gandhi the Congress remained what it had been in the past, an amorphous and eclectic organization with a pragmatic leadership which tried to accommodate various strands of thought and commitment in order to gain the widest possible support for its chief objective of *swaraj*, it did not fail to acquire a distinctive ideology which went beyond the mere winning of independence and which stood India in good stead even after she became independent.

Gandhi broke the hypnotic spell of the British Raj in India. He tried to rid the Indian people of the pervasive, perpetual and paralysing fear with which they were seized. He taught them to say 'no' to their oppressors, both foreign and indigenous. He uplifted the spirit and exalted the dignity of a vast people by teaching them to straighten their backs, to raise their eyes, and to face circumstances with steady gaze.[99]

Gandhi aimed at bringing about both a political and a social revolution in India, though he tried to harmonize the demands of the one with those of the other. He took up with vigour and power the cause of the untouchables and brought it into the forefront of Indian politics. Though a *brahmachari*, Gandhi made women his close allies and co-workers. Their emancipation in India was mainly his doing. Gandhi did not believe in deliberately stoking the fire of class conflict, but he laboured hard to teach the Indian people that the measure of their capacity for self-government was their ability to feel for the lowliest among them. 'Throughout his life', said Nehru, 'he [Gandhi] thought of India in terms of the poor and the oppressed and the downtrodden. To raise them and free them was the mission of his life. He adopted their ways of life and dress so that none in the country may feel lowly. Victory to him was the growth of freedom of these people.'[100] It is ridiculous to describe Gandhi as an agent of the *bourgeoisie* or a champion of the rich.

Gandhi did not allow the Indian national movement to become narrow, racial and isolationist. He was the strangest rebel the world has ever known. Day in and day out he told his countrymen that they should regard Englishmen as their friends and not enemies, that their fight was against the system and not against the men administering it, and that in so far as they failed to understand this distinction they harmed their own cause. Even a man like Jawaharlal Nehru, who did not stand much in need of such preaching, admitted its corrective effect in his life and thinking.[101]

Mass politics is impossible without violence. Gandhi carried on a mass movement for many years with the minimum use of violence. Only those who believe in the therapeutic qualities of blood-letting would regret that the Indian national movement had a leader like Gandhi who combined liberty as aim with non-violence as the method. Competent British observers have testified that Gandhi, by bringing the Indian national movement into the open and keeping it non-violent, freed it from secret terroristic activities and rid the British of the 'Mutiny complex'.[102] Had the Indian national movement turned violent, it would have, in its turn, invited violent repression, and ended by leaving a legacy of bloodshed which would have been extremely hard to overcome. If there was no 'Mutiny' or 'Amritsar' after 1919, and if the transfer of power in India in 1947 could be what Lord Samuel called it 'a treaty of peace without a war',[103] credit is as much due to Gandhi's leadership as to enlightened British statesmanship. Any large-scale use of violence in the Indian national struggle would have almost certainly sabotaged the development of Indian polity on constitutional lines and prevented the emergence of independent India as a democratic and secular state.

Gandhi had in him, as Gokhale had observed, 'the marvellous spiritual power to turn ordinary men around him into heroes and martyrs'.[104] He himself believed that the sagacity of a general consisted in the choice of his lieutenants.[105] He could pick capable men and was not afraid to give them responsibility. One of his greatest contributions to the national movement in India was that he provided it with able leaders at various levels and ultimately made himself dispensable.

Gandhi did not believe in petty manoeuvrings and manipulations for gaining temporary advantages. Despite all his tactical mistakes—real or alleged—his essential strategy continued to be right. Indians must develop internal strength—both material and moral. The British would relent and retire when India became strong. Disciplined agitation is the condition of national growth. Means are more important than ends.

Gandhi did not, as is commonly believed, mix religion with politics. He tried to spiritualize politics. He refused to separate ethics and politics. He reinforced the religious spirit of Indian nationalism and made patriotism synonymous with religion. He was himself a deeply religious man and an avowed Hindu. But his religious faith was of the most liberal, eclectic, non-ritualistic and tolerant kind. He lived and died for the sake of promoting communal harmony and national unity in India. 'He was', as Nehru remarked, 'a great unifier in India who taught us not only bare tolerance of others but the willing acceptance of them as our friends and comrades in common undertakings.'[106] It is the height of ignorance and intellectual perversity to accuse Gandhi of indulging in communal or communitarian politics and thereby bringing about the partition of the country.

Though Gandhi's lasting claim to greatness and fame would rest primarily upon his leadership of the Indian national movement, it is possible to argue—as, in fact, it has been argued[107]— that Indian independence would have come even without him, and that instead of hastening its advent, he actually delayed it by a few years. It is true that India would have been free sooner or later even if Gandhi had never lived. But without Gandhi's leadership the national movement in India would have been deprived of a great deal of its poetry, high drama, moral elevation and spiritual enthusiasm. The special impress of Gandhi's personality on the Indian national movement and on modern India can neither be effaced nor ignored. Whether he is deified or denigrated by his own people, whether they regard him as a splendid success or as a magnificent failure, Gandhi has, in a strange and subtle manner, become, as Nehru pointed out in 1948[108] and as recent events in India have confirmed, a significant part of the stuff of which India's spirit is made.

9

THE GROWTH OF LEGISLATIVE COUNCILS IN INDIA, 1833-1935

Introductory

The British began in India by establishing factories in various places—particularly in the west, the south and the east—in Bombay, Madras and Bengal. When traders became rulers, these were transformed into the three presidencies of Bombay, Madras and Bengal. To these were later added the following provinces: the North-Western Provinces, the Central Provinces, and Panjab. In the beginning the three presidencies were virtually separate and autonomous. They were controlled only from London. Instead of communicating with one another they preferred to correspond with London.

In 1773 and 1784 Acts were passed—the first called the Regulating Act of 1773[1] and the second called Pitt's India Act of 1784[2]—which centralized the British administration in India. The Acts of 1773 and 1784, in fact, did so many things: (*a*) the presidency of Bengal became the premier presidency; the governor of Bengal became the governor-general of India; Calcutta became the capital of the British Raj; (*b*) the governor-general became master of his own house, i.e. he could now overrule his council, consisting of four members in all; and (*c*) the British Parliament began indirectly controlling and superintending the Company's government in India.

The Charter Act of 1833

The process of centralization which began in 1773 reached its culmination in 1833, when the Charter Act of 1833[3] was passed and the legislative powers of the governors of Bombay and Madras were abolished. All laws now began to be made in Calcutta. For this immense task of making laws for the whole of British India all that was done was to add another member—the 'fourth' or 'ordinary' member, as he was called—to the council of the governor-general in Calcutta. In place of three law-making bodies, India thus acquired one central, though rudimentary, legislature.

The Charter Act of 1833 also marked the first attempt at differentiating the legislative from the executive functions of government. For purposes of administration the governor-general and only one ordinary member needed to be present. But when the council met for purposes of legislation, the presence of at least three ordinary members was essential. In fact, the fourth member, who had been added to the council, attended its meetings only when laws were to be made. This fourth member in 1834 was no other than the famous historian and jurist, T.B. Macaulay. He was also known as the 'legislative' or 'law member'.

The Charter Act of 1853

No sooner did laws for the whole of British India begin to be made in Calcutta than the peoples and governments of the other provinces started complaining that the governor-general in council was making laws without due knowledge of and regard for local conditions and needs. Before the Company's charter came up for renewal in 1853, there was a general feeling, both among educated Indians and enlightened British, that the various provinces in India should have their own legislative councils and that both the central and the provincial councils should include non-officials, preferably elected ones.[4]

The Charter Act of 1853,[5] therefore, provided that each provincial government would send one of its experienced officials to the governor-general's council in Calcutta. In fact, the governor-general's council, when acting in its legislative capacity, was enlarged by the addition of six members, of whom two were judges of the Calcutta Supreme Court and the other four were officials of at least ten years' standing appointed by the local governments of Bengal, Madras, Bombay and the North-Western Provinces. This was the first recognition of the principle of local representation in the Indian legislature, even though the representatives of the provinces were officials and Englishmen. The fourth ordinary member now became a full-fledged part of the executive. The additional (six) members were entitled to sit and vote only at the meetings of the council of the governor-general held for legislative purposes.

The council created by the Act of 1853 assumed in practice a distinct character, though the position of the additional members was similar to that of the fourth ordinary member of 1833. Discussions became oral instead of being conducted in writing. The examination of bills was performed by select committees instead of by a single member, and, for the first time, the legislative business of India was conducted with open doors. The council began to behave like a 'quasi-independent body', a 'miniature representative assembly' or a 'petty parliament', and its debates began to be regularly published.[6] But the council was composed entirely of British officials (even judges were officials, after all). Moreover, the huge extent of the territory for which it legislated made it impossible for matters to be handled with adequate information and experience.

The Indian Councils Act of 1861

The revolt of 1857 underlined the need for associating Indians with the process of law-making in India. The British government in India realized that it was dangerous to continue 'to legislate for millions of people with few means of knowing, except by rebellion, whether the laws suit them or not'.[7] The revolt also proved to be a financial disaster for the British government in India. It badly needed additional funds. It tried to increase taxation, especially direct taxation. At once the cry of 'no taxation without representation' was raised, and the old demand was revived for an introduction of non-officials into the legislative council. Non-official Anglo-Indians were far more prominent in this agitation than Indians. The former were also a clamant and powerful body. The government was naturally anxious to mollify them lest they unite with Indians against it. But any inclusion of representatives of non-official Anglo-Indians in the legislative council would have, besides being bitterly resented by Indians, meant an undesirable increase in their influence in the government. It was, therefore, felt necessary to include Indians also as a counterweight to non-official Anglo-Indians.[8]

The Indian Councils Act of 1861[9] provided that for legislative purposes the governor-general's council should be enlarged by the addition of not less than six and not more than twelve members, nominated for two years, of whom not less than half were to be non-officials. The Act also gave limited powers of legislation to the presidencies of Bombay and Madras, and provided for the addition of not less than four and not more than eight members, of whom not less than half were to be non-officials, to the councils of the governors of Bombay and Madras when they met for the purpose of making laws and regulations. The governor-general was authorized to create similar local councils for Bengal, the North-Western Provinces and Panjab.

The legislative council at Calcutta had latterly exhibited a spirit of too much independence and behaved almost like a 'petty parliament'. The passage of the Indian Councils Act of 1861 gave the secretary of state an opportunity to clip the wings of the Calcutta council and to define precisely its constitutional position. The Act introduced the safeguard of requiring the governor-general's prior sanction for the introduction of bills or contentious subjects and preserved his veto. Further, the council could only discuss motions for leave to introduce a bill, or bills actually before it. Judges, who had proved to be thorns in the side of the executive, ceased to be *ex-officio* members of the council. In his communications to the viceroy, the then secretary of state, Sir Charles Wood, was insistent that every care should be taken to prevent the council from developing into an independent body or miniature parliament. No rules were to be made and no expressions used which tended to create an impression that there was a legislative council separate and distinct from the executive council. The additional members were to be treated as members of the governor-general's council when it met for the purpose of making laws and regulations.[10] The Indian Councils Act of 1861 was thus both a progressive and a retrogressive measure.

The additional members of the councils were carefully hand-picked and their role and status were advisory. The legislative councils were more like *darbars* than representative bodies. Officials still dominated their proceedings. Non-officials were few and they could only make speeches. They could neither consider the budget nor question the policies of the executive. Only when a bill was required for the levy of a new tax, was the legislature entitled to discuss any part of financial management. And the presence of one or two Indians could hardly make much difference in the functioning of the councils. But, as the Chinese say: 'Even the longest journey begins with one small step.' Once Indians were admitted into the legislative councils, the demand naturally grew that there should be more of them, that they should be representative, preferably elected, men, and that the councils should have wider powers.

The Growth of Local Self-Government

Finance often plays a more important role in determining government policies than is generally admitted by politicians or realized by historians. It was financial considerations which really forced the hands of the viceroy and the secretary of state after the revolt of 1857 to attend urgently to the question or reforming the legislative council. The tendency of the Indian Councils Act of 1861 was towards decentralization of legislative authority. This tendency was further reinforced because of the financial difficulties of the British government in India. And the more the government increased taxation the more unpopular it became both with the people and with the subordinate provincial governments. The situation was becoming impossible financially as well as politically. The imperial government had to go in for financial decentralization. The process began with Lord Mayo in the early 1870s. He transferred heads of expenditure and certain revenues to the provinces. He also provided for the provincial governments to enlarge the powers of municipal bodies and to encourage the recruitment of non-official members to them. Lord Ripon carried the process of decentralization further and gave it a pronouncedly political and democratic purpose.

Pressure for Reform of the Councils

Ripon also suggested in December 1881 to the then secretary of state for India, Lord Hartington, the desirability of allowing the municipalities, some of which contained elected members, to elect Indians to the central and provincial legislatures. The reform would, the viceroy argued, be appreciated by the people of India and promote their 'political education'; it would prevent the councils from becoming shams and subject government bills to real discussion; it would be 'a substantial assistance to the Government', for it would enable them to ascertain the views of the public and give them an opportunity of expressing their real intentions and removing misunderstandings.[11] Hartington, however, thought the suggestion premature and risky and rejected it.[12] Ripon's successor to the viceroyalty, Lord Dufferin, was impressed with the rapid growth of political aspirations in India and the need for satisfying them. He felt that it would be both prudent and profitable from the point of view of the administration to associate qualified Indians with itself and provide them with regular, constitutional channels for the expression of their wants and feelings.[13] The Indian National Congress and other political bodies in India were already agitating for the reform of the legislative councils. Dufferin regarded 'the objects even of the more advanced party' in India as 'neither very dangerous nor very extravagant', and he favoured giving 'quickly and with a good grace whatever it may be possible to accord'.[14] The Liberal secretary of state, Lord Kimberley, to whom Dufferin communicated his proposals for the reform of the legislative councils in March-April 1886 was not opposed to 'some very cautious step in this direction',[15] but, unfortunately, before any step could be taken the government of which he was a member went out of office in July 1886. Dufferin wasted about two years more in persuading the new Tory secretary of state for India, Lord Cross, to permit him to submit his recommendations for the reform of the provincial legislative councils. And when in November 1888 Dufferin submitted his recommendations[16] for the introduction of the elective principle, the increase in the non-official element of the councils, and the grant to the latter of the right of interpellation and partial control of the finances, they did not commend themselves to the secretary of state.[17] It required another viceroy—Lord Lansdowne—and three more years of persistent pressure on his part to compel a rather reluctant ministry in Britain to go to Parliament with a half-hearted measure which did not even go as far as the government of India desired and which could hardly be expected to satisfy Indian public opinion.

The Indian Councils Act of 1892

The Indian Councils Act of 1892[18] increased the number of additional members in the governor-general's council, that is to say, the number of members added to the executive council when it went into legislative session, from a maximum of twelve to a maximum of sixteen, and that in the governors' councils from a maximum of eight to a maximum of twenty. All the additional members were still nominated, but the regulations framed under the Act allowed the non-official members of the provincial councils to make recommendations for four seats in the governor-general's council, and the municipalities, district boards, chambers of commerce and universities to make recommendations for eight seats in the provincial councils. The provincial councils, though not the supreme council, were empowered to discuss the budget and raise administrative questions, though not to vote on them.

The Indian Councils Act of 1892 was a 'cautious extension' of the Act of 1861. It increased the Indian membership of the councils and widened the non-officials' power to question the executive. The provision for election was implicit, indirect and limited. The government was anxious to provide representation to the views of 'different races, classes and localities', but on account of the very small number of seats available for non-officials, little room was left for territorial representation. The Act failed to make any profound impact on the politically-conscious Indians. The more extensive employment of Indians in the higher administrative posts and the steady development of representative institutions in India were the two main demands of the early Indian nationalists. The Indian Councils Act of 1892 was a small and slow measure of reform aimed at conciliating the Indian nationalists in respect of their second demand. It came too late and it gave too little. It did not succeed in forestalling radical nationalist demands by offering timely concessions. But it did offer a useful inducement to the Congress to continue pursuing its objectives by peaceful and constitutional means.

The Morley-Minto Reforms of 1909

The reform of 1892 came thirty-one years after that of 1861. The next reform came only seventeen years later, in 1909. In the meantime the tempo of Indian nationalism had quickened. An extremist party had emerged. The bomb had made its appearance in India. Japan had defeated Russia. A Liberal ministry had come to power in Britain with an overwhelming majority and committed to reform. John Morley was the secretary of state for India and Lord Minto was the viceroy. The moderates in India were losing ground. The reforms were aimed at rallying them. And while making concessions with one hand, the British used the other hand to put down terrorism and sedition.

The Morley-Minto reforms[19] increased the number of Indians in the councils, made more seats elective, and gave the councils more powers, though not enough to enable them to control the executive. The principle of election, implicit in the Act of 1892, was now frankly recognized. The legislative councils were allowed more time to discuss the budget, to move resolutions and to call for a division. The right of interpellation was extended and members could ask supplementary questions. Morley and Minto, however, repudiated the suggestion that these enlarged legislative councils were intended to pave the way for anything resembling parliamentary institutions in India. The councils being already in existence, they tried to make them better vehicles for expressing the opinions of the different classes and communities in India. The liberalization of their procedure was intended to afford the British government in India 'additional opportunities both of becoming acquainted with the drift of public opinion, and of explaining their own actions'.[20] Indians were to be more closely associated with the tasks of administration and legislation, they were to be given better opportunities of influencing the alien government, but they were not yet to govern themselves or to be trained for doing so.

The elections to the legislative councils were indirect, except in the case of landlords and Muslims; the electorate was indefinite and severely restricted. The constituencies for the imperial legislative council were the provincial legislative councils, landholders, Muslims, and chambers of commerce. For the provincial legislative councils, the electors were municipal and district boards, landholders, planters, universities, Muslims, and the trading community. For the 27 elective seats on the imperial legislative council there were only 4,818 electors. Of these 2,406 were directly landlords and 1,901 Muslims. Thirteen of the twenty-seven elected members were elected by the non-official members of the provincial legislative councils, six by landlords, six by Muslims, and two by chambers of commerce. Eight electors chose the representative from Burma, fourteen from the Central Provinces, and fifteen from Panjab. The non-official majorities in the provincial legislative councils were unreal and an attempt was made to counteract the influence of the advanced political classes by special electorates created and weighted in favour of the landed gentry and the Muslims.

The Indian Councils Act of 1909 was, in the main, an extension of the Act of 1892. It doubled the number of Indians in the provincial legislative councils and gave the latter non-official (nominated plus elected) majorities. The number of additional members was increased to a maximum of fifty in the larger and thirty in the smaller provinces. In Bombay, for example, of the total membership of forty-seven, five were *ex-officio* members, twenty-one were nominated (of which not more than fourteen could be officials) and twenty-one were elected. In Bengal alone there was a clear elected majority, but there the European representatives held the balance. The imperial legislative council also received an addition of Indian members, but here an official majority was retained. Out of its total membership of sixty-eight, there was thirty-six officials and thirty-two non-officials; forty-one seats were filled by nomination and twenty-seven by election.

The Morley-Minto reforms were a typical product of that nineteenth century British liberalism which believed that statesmanship was mainly a question of determining how far popular demands should be conceded, but which seldom bothered to think out the fundamentals of policy, or relate it to a well-defined larger purpose. 'Lacking a clearly distinguishable and steadily developing policy towards the growth of politics in India,' justly comments Professor C.H. Philips, 'Morley and Minto were driven to devising not so much a coherent plan as a series of expedients to meet the particular and admittedly difficult situation.'[21] Morley's maxim 'Order *plus* Progress,[22] was excellent, but it could not be a substitute for a well-thought-out and far-seeing policy.

The second major defect of the Morley-Minto reforms was that they brought the Indian government to a constitutional blind alley. They expanded the legislative councils, increased the number of non-officials in them and gave them greater powers. The reformed councils were bound to clash with the irremovable executives. The main function of the councils was to oppose and criticize the government while remaining completely free from responsibility for the results of their action. It was not long before British statesmen realized that any further progress on the lines of the Morley-Minto reforms would lead to disaster, for a further increase in the non-official element in the legislative councils would give the latter the power of paralysing government at every turn, but not the power and responsibility of conducting government for themselves.

The third major defect of the Morley-Minto reforms was the grant of separate electorates to the Muslims. The British encouraged the Muslims to demand their being placed on a separate register and readily allowed the demand when it was actually made. Their motive clearly was to 'divide and rule'. A backward conservative minority was placated and used against an increasingly radical Indian nationalism. A cultural minority was transformed into a political minority. Separate electorates cut at the very root of Indian nationalism. Their evil consequences 'unfolded themselves with the remorseless march of a Greek tragedy'.[23] The poison worked steadily.

The Montagu-Chelmsford Reforms of 1919

Why were the British in India? What did they mean to do with India? What would be next instalment of reforms? Questions such as these which Morley and Minto parried, British statesmen were required to answer during the First World War and in the changed atmosphere that the war created. The goal of British rule in India was declared on 20 August 1947 to be 'the increasing association of Indians in every branch of the administration, and the gradual development of self-governing institutions with a view to the progressive realisation of responsible government in India'.[24] But there was yet no timetable for the achievement of this goal. Most Britons were inclined to believe that it would take centuries before India could be self-governing.

In July 1918 the secretary of state for India, E.S. Montagu, and the viceroy of India, Lord Chelmsford, published their joint 'Report on Indian Constitutional Reforms'. Its main recommendations were incorporated in the Government of India Act, 1919,[25] which became operative in 1921.

The Montagu-Chelmsford reforms were in the nature of a control experiment. A beginning in responsible government was made in the provinces (now numbering eight: Bombay, Madras, Bengal, U.P., Panjab, C.P., Bihar and Orissa, and Assam). Provincial government was divided into two compartments: reserved and transferred. The reserved subjects were finance, land revenue, law and order, forests and commerce. The transferred subjects were agriculture, health, education, and local government. True, most of the development departments were transferred but they required money and fresh taxation. The more important and revenue-yielding departments were reserved. The reserved subjects were in the charge of the governor and his executive council, which in all save two provinces now consisted of four members, two British and two Indian. The transferred subjects were in the charge of the governor acting through his ministers, who were all Indians.

The provincial legislative councils were enlarged. Bengal, for example, had 139 members; Madras, 127; and Bombay, 111. Of these about 70 per cent were elected, 20 per cent were officials, and 10 per cent were nominated. The franchise was extended. There were $5\frac{1}{2}$ million voters for the provincial legislatures, and 1 million for the central legislature. There was a property and educational qualification for voters. The number of separate/communal electorates increased despite the explicit recognition by Montagu and Chelmsford in their joint report that they were inimical to the growth of democracy and unity in the country. Muslims, Sikhs, Europeans, Anglo-Indians (i.e. Eurasians), and Indian Christians—all were put on separate registers. The devolution of authority from the centre to the provinces was now given a precise and legal form. The central government retained defence, foreign affairs, relations with the Indian princely states, communications, customs, commerce and banking, and the control of the all-India services. Customs and income tax were to be the major sources of central revenue, and land revenue the major provincial source. The provincial governments were required to make fixed annual contributions to the central funds. The central legislature was divided into two houses. The lower house, called the Assembly, had 145 members (104 elected [52 general, 30 Muslims, 9 Europeans, 7 landowners, 4 commerce, 2 Sikhs]; 25 nominated officials; and 16 nominated non-officials). At the centre no such advance was made as in the provinces, but measures were taken to further Indian unity and to pave the way for the introduction of responsible government by the creation of an Assembly and a Council of State, the majority of whose members were elected. If they could not determine policy, they could debate it.

There were two main conditions for the success of the difficult and delicate machinery created by the Act of 1919. The first—it was emphasized by the government of India—was 'a sufficiently long truce in the struggle for power'.[26] The second—it was emphasized by Ramsay MacDonald—was to persuade India that 'a really substantial beginning' was being made and an organization created which would by its own momentum lead progressively to complete self-government for India.[27] Unfortunately, neither of these two conditions was satisfied in the event.

Even under the most favourable circumstances dyarchy would have been a 'a high test of human nature,'[28] on all sides. In point of fact, the ironical imp who turns the wheel of fortune in human affairs could hardly have devised a setting less favourable to the inauguration of the reforms of 1919. The reflex action of the war, a devastating influenza epidemic, scarcity, high prices, stifled trade, the painful events of 1919, the uneasiness of the Muslims about the future of Turkey, and finally the non-co-operation movement—all combined to ruin the chances of their success.

Whereas most British officials and politicians believed that the concession of 1919 had been made by Parliament 'in the extreme of its generosity',[29] most Indians thought that it had not given them even 'four annas of genuine *swaraj*'.[30] What Montagu had feared came to pass; his scheme proved to be 'much too small for the situation' in India.[31]

There was no more unfortunate remark in the Montagu-Chelmsford Report than that which told Indians '*Hanoz Dihli dur ast*'[32] (Delhi is yet far away), for their eyes were now set on the citadel of power. The demand of Indian politicians for the fixing of a time limit for the achievement of complete self-government arose from a disbelief in the intentions of the British government to transfer power to them in any foreseeable future. No such time limit could obviously be fixed, and it is no easy matter to remove distrust and suspicion. But unless Indians had some definite vision of the goal which they were going to reach in some foreseeable future, it is difficult to see how that goodwill and co-operation between the rulers and the ruled could be secured which was so necessary for the success of the Montagu-Chelmsford reforms. The tragedy of later years—so full of agonizing conflict— was due in the main to the failure of Indian politicians to realize that these changes had put into their hands the ultimate lever of power if only they knew how to use it; and the failure of most British statesmen, on the other hand, to recognize that the Act of 1919 marked the beginning of the end of British rule in India, to visualize the full implications of this process, and to be prepared for all its consequences.

Early in the 1920s Indian public opinion became unanimous on the point that the time had come for a more or less final settlement—a settlement by which the provinces would attain full responsible government and at the centre all subjects, except foreign affairs, defence and relations with the Indian princely states, would be transferred to an Indian government responsible to an elected majority. It demanded that schemes should be framed which would ensure complete Indianization of the army and the civil service within a reasonable period of 25 or 30 years. By the end of that period it hoped to see the remaining subjects at the centre also to be transferred to a responsible Indian government. For any such quasi-final arrangement the British government were not yet prepared; nor did they think that India was ripe for it. Indians wanted to have a definite vision of the goal with the milestones on the journey clearly marked out. The traditional dislike of the English for any such definite and explicit arrangement was reinforced by a vivid recognition of the immense difficulties and complexities of the Indian problem. Moreover, as has already been pointed out, most British statesmen failed to take into account the full implications of the announcement of 1917 and the reforms of 1919. It was generally assumed that the introduction of responsible government in India would be slow and long-drawn-out affair. Once this plan of slow-motion advance had been rudely disturbed by the march of events in India, there developed a tendency on the part of British statesmen to wait on events instead of thinking out and working out a bolder plan of campaign. The British not only did not declare their timetable; they had no timetable. And their proclaimed schemes of Indianizing the army and the civil service in India—which would have taken a few hundred years to materialize—only served to confirm and deepen Indian suspicions of British intentions. The British attempted to deal with the Indian problem more as political engineers than as psychologists. The dangers of going fast were realized but not those of delay.

In 1922 Lloyd George, as British prime minister, still spoke of the British element in the Indian Civil Service as 'the steel frame' of the Raj and remarked that he could see no time when India could dispense with its guidance and assistance.³³ In 1925, the secretary of state for India, Lord Birkenhead, admitted that the implications of provincial autonomy had 'never yet been closely analysed'.³⁴ No attempt was made to grapple with the problem of the princely states until 1930. Plans for the Indianization of the army remained halting, leisurely and unconvincing. Defence was often called 'the very article by which the republic stands or falls'.³⁵ Indian incapacity in the matter was repeatedly emphasized as constituting as almost insuperable block on her rapid constitutional advance, but the British government, in the 1920s or even in the 1930s, had not reconciled themselves to the idea of handing over the control of the Indian army to a government responsible to an Indian legislature in the foreseeable future.³⁶ In 1930 the Simon Commission proposed that the subject of Indian defence should be reserved indefinitely as an imperial responsibility and transferred to the imperial government.³⁷

It was ironical and tragic that Indian public opinion morally broke with Britain at the very moment when she committed herself publicly and definitely to the policy of self-government for India. But should not part of the explanation for this unfortunate happening be sought in the failure of British statesmen to show Indians clearly the steps by which they proposed to reach a definite goal? Did not the lack of a settled policy and a denfinite programme on the part of the British government contribute largely towards the exasperation and intransigence of political India?

Surprisingly enough, dyarchy did not prove to be a mechanical failure. Though clumsy, the dual machinery created in the provinces by the Montagu-Chelmsford reforms did function. Legislative and administrative work continued. But dyarchy failed in its primary purpose of providing Indians with real training in responsible government. No real party system developed. There was little political education of the electorate. The dyarchic division in the executive councils did not work, as government is one and cannot be easily divided. Ironically enough, the Act of 1919 worked better in those provinces where dyarchy was not observed. From the point of view of the British government, the reforms of 1919 were not altogether a failure. They withstood the extremist assault for sixteen long years.

The Government of India Act of 1935

The process of revising the Act of 1919 began in 1927 with the appointment of the Simon Commission. The Commission reported in 1930. The Round Table Conferences met from 1930 to 1932. It was not until 1935 that 'the monstrous boat' of the new Government of India Act was ready. The Act went into operation in the provinces in 1937. The federal part of the Act could never become effective. On the outbreak of the war in 1939 it was shelved. So at the centre India continued to be governed until 1947 by the Act of 1919 which even its authors thought would not last for more than five to ten years.

The main provisions of the Government of India Act of 1935[38] were as follows:

Two new provinces—Sindh and Orissa—were created, and together with the North-West Frontier Province, they were placed on an equal footing with the older provinces and presidencies. The number of provinces in India now became eleven. Burma now ceased to be a part of India. In the provinces dyarchy was abolished and they gained virtually complete autonomy. They acquired a separate legal personality and were now substantially liberated from 'the superintendence, direction and control' of the government of India and the secretary of state in London.

The executive authority of a province was vested in the governor as the representative of the Crown. He was provided with a council of ministers to aid and advise him in the discharge of the functions conferred on him by the Act. These functions included almost the entire sphere of provincial government, except in matters like law and order for which he had a special responsibility and for which he could act at his own discretion. All departments of provincial administration were now to be controlled by ministers responsible to their legislatures. The governors were to accept their ministers' advice in all matters except those in which they had 'special responsibilities', for example, the prevention of any grave menace to the peace and tranquillity of the province and the safeguarding of the legitimate interests of the minorities (these were known as 'safeguards'). In case it became impossible to carry on the government of a province in accordance with the provisions of the Act, the governor could (under section 93) assume control of the whole administration of the province at his discretion for a specified period. The governor was also invested with some extraordinary powers. Under certain conditions he could refuse his assent to bills passed by the legislature. He could promulgate ordinances when the legislature was not in session if he thought that circumstances rendered it necessary for him to take immediate action, and also at any time with regard to certain subjects. Moreover, under certain conditions he could issue permanent Acts either with or without consulting the legislature if he so pleased. The special powers of the governor were regarded as serious limitations on real responsible government in India.

Provincial legislatures consisted of one or two chambers. Madras, Bombay, Bengal, the United Provinces, Bihar and Assam had each two chambers, known as the legislative council and the legislative assembly. Panjab, the Central Provinces, the North-West Frontier Province, Sindh and Orissa had only one chamber, known as the legislative assembly. The strength of the legislative assembly or the lower chamber varied from 50 to 250 members, almost all of whom were elected. It was to sit for five years, though it could be dissolved earlier by the governor.

Representation in the legislatures was arranged in accordance with the 'communal award' as modified by the Poona Pact. Special electorates were retained and certain seats were reserved for the 'scheduled castes'. About ten per cent of the population of India—roughly 30 million—was enfranchised.

The legislative council, or the upper chamber, was a permanent body, not subject to dissolution, but approximately one-third of its members were to retire every third year. The powers of the two chambers were co-ordinate, except in the matter of certain grants and introducing financial bills, which were within the purview of the legislative assembly. In case of a difference of opinion between the two chambers the governor could convene a joint session of the two chambers and form a decision according to the opinion of the majority of the members of the joint meeting.

As regards the central government in India the Act of 1935 provided two alternate constitutions. It contemplated the establishment of a federation of India—including both the provinces and the Indian princely states. But if such a federation failed to materialize, the Government of India Act, 1919, with some minor amendments, was to remain in force at the centre.

The federal proposals of the Government of India Act, 1935,

may be summarized as follows:

The federation of India could only come into operation if and when a sufficient number of states (*i*) to occupy 52 of the 104 seats allotted to the states in the upper house of the federal legislature and (*b*) to make up half the total population of the states had acceded to the federation.

A state would accede to the federation when its ruler had executed the instrument of accession empowering the federal government and the legislature to exercise authority over it in accordance with the Act; but this authority could be exercised only in respect of those matters in the federal list, and with such limitations, which the ruler enumerated in his instruments of accession. In the conduct of their affairs as members of the federation, the states were to deal with the governor-general as head of the federal government, but in their relations with the British government apart from federal affairs, they were to deal with 'His Majesty's Representative for the exercise of the functions of the Crown in its relations with Indian States'. This meant in effect that paramountcy was not to be transferred to the federation of India.

The federal legislature was to be bicameral. The council of state, or the federal upper house, was to consist of 156 representatives of British India and not more than 104 of the states. One-third of its members were to retire in every third year. The states' representatives were to be appointed by their rulers, the smaller states were to be grouped together as units for electoral purposes. Six of the British Indian representatives were to be nominated by the governor-general. Ten seats were allotted to the Eurasian, European and Indian Christian communities in British India as a whole. Of the remaining 140 seats, 20 were allotted to Madras, Bengal and the United Provinces; 16 to Bombay, Panjab and Bihar; 8 to the Central Provinces; 5 to Assam, the North-West Frontier Province, Orissa and Sindh; and one each to the four large commissioners' provinces. In the distribution of seats both population and communal interests were taken into account. The General, Muslim and Sikh seats were to be filled by direct election by members of those communities in territorial constituencies. The representatives of the Depressed Classes, Indian Christians, Eurasians, and Europeans were to be elected by the members of those communities who were members of the provincial legislatures. Of the 140 seats mentioned above, 75 were for the General electorate, 6 for the scheduled castes, 4 for Sikhs, 49 for Muslims, and 6 for women.

The federal assembly was to be elected every five years. It was to consist of 240 representatives of British India and not more than 125 of the Indian princely states. The distribution of seats allotted to the states was based mainly on population (for example, Hyderabad was given 16 seats, Mysore 7, and Travancore 5). Comparatively few of the states were to be represented individually. In most cases there was to be one representative for a group of states. The British Indian seats were allocated on the same basis as those in the upper house, but in the federal assembly the General, Muslim and Sikh seats, which numbered no less than 193, were to be filled by indirect election, that is by the members of those communities who were members of the provincial legislative assemblies on the principle of proportional representation with the single transferable vote. The Indian Christian, Eurasian and European representatives and women were to be elected by members of those classes in the provincial assemblies. The representatives of the scheduled castes were to be elected by the holders of the General seats in the assemblies from candidates previously elected —four for each seat—by the scheduled caste votes only.

The scope of federal legislation was limited to the subjects enumerated in the federal and concurrent lists. The federal legislature could not make laws for a princely state otherwise than in accordance with its instruments of accession; nor could it make laws to have effect in a province on the subjects enumerated in the provincial list. As to 'residuary powers', they were allocated neither to the centre nor to the provinces; instead the governor-general was to determine 'in his discretion' which legislature would deal with a subject not mentioned in any of the lists. In the event of a conflict between a federal and a provincial law, the former was normally to prevail. The governor-general was also empowered to proclaim 'in his discretion' that 'a grave emergency exists whereby the security of India is threatened, whether by war or internal disturbance'; and on the issue if such a proclamation the federal legislature was entitled to legislate with the previous sanction of the governor-general on any subject in the provincial list.

As regards finance, certain items were charged on the federal revenues, and were, therefore non-votable, but discussion on most of them was allowed in the legislature. The federal legislature was, however, debarred from even discussing the expenses of the governor-general and the expenditure arising from the Crown's relations with the princely states. Further, no legislation could be introduced affecting coinage, currency or the constitution or functions of the Reserve Bank of India without the previous sanction of the governor-general.

The governor-general was to have a council of ministers of not more than ten. He was charged with eight 'special responsibilities', seven of which were the same, *mutatis mutandis*, as the governors'; the eighth was 'the safeguarding of the financial stability and credit of the Federal Government'. The governor-general was required to act 'in his discretion' not only, like the governor, in such matters as the appointment of ministers and the summoning of the legislature, but also as regards defence, external affairs, and ecclesiastical affairs. These matters could be discussed in the legislature, but the supplies for dealing with them would not be subject to vote. Moreover, on these matters—called 'reserved'— the governor-general was to be assisted not by the ministers responsible to the legislature, but by 'counsellors', responsible only to him. These counsellors did not need to be members of the legislature, but they were entitled to take part in its proceedings. The dyarchy which was abolished in the provinces was reproduced at the centre. For the administration of the 'reserved' departments, as for the discharge of the 'special responsibilities', the governor-general was given similar powers of legislation as those given to the governors for similar purposes. The governor-general was also empowered to appoint a financial adviser who was to be responsible to him and was to assist him in the discharge of this special responsibility for 'safeguarding the financial stability and credit of the Federal Government'. Finance in general was, however, to be entrusted to a finance minister, responsible to the legislature.

The Indian Civil Service, the Indian Police Service and the civil branch of the Indian Medical Service were to continue to be recruited by the secretary of state and their rights and conditions of service were protected by special laws.

The secretary of state's council in London was to be abolished and he was to be provided in its place with a body of advisers, not less than three and not more than six. The India Office remained, but its cost was to be charged to the British revenues.

Reactions to the Act of 1935

A great deal of time and effort was spent in the making of the Government of India Act, 1935. It was a long, complex and comprehensive document. But it was 'far behind the times for which it was legislating',[39] and it had few friends in Britain or in India. Sir Winston Churchill, who was not sympathetic to Indian aspirations, called it 'a gigantic quilt of jumbled crotchet work' and asked the pertinent question: 'Who in India wants it?'[40] According to Clement Attlee, the keynote of the Act was 'mistrust' of the Indian people. And he warned: 'It is quite impossible to get the real changes which are demanded in India by setting up a constitution which is merely acquiesced in by a certain number of people, which may be worked by a privileged class, but which will not be supported by any of the advanced parties in India or any of the people who really want a change.'[41] A.B. Keith commented: 'It is difficult to resist the impression that either responsible government should have been frankly declared impossible or the reality conceded; it is not surprising that neither gratitude nor co-operation is readily forthcoming for a hybrid product such as is the provincial system of special responsibilities and acts to be done according to individual judgment.... For the federal scheme it is difficult to feel any satisfaction... on the British side the scheme is favoured in order to provide an element of pure conservatism in order to combat any dangerous elements of democracy contributed by British India.... It is difficult to deny the justice of the contention in India that federation was largely evoked by the desire to evade the issue of extending responsible government to the central government of British India.'[42] The Indian Liberal leader, Sir C.Y. Chintamani wrote: 'I venture to describe the Government of India Act of 1935 as the anti-India Act. We are given a limp federation full of undesirable features, ill-balanced as between the States and the Provinces and denied powers which are vital to every government worth the name.'[43] Congress leaders described the Act as a 'slave constitution' and 'a new charter of bondage'. They denounced the 'safeguards' as rendering responsible government nugatory. They condemned the yoking of democracy and autocracy in the proposed federation. They resolved 'not to submit to this Constitution or to co-operate with it, but to combat it, both inside and outside the legislatures, so as to end it'. They coupled their condemnation of the Act of

1935 with the demand that the future constitution of India should be framed by Indians themselves by means of a constituent assembly elected on the basis of universal adult franchise.⁴⁴

The Muslim League also condemned the Government of India Act, 1935, but its reasons for doing so were very different from those of the Congress. The League was not entirely dissatisfied with the provincial part of the Act, though it would have liked the provinces to enjoy greater autonomy and the Muslim share in the provincial ministries to be fixed by statutory enactment, and decided to work it 'for what it was worth'. The League was not at all enamoured of the idea of a federation of India, though it still paid lip service to that idea. The Muslim League realized that in the proposed federation of India the numerical majority of the Hindus would increase, for most of the states were predominantly Hindu. In order to ward off this danger the leaders of the Muslim League and other Muslim organizations had put forward certain proposals even while the Act of 1935 was in the making. These included (*i*) a very loose federation in which the functions of the federal government would be confined to minimum common purposes, namely defence, foreign affairs and communications; (*ii*) the transfer of power from the British government in London to the provinces and not to any central government in India; (*iii*) utmost autonomy for the provinces with residuary powers vested in them; and (*iv*) safeguards for the Muslims in the Hindu majority provinces. In fact, Muslim leaders had already begun to demand the creation of a block of autonomous Muslim states in the east and the north-west and an extremely loose federation of sovereign states.⁴⁵ A British cabinet paper of 25 December 1932 examined the communal problem in India and wondered whether 'the Muslim provinces, or the provinces in which the Muslims hope to consolidate their power, should be under any degree of control from a centre which will be predominantly Hindu'. The paper considered the Muslims' 'primary object' to be the creation of 'a Muslim India'; their secondary object was to secure Muslim interests elsewhere by the operation of the hostage theory.⁴⁶ The Muslim approach to the question of federation was examined by a *Manchester Guardian* correspondent, who reported on 18 June 1931: 'The Moslems see that the new Federal Government, if and when it comes into existence, will have a large Hindu majority. The entrance of the States has increased the majority, for the States are chiefly Hindu. There is a strong tendency to counteract the permanent majority by trying to form a large northern block of provinces which will be Moslem, and in which the Hindus will be, as it were, hostages for the good behaviour of their co-religionists in the centre and the South.... Many Moslems do not believe in the permanence of a Federal India, and they foresee a Moslem state in the North stretching from Karachi to North Bengal.... This idea may help to explain their insistence on... the separation of Sind;... that the Moslem N.W.F.P. should become an ordinary province; ... [and the securing of] a permanent majority in the Punjab, and if possible in Bengal.'[47]

The apparent enthusiasm which some of the Indian princely states had shown for the idea of a federation in the early stages of the Round Table Conference had cooled off by the time the Act of 1935 came to be enacted. The states had been very generously treated by the framers of the Act and they had been given a virtual veto on the federation. But they tried to exact more concessions. The government of India, under the viceroyalties of Willingdon and Linlithgow, showed neither urgency nor firmness in dealing with the states. The negotiations dragged on leisurely for years until the Second World War broke out in September 1939 and the federation was shelved.

Despite the claims of some contemporary and latter-day commentators, it is impossible to regard the Act of 1935 as a major constructive achievement of the British in India, designed to promote Indian unity and independence. In the early stages of the consultations which led to the framing of the Act, Sir Samuel Hoare, the then secretary of state for India, drew up, on 12 December 1930, a memorandum for the consideration of the Conservative Party Business Committee, in which he presented all-India federation as an opportunity of avoiding democracy and responsibility in the central government of India, of extricating 'British India from the morass into which the doctrinaire liberalism of Montagu had plunged it'. Hoare pointed out that the British would be yielding 'a semblance of responsible government and yet retain in our hands the realities and verities of British control'. The viceroy would have large overriding powers. The army would be reserved to British control. Some eighty per cent of the Indian revenues would be kept out of the hands of an Indian finance minister. The federal executive would not be responsible or removable in the British sense.[48] In December 1939 Lord Linlithgow, the viceroy, wrote to Lord Zetland, the secretary of state for India: 'But there is also our own position in India to be taken into account. After all we framed the Constitution as it stands in the Act of 1935, because we thought that way the best way—given the political position in both countries—of maintaining British influence in India. It is no part of our policy, I take it, to expedite in India constitutional changes for their own sake, or gratuitously to hurry the handing over of controls to Indian hands at any pace faster than we regard as best calculated on a long view, to hold India to the Empire.'[49] The draftsman of the 1935 Act was being absolutely honest and correct when he described it as an Act 'to make further provision for the government of India'[50] by the British.

10

THE CONGRESS AND THE PARTITION OF INDIA

The Congress and the Government of India Act, 1935

The Government of India Act of 1935 provided for the establishment of full responsible government, subject to 'safeguards', in the eleven provinces of British India; it provided also for a federation of India, comprising both provinces and states, with a federal central government and legislature for the management (subject to 'safeguards' similar to those which were to operate in the provinces) of all central subjects except foreign affairs and defence. While the provincial part of the Act was to come into force on 1 April 1937, the federal part of the Act was to become operative only if and when a sufficient number of states (*i*) to occupy 52 of the 104 seats allotted to the states in the upper house of the federal legislature and (*ii*) to make up half the total population of all the states, had acceded to the federation.

If the Act of 1935 had been enacted soon after the First World War it would have been hailed as a welcome step along the road to self-government. In the temper of the 1930s the Act received a frigid reception in India. It was condemned by almost all political groups and parties in India, though not always for the same reasons. As was to be expected, the Indian National Congress, with its pronounced nationalist and democratic-socialist outlook, was the most vehement in its denunciation of the Act.[1] The Congress denounced the 'safeguards' as rendering responsible government nugatory. It demanded complete responsibility in the provinces and at the centre. The Congress particularly denounced the excessive weightage given to the states in the proposed federation—40 per cent in the Council of States and $33\frac{1}{3}$ per cent in the

Federal Assembly, whereas the population of the states was only 25 per cent of the total population of India at that time. It denounced also the manner of the states' representation. The Congress wanted the representatives of the states in the federal legislature to be elected by their people and not, as provided for in Act, nominated by their rulers.

The Congress coupled its condemnation of the Act of 1935 with the far-reaching demand that the future constitution of India should be framed by Indians themselves by means of a 'constituent assembly' elected on the basis of universal adult franchise. But, while the Congress 'rejected' the Act of 1935 and resolved 'not to submit to this Constitution or to co-operate with it, but to combat it, both inside and outside the legislatures, so as to end it',[2] there was an influential section within the Congress which felt that the provincial portion of the Act should be permitted to function. Both the right and the left in the Congress were agreed on the desirability of contesting the elections for the provincial legislatures, but they were divided on the question of 'acceptance of office'. The Congress, at its Faizpur session in December 1936, accordingly, decided to contest the elections to the provincial legislatures due early in 1937, but postponed decision on the controversial issue of 'acceptance of office' till after the elections.

The Elections of 1937

With able leaders, an effective organization and a simple yet attractive programme, the Congress won a notable victory at the polls early in 1937.[3] Of the 1,585 seats in the provincial legislatures the Congress contested 1,161 and won 716.[4] The Congress victory is all the more impressive when it is borne in mind that of the 1,585 seats less than half, 657, were 'general' or open, that is not allotted to a separate, closed elect group such as Muslims, Sikhs, Christians, Europeans, Anglo-Indians and landholders. Of the eleven provinces in British India the Congress secured a clear majority in six and was the largest single party in three others.

By contrast, the Muslim League won only 109 of the 482 seats allotted to the Muslims, securing only 4.8 per cent of the total Muslim votes.[5] It did not win a majority of seats in *any* of the four Muslim-majority provinces. In fact, its performance in certain Muslim-majority provinces was far worse than that in the Muslim-minority provinces.

But the success of the Congress, though impressive, was by no means unqualified. While the Congress virtually routed the Hindu communalists and reactionary landlords in the Hindu-majority provinces, it failed to do so in the Muslim-majority provinces. Its performance in Bengal and the North-West Frontier Province was not bad, but it cut a rather sorry figure in Sindh and the Panjab. Its greatest failure, however, lay with the Muslim electorate. The Congress in 1937 had probably many more Muslims on its rolls than did the Muslim League and some of them were individually quite distinguished, but, except in the North-West Frontier Province, they were not very popular with the Muslim masses in general. The Congress ran only 58 candidates for the 482 separate Muslim seats and won 26. The elections of 1937 showed that Hindu communalism was stronger in the Muslim-majority provinces than in the Hindu-majority provinces and that Muslim communalism was more firmly entrenched in the Hindu-majority provinces than in the Muslim-majority provinces. But, on the whole, the electorate all over India had preferred non-communal parties and individuals to the purely communal parties and individuals. This was a result which could not fail to delight the Congress and encourage its hopes for the future. The Congress, tired of trying to promote an agreement between the various communities of India by means of private parleys and public conferences, had appealed directly to the masses over the heads of communal leaders on the basis of its own political and economic programme and scored a notable triumph. The results of the 1937 elections, besides proving the effectiveness of Congress organization and the popularity of its programme, had apparently vindicated the correctness of its new approach to the solution of the communal problem in India. The leaders of the Congress naturally concluded that if they persisted in their efforts they could without much difficulty wean the masses away from their communal organizations and rally them under the banner of the sole national organization in India. They therefore intensified their campaign of contacting the masses, especially the Muslims. The communal leaders saw in the Congress move a threat to their very existence. They felt that, unless they organized themselves like the Congress and regained their popularity with the masses, they might get up one fine morning to find that the Congress had walked away with their flock.

The spectacular success of the Congress in the elections of 1937—especially when contrasted with the miserable performance of the Muslim League—was not only galling to the pride of the leaders of the Muslim League, it also disturbed many of their comfortable assumptions. For example, one of the reasons why League leaders had agreed to work the Act of 1935, for what it was worth, was their calculation that they would be able to dominate the Muslim-majority provinces and that the divisions amongst the Hindus would enable 'the solid Muslim bloc', elected on the basis of separate electorates and the 'communal award', to play an effective and even balancing role in the legislatures of the Hindu-majority provinces. The results of the 1937 elections disproved this calculation. They showed that, while the vast majority of the Hindus, especially those in the Hindu-majority provinces, were behind the Congress, only a very small percentage of the Muslims supported the Muslim League, and that, despite their numerous divisions, the Hindus were capable of greater unity in political action than the socially more homogeneous Muslims. In none of the four Muslim-majority provinces was the League in a position to form a ministry. In the legislatures of three Hindu-majority provinces (Bihar, Orissa and the Central Provinces) there was not a single Muslim member elected on the League ticket. In the legislatures of the four other Hindu-majority provinces (Assam, the United Provinces, Bombay and Madras) Muslim League members were in such a minority that they could safely be neglected by the Congress party in the formation of ministries. While Congress leaders occupied the centre of the polictical stage in India in 1937 and decided the fate of ministries, M.A. Jinnah and his colleagues in the Muslim League were in the political wilderness, sadly learning the lessons of their debacle and struggling hard to check their small following from defecting to the Congress.

The results of the 1937 elections also underlined the fact that, while the Hindus enjoyed an overwhelming numerical superiority in almost all the provinces in which they were in a majority, the Muslims did not enjoy the same superiority in at least two of the provinces in which they were in a majority, namely Panjab and Bengal. These provinces accounted for forty million out of the eighty million Muslims in British India. This meant, according to the calculations of the Muslim communalists, that, while the

Hindus would dominate all the Hindu-majority provinces, the Muslims could not be sure of dominating two of the Muslim-majority provinces which they considered to be their mainstays. Unpromising as the situation was in the provinces from the point of view of the Muslim League, it was likely to be far worse in the future federation of India, for there the Muslims had only one-third of the total seats allotted to British India. If the last elections were any indication, the Congress was sure to capture the majority of the non-Muslim seats in British India and, if it succeeded in coercing the princes (the vast majority of whom were Hindus anyway), it would capture most of the seats allotted to the states in the federal legislature.

The lessons of the 1937 elections were clear and unmistakable and the Muslim League did not fail to learn them. The prospect that was starkly obvious to the leaders of the League was this; either they must cease to be the leaders of the League or they must accept a position of permanent inferiority and exclusion from office in the Hindu-majority provinces and the proposed all-India federation. Only in the Muslim-majority provinces was there some chance for the leaders of the League, provided they could make their organization as effective as the Congress, to be able to exercise the kind of power which the leaders of the Congress exercised in India. Not unnaturally, the leaders of the League clutched at this off-chance, but very soon they realized that their ambition could not be fulfilled without detaching the Muslim-majority provinces from the rest of India.

The notable victory of the Congress at the polls strengthened the hands of those Congress leaders who had been in favour of working the provincial part of the 1935 Act. On 18 March 1937 the All-India Congress Committee, meeting at Wardha, permitted, despite the determined opposition of its small but influential left wing, 'the acceptance of offices in provinces where the Congress commands a majority in the legislature provided... the leader of the Congress party in the legislature is satisfied and is able to state publicly that the Governor will not use his special powers of interference or set aside the advice of ministers in regard to their constitutional activities'.[6] Not until 21 June 1937 did the governor-general, Lord Linlithgow, make a public statement which was regarded by the Congress as satisfactory on this point. In July 1937 Congress ministries were formed in six provinces (Bihar, Orissa, the United Provinces, the Central Provinces, Bombay and Madras). Later in the same year the Congress was able to form a ministry in the North-West Frontier Province and in March 1938 in Assam as well. In forming their ministries the leaders of the Congress party in the various provincial legislatures took special care to include a fair proportion of Muslims. The latter were either Congressmen elected on the Congress ticket or Independents and pro-Congress Muslim Leaguers who had signed the Congress creed.

The Congress expressed its readiness to co-operate with any other party or group in the provincial legislatures on the basis of its published economic and political programme, but it set its face firmly and definitely against the recently revived proposal of 'communal coalition cabinets',[7] the proposal that the Congress ministries should contain 'an adequate number of Muslims possessing the confidence of their community', which in effect meant that the latter should be either elected by the Muslim legislators or nominated by the Muslim League. The Congress could never be expected to accept this proposal, which it rightly regarded as an extension of the vicious principle of communal representation and a negation of democracy.

The Congress and the Muslim League

Except for a short and rather unusual period of six years (1915-21) during and after the First World War, when the Muslim League came to be dominated by Muslim Congressmen and temporarily subordinated its creed of communal separatism to the demands of Indian nationalism, its relations with the Congress had never been cordial. The Congress stood for democracy, secularism and a common Indian nationality. The Muslim League existed primarily to safeguard and promote the interests of the Indian Muslims as a separate political entity. In the circumstances created by the basic conflict between the ideologies and objectives of the two organizations there were possibilities for manoeuvre, but little ground for compromise on essentials. Scores of attempts were made in the 'twenties and 'thirties to arrive at a settlement between the Congress and the Muslim League, but they foundered on the rock of mutual incompatibility. The Congress was not prepared to give up its national character; the Muslim League refused to give up its communal character. As the introduction of representative and responsible government proceeded in India, the Muslim League, as the champion of Muslim interests, demanded that the share of the Muslims in the services, elected bodies and cabinets should be fixed by statutory enactment. The Congress, while prepared to concede the substance of this demand in practice and as a matter of temporary political expediency, could never accept it in principle and in perpetuity, because it militated against the Congress objective of a secular, democratic and united Indian nation. There could be no lasting co-operation between the Congress and the League unless either one or the other changed its character. From the point of view of the Congress the price demanded by the League for its temporary co-operation was not only too high, it was also not worth paying, for it did not subserve the ultimate purpose of the Congress.

Too much has been made by certain writers, who seem to be more eager to apportion blame than to ascertain facts, of the alleged refusal of the Congress to form coalition ministries with the Muslim League in 1937. It has been said[8] that the Congress, because of the 'intoxication of victory' or its foolish adherence to 'orthodox parliamentarianism', 'socialism' and 'totalitarianism', lost a great opportunity in 1937 of winning over the Muslim League by unceremoniously turning down the latter's offer of coalition.

It is entirely untrue to suggest, as has been done by some latter-day writers, that there was any understanding between the Congress and the League about the elections or the coalition ministries to be formed after the elections of 1937. The slight apparent similarity between the election manifestos of the Congress and the League was not the result of any desire on the part of the two organizations to arrive at an electoral or post-electoral arrangement. On many economic and political issues there was little difference between the right wing of the Congress and the left wing of the Muslim League, and quite a few radical Muslim Leaguers were also members of the Congress. In fact, the election manifestos of almost all political parties in India in 1937 were impeccably progressive. The election manifesto of the Muslim League was meant to conciliate the radical Muslims who considered the League to be conservative and reactionary and who were, therefore, inclined to be pro-Congress. It was drafted also with an eye on the Muslim peasant and middle class voter, for in a good many constituencies the Muslim League candidates were pitted against the Khan Bahadurs and the Khan Sahibs. On important issues like the separate electorates, the 'communal award', the safeguards for minorities, the Act of 1935, the idea of a constituent assembly and the abolition of landlordism, the Congress and the League were in complete disagreement and their leaders made no secret of their disagreement. It was significant that Jinnah inaugurated the Muslim League election campaign in Bengal by emphasizing the differences between the Congress and the League. Speaking in Calcutta on 3 January 1937 he remarked: 'Pandit Jawaharlal Nehru is reported to have said in Calcutta that there are only two parties in the country, namely, the Government and the Congress and the others must line up. I refuse to line up with the Congress. There is a third party in this country and that is the Muslims.'[9] In a speech at Dacca on 8 January 1937 he said that 'at present there was a fundamental difference between the League and the Congress'.[10]

In the elections held in January-February 1937 Congress Muslim candidates were pitted against the Muslim League candidates in almost all the provinces.[11] As Muslim seats were on a separate register and the Congress contested only 58 of the total 482 Muslim seats, the elections of 1937 were only partly a Congress-League trial of strength. But the decision of the Congress to contest Muslim seats gave great offence to Jinnah, who publicly warned the Congress early in January 1937 'to leave the Muslims alone'.[12] This sparked off a bitter controversy between Jinnah and Nehru which dragged on for months and served only to widen the gulf that already separated the Congress and the Muslim League and their respective leaders. 'Our policy and programme differ in vital respects from those of the Congress',[13] asserted the leader of the Muslim League. 'Let us agree to differ',[14] replied the leader of the Congress. 'We shall not bow our head before Anand Bhavan',[15] said Jinnah. 'In the hour of trial when we faced the might of a proud Empire many prominent leaders of the Muslim League sought alliance with the die-hard leaders of the Conservative Party in England, than whom there are no greater enemies of Indian freedom. Are we to submit to them now, we who have refused to submit to the embattled power of that Empire, and who prepare afresh for fresh trials and tribulations in the struggle for independence which has become the life-

The Congress and the Partition of India

blood of our activities?'[16] asked Nehru.

In this environment of growing political antagonism and personal invective, it would have been a miracle if the All-India Muslim League had offered to join the Indian National Congress in forming coalition ministries. Actually, the League made no such offer and so there was no question of the Congress accepting or rejecting any offer of the League.

Of the six provinces in which the Congress secured clear majorities, the Muslim League had not a single elected member in three (Bihar, Orissa and the Central Provinces), where the problem of including Leaguers in the ministries did not simply arise. Only in the three other provinces (the United Provinces, Bombay and Madras) had the Muslim League any members who could be included in the ministries formed by the Congress. But in Bombay and Madras no move was made by either party even to initiate talks for a possible coalition.[17] Only in the United Provinces was some attempt made to negotiate a Congress-League settlement, but it failed. The full story of the negotiations in the United Provinces in 1937 is not yet known and probably will never be known, but the following brief account, based mainly on newspaper reports and other published sources, should suffice for our purposes.

Before the elections of 1937 Jinnah tried, though not with much success, to organize Muslim League Parliamentary Boards in the various provinces of British India, comprising leaders of all shades of Muslim opinion. The complexion of these Parliamentary Boards differed from province to province. In Bengal, for example, the provincial Muslim League Parliamentary Board was dominated by the reactionary landlords—a fact which made it difficult for the local Muslim League to have an electoral agreement with Fazlul Huq's Krishak Proja Party. In the United Provinces, on the other hand, the provincial Muslim League Parliamentary Board was dominated by the progressives—the representatives of the Ahrars, the Jamiat-ul-Ulema, the Momins, the Shia Political Conference, and the pro-Congress Muslims. It was headed by Chaudhry Khaliquzzaman, who was also a Congressman with pronounced socialist leanings and close personal relations with many Congress leaders. But hardly was the Muslim League Parliamentary Board formed in the United Provinces when differences arose and a few leaders of the Ahrars, the Momins, the Jamiat-ul-Ulema and the Shia Political Conference resigned from it, expressing their dissatisfaction with its proceedings. This process was accelerated during and after the elections and the result was that the position of the few progressive Muslims who still remained on the Board became precarious. There were three main elements within the Board and they were trying to pull it in different directions. One element favoured an alliance with the National Agriculturalist Party—the party of the landlords in the United Provinces—whose leader, the Nawab of Chhatari, had formed the interim ministry in the province. The second element, which came increasingly to dominate the proceedings of the Board, wanted to pursue a purely communal and anti-Congress policy under the direction of Jinnah and was anxious to unite all the Muslim M.L.A.s The third element, which was in a minority and consisted of men like Khaliquzzaman, Hafiz Muhammad Ibrahim, Suleman Ansari, Saiduddin Khan and Ali Zaheer, favoured co-operation with the Congress. What was true of the United Provinces Muslim League Parliamentary Board was also true of the United Provinces Muslim League and its Legislature Party. In all the three bodies the progressives were fighting a losing battle against the reactionaries composed of the landlords and the pure communalists.

It was in these circumstances that some Muslim League progressives, chief amongst whom was Chaudhry Khaliquzzaman, opened negotiations with the local Congress leaders in March-April 1937, offering their co-operation in the legislature on the basis of the Congress programme as laid down by the Congress Working Committee at its meeting at Wardha on 28 February 1937. Congres leaders reacted favourably to the offer, though some of the younger socialist Congressmen, especially Muslims, did not conceal their dislike of any parleys with Muslim Leaguers. The reaction of Khaliquzzaman's more communally-minded associates in the United Provinces Muslim League was positively hostile to any idea of co-operation with the Congress. They openly accused Khaliquzzaman of hatching 'a dreadful plot against both the Muslim League and Mr. Jinnah', of trying to wreck the latter's plan 'to organize the Muslims to stand against the Congress', and of 'hoisting the Congress colour on the Muslim League Parliamentary Board'.[18] They complained to Jinnah, who issued a public statement on 25 April 1937 condemning Khaliquzzaman's

The Congress and the Partition of India 191

move. 'I want to make it clear', said Jinnah, 'that it will be useless for any individual or individuals to effectively carry the Muslims behind them if any settlement is arrived at with a particular group or even for the matter of that with a particular province. I say that it is a pity that these roundabout efforts are being made. The only object of it can be to create some differences between Mussalmans. It is no use deciding with those men who are in and out of the Congress and in and out of the Muslim League, one time with one and another time with the other as it suits them. I am sure that the Muslims of the United Provinces will not betray the Mussalmans of India and therefore any effort to settle by individuals which may be advantageous to them for the time being will not carry us anywhere.... I only trust that he [Khaliquzzaman] will not enter into any commitments which may be repudiated by the Muslims of all India.'[19] A stormy meeting of the Working Committee of the United Provinces Muslim League Parliamentary Board took place at Lucknow on 25 April 1937 at which Khaliquzzaman and his friends were severely criticized for their flirtations with the Congress and a resolution was passed wh'ch said that 'it is not possible for the Muslim League Parliamentary Board or the members elected on its ticket to join the Congress in its policy of wrecking the constitution, but [they] can co-operate with the Congress or any other progressive party in the legislature whose policy and programme are approximately the same as of this Board'.[20] On 4 May 1937 the Committee of the Bombay Provincial Muslim League, meeting under the chairmanship of Jinnah, passed a resolution which 'appealed to the Muslim members of the United Provinces Legislative Assembly who had been elected on the League ticket not to act in such a way as to cause disunion among the Muslim of India by arranging sectional or provincial settlements with the Congress'.[21] Speaking at the meeting Jinnah remarked: 'We shall face the challenge of the Congress if they think that the Muslims will accept their policy and programme because our policy and programme are different in vital respects.'[22] A couple of days later Jinnah visited Lucknow and reasserted his authority over the local Muslim League, though his efforts to bring about unity among the different groups of Muslim M.L.A.s did not quite succeed. He was reported to have rebuked those 'who talked loosely of co-operating with the Congress' and to have said that 'for the time being they would join hands neither with the Congress nor with the Government, but wait till they had gained strength by organizing the Muslims'.[23] On 7 May 1937 the United Provinces Muslim League Parliamentary Board reaffirmed, with certain significant alterations and additions (which were indicative of the increasing dominance of the anti-Congress element in the counsels of the Board), the earlier resolution of its Working Committee, dated 25 April 1937, about the possibility of the League's co-operation with other parties in the legislature. The resolution adopted by the Board said 'that the Muslim League Party in the Legislature cannot and should not join the Congress in its policy and programme of wrecking the constitution, but that co-operation and coalition with the Congress or any other party on the basis of work in the legislature upon a programme that may be agreed upon in conformity with the programme of the Board should be explored, provided the communal award and separate representation in the local self-governing bodies be allowed to stand till an agreed settlement is arrived at between the communities concerned on an all-India basis'.[24]

These developments must have indicated to Khaliquzzaman and his friends how far they could hope to carry the local Muslim League party and the All-India Muslim League with them in their efforts to co-operate with the Congress in the United Provinces. Nor should it be forgotten that the Congress had not yet formed ministries in the provinces where it had secured majorities, that the elements within the Congress who were bitterly opposed to the formation of Congress ministries were the strongest in the United Provinces and that the official policy of the Congress about wrecking the constitution of 1935 had remained unchanged.

In the meantime the relations between the Congress and the League had further deteriorated. On 26 March 1937 Jinnah had issued a statement directing the Muslims not to participate in the demonstrations proposed to be organized by the Congress to mark 'the Anti-Constitution Day' on 1 April 1937.[25] The war of words between the leaders of the Congress and those of the Muslim League had continued unabated. League leaders had deprecated the assurances demanded of the governors by Congress leaders as a condition of their accepting office and instead suggested that the latter should give assurances to the minorities in the Congress-majority provinces.

Early in May 1937 the Congress organized conventions of the

newly elected legislators at the provincial capitals and at New Delhi which were boycotted by the Muslim League, though a few isolated pro-Congress Muslim Leaguers did take part in them. The leaders of the Muslim League also toyed with the idea of organizing conventions of Muslim or non-Congress M.L.A.s. In mid-May 1937 some Nationalist Muslims met in a conference at Allahabad. They criticized the 'separatist' and 'anti-Congress' policy of the Muslim League and advised their co-religionists 'to unconditionally join the Indian National Congress and participate in the struggle for the freedom of the country'.[26] Those who figured prominently at the Allahabad conference included not only the well-known Congress Muslims such as Maulana Abul Kalam Azad and Dr Syed Mahmud and the leaders of the pro-Congress Muslim organizations (Jamiat-ul-Ulema and others), but also Syed Wazir Hasan, who had presided over the last session of the All-India Muslim League held at Bombay in April 1936. Early in June 1937 a prominent pro-Congress Muslim who had been elected to the United Provinces legislature on the Muslim League ticket, Hafiz Muhammad Ibrahim, resigned from the Muslim League, complaining of the League's 'anti-national' and 'anti-Congress' policy, and joined the Congress party.[27] Ibrahim's example was followed a few weeks later by four other Muslim M.L.A.s in the United Provinces (2 elected on the League ticket—Muhammad Suleman Ansari and Saiduddin Khan—and two as Independents—Abdul Hakim and Aqbal Suhel).[28] When, therefore, the Congress ultimately formed ministries in the six provinces where it had secured clear majorities, its strength in the United Provinces legislature had increased to 139, including 7 Muslims (2 elected on the Congress ticket and 5 Muslim M.L.A.s who had recently defected to the Congress).

 Congress-League relations in the United Provinces touched a new low in June-July 1937 when the two parties set up rival candidates to contest the Jhansi-Jalaun-Hamirpur Muslim seat in a by-election. The contest became a veritable trial of strength between the Congress and the League which strained all their available resources to win it. Congress leaders were greatly annoyed at the manner in which League leaders conducted their election campaign, particularly the appeals openly made by the latter to the communal feelings of the electorate,[29] and the result was that personal relations even between the few local leaders on bothsides who had hitherto managed to remain friends were badly damaged. As against the superior organization and resources of the Congress, the League depended—as Shaukat Ali later confessed[30]—entirely on the cry of 'Allah-o-Akbar', and carried the day.

The defeat of the Congress candidate in a bitterly contested by-election, coming as it did almost on the eve of the formation of the Congress ministry in the United Provinces, could not have been conducive to the success of the negotiations for a 'Congress-League coalition' which had recently been resumed, mainly at the instigation of Khaliquzzaman. A rather slippery politician who had a foot in almost every camp, Khaliquzzaman was torn between his old loyalty to the Congress and his new loyalty to the League, between his attraction to a ministership and his fear of being repudiated by his colleagues in the Muslim League. He persisted in continuing his negotiations with the Congress leaders but these negotiations ultimately failed on 28 July 1937, not, as has been alleged by some latter-day writers, because the Congress laid down any impossible conditions,[31] but because of Khaliquzzaman's insistence that communal questions should be specifically excluded from the scope of the agreement[32] and that a colleague of his in the Muslim League legislature party—Nawab Muhammad Ismail Khan—who was not acceptable to Congress leaders both on personal and political grounds, should also be included along with him in the ministry.[33] The breakdown of the talks between Khaliquzzaman and the Congress leaders in July 1937, though regretted by some, caused little surprise and elicited few comments at the time. The most significant commentary on the whole episode was provided by Khaliquzzaman himself. 'I am afraid,' he said in a statement issued on 30 July 1937, 'I was trying to accomplish the impossible.'[34]

The Schism Widens

After the elections of 1937 Jinnah redoubled his efforts to make the Muslim League the sole representative organization of the Muslims so as to enable him—as the leader of the League—to bargain on a level of equality with the leaders of the Congress. There is reason to believe that Jinnah was in 1937 still thinking in terms of reaching an ultimate settlement with the Congress, but he was not sure what this settlement could be or of his ability to get it endorsed by his community. This may well explain why he never really cared to spell out his conditions for a possible settlement, though he was repeatedly asked by Congress leaders to do so. A vigorous campaign was launched to organize the Muslim League at various levels all over the country. The cry was raised—even before the Congress formed ministries in the six provinces where it had secured clear majorities—that Islam was in danger and that the Congress was trying to divide the Muslims in its bid to establish Hindu *raj* throughout the country. The Muslims were asked to rally under one banner for their survival and an attempt was made to coerce or cajole Muslims of other political persuasions to fall in line with the League. The decision of the Congress to accept office was represented as a crowning piece of Hindu hypocrisy and the result of a sinister understanding between the Congress and the British government. The formation of a Congress ministry in the predominantly Muslim North-West Frontier Province later in the year was treated as an insult to the Muslims and as a warning that very soon the Congress would capture governments even in the remaining Muslim-majority provinces. Governors were denounced for not using their special powers to nominate Muslims ministers who were truly representative of their community in the Congress-governed provinces. The League, which had earlier condemned the scheme of federation embodied in the Act of 1935 as being not democratic enough, now changed its ground and condemned the Act as being detrimental to the interests of the Muslims in particular, for it meant their subjugation to the vast Hindu majority, propped up by British bayonets. Pressure began to be secretly exercised on Muslim states, especially Hyderabad, to stay out of the proposed federation.[35] The League skilfully exploited every act of omission or commission by Congress governments to build up the image of the Congress in the eyes of the Muslims as that of a party of the tyrannical Hindu majority bent upon oppressing the Muslims, denying them their due rights and privileges and destroying their religion and culture.

Jinnah steadily succeeded in achieving his objective of making the League the most powerful organization of the Muslims, but in the very process of doing so he ruined all chances of reaching an amicable settlement with the Congress. The more he tried to rally the Muslims under the banner of the League by appealing to their communal hopes and fears, the more he had to succumb to and identify himself with those communal hopes and fears, thus abandoning his old role of 'the ambassador of Hindu-Muslim unity'. Congress leaders, too, were embittered by what they considered to be a systematic and malicious campaign of vilification against the Congress launched by the Muslim League. Efforts were none the less made by Congress leaders in 1937-8 to open negotiations with Jinnah, but they failed to make any headway. Having consolidated his position to a considerable extent, Jinnah now insisted that before negotiations could begin the Muslim League should be recognized as the one and only organization that represented the entire Muslim community in India and that the Congress should speak only on behalf of the Hindus. The Congress refused to accept Jinnah's condition, for it would have meant its committing suicide as a national organization. As Rajendra Prasad rightly pointed out, it 'would be denying its past, falsifying its history, and betraying its future'.[36] Lacking any common ground or common approach, staking exaggerated claims and working at cross-purposes in an increasingly unpropitious atmosphere, the Congress and the League steadily became two absolutes between whom no compromise was possible.

As long as Congress ministries remained in office, the League derived and extended its power by resistance to and negation of Congress rule, but when Congress ministries resigned in October 1939 over the war issue, negation alone left the League static. For this reason as well as any other, Jinnah and his associates had inevitably to evolve a positive procedure. The circumstances, too, were favourable: the Congress was out of office, the British government was engaged in war and was in search of friends, the federation was shelved, and there was a clear prospect of the transfer of power at the end of the war. In March 1940, at its Lahore session, the All-India Muslim League formally demanded the partition of India and the creation of a separate, independent Muslim state.

The Emergence of the Demand for Pakistan

The demand as such was neither new nor sudden. The idea of 'Pakistan' or a separate homeland for the Indian Muslims had been floating in the imagination of many educated Muslims for quite a long time. It was born of the feeling entertained and sedulously propagated by certain Muslim intellectuals that their community formed a distinct cultural and political entity, different from the other Indian communities, especially the Hindus. It was encouraged and fortified by the sentiment of pan-Islamism, the grant of separate electorates and the fear that in a united India the Muslims would inevitably be placed under the domination of the Hindus, who out-numbered them by three to one. It received its real strength and substance, however, from the fact that there were certain regions in India, particularly in the north-west and the north-east, where the Muslims formed a majority of the population and which they thought they must dominate. But for this accident of geography, the idea of Pakistan—even if it were born—would never have materialized. If the Muslim population in India had been more evenly distributed throughout the sub-continent, it would have been a minority everywhere which could have neither dreamt nor been in a position to dominate—as a community—any region.

The myth of the inevitability of Pakistan has already grown and historians have, as is their wont, been of late busy proving and perpetuating it. They have traced the idea of Pakistan back to Sir Syed Ahmed Khan in the nineteenth century, to Shah Wali-ullah and Shah Abdul Aziz in the eighteenth century, and even to Muhammad bin Qasim, the first Muslim invader of India early in the eighth century. They have attributed its emergence to the ancient and allegedly incurable religious and cultural schism between the Hindu and the Muslim, to the British policy of divide and rule (which later took the form of 'divide and quit') to the working of the inexorable logic of the separate electorates conceded to the Muslims in 1909, to the theory of 'two nations', to the determination of the Muslims in India not to submit to the Hindu majority and instead secure a homeland for themselves, and to the lapses on the part of the Hindu and Congress leaders.

These theories are often illuminating. But, while they may explain the historical phenomenon of Muslim separatism in India, they do not really explain the emergence of Pakistan as a geographical and political phenomenon. Muslim separatism in India had a long history, but it was not the only separatism that afflicted India. It had created many complications in the past and it could create many more in the future. It might have even led to a civil war. But Muslim separatism in itself could not have led to Pakistan, unless there were Muslim-majority regions in India which could be easily separated from the rest of India. The Muslim desire for a separate homeland of their own could not, even if it had arisen, have found fulfilment in the manner in which it ultimately did unless there were clearly demarcable regions in which the Muslims were in a majority and which they could turn into their own separate homeland. Further, even the existence of well-defined and easily separable Muslim-majority provinces and the Muslim desire to dominate them as a community would not necessarily have led to the partition of India. For, without great difficulty, some form of loose all-India federation could have taken cognizance of both these facts. After all, the Muslims were dominant in the Muslim-majority provinces—this dominance could have been made more effective by making some territorial and other adjustments—and the strong sense of Muslim solidarity militated against the idea of a division of India. But it was the alliance of Muslim separatism with the Muslim will to power which proved decisive. It was the determination of the All-India Muslim League, the carrier of the ideology of Muslim separatism in India, to dominate the Muslim-majority provinces which led directly and inevitably to the partition of India and the creation of Pakistan. The fact of Jinnah's leadership has relevance in this context only in so far as he became both the architect and the symbol of the alliance between Muslim separatism and the Muslim will to rule the Muslim-majority provinces. In their reckless pursuit of power the leaders of the League not only divided India, they also divided the so-called Muslim nation in whose name they had claimed a separate homeland. History offers few better examples of poetic justice than this.

As long as constitutional reforms in India were limited to the introduction of representative institutions, the Muslims as a minority community felt their position fully safeguarded by separate electorates. But no sooner did the prospect of responsible government in India appear on the horizon after the First World War than the Muslims began to fear for their own future in a state in which, under any system of popular election, they would be in a position of perpetual subordination to the Hindu majority. There was, however, one redeeming feature in the grim prospect that awaited them. The Muslims were not in a minority in all the provinces. In Bengal, Panjab, Sindh and the North-West Frontier Province they actually formed a majority of the population. If, therefore, the powers of the central government could be reduced to the minimum and the provinces given the utmost autonomy, there was a chance that the four Muslim-majority provinces could provide some sort of a balance to the seven Hindu-majority provinces in British India. As for the Muslim minority in the Hindu-majority provinces, its position could be safeguarded by statutory enactment or by the threat that whatever treatment was meted out to it would be given also to the Hindu minority in the Muslim-majority provinces. Early in the 1920s Muslim opinion began to veer round to this simple solution of the political and communal problem in the country as their only hope of security in a future self-governing India. Some Muslims began to think in terms of a loose federation, with a weak centre for minimum common purposes and written safeguards for the minorities, and of fully autonomous provinces, vested with the residuary powers, so as to enable the Muslims to play an effective role at the centre and to dominate at least four provinces in which they formed a majority of the population.

This Muslim solution of the Indian political and communal problem was put forward publicly—probably for the first time—by Maulana Hasrat Mohani in his presidential address to the Muslim League session held at Ahmedabad towards the end of December 1921.[37] With slight variations of emphasis or detail, it formed the substance of the various demands put forward in the 'twenties and 'thirties by most of the prominent Muslim organizations and leaders on behalf of their community. Attempts were being made concurrently to provide with an adequate rationale the Muslim demand to dominate the provinces where the Muslims were in a majority. The Indian Muslims, it was urged, were a 'nation' by themselves, totally different from the other 'nations' in India, and as such entitled to exercise their right of self-determination and to establish a homeland for themselves where they could work out their destiny according to their own ideas of Islamic culture and polity. While some, such as Muhammad Iqbal[38] in 1930, favoured 'the creation of a Muslim India [with-] in India', others, such as Rahmat Ali[39] in 1933, advocated the total separation of 'Muslim India' from the rest of India and the creation of a new Muslim state ('Pakistan'). The results of the 1937 elections came as a great shock and surprise to the communally-minded Muslims. They showed that the Muslims were weak, divided and disorganized. They had no strong and effective all-India organization like the Congress. They were a negligible quantity in the Hindu-majority provinces. Even in the Muslim-majority provinces their position was far from being invulnerable. In two of the Muslim-majority provinces—Bengal and Panjab —they had no effective majorities and were dependent on the support or sufferance of the non-Muslims. While the separate electorates, which they had so far regarded as their Magna Carta, precluded them from influencing the results of the elections in the non-Muslim constituencies, the Congress could, if it tried and as the 1937 elections proved, influence the results of the elections in the Muslim constituencies. The proposed all-India federation, instead of off-setting, as many Muslim leaders had hoped it would, the vast Hindu majority in India as a whole, was likely to reinforce it. The writing on the wall was clear. And it read: Muslims as a community could not be sure of dominating even the Muslim-majority provinces in India. 'The creation of a Muslim India [with-] in India' was impossible.

Soon after the elections—on 28 May 1937—Iqbal was writing to Jinnah: '... the enforcement and development of the Shariat of Islam is impossible in this country without a free Muslim State or States ... it is necessary to redistribute the country and to provide one or more Muslim States with absolute majorities. Don't you think that the time for such a demand has already arrived?'[40] On 21 June 1937—almost a month before Congress ministries were actually formed in six provinces—we again find Iqbal writing to Jinnah that 'the idea of a single Indian federation' was 'completely hopeless' and that Muslim leaders 'ought at present to ignore Muslim-minority provinces' and instead concentrate on the creation of 'a separate federation of Muslim [-majority] provinces' in the north-west and the north-east.[41] Iqbal once again urged upon Jinnah the need for making known publicly the new objective of the Muslims. But Jinnah was no visionary like Iqbal and apparently decided to wait until the Muslims were 'sufficiently organized and disciplined'.[42] As a practical politician he knew that before demanding the creation of 'a separate federation of Muslim [-majority] provinces' he should have a strong and united Muslim party, preferably in control of the governments in the Muslim-majority provinces and some definite prospect of British withdrawal from India.

But, while Jinnah held his hand, others did not hesitate to show theirs. It was not long before an increasing number of Muslim politicians and publicists got busy with their scissors, cutting and rearranging the map of India according to their individual fancy.[48] Some of them were separationists pure and simple, others were separationists-cum-confederationists. The idea of a 'Muslim India'—within or without India—proved to be a catch-all. It made a tremendous appeal to the hopes and fears of the Muslims. The desire to have undisputed sway over the Muslim-majority provinces, the prospect of undisturbed place and power, the attraction of a separate homeland and an Islamic state, probably forming part of a future pan-Islamic federation, fear of Hindu competition and domination, anxiety about the preservation of their communal way of life, and annoyance with the Congress made a steadily growing number of thinking Muslims favour the idea of a separation of 'Muslim India' from 'Hindu India'. While most of them took up the idea enthusiastically, at least a few accepted it rather regretfully as offering an easy and perhaps the only practicable solution to the chronic and extremely intractable Hindu-Muslim problem.

Still very weak and inchoate, the Muslim League in 1937-8 was probably not in a position to commit itself definitely on the issue, but it could not afford to postpone its commitment for long. The British government had its plan of establishing an all-Jndia federation embodied in the Act of 1935. The Congress had countered it with its own plan of a 'constituent assembly'. The Muslim League, while opposing both the British and the Congress plans, had in 1937 virtually no alternative plan of its own. Hitherto, it had at least nominally subscribed to the idea of a loose federation for India, but the results of the 1937 elections, by indicating what the position of the Muslims and of the Muslim League—even with separate electorates and the reservation of seats—was likely to be in the proposed federation, had forced it to reconsider its stand. There was a growing realization in Muslim League circles that the League's earlier adherence to the idea of an all-India federation as such, however qualified, had been a mistake. This was accompanied by an increasing apprehension—not entirely unfounded—that the Congress might ultimately agree to work the federal part of the 1935 Act. The League, therefore, became more firmly and unitedly opposed to the federation envisaged by the Act of 1935 than the Congress.

But mere opposition to the British plan of an all-India federation—and to the Congress plan of a 'constituent assembly'—was not sufficient. The Muslim League had to put forward an alternative plan of its own. Already the League rank and file were pressing for it and a good many Muslim Abbes Sieyes were busy trying to fill in the gap.

At its annual session held at Lucknow in October 1937 the Muslim League officially proclaimed its 'emphatic' disapproval of the federal scheme of the 1935 Act as being 'detrimental to the interests ... of the Muslims in particular'.[44] While, in redefining its creed at this session as 'the establishment in India of full independence in the form of a federation of free democratic states, in which the rights and interests of the Muslims and other minorities are adequately and effectively safeguarded in the constitution',[45] the League apparently reiterated its continued adherence to the idea of a federation as such, the proceedings of the Lucknow session left no doubt as to the direction in which the current of League politics was set. Jinnah and other prominent speakers at the session breathed fire and sword against the Congress and the Hindus. They accused the British of aiding the Congress in its design of establishing Hindu *raj* and perpetrating 'atrocities' on the Muslims. They denied that India was a nation and talked of establishing 'Muslim *raj*' in opposition to 'Hindu *raj*'. Reviewing the Lucknow session of the League, a competent Muslim observer—Dr Mahmudulla Jung—wrote: 'The doctrine of aloofness was preached *ad nauseam* in a most unrestricted and irresponsible language. Out of the clouds of circumlocution and confusion arose the cry of Islam in danger. The Muslims were told that they were disunited and were about to be crucified by the Hindus. Religious fervour was raised to a degree where it exhibited itself in blind fanaticism. ... In the name of Muslim solidarity Mr. Jinnah wants to divide India into Muslim India and Hindu India.'[46] Nehru's comment on the Muslim League annual session of 1937 was equally significant: 'The League and its supporters stand clearly and definitely today for the division of India, even on the political and economic planes, into religious groups. Whatever it may be, it is the antithesis of the nationalist idea of the unity of India. It is a reduction to absurdity of modern life and its problems. It is mediaevalism in excelsis.'[47]

A clearer picture of the aims and intentions of the Muslim League emerged at the Sindh Provincial Muslim League Conference held at Karachi in the second week of October 1938. The conference was presided over by Jinnah and attended by many prominent Muslim leaders from all over India. Speaking at the conference, Shaukat Ali remarked: 'If the Congress will not allow the Muslim League to have ministries in the four provinces where the Muslims are in a majority, vagabonds like me will run amuck.'[48] Jinnah accused the Congress of trying 'to destroy the Muslim League, divide the Muslims and dominate them', and he added in warning: 'This will result in India being divided.'[49] The chairman of the reception committee of the conference, Sir Abdulla Haroon, hinted at the possibility of 'an independent federation of Muslim States'.[50] Fazlul Huq, the premier of Bengal, was greeted with 'a wild burst of cheering' by the audience when he remarked: 'If Muhammad bin Qasim, an eight year old lad, with 18 soldiers could conquer Sindh then surely nine crores of Muslims can conquer the whole of India.'[51] Sheikh Abdul Majid threatened 'that if the Congress did not concede Muslim rights, Muslims would have no alternative but to fall back upon the Pakistan scheme' and that 'nothing would prevent Muslims, from Karachi to Calcutta, to march to their own self-determination'.[52]

The most significant episode of the conference was the tabling of a long resolution which, after cataloguing all the possible sins of the Congress and the Hindus, said: 'The Sindh Provincial Muslim League Conference considers it absolutely essential in the interests of an abiding peace of the vast Indian continent and in the interests of unhampered cultural development, the economic and social betterment and political self-determination of the two nations, known as Hindus and Muslims, that India may be divided into two federations, namely, the federation of Muslim States and the federation of non-Muslim States.

'The Conference therefore recommends to the All-India Muslim League to devise a scheme of constitution under which Muslim-majority provinces, Muslim Indian States and areas inhabited by a majority of Muslims may attain full independence in the form of a federation of their own with permission to admit any other Muslim State beyond the Indian frontiers to join the Federation and with such safeguards for non-Muslim minorities as may be conceded to the Muslim minorities in the non-Muslim Federation of India.'[53]

At the subjects committee stage of the proceedings of the conference, however, this particular portion of the resolution was altered to read as follows:

'This Conference considers it absolutely essential, in the interests of an abiding peace of the vast Indian continent and in the interests of unhampered cultural development, the economic and social betterment and political self-determination of the two nations, known as Hindus and Muslims, to recommend to the All-India Muslims League to review and revise the entire conception of what should be the suitable constitution for India which will secure honourable and legitimate status to them.'[54]

We do not precisely know the reasons which prompted this alteration. Probably some League leaders felt that the resolution as originally tabled was too explicit and premature. A remark made by Jinnah at the conference is highly significant in this connexion. 'The Government', he said, 'is still in the hands of the British. Let us not forget it. You must see ahead and work for the ideal which you think will arise 25 years hence.'[55]

In December 1938 the annual session of the All-India Muslim League, held at Patna, reiterated its opposition to the scheme of an all-India federation embodied in the 1935 Act and authorized its president, Jinnah, to adopt such courses as might be necessary with a view to exploring a suitable alternative to the aforesaid scheme which would safeguard the interests of the Muslims.[56] The idea of the physical division of India was discussed at almost every gathering of Muslim Leaguers during 1939. On 26 March 1939 the Working Committee of the Muslim League appointed a committee, headed by Jinnah, to examine and report on the various draft schemes 'already expounded by those who are fully versed in the constitutional developments of India and other countries and those that may be submitted hereafter to the President and report to the Working Committee their conclusions at an early date'.[57] The committee appointed by the Working Committee of the Muslim League presumably examined the 'several schemes in the field including that of dividing the country into Muslim and Hindu India',[58] but there is no evidence to suggest that its year-long deliberations enabled it to reach a final decision and to recommend a particular scheme of its own to the

Muslim League Working Committee. Opinion in the committee—as in Muslim League circles generally—was apparently divided on three main questions: What areas should form part of 'Muslim India'? Should 'Muslim India' be completely separate and independent? Should there be a transfer of population between 'Muslim India' and 'Hindu India'? This division of opinion probably accounts for the vagueness and imprecision of the famous resolution passed by the All-India Muslim League at its annual session in Lahore on 23 March 1940, which affirmed 'that no constitutional plan would be workable in this country or acceptable to the Muslims unless it is designed on the following basic principles, viz., that geographically continuous units are demarcated into regions which should be so constituted, with such territorial readjustments as may be necessary, that the areas in which the Muslims are numerically in a majority as in the North-Western and Eastern zones of India should be grouped to constitute "Independent States" in which the constituent units shall be autonomous and sovereign'.[59]

The usual arguments, with which we have become familiar, were urged in favour of the resolution adopted by the League at Lahore in March 1940: that the Muslims must dominate the areas in which they were in a majority and that this dominance could not be assured in a united India with its 'hostile' and 'tyrannical' Hindu majority, that India was not one nation, that the Muslims of India constituted a separate nation and were as such entitled to a separate homeland of their own where they could work out their destiny according to their cherished ideals, and that western democracy was not suited to Indian conditions. Whatever the views of other League leaders, there can be no doubt that Jinnah had now crossed the Rubicon and that what he demanded was the partition of India pure and simple and the creation of a separate, sovereign Muslim state, popularly known as Pakistan. With him at least the demand for Pakistan was neither a bluff nor a bargaining counter, but a solemn and irrevocable decision.

The Congress and the Muslim League's Demand for Pakistan

The Muslim League's demand for Pakistan was open—and in fact subjected—to many obvious criticisms. It was a grave blow to the ideal of a united India which generations of Indians had cherished and laboured for. The vivisection of India was an outrageous idea to all those who had become accustomed to the geographical, political, economic and cultural unity of the country. It was considered to be retrograde, impracticable and dangerous. If religion were to be acknowledged as the criterion of nationality and each nationality allowed to have a separate homeland for itself, it would mean the Balkanization of India. If the non-Muslims were to continue staying—as most League leaders assured they would—in the areas claimed for Pakistan, how would those areas be different in political composition and power from what they were at present and in what sense would they become Islamic? If Hindus and Muslims were two separate and antagonistic nations in India, how would they become one peaceful nation in Pakistan? Similarly, if democracy was not suited to India, how would it become suited to Pakistan? The division of India would not improve the position of the minorities. It would in fact worsen their position by converting them into hostages. Smaller minorities would be subjected to the domination of bigger majorities. Instead of solving, the creation of Pakistan would perpetuate and even aggravate communal differences. It would not bring peace but the sword. The Muslims in India would raise the cry of oppression at the hands of the Hindus and the Hindus in Pakistan would raise a similar cry, and there would be retaliatory wars. Instead of peace and harmony there would be aggression of one state against the other and the subcontinent would for ever remain exposed to third-party intervention. The creation of Pakistan would be detrimental even to the best interests of the Muslims, for it would permanently divide and weaken them.

These and similar other weighty objections were raised against the Muslim League demand for Pakistan by the leaders of almost all the other political parties and groups in the country, but they failed to make any impact on Jinnah and his followers. To Congressmen the idea of Pakistan was particularly distasteful, for it threatened to undo the effort the Congress had been making for over half a century. In the same week of March 1940 in which Jinnah put forward the demand for Pakistan on the basis of the two-nation theory at the Lahore session of the Muslim League, another—and a more learned and devout—Muslim, Maulana Abul Kalam Azad, reiterated the creed of Indian nationalism at the Ramgarh session of the Congress: 'It was India's historic destiny that many human races and cultures and religions should flow to her, finding a home in her hospitable soil, and many a caravan should find rest here.... One of the last of these caravans, following the footsteps of its predecessors, was that of the followers of Islam. This came here and settled here for good. This led to a meeting of the culture-currents of two different races. Like the Ganga and Jamuna, they flowed for a while through separate courses, but nature's immutable law brought them together and joined them in a *sangam*. This fusion was a notable event in history. ... Eleven hundred years of common history have enriched India with our common achievements. Our languages, our poetry, our literature, our culture, our art, our dress, our manners and customs, the innumerable happenings of our daily life, everything bears the stamp of our joint endeavour. This joint wealth is the heritage of our common nationality and we do not want to leave it and go back to the time when this joint life had not begun.... The cast has now been moulded and destiny has set its seal upon it. Whether we like it or not, we have now become an Indian nation, united and indivisible. No fantasy or artificial scheming to separate and divide can break this unity. We must accept the logic of fact and history and engage ourselves in the fashioning of our destiny.'[60]

Gandhi called the two-nation theory 'an untruth' and wrote: 'The vast majority of Muslims of India are converts to Islam or are the descendants of converts. They did not become a separate nation as soon as they became converts. A Bengali Muslim speaks the same tongue that a Bengali Hindu does, eats the same food and has the same amusements as his Hindu neighbour. They dress alike. I have often found it difficult to distinguish by outward sign between a Bengali Hindu and a Bengali Muslim. The same phenomenon is observable more or less in the south among the poor, who constitute the masses of India.... Hindus and Muslims of India are not two nations. Those whom God has made one, man will never be able to divide.'[61]

But, while Congressmen flatly refused to countenance the two-nation theory and the proposed partition of India and continued nourishing the hope that League leaders would finally turn back from the brink, they also made it clear that they would not use coercion to resist the demand for Pakistan. 'Unless the rest of India', wrote Gandhi in April 1940, 'wishes to engage in internal fratricide, the others will have to submit to the Muslim dictation, if the Muslims will resort to it. I know no non-violent method of compelling the obedience of eight crores of Muslims to the will of the rest of India, however powerful a majority the rest may represent. The Muslims must have the same right of self-determination that the rest of India has. We are at present a joint family. Any member may claim a division.'[62] Again in the same month he wrote: 'As a man of non-violence, I cannot forcibly resist the proposed partition if the Muslims of India really insist upon it. But I never can be a willing party to the vivisection.... For it means the undoing of centuries of work done by numberless Hindus and Muslims to live together as one nation. Partition means a patent untruth. My whole soul rebels against the idea that Hinduism and Islam represent two antagonistic cultures and doctrines.... But that is my belief. I cannot thrust it down the throats of the Muslims who think that they are a different nation. I refuse, however, to believe that the eight crores of Muslims will say that they have nothing in common with their Hindu and other brethren. Their mind can only be known by a referendum made to them duly on that clear issue. The contemplated constituent assembly can easily decide the question.'[63]

The Congress did not formally express its attitude to the demand for Pakistan until April 1942—and then, too, indirectly—but there is reason to believe that Gandhi's views, quoted above, were shared by a great majority in the Congress. As a nationalist organization, which had unfortunately failed to secure the confidence of the Muslim community, wedded to democracy and non-violence, the Congress could not afford to resist the demand for Pakistan by force, especially while it was still engaged in fighting the British for the political freedom of India. The Congress, however, could not accept the two-nation theory. It could not be a willing party to the division of India. But, if the Muslims were really insistent upon Pakistan, they could have it. Let them send their representatives to the proposed constituent assembly with a clear mandate and let these representatives settle the issue.

Jinnah, however, insisted that the Congress should first concede the principle underlying the demand for Pakistan. Probably he was just biding his time, for he was as yet not sure of securing a decisive verdict in favour of Pakistan from his own community.

The annoyance and distress caused in Congress circles by the Lahore resolution of the League was not unmixed with a certain amount of relief, especially at the thought that League leaders had at last given up their frivolous demands and shown their real hand and that this had cleared the air. Nehru, for example, was reported to have remarked that, instead of feeling sorry at the Muslim League's new demand, 'he was pleased, not because he liked it—on the contrary he considered it to be the most insane suggestion—but because it very much simplified the problem. They were now able to get rid of the demands about proportionate representation in legislatures, services, cabinets, etc.... [He] asserted that if people wanted such things, as suggested by the Muslim League at Lahore, then one thing was clear, they and people like him could not live together in India. He would be prepared to face all consequences of it but he would not be prepared to live with such people.'[64]

Having more or less resigned themselves to the distasteful possibility of the partition of India, if the vast majority of the Muslims insisted upon it, Congress leaders decided to concentrate almost all their attention on securing the political freedom of India as early as possible and on preserving the political unity of as large a part of the country as possible. They could not coerce the Muslim League into giving up its demand, but they could not also allow the Muslim League to coerce them into giving up their own cherished ideals. Their fight for the independence and unity of India was to continue with unabated vigour and they were not to enter into any temporary or patchwork settlement with either the Muslim League or the British government which was likely to damage their ultimate objective. As often in the past, Gandhi gave clear expression to this new mood of Congressmen in a series of articles in the *Harijan*.

'The British,' he wrote in the *Harijan* of 4 May 1940, 'can retain their hold on India only by a policy of "divide and rule". A living unity between the Muslims and Hindus is fraught with danger to their rule. It would mean an end to it. Therefore, it seems to me that a true solution will come with the end of the rule, potentially, if not in fact. What can be done under the threat of Pakistan? If it is not a threat but a desirable goal, why should it be prevented? If it is undesirable and is meant only for the Muslims to get more under its shadow, any solution would be an unjust solution. It would be worse than no solution. I, therefore, am entirely for waiting till the menace is gone. The whole world is in the throes of a new birth. Anything done for a temporary gain would be tantamount to an abortion.

'I cannot think in terms of narrow Hinduism or narrow Islam. I am wholly uninterested in a patchwork solution. India is a big country, a big nation composed of different cultures, which are tending to blend with one another, each complementing the rest. If I must wait for the completion of the process, I must wait. It may not be completed in my day. I should love to die in the faith that it must come in the fullness of time. I should be happy to think that I had done nothing to hamper the process. Subject to this condition, I would do anything to bring about harmony. My life is made up of compromises, but they have been compromises that have brought me nearer the goal. Pakistan cannot be worse than the foreign domination. I have lived under the latter, though not willingly. If God so desires it, I may have to become a helpless witness to the undoing of my dream. But I do not believe that the Muslims want to dismember India.

'The partition proposal has altered the face of the Hindu-Muslim problem. I have called it an untruth. There can be no compromise with it. At the same time I have said that, if the eight crores of Muslims desire it, no power on earth can prevent it, notwithstanding opposition, violent or non-violent. It cannot come by honourable compromise.'[65]

Again, in another issue of the *Harijan*, dated 15 June 1940, Gandhi underlined the difficulty of achieving a common measure of agreement between parties which did not have a common ground or a common approach and asserted that the Congress could not afford to betray its trust just for the sake of achieving such an agreement. He wrote: '... if the Congress loses hope and faith and comes to the conclusion that it must surrender its original position for the purpose of getting a common measure of agreement, it will cease to be the power it is. Today it is the sheet-anchor of India's hope and faith. It will be well for it, if it refuses to move away from its moorings, whether it is in a minority or a majority.'[66]

The reaction of Congress leaders to Jinnah's demand for Pakistan must have convinced him that though Congress leaders might not willingly concede it—at least not on principle—they would not forcibly resist it, and that all that he really needed to do in order to achieve his objective was to produce evidence of over-

The Congress and the Partition of India

whelming support for the demand among the Muslims and to persuade the British government to agree to it. This he could easily do. The cry of Pakistan swept the Muslims off their feet. That it should have been popular with the Muslims of the Muslim-majority provinces is easily understandable, but the extent to which Muslim Leaguers were able to delude themselves and their co-religionists in the Hindu-majority provinces into believing that Pakistan was good for them, is one of the most astonishing phenomena of modern times—a phenomenon which students of mass psychology might study with benefit. It was, however, not until the elections of 1945-6 that Jinnah could effectively establish his claim that the vast majority of the Muslims supported the demand for Pakistan.

British attitude to the demand for Pakistan had, of necessity, to be equivocal. Though few Britons ever believed that India could be governed as 'one and indivisible' by their brown successors, the prospect of the partition of India could not be pleasing to those who took pride in the creation of the administrative and political unity of the subcontinent as being one of the greatest of British imperial achievements. On the other hand, as the viceroy, Lord Linlithgow, publicly affirmed on 8 August 1940, the British government 'could not contemplate the transfer of their present responsibilities for the peace and welfare of India to any system of government whose authority is directly denied by large and powerful elements in India's national life'.[67] It had not been British policy in the past 'to expedite in India constitutional changes for their own sake, or gratuitously to hurry the handing over of controls to Indian hands'[68] and the British government saw no reason to alter that policy at a moment when it was 'engaged in a battle for existence'. Faced with conflicting claims and lacking a plan of its own, the British government adopted the not uncongenial attitude of giving its ear to all and its mind to none. To many Britons in India, who found the Congress either incomprehensible or irritating, the demand for Pakistan appeared to be a condign punishment to the Congress for its impudence in asking the British to quit India. They regarded the partition of India as inevitable and not entirely unwelcome. Commenting upon the Lahore resolution of the Muslim League, the *Statesman* of Calcutta wrote on 26 March 1940: 'Partition, we have to recognize, is becoming a live issue. If India receives Dominion Status partition seems the inevitable result in view of the attitude which the Muslim community appears disposed to adopt. If that really represents their position neither the Congress nor the Hindu Mahasabha would be able to hold them. There would probably be fighting, but in any case there would be partition. The situation would be further complicated by other facts. The Congress resolution repudiates association with Great Britain and aims at severing economic links, and the most vocal section of the Congress, the Leftists, demand a new economic orientation and affiliation with Soviet economy, while the Rightists are in economics purely reactionary and talk of reversion to the spinning wheel, and village economy to replace national industry. The Muslims on the other hand propose that their independent Northern and Eastern federation shall be permanently allied with Great Britain and free from fads either about the spinning wheel or the dictatorship of the proletariat. Actually at the back of their minds is probably the intention of making an easy meal of the other half of India, while it is busy with the quarrel between the spinners and the Marxists, and establishing an Islamic empire to be a glory of the modern world.'[69]

Towards Partition

The story of the various efforts made to solve the Indian problem during and after the war is long and complicated, but for the purposes of this paper it can be easily told. While the Muslim League examined every proposal from its own point of view, namely, whether or not it led directly and speedily to the creation of Pakistan, the Congress examined the same proposal from its own point of view, namely, whether or not it ensured the freedom and the maximum possible unity of India. The Congress did not regret the shelving of the federal part of the 1935 Act for it had never regarded it as capable of leading to the emergence of a united and free India. The Congress turned down the long-term proposals of the Cripps Mission of 1942 for similar reasons. In its resolution dated 2 April 1942 the Working Committee of the Congress said: 'The complete ignoring of ninety millions of people in the Indian States, and their treatment as commodities at the disposal of their rulers, is a negation both of democracy and self-determination. While the representation of an Indian State in the constitution-making body is fixed on a population basis, the people of the State have no voice in choosing those representatives, nor are they to be consulted at any stage while decisions vitally affecting them are being taken. Such States may in many ways become barriers to the growth of Indian freedom, enclaves where foreign authority still prevails, and where the possibility of maintaining foreign armed forces has been stated to be a likely contingency and a perpetual menace to the freedom of the people of the States as well as the rest of India.

'The acceptance beforehand of the novel principle of non-accession for a Province is also a severe blow to the conception of Indian unity and an apple of discord likely to generate growing trouble in the Provinces, and which may well lead to further difficulties in the way of the Indian States merging themselves into an Indian Union. Congress has been wedded to Indian freedom and unity and any break of that unity especially in the modern world when people's minds inevitably think in terms of ever larger federations would be injurious to all concerned and exceedingly painful to contemplate. *Nevertheless, the Committee cannot think in terms of compelling the people of any territorial unit to remain in an Indian Union against their declared and established will. While recognising this principle, the Committee feel that every effort should be made to create a common and co-operative national life. Acceptance of this principle inevitably involves that no changes should be made which would result in fresh problems being created and compulsion being exercised on other substantial groups within that area.* Each territorial unit should have the fullest possible autonomy within the Union consistently with a strong national state.

'The proposal now made on the part of the British War Cabinet encourages and will lead to attempts at separation at the very inception of the Union and thus create great friction just when the utmost co-operation and goodwill are most needed. This proposal has been presumably made to meet the communal demand, but it will have other consequences also and lead politically reactionary and obscurantist groups among the different communities to create trouble and divert public attention from the vital issues before the country.'[70]

A careful perusal of this resolution would reveal that, while the Congress Working Committee rejected the long-term proposals of the Cripps Mission because it feared that they might lead to the disintegration of India, it had implicitly conceded (in the italicized portion of the statement) the Muslim League's demand for Pakistan, provided, first, that a common centre was maintained, and, second, that the non-Muslim-majority areas in Assam, Bengal and Panjab were not to be compelled to join Pakistan. Had the Muslim League been willing to accept Pakistan in association with the rest of India it could have easily struck a bargain with the Congress in 1942. But obviously it was not willing to do so.

During his talks with Jinnah in 1944 Gandhi further spelled out the terms of the Congress offer. Gandhi wrote to Jinnah on 24 September 1944: 'I proceed on the assumption that India is not to be regarded as two or more nations, but as one family consisting of many members of whom the Muslims living in the north-west zones, i.e., Baluchistan, Sindh, the North-West Frontier Province, and that part of the Punjab where they are in absolute majority over all the other elements, and in parts of Bengal and Assam where they are in absolute majority, desire to live in separation from the rest of India.

'Differing from you on the general basis, I can yet recommend to the Congress and the country the acceptance of the claim for separation contained in the Muslim League Resolution of Lahore, 1940, on my basis and on the following terms:

'(a) The areas should be demarcated by a commission approved by the Congress and the League. The wishes of the inhabitants of the areas demarcated should be ascertained through the votes of the adult population of the areas or through some equivalent method.

'(b) If the vote is in favour of separation, it shall be agreed that these areas shall form a separate State as soon as possible after India is free from foreign domination and can, therefore, be constituted into two sovereign independent States.

'(c) There shall be a Treaty of Separation which should also provide for the efficient and satisfactory administration of Foreign Affairs, Defence, Internal Communications, Customs, Commerce and the like, which must necessarily continue to be matters of common interest between the contracting parties.

'(d) The Treaty shall also contain terms for safeguarding the rights of minorities in the two States.'[71]

Jinnah rejected Gandhi's proposals as being 'fundamentally

opposed to the Lahore Resolution' and insisted that the Muslims of India should be recognized as a nation, with an inherent right of self-determination which they alone were entitled to exercise; that Pakistan should comprise six provinces, namely, Sindh, Baluchistan, the North-West Frontier Province, Panjab, Bengal and Assam, subject only to minor territorial adjustments; and that vital matters like foreign affairs, defence, internal communications, customs and commerce, 'which are the life-blood of any State, cannot be delegated to any Central authority or Government'.[72]

The Gandhi-Jinnah talks (July-October 1944)—and the correspondence which punctuated the talks and was later made public—brought into full relief the differences between the Congress and the Muslim League and to that limited extent they served an extremely useful purpose. It was now clear to Congress leaders—and to the public at large—that Jinnah's three main demands were, in fact, the recognition of the two-nation theory as a condition precedent to the discussion of the details of any possible settlement; the inclusion, almost in their entirety, of six existing provinces within the proposed state of Pakistan; and the creation of two completely independent sovereign states with no connexion between them, except probably by treaty.

Having known Jinnah's mind, Congress leaders began to think out their own line of action for the future. It was generally felt that they could not yield to Jinnah on his first two demands and that any further concession they could make would have to be on his third demand

As regards Jinnah's first demand—the recognition of the two-nation theory—there was absolute unanimity in Congress circles that it should not and could not be conceded. It ran counter to the creed of the Congress and to the facts of Indian life. It was mischievous and potentially dangerous. It would give Pakistan a handle to interfere in the affairs of India, undermine the basis of India's existence and encourage other groups and communities in the country to emulate the Muslim League. The future state of independent India could not stand on the theory of disintegration and, whatever its enemies might say, the Congress had no ambition to establish a Hindu state.

As regards Jinnah's second demand—the inclusion in Pakistan of almost the entire area covered by six existing provinces—Congress leaders became determined that if Jinnah had Pakistan it should not be Pakistan with those districts of Assam and Bengal and of Panjab in which the population was predominantly non-Muslim. They decided to hoist Jinnah with his own petard. Every argument that could be used in favour of Pakistan could equally be used in favour of the exclusion of the non-Muslim areas from Pakistan. Moreover, Jinnah had already compromised his position on this point. The Lahore resolution of the Muslim League had spoken only of the demarcation of 'geographically contiguous units' and admitted the necessity of 'territorial readjustments'.[73] The non-Muslim majority districts of Assam and Bengal and of Panjab were equally contiguous to the rest of India and with popular feeling there being strong against their inclusion within Pakistan, the Congress was in a formidable bargaining position *vis-a-vis* the Muslim League.

As regards Jinnah's third demand, namely, the total separation of Pakistan from the rest of India and the elimination of a common centre in any form, the Congress had already gone a long way in meeting it. In fact, Gandhi in his talks and correspondence with Jinnah in 1944 had studiously avoided mentioning the term 'central government' and had instead suggested 'a Board of Representatives of both the States' or any other 'authority acceptable to both the parties' whose effectiveness would largely or solely depend upon mutual goodwill.[74] But Jinnah had insisted 'first on complete partition as between two nations, and then an agreement between them as on Foreign Affairs, etc. He would not agree to anything simultaneous.'[75] Congress leaders, therefore, did not need to make any further material concession in order to meet Jinnah's third demand in full. All that they were now required to do was to reconcile themselves—and their followers—to the painful prospect of the complete separation of Pakistan from the rest of India. It was, however, by no means an easy task. For over half a century the Congress had cherished the dream of a united India and struggled, according to its lights, to realize that dream. For the Congress, to accept the partition of India was to accept the destruction of its dream and the failure of its struggle. Nor was the feeling for Indian unity confined to Congressmen. As the Cabinet Mission noted in 1946, there was 'an almost universal desire, outside the supporters of the Muslim League, for the unity of India'.[76] If the idea of Pakistan was repugnant to the Hindus because, as Muhammad Ali once said, they worshipped the map of India, it was equally repugnant to those Muslims who realized that it meant the vivisection of their community. The partition of India was not only painful to contemplate, it was also fraught with grave risks. The Muslim League's demand for Pakistan had given a dangerous encouragement to the forces of communal, cultural, linguistic and political separatism in India. Already demands were being made for a separate homeland for the Sikhs ('Khalistan') and Dravidians ('Dravidistan') and for the creation of linguistic provinces such as Andhra and Maharashtra. Some of the princes were known to be dreaming of independence. Congress leaders therefore had to walk warily. They had to ensure that the establishment of Pakistan would not lead to the disintegration of the rest of India. They had to consolidate the forces working for Indian unity and to contain the menacing forces of separatism—both old and incipient—in India. They were fortunate in being aided in their difficult task by the accidents of time and circumstance. The Pakistan issue came to overshadow every other issue in the country. The very extremism of the Muslim League annoyed and alienated many moderate groups and parties in India and drove them closer to the Congress. The new viceroy, Lord Wavell, was a believer in the geographical unity of India. The Labour government, which came to power in Britain in July 1945, was not entirely unsympathetic to the aims and aspirations of the Congress. The elections of 1945-6 in India simplified the political scene by virtually eliminating the minor parties and leaving the Congress and the Muslim League as the two real contenders for power in India.[77] While the triumph of the Muslim League in the elections loaded the dice heavily in favour of Pakistan, the far more impressive triumph of the Congress in the elections held out a fair hope that the Congress would be able to hold together the rest of India even after the creation of Pakistan and to thwart the Muslim League's design to include the predominantly non-Muslim areas of Assam and Bengal and of Panjab within Pakistan.

Having failed to settle their dispute in 1944, the Congress and the League naturally awaited the reaction of the British government. It was not, however, until mid-1945—with the end of the war already in sight—that the British government felt able and willing to make a positive reaction. Rather unexpectedly, instead of acting as an arbitrator, the British government decided to act as a peacemaker. But it was too late for peacemaking in India in 1945. Not all the King's horses and all the King's men could now reconcile the Congress and the League. Congress leaders knew that Jinnah was determined to have a fully sovereign independent Pakistan and they, on their part, were equally determined that such a Pakistan should be confined to the Muslim-majority areas alone, that is, it should exclude those districts of Assam and Bengal and of Panjab in which the population was predominantly non-Muslim. Jinnah knew that the Congress—through Gandhi—had already offered him, what he had contemptuously described as, 'a maimed, mutilated and moth-eaten Pakistan'[78] and all that he was interested in knowing was whether the British government could offer him anything better. Neither party was willing to accept any temporary settlement which might prejudice its ultimate objective. Undeterred by the fiasco of the Simla Conference (June-July 1945), the British government sent out to India early in 1946 a special mission of cabinet ministers to make yet another attempt at peacemaking, but it met with no better success. The Cabinet Mission frankly told Jinnah that if he wanted a separate and fully independent sovereign state he would have to be satisfied with the smaller Pakistan offered to him by Gandhi in 1944, for, in the Mission's view, there was no justification for including within such a state those districts of Panjab and of Assam and Bengal in which the population was predominantly non-Muslim.[79] The Cabinet Mission also tried to demolish Jinnah's case for the partition of India by arguing that, apart from providing no acceptable solution for the communal problem, there were 'weighty administrative, economic and military considerations' against it.[80] But the Mission 'were greatly impressed by the very genuine and acute anxiety of the Muslims lest they should find themselves subjected to a perpetual Hindu-majority rule' and they were led to believe that this feeling had become so strong and widespread amongst the Muslims that it could not be allayed by mere paper safeguards.[81] They therefore proceeded, despite continuing objections from the Congress and the League, to recommend certain complicated and 'purposely vague'[82] proposals of their own[83] which offered the League the temptation of securing a bigger Pakistan, provided it was willing to try and work for some time the constitution of an 'Indian Union', and at the same time offered the Congress the temptation of preserving at least a semblance of Indian unity, provided it was willing to run the risk of India being divided not only into two but three or more parts in the future. Not unnaturally, both the Congress and the League at first showed interest in the proposals of the Cabinet Mission and then shied away from them.

Though the Cabinet Mission's long-term proposals of 16 May 1946 were drowned in a welter of conflicting alarms and interpretations, their short-term proposals—for the establishment of a Constituent Assembly and an Interim Central Government— were duly implemented. The League at first stayed away from both the Constituent Assembly and the Interim Central Government and resorted to 'direct action' to secure Pakistan. Later, realizing the risks of continued abstention, the League entered the Interim Central Government and turned it into another battlefront of 'the holy war'. Meanwhile, in the prevailing atmosphere of uncertainty and fear, mounting communal passions burst out into spasmodic rioting which threatened to develop into civil war. Lord Wavell was apparently so disgusted at the sight of riotous mobs and squabbling politicians in India that, soldier as he was, he advised the British government either to allow him to re-establish British authority in India or to march out of the country and let the Indians stew in their own juice. This advice cost the viceroy his recall in February 1947.

Partition and Independence

Lord Mountbatten did not, like Lord Wavell and the Cabinet Mission, attempt to erect matchwood dams against the Indian political torrent. He squarely faced the realities of Indian politics and persuaded the politicians in India to do the same. The partition of India was carried out with exemplary speed and smoothness, amidst circumstances which would have deterred a lesser man.

On 20 February 1947 the British prime minister, Clement Attlee, had announced His Majesty's Government's 'definite intention to take the necessary steps to effect the transfer of power into responsible Indian hands by a date not later than June 1948'[84] and clearly hinted at the possibility of partition. On 8 March 1947 the Congress Working Committee had passed a resolution welcoming Attlee's announcement and implicitly recognizing the necessity of partition.[85] In April 1947 Nehru publicly stated what had in fact been the view of the Congress at least ever since 1944. 'The Muslim League', he said, 'can have Pakistan if they want but on the condition that they do not take away other parts of India which do not wish to join Pakistan.'[86] But the first partition plan which Mountbatten's staff produced in May 1947 in accordance with the instructions of the British cabinet was so wrong-headed that Nehru angrily rejected it.[87] It provided for the transfer of power to the provinces or to such confederations of provinces as the latter might decide to form. As Nehru rightly pointed out to Mountbatten, the plan 'would encourage disruptive tendencies everywhere and chaos and weakness'.[88] It is difficult to believe that in May 1947 a group of British civil servants and statesmen could have seriously put forward a plan which would have encouraged units to cut adrift from the Union and the princely states to stand out and might have easily led to the total disintegration of India. Jinnah fought hard against another feature of the plan, namely, the proposed division of Bengal and Panjab, but ultimately reconciled himself to the inevitable. Almost as a consolation prize he was allowed to have the predominantly Muslim district of Sylhet in Assam for Pakistan. Jinnah also demanded a 800-mile corridor to link East and West Pakistan, but, in the face of firm Congress opposition, he did not press the issue.

In the framing of the second plan—better known as the 3 June or the Mountbatten plan—a distinguished Indian civil servant, V.P. Menon, appears to have played a crucial role.[89] It was accepted by all the parties concerned and finally became the basis of the Indian Independence Act, 1947. It provided for the transfer of power to India and Pakistan on the basis of dominion status, without disturbing constitutional continuity. In a certain sense this particular arrangement supported the claim of Indian leaders that the Union of India was the rightful successor to the British Raj and that Pakistan was merely the secession of a few provinces and parts of provinces from British India. This proved to be of some importance for the subsequent international status of the Indian Union: the U.N. recognized this claim.[90] Jinnah's two-nation theory found no mention either in the 3 June plan or in the Indian Independence Act and Congress leaders could legitimately claim that, far from vindicating the two-nation theory, the partition of India was really in accordance with the view which they had consistently adopted towards the demand for Pakistan, namely, that India was not to be regarded as two or more nations, but as one family consisting of many members of whom the Muslims living in certain areas desired to live in separation from the rest of India.

Congress leaders were extremely critical of the declaration made by the British government that paramountcy was to lapse on 15 August 1947 and the rulers of the Indian states were to become technically and legally independent, because they felt that it posed a grave threat to the stability and integrity of India for all but a dozen of the six hundred odd states were contiguous to Indian territory. They argued that paramountcy came into being as a fact and not by agreement and that on the British withdrawal the successor authority must inherit the fact along with the rest of the context. They insisted that no state should be allowed to declare independence, and that the princes must make up their minds to accede to India or Pakistan, taking into account their geographical situation, before 15 August 1947.[91] Jinnah, on the other hand, insisted that the rulers had absolute freedom of decision.[92] By their firm and tactful handling of the situation, Congress leaders were able to persuade nearly all the rulers to accede to the Dominion of India. The notable exceptions were Hyderabad, Kashmir and Junagarh; these also later acceded to the Dominion of India, but the circumstances under which this happened do not fall within the scope of this paper.

In agreeing to the partition of India, Congress leaders chose the lesser evil. Partition was bad, but the alternatives to partition in 1947 were worse. Continued slavery, civil war, chaos and the fragmentation of India—these were the only alternatives to partition in 1947. Nor was partition, in the judgement of many Congress leaders, an unmixed evil. India was at long last free. The unity of at least two-thirds of India had been preserved. The Congress had not compromised its ideals of secularism, democracy and a common Indian nationality. In fact, it had ensured that these ideals would find freer play in the Indian Union of the future. Some Congress leaders also hoped that partition would be transitory and that, instead of permanently barring, it might even clear the way to a real reunion. 'The division', said Maulana

Azad, 'is only on the map of the country and not in the hearts of the people, and I am sure it is going to be a short-lived partition.'[93] Nehru remarked: 'The united India that we have laboured for was not one of compulsion and coercion but a free and willing association of free peoples. It may be that in this way we shall reach that united India sooner than otherwise and then she will have a stronger and more secure foundation.'[94] Doubts and fears about the future were expressed by certain other Congress leaders, but these were submerged in the intense agony and ecstasy of the hour.

Most foreign observers applauded the wisdom of all the parties concerned in reaching a settlement. There were, however, two notable exceptions. The newspapers of northern and southern Ireland compared the proposed partition of India with the partition of their country, warning that Ireland had been materially and spiritually weakened by the division, which time had done nothing to heal.[95] From neighbouring Burma came a more ominous warning. 'A divided India', remarked Aung San, 'augurs ill not only for the Indian people but also for all Asia and world peace.'[96]

11

THE PARTITION OF INDIA: SOME MYTHS AND MIGHT-HAVE-BEENS

'If men could learn from history—what lessons it might teach us! But ... the light which experience gives is a lantern on the stern, which shines only on the waves behind us.' Samuel Taylor Coleridge, *Table Talk*.

'To forget and—I will venture to say—to get one's history wrong, are essential factors in the making of a nation; and thus the advance of historical studies is often a danger to nationality.' Ernest Renan, *What Is a Nation?*

'There is an element of political determinism in the working out of majority-minority relations in dependent societies as the time for a transfer, or possible transfer, of power approaches and the pattern of Ireland had so much in common with events as they unfolded in India, in Cyprus and in parts of Africa, as to suggest that the freedom of choice before the majority and minority community leadership was more limited than may retrospectively be supposed.' Nicholas Mansergh, *The Irish Question*.

Let me begin with the Government of India Act, 1935, and with that great 'if' of modern Indian history, namely that if the federal part of that Act had become effective before the Second World War broke out in 1939, the partition of India, with all the turmoil and bloodshed which it brought, would have been avoided. Some Englishman with guilty consciences started the myth, and it was readily swallowed by many Indian Liberals. Of late Indian journalists and historians have been busy turning it into a commonplace. It runs somewhat like this. The Act of 1935 was meant to give freedom and unity to India. If it had become fully operative, communities and parties would have learnt to work together through the necessary compromises and coalitions imposed by the very nature of the Act, and in due course power would have been transferred peacefully to a united India.

We know a little more now about the making of the Government of India Act, 1935, than we did ten years ago. From the records recently made available one thing clearly emerges: the Act of 1935 was not conceived either to give India freedom soon or to preserve its unity. The chief aim of the framers of the Act was to divert the demand of the Congress and the Indian Liberals for an early transfer of power at the centre. And they did so by a nodding assent to the nebulous formula: central responsibility with reservations and safeguards, upon the creation of an all-India federation.[1] Probably the only Englishman who was absolutely honest about the Act of 1935 was its draftsman, who described it as 'an Act to make further provision for the government of India'.[2]

But it might be argued: 'Whatever might have been the intentions of the British, Indians could have used the federation to promote unity and to extract more concessions from the British. The British proposed, Indians could have disposed.' This is more or less what actually happened. The Congress was critical of the Act of 1935, but it was not opposed to the idea of federation. So, despite its dissatisfaction with the federal part of the Act, the Congress became inclined, especially after its sweeping victory in the provincial elections of 1937, to work the federation. Its leaders even began persuading the princes—using both the carrot and the stick—to enter the federation. No sooner was this known —that the Congress was trying to realize the federation—others like the British and the Muslim League, who had so far pretended to favour the idea of a federation of India, began opposing it tooth and nail. The proposed federation failed to materialize because the British and the Muslim League opposed it. The former wanted a federation which they would be able to control, and the latter wanted a federation which would not control the provinces.

It is a fact not fully appreciated by most historians of recent Indian history that by the 1920s and the 1930s Muslim politicians in India had become united in their determination not to be dominated by the Hindus in any form of central government which might come into being. Whether one examines the pronouncements of leading Muslim politicians from 1921 onwards, or the demands officially put forward by leading Muslim organizations, or the assessments of Muslim attitudes made by competent foreign observers, they all point in the same direction: the Muslims wanted power to be transferred from London to the provinces, and not to any central authority in India; they wanted a bloc of autonomous states in the east and the north-west; and they insisted on an extremely loose confederation of sovereign states.[3]

The federation proposed in the Act of 1935 was, as Professor R.J. Moore has ably argued,[4] not only not meant to work, it was, in fact, unworkable. It gave the Muslims one-third of the seats in the federal legislature, though they were only a quarter of the British Indian population. The states were even more generously treated. They had 40 per cent representation in the upper house and 33.3 per cent in the lower house, though their population was less than a quarter of the total population of India. The representatives of British India were to be elected, while the representatives of the states were to be nominated by their rulers. There was also a provision that all powers connected with the exercise of the functions of the Crown in its relations with the states were not to be transferred to the federation—that is, paramountcy was not to be transferred to the federal government in India. Moreover, the states were free to join or not to join the federation. As was generally known at the time, the bigger states like Hyderabad and Kashmir had no intention of joining the federation. The federation could not come into existence until a sufficient number of states had joined to ensure that half the states' quota of seats had been filled in the upper house and half the total population of the states had been included. This was a condition almost impossible to be fulfilled. The states were virtually given a veto over the question of federation. The story of the appeasement of the states did not end there. The federation could exercise in the several states only those powers and functions which they agreed to confer upon it by their instruments of accession. A federation which included some states and excluded others, which exercised different powers and functions in different states, was unlikely to promote Indian unity. Moreover, if the integrity, autonomy and sovereignty of the Indian states had been recognized and institutionalized by some federation in the late 1930s, it would have been extremely difficult, if not impossible, to reverse the process after the Second World War. The relative ease with which the states were integrated and absorbed by the Indian Union after the transfer of power in 1947 should not make us forget the enormity and complexity of the problem created by the Indian states in the 1930s.

But the most important point is this. By the 1930s the Muslim demand for a bloc of autonomous states in the east and the north-west of India had clearly emerged; only it had not yet been formally adopted by the Muslim League. The establishment of a federation of India in the late 1930s could not have prevented the adoption of the demand for Pakistan by the Muslim League; it could easily have hastened it. We would thus be justified in concluding that even if the federation had materialized in the 1930s it could not have prevented the partition of India.

Having disposed of a 'might-have-been', let us consider a myth. It is the most preposterous, but the most persistent, myth. It is also an elaborate myth, the work of many hands, and people are still busy embellishing it. It runs somewhat as follows. Before the 1937 elections M.A. Jinnah was a good nationalist. He was eager for a settlement between the Congress and the Muslim League. The election manifestos of the Congress and the League were very similar. In the United Provinces there was even an understanding between the Congress and the Muslim League. They helped each other in the elections and looked forward to forming a coalition ministry in the province. But after its unexpectedly sweeping victory in the 1937 elections, the Congress became power-mad; it refused to give even two seats in the cabinet to the League and imposed impossible conditions for a coalition with it. If only the Congress had been generous enough to take two Muslim Leaguers into the U.P. cabinet, the Muslim League would have first disintegrated in the United Provinces, which was its stronghold, and later all over India, and there would have been no demand for Pakistan.

Only a complete ignoramus in recent Indian history would accept the statement that the League and the Congress were very close to each other in 1937. The Congress and the League represented two contradictory urges: the Congress stood for democracy, secularism and a common Indian nationality; the League existed primarily to safeguard the interests of Muslims in India as a separate political entity. They were never close to each other except for a brief period during 1915-21, under very exceptional circumstances, and it proved to be a disaster, for the Congress was persuaded, as a matter of expediency, to agree to the Lucknow Pact of 1916 which was a surrender to Muslim communalism and separatism. Jinnah was no doubt eager in the 1930s for a settlement between the Congress and the Muslim League, but he wanted this on his own terms: a weak centre for minimum common purpose; complete autonomy for the provinces, with residuary powers vesting in the provinces; the share of the Muslims in the services, elected bodies and cabinets to be fixed by statute; and the Congress to admit that it was—and function as—a Hindu body and to recognize the League as the sole spokesman for the Muslims. And almost in the same breath in which Jinnah used to speak of his desire for a settlement with the Congress, he would warn it that it must keep its hands off the Muslims. Students of history should be suspicious of rhetoric and they must not treat general declarations of availability as firm proposals for marriage.

As for the alleged similarity between the election manifestos of the Congress and the Muslim League, it hardly needs pointing out that to the superficial observer most election manifestos would look alike, for they promise all sorts of things to all sorts of men. However, as has been well said, there is very little difference between the nose of one man and that of another, but the little that is, is important. There was some apparent similarity between the manifestos of the Congress and the League, but this was accidental, and on important issues like the separate electorates, the 'communal award', the safeguards for the minorities, the Act of 1935, the idea of a constituent assembly and the abolition of landlordism, the Congress and the League were in complete disagreement and their leaders made no secret of this disagreement. Significantly enough, Jinnah inaugurated the Muslim League election campaign in Bengal in January 1937 by saying: 'Pandit Jawaharlal Nehru is reported to have said ... that there are only two parties in the country, namely, the Government and the Congress and others must line up. I refuse to line up with the Congress. There is a third party in this country and that is the Muslims.'[5] In a speech at Dacca on 8 January 1937 he said that 'at present there was a fundamental difference between the League and the Congress'.⁶

There is no tangible evidence to suggest that any understanding existed between the Congress and the League about the elections or the ministries to be formed after the elections of 1937. Minor personal and local instances of adjustment, arrangement and even co-operation between individual Congressmen and Leaguers should not be elevated to the position of a 'pact' or 'understanding' between the two organizations and their leaders. The fact of the matter is that in most provinces Congress Muslim candidates were pitted against Muslim League candidates. In the United Provinces, where this alleged understanding is said to have existed, the Congress set up 14 Muslim candidates, four of whom contested against Muslim League rivals and lost. In the very capital of the province, Lucknow, the Congress Muslim candidate fought and lost against a Muslim League candidate. This was the limit of the cordiality and co-operation which is alleged to have existed between the Congress and the League in 1937.

The core of this myth is that certain talks did take place between some Congress and League leaders for a possible coalition ministry in the United Provinces after the elections of 1937, but they failed to produce any positive result. Before we go on to discuss why these talks failed, we must recapitulate certain important facts of the situation in the United Provinces at the time. The total number of seats in the U.P. legislative assembly was 228, of which the Congress had won 133 and the League only 27 (out of a total of 64 Muslim seats). The Congress did not need the support of Muslim Leaguers in order to be able to form a ministry. It also had a few Muslims of its own, so it was not required to court the Muslim League in order to vindicate its national and secular character. The League's bargaining power in the United Provinces and elsewhere in the country was very weak. It could offer the Congress little in return for any possible favour done to it. Jinnah threatened the chief Muslim League negotiator in the United Provinces, Chaudhry Khaliquzzaman, with dire consequences if he persisted in his efforts to have an isolated and piecemeal agreement with the Congress. The talks failed not because the Congress tried to impose any 'impossible' or 'humiliating' conditions on the Muslim League, but because it was impossible for the Congress to grant what the Muslim League in the United Provinces demanded. The Congress wanted to have a cabinet of six or eight ministers in the United Provinces. The Muslim League demanded that one-third of the ministers in the cabinet—two in six or three in eight—must be Muslim Leaguers. The Congress did not—it could not—accept this demand. Why? Unless the Congress was prepared to give up its own Muslims, it was bound to include at least one Nationalist or Congress Muslim in the U.P. cabinet. If the Congress accepted the demand of the Muslim League also, in a cabinet of six there would have been three Muslims (2 Leaguers and 1 Nationalist Muslim), and in a cabinet of eight there would have been four Muslims (3 Leaguers and 1 Nationalist Muslim). Giving fifty per cent representation to the Muslims in a province where they formed only 14 per cent of the total population was a proposition which the Congress could not sell to its constituents. Moreover, the Congress did not fail to realize that the acceptance of the Muslim League demand would result in giving the League a prescriptive right to nominate the Muslim members of cabinets, in forcing all Muslim legislators to rally round the banner of the League, in admitting that the League was the sole spokesman for the Muslims, in encouraging the other communities to demand similar representation, and in writing not only the two-nation but the multi-nation theory into the constitution of India.

It was not just a question of giving two seats, instead of one, to Muslim Leaguers in the U.P. cabinet in 1937, as Maulana Abul Kalam Azad argued in his famous book, *India Wins Freedom*.[7] Far more momentous consequences would have flowed from the acceptance by the Congress of the Muslim League demand for one-third representation in the U.P. cabinet. The Muslim League wanted the Congress to accept the vicious principle of communal coalition cabinets. It would not have prevented the partition of India, but it could have caused infinite mischief in India after 1947. Maulana Azad's belief that if the Congress had been generous enough to give one more seat to the Muslim League in the U.P. cabinet in 1937, the Muslim League party in the province would have disintegrated and the demand for Pakistan would not have arisen[8] is too naive to merit serious consideration.

Let us move on to the examination of another great 'if' connected with the history of the partition of India. It is said that if the proposals of the Cripps Mission in 1942 had been accepted by Indian political parties, the partition of India could have been avoided. Briefly stated, the long-term proposals made by Sir Stafford Cripps in March 1942 to Indian leaders were as follows: at the end of the war a constitution-making body would be set up for the Indian Union; any province that was not prepared to accept the new constitution could retain its present position; with such non-acceding provinces the British government would enter into a new constitutional arrangement, giving them the same full status as allowed to the Indian Union; the Indian princely states would have the same rights as the British Indian provinces of non-accession and of forming new unions.[9] It does not require much intelligence to realize that if Indian leaders had accepted these proposals made by Cripps in 1942 there would have been a bigger Pakistan today and many Indian princely states would have gone the way of Pakistan. Far from negating the Muslim League demand for Pakistan, the offer made by Cripps in 1942 amounted to the first formal acceptance by the British government of the principle of Pakistan.

Some people believe that if the Cabinet Mission plan of 1946 had been allowed to be worked, the unity of India would have been preserved. They say that Pandit Jawaharlal Nehru made a great tactical blunder when he remarked on 7 July 1946: 'We are not bound by a single thing except that we have decided to go to the Constituent Assembly.'[10] This remark is alleged to have scared the Muslim League into withdrawing its earlier acceptance of the Cabinet Mission plan. Maulana Azad called it 'one of those events which change the course of history'.[11] People who maintain that the Muslim League had accepted the Cabinet Mission plan as a final solution of the Indian problem have probably never cared to look at League documents. The League accepted the Mission plan with its own interpretation of grouping, and it accepted it only as a stepping-stone to full, complete and sovereign Pakistan.[12]

By the time the Cabinet Mission came to India in 1946 the British had decided to 'divide and quit' India. They feared that there was going to be 'a revolution' in the country and they were anxious to evacuate as early as possible.[13] But they were also anxious that the responsibility for the partition of India should be firmly fixed on Indian shoulders. When the Mission arrived in India, they first offered Jinnah the small Pakistan which he ultimately got, but Jinnah refused to accept it at the time because he regarded it as 'a maimed, mutilated and moth-eaten Pakistan'.[14] The Mission then tried to give Jinnah his 'big' Pakistan through the backdoor. The Cripps proposals had given the provinces the right of secession. This was dangerous from the point of view of the Muslim League, because the North-West Frontier Province and Assam were controlled by the Congress. So the Cabinet Mission allowed the right of secession both to provinces and to groups of provinces by a simple majority.

The Cabinet Mission did not prescribe a constitution for India. It only arranged for a machinery to frame the constitution for India in three tiers: first, the constitution for India (and here it was understood that the centre will have no other powers except those for defence, foreign affairs and communications); second, the constitutions for all the provinces; and, third, the constitutions for groups of provinces.[15]

The most important part of the Mission plan was the grouping of provinces. The Mission proposed to call them 'Hindustan' and 'Pakistan' provinces, but at the suggestion of V.P. Menon and B.N. Rau it was agreed to call them A, B, and C groups of provinces.[16] The A group included Madras, Bombay, C.P., U.P., Bihar, and Orissa; the B group included N-W.F.P., Panjab, and Sindh; and the C group included Bengal and Assam. The plan provided that provinces or groups of provinces could leave the Union after every ten years.

The proposals of the Cabinet Mission were, as Sir Stafford Cripps later admitted, deliberately kept vague[17] in order that they might mean different things to different parties. For example, in one place it was said that provinces might form groups (this made grouping optional), but in another place it was laid down that provinces would form groups (this made grouping compulsory).[18] The Congress accepted the proposals believing that grouping was optional and, as it controlled Assam and the North-West Frontier Province, it felt confident that there would be no grouping. The Muslim League insisted that grouping was compulsory, and the British government later upheld the League's interpretation. If the Congress had accepted compulsory grouping, the proposed B and C groups of provinces would have, in effect, given the Muslim League after ten years—at the latest— the 'big' Pakistan which it wanted, and India would have been left with a weak minimal centre. The Congress very wisely decided not to take the risk.

The Cabinet Mission plan was meant not to preserve the unity of India, but to give the Muslim League a 'big' Pakistan through the backdoor. This view is confirmed by a fact which has recently become fairly well known. While the Cabinet Mission was still in India, the then viceroy, Lord Wavell, and his advisers prepared in late May 1946 what was called 'a breakdown plan'. According to this plan, the British were to 'hand over the Hindu Provinces [Madras, Bombay, C.P., U.P., Bihar, and Orissa], by agreement and as peaceably as possible, to Hindu rule, withdrawing our troops, officials and nationals in an orderly manner; and ... at the same time support the Muslim Provinces of India [N-W.F.P., Panjab, Sindh, Bengal, and Assam] against Hindu domination and assist them to work out their own constitution'.[19] Luckily for India, the British prime minister, Clement Attlee, did not approve of the plan.

As an Indian, I feel happy that the Cabinet Mission plan failed. The people who feel most unhappy about it are the Pakistanis and their friends. And they feel unhappy because it robbed the Muslim League of its last chance of getting the 'big' Pakistan which it wanted. When ultimately, in 1947, India was partitioned, our leaders made sure of so many vital things: first, that Pakistan did not get the whole of Assam, Bengal, and Panjab; second, that almost all the princely states in India acceded to the Dominion of India; third, that we had a strong centre which could promote the unity and stability of the country; and, fourth, that we were not required to abandon our ideals of liberal nationalism.

'We cannot choose situations in life,' Mahadev Govind Ranade used to say, 'our duty is to do the best we can according to our lights in any situation in which we find ourselves.'[20] In politics, as in life generally, we have often to be satisfied with the second, or even the third, best. The freedom of choice before our national leaders in the 1930s and the 1940s was more limited than may retrospectively be supposed. And, situated as they were, they did their best according to their lights.

12

THE PROBLEM OF THE INDIAN STATES IN HISTORICAL PERSPECTIVE

The story is told to a Cambridge professor who was an expert in ancient history, but who was once required to deliver lectures on modern economic history. He found a way out. In his first lecture he explained how the understanding of all modern problems depended on the knowledge of historical foundations, and then in this happy escape, he devoted the entire series of lectures to the Barbarian invasions of Rome. When I was asked to write a paper for this seminar on Sardar Patel,* I tried to find a similar escape and offered to do a paper on 'The Problem of the Indian States in Historical Perspective'.

But what should be my historical perspective? Where should I begin? After all, the problem of the Indian states has been with us for a very long time. From very early times this old and vast subcontinent of ours has been divided into numerous states of all kinds and sizes. Take our own region of the Panjab and Simla hill states. This is what J. Hutchinson and J.Ph. Vogel have written about its history: 'The history of these Hill States is one of almost continuous warfare. When a strong ruler rose to power, the larger States absorbed or made tributary their smaller neighbours, but these again asserted their independence as soon as favourable opportunity arrived.'[1]

Taking the country as a whole, *matsyanyāya* (the bigger fish swallowing the smaller fish) was the narrative. All-India empires were episodes in our history (e.g., the Maurya empire in the 4th

---

*Organized in 1975 by Panjab University, Chandigarh, in connexion with the birth centenary of Sardar Vallabhbhai Patel.

century B.C.; the Gupta empire in the 4th century A.D.; the Mughal empire in the 16th century; and the British empire in the 19th century). And the problem of the states was always there: the problem of controlling from one imperial centre the numerous and far-flung states of the Indian subcontinent. It is significant that the Indian empires were compared to a hide: you tried to press it on one side, the other side would rise.

There is no limit to going back in history. One has to choose some date arbitrarily. I have chosen to begin with 1765. In that year the East India Company acquired *diwani* rights in Bengal, Bihar and Orissa and emerged as a recognized political power in the country.

At first the British tried to establish a balance of power among rival forces (Indian and foreign) contending for supremacy on the ruins of the Mughal empire. They also tried to safeguard their territories by adopting what has been called a 'policy of the ring-fence';[2] that is, to guard the frontiers of the neighbouring states by way of precaution. In pursuance of this two-fold policy the East India Company entered into defensive treaties with Hyderabad and Travancore in the south; with Avadh in the north; and with Baroda in the west. The British avoided a headlong collision with the Marathas until they had subjugated Mysore. These treaties (with Hyderabad, Travancore, Avadh and Baroda) were, however, concluded on a footing of equality.

By the time we come to Lord Wellesley (1798-1804), British power is more firmly established in India and over a larger territory; he could therefore speak to the Indian states in a different language. Wellesley initiated a new policy towards the Indian states. He refused to treat them as equals of the British. As he remarked in 1804: 'A general bond of connexion is now established between the British Government and the principal states of India on principles which render it the interest of every state to maintain its alliance with the British Government . . . and which secure to every state the unmolested exercise of its separate authority within the limits of its established dominion, under the general protection of the British power.'[3] Wellesley did not invent it, but he perfected the system of subsidiary alliances as a part of his technique of supremacy. What was the system of subsidiary alliances?

An Indian prince in danger from his neighbours was encouraged to seek British help. The British guaranteed his independence against all comers, and in order to make the guarantee effective, stationed a detachment of Company's troops within his state. The cost of these troops was met by the Indian prince by a subsidy or cession of territory to the British. Those who were thus allied to the British at this period (the first decade of the 19th century) included Hyderabad, Travancore, Mysore, the Peshwa at Poona, Baroda, and Avadh. The system of subsidiary alliances gave security to those who accepted it, but 'the princely fly was firmly enmeshed in the British political web, and any hope of escape was idle'. It meant an assertion of the fact that politically and militarily the British were supreme in India by the turn of the century.

A third stage in the British relations with the Indian states began with Lord Hastings (1812-23), who carried Wellesley's policy to its logical conclusion. Hastings abandoned the fiction of 'reciprocity and mutual amity'. The series of treaties which he concluded with the Rajput and Maratha states clearly defined the status of the Indian states in relation to the Company as one of 'subordinate co-operation'. British paramountcy was established by compelling the Indian states to surrender their rights of making war and peace and of negotiating agreements with other powers. In theory, the Indian states retained their internal sovereignty, but in actual practice they became subject to frequent interference in their internal affairs by British Residents. The British now stood forth as the paramount power in India. They assumed feudal superiority of wardship, escheat and the right of confirming succession.

The system of subsidiary alliances secured British authority in India at the lowest possible cost. It also provided a cheap, simple and effective method of developing British military strength. Almost half of the British army in India in 1818 was composed of the subsidiary forces of the states. But the system undermined the independence of the Indian rulers and contributed to extravagance and misgovernment. Moral degeneration and administrative chaos set in wherever the Indian ruler was made secure in his throne and protected from foreign invasion. Deprived even of the right of insurrection, the Indian people in many states became worse off than what they were before.

From 1823 to 1856 British policy towards the Indian states may be described as being frankly annexationist. But there is a qualitative difference between the policy pursued by Dalhousie (1848-56) and that of his immediate predecessors. While the annexations of Bentinck, Auckland, and Ellenborough were the result of political and military necessity, in Dalhousie's time annexation became a deliberate goal of British policy in India. Dalhousie was convinced that British rule was superior to Indian and that the Indian states were an anachronism in an age of progress. In a famous minute, dated 30 August 1848, Dalhousie wrote: 'I cannot conceive it possible for anyone to dispute the policy of taking advantage of every just opportunity which presents itself of consolidating the territories which already belong to us, by taking possession of States that may lapse in the midst of them; for thus getting rid of those petty intervening principalities, which may be made a means of annoyance, but which can never, I venture to think, be a source of strength, for adding to the resources of the public treasury, and for extending the uniform application of our system of government to those whose best interests, we sincerely believe, will be promoted thereby.'[4]

Dalhousie annexed seven Indian states in seven years. How did he do it? The first device which Dalhousie used was the doctrine of lapse. According to this doctrine, on the failure of natural heirs, the sovereignty of the 'dependent' states—of those created by the British government, or held by a subordinate tenure—lapsed to the paramount power. The doctrine was not new. Dalhousie did not invent the doctrine of lapse. He only applied it more vigorously. And he annexed Satara, Sambhalpur, Baghat, Udaipur, Jhansi, and Nagpur in pursuance of this policy. (Baghat and Udaipur were later restored by Lord Canning.) The doctrine of lapse was also used to do away with the titles and pensions of the rulers of some states (e.g., the Nawab of Carnatic, the Raja of Tanjore, and the Nana Sahib's pension of Rs 800,000 after the death of Baji Rao II in 1853).

The second excuse which Dalhousie used for annexation was the old and familiar one of misgovernment. He regarded persistent misgovernment by Nawab Wajid Ali Shah as a sufficient justification for annexing Avadh in February 1856 in violation of the solemn treaty made in 1837.

By the middle of the 19th century the British were masters of all they surveyed in India. They thought they could do whatever they liked in the country. They annexed kingdoms and overthrew established rights without much fear of consequences. The Indian princes trembled on their thrones as they saw one princely state after another annexed on the ground of misgovernment or the failure to produce a natural heir. The cry had gone forth that the British Empire in India should be 'one and indivisible'. Powerful organs of the British press hounded on the Indian government to a career of spoliation in the name of duty, of justice, and of manifest destiny. Titles and treaties were denounced as antiquated parchments and the approaching doom of every Indian kingdom was loudly proclaimed.

The Indian princes were terrified by the writing on the wall. It was Ranjit Singh who gave expression to their fear. He was once shown the map of India with parts coloured red. He asked what the red colour represented, and on being told that it represented British territory he said: *'Sab lal ho jayega'* ('All will become red'). The alarm of the princes was shared not only by the people in their own states, but also by those in British India. Crowns do not crumble without a clamour from the crowd. Even if there be no love for a particular bearer, his name is still a flag, a symbol, the representative of some principle. This was especially true in India, with her conservative and legitimist people. Dalhousie's annexation of Panjab after victory in battle was stoically accepted by the people of India, but his annexation of Avadh in violation of a solemn treaty and that of Nagpur, Satara, Jhansi, etc., in pursuance of the doctrine of lapse was universally denounced by the people of India as unjust and unfair. Let us also not forget that the people of India were interested in the survival of their princes not only for sentimental reasons, but also because they considered it somehow to be a safeguard of their religion and nationality. T. R. Metcalf has rightly observed: 'Foremost among the causes of the revolt [of 1857] was Lord Dalhousie's policy of annexing the princely states of India. The fate which befell so many states during his tenure of office excited widespread apprehension, not least among the remaining princes, and contributed largely to that spirit of unrest from which the revolt gathered strength.'[6]

One of the most important lessons which the revolt of 1857 taught the British was that the political value of maintaining the princely states in India far outweighed any moral or administrative shortcomings they might possess. Dalhousie's policy of annexation had created widespread alarm and dissatisfaction and the dispossessed princes had provided leadership to the revolt. The remaining princely states, on the other hand, had proved themselves, as Canning said, 'breakwaters to the storm which would otherwise have swept over us [the British] in one great wave'.[7] Wiser from their experience of the revolt of 1857, the British gave up the policy of annexation. They conceded to the princes the right of adoption. And they tried in all sorts of ways to enlist the influence and loyalty of the princes in the interests of the British Raj.

This new British policy towards the Indian states was not only welcomed by the princes and their subjects, but also by the people of India in general. To the average Indian the states were islands of self-government in a sea of alien rule. He looked upon the survival of the princely states as a safeguard of his religion and nationality. The states also provided an outlet for political ambition denied in British India. Indians could rise to the highest positions in the states—something which they could not do in British India. Not surprisingly, many patriotic and liberal-minded Indians had a soft corner for the princely states, despite their illiberal and despotic governments.

Though the British gave up the policy of annexation after 1858, they did not give up the right of intervening in the affairs of the Indian states, especially in order to set right abuses in the administration. And as paramount power, the British remained the sole judge of the extent and occasion of their intervention. The effective powers of the Indian princes were severely circumscribed by the British Residents. The British government occasionally intervened to retain a particular minister in office (e.g., Salar Jang in Hyderabad) against the will of the ruler, to regulate succession, and to depose refractory or oppressive rulers (e.g., Gaikwar Malharrao of Baroda in 1875). But the British usually kept their interference to a minimum and their power in the background. They had realized the advantages of maintaining the princely order in India as a bastion of conservatism and imperialism. The new British policy towards the Indian states after the revolt of 1857 paid off. The states remained loyal to the British Raj until 1947.

If the Indian states survived for such a long time, they did so not because of any intrinsic strength of their own, but because the British deemed it politically expedient to allow them to survive.

But this was only one reason why the states survived in India. The other reason was that Indians—both in the states and in British India—wanted them to survive. We have already seen how the Indian states were saved from total extinction because the people of India rose in rebellion in 1857. And after the revolt whenever it appeared that the British government was being high-handed in dealing with the ruler of any Indian state—whether it was Baroda in the 1870s or Kashmir in the 1890s—the people of India—particularly those of British India with their newspapers and agents and associations—raised such a hue and cry that the British government had to be very careful in its intervention. Indians knew that the rulers of many princely states were oppressors, but they were inclined to make all sorts of allowances for them, because at least these oppressors were of their own kind.

So the Indian states survived not because of their own vitality or capacity for survival, but because (*i*) the British wanted them to survive to serve their own ends; and (*ii*) because the people of India also wanted them to survive.

The Indian states were giants with feet of clay. They had little strength of their own. They were really propped up by the British and the people of India (both of Indian India and of British India). Pandit Jawaharlal Nehru, in his presidential address to the annual session of the All-India States' People's Conference, 15 February 1939, observed: 'Offspring of the British power in India, suckled by imperialism, for its own purposes, it has survived till today.... That system has no inherent importance or strength, it is the strength of British imperialism that counts. For us in India, that system has in reality been one of the facets of imperialism. Therefore, when conflict comes, we must recognize who our opponent is. ... It is clear that the problem of the States would be easy of solution if the conflict was confined to the people and the Ruler. Many of the Rulers, left to themselves, would ultimately line themselves with the people and if they hesitated to do so, the pressure from below would soon induce them to change their minds. Not to do so would imperil their position and the only alternative would be complete removal.'[8]

Once the British bayonets were withdrawn, and the people of India withdrew their support, the princes collapsed. Those who had made or saved them also unmade and integrated them.

But we are anticipating developments. Let us now try to understand the problem of the Indian states in the context of the Indian struggle for freedom and unity. In the later 19th century there were no fewer than 562 states in India and they formed a good third of the whole country. They differed from each other enormously in size and importance. The Nizam of Hyderabad ruled over an area of 83,000 square miles and a population of 11,500,000. There were petty chiefs in Kathiawar whose territories consisted only of a few acres. The sovereignty over the states was divided between the British government and the ruler of the state in proportions which differed greatly according to the history and importance of the several states, and which were regulated partly by treaties or less formal engagements, partly by *sanads* or charters, and partly by usage. The maximum of sovereignty enjoyed by any Indian prince was represented by the Nizam of Hyderabad, who coined money, taxed his people, and inflicted capital punishment without appeal. The minimum of sovereignty was represented by the lord of a few acres in Kathiawar, who enjoyed immunity from British taxation and exercised some shadow of judicial authority.

As paramount power, the British government exercised exclusive control over the foreign relations of the state; assumed a general but limited responsibility for the internal peace and security of the state; assumed a special responsibility for the safety and welfare of British subjects resident in the state; and required subordinate co-operation in the task of resisting foreign aggression and maintaining internal order. The Indian state did not have any international existence. It could not make war. It would not enter into any treaty or arrangement with any of its neighbours. (Indian princes could not even directly communicate with each other.) It could not initiate or maintain diplomatic relations with any foreign power.

The territories of British India and of the Indian states were inextricably interlaced. The territories of the Indian states were intersected by British railway lines, postal lines and telegraph lines. For each state there was a British political officer, representing the civil authority exercised by the paramount power, and in each of the more important states there was a resident political officer with a staff of subordinates. Detachments of British troops occupied cantonments in all the more important military positions. The states maintained a number of selected troops in such a condition of efficiency as would make them fit to take the field side by side with British troops. The officers and men of these troops were largely natives of the state, and they were under the command of the ruler of the state, but they were inspected and advised by British officers. All these were limitations on the powers of the states.

The creation of an historical accident, the states were scattered haphazard over the map of India, though they could be grouped in eight or nine distinct blocks. Though the geographical layout of the Indian states was a patchwork, it had a certain broad coherence. Taken together the states constituted a great cruciform barrier, broken by gaps of varying width, but more or less effectively separating the different parts of British India from one another. This fact had obvious strategic and political importance.[9]

Most of the rulers of the states were Hindus, but their religion was not necessarily that of the majority of their subjects. Whereas Muslims numbered one-fourth of the total Indian population, they numbered only about one-sixth of the population of the states.

Though the points of contact between British India and princely India were many, the latter were slow in assimilating the new principles and ideas, methods and practices current in the former. But the growing influence of modern conditions of life was busy breaking down the isolation of the states from one another and from the rest of India. New forces of constitutional development and national movement were beginning to pose problems which could not be solved by keeping India divided into two watertight compartments. It was an artificial division, artificially maintained. But even with the best will in the world, the marriage of Indian India with British India would not have been an easy task. And the British surely were not eager to act as the priest and bring about a happy union. In fact, they had a vested interest in perpetuating the division.

In order to counter the Indian nationalist movement, the British played two trump cards: one was that of the Muslims; and the other that of the states. In the long run, the first proved to be a success; but the second proved to be a failure. The relative failure of the British in using the states against the Indian struggle for freedom and unity was due to many factors: (*i*) the lack of unity among the Indian states; (*ii*) the lack of support from the subjects of the Indian princes; (*iii*) the dissatisfaction of the Indian princes with the government of India's Political Department; and (*iv*) the patriotism of some of the Indian princes. But the British did not fail to try.

From Lytton in the 1870s to Hardinge in the second decade of the 20th century repeated attempts were made to organize the Indian princes as a conservative bloc against the Indian nationalist movement, but they were not very successful. With the appearance of Gandhi on the Indian stage and the introduction of the Montagu-Chelmsford reforms, the British became more anxious than ever before to use the princes as a counterweight to Indian nationalism. Under the smokescreen of bringing together Indian India and British India and of working towards an ultimate federation of India, the British organized a Chamber of Princes on 8 February 1921 which did little more than promoting joint action on the part of the Indian states and bringing them closer to the Political Department of the government of India. But it had another and a far more important consequence. So far the Indian questions had been triangular (involving the British, the Indian nationalists, and the Muslim communalists). From now onwards another element was introduced into the conflict (that of the Indian states) and it became quadrangular. It is this quadrangular situation which we encounter at the Round Table Conference in the early 1930s and in the Government of India Act of 1935.

When in the 1930s the British, under pressure from the Indian Liberals, agreed to the idea of an Indian federation, they saw to it that if at all the federation came into existence, it would be controlled by them and not by the Congress. We know how the federal provisions of the Government of India Act of 1935 gave the Muslims one-third of the seats in the central legislature, though they were only a quarter of the British Indian population. The princely states were even more generously treated. They had 40 per cent representation in the upper house and 33.3 per cent in the lower house, though their population was less than a quarter of the total population of India. The representatives of British India were to be elected, but the representatives of the states were to be nominated by their rulers. There was also a provision that all powers connected with the exercise of the functions of the Crown in its relations with the states were not to be transferred to the federation, i.e. that paramountcy would not be transferred to the federation.

That was not all. The states were free to join or not to join the federation. And everybody knew that the bigger states like Hyderabad and Kashmir would never join it. The federation could not come into existence until a sufficient number of states had joined it to ensure that half the states' quota of seats had been filled in the upper house and half the population of the states had been included. This was a condition almost impossible to be fulfilled. The states were thus given a veto over the question of federation. The friends of the princes in Britain, Winston Churchill and others, had got a promise from the British government that the princes would not be coerced, and unless the princes were coerced they would not join the federation.

The story of the appeasement of the states did not end there. The federation could enjoy in the several states only those powers and functions which they agreed to confer upon it by their instruments of accession.[10]

Could this 'gigantic quilt of jumbled crotchet work',[11] as Winston Churchill called it, really function? I personally believe that the federation proposed by the Government of India Act, 1935, was not only not meant to work, it was in fact unworkable.

Some persons have blamed Willingdon and Linlithgow for not pressing ahead with the scheme of federation speedily enough. They have regretted that the Second World War intervened and the federal proposals had to be shelved. They have gone further and asserted that if the federation had materialized by 1939 the partition of India, with all the turmoil and the bloodshed which it brought, would have been avoided.

I have argued elsewhere[12] that the creation of an Indian federation, such as postulated by the Government of India Act, 1935, before 1939 would not have prevented the partition of India. The demand for Pakistan had already emerged. Only the Muslim League did not officially adopt it as its goal until March 1940. If there was any prospect of the federation materializing earlier, the Muslim League would have adopted the slogan of Pakistan also earlier. But this is not the point which I wish to discuss here.

Believing as I do in the unity of my country and rejoicing in the fact that the Indian states have been integrated with the rest of India to form the present Indian Union, I do not regret that the federal provisions of the Act of 1935 were never put into effect. I am glad that the princes were not wise enough in their time and were ultimately swept away. It would have been a disaster if they had seen their way to join in the making of an Indian federation in the late 1930s. A federation which included some states and excluded other states, which enjoyed different powers and functions in different states, was unlikely to promote Indian unity. If the integrity, sovereignty and autonomy of the Indian states had been recognized and institutionalized by some federation in the 1930s, it would have been impossible to reverse the process in 1947.

I do not want to discuss here the question, 'Who killed the federation idea?' Personally, I am inclined to believe that after their sweeping victory in the elections of 1937 many Congressmen became eager to try even the wretched federation proposed by the Government of India Act of 1935, because they thought they could dominate it.

The Congress tried both the stick and the carrot with the princes. The stick was an intensification of the agitation by the All-India States' People's Conference and the local Praja Mandals against the princes for constitutional privileges. Even Gandhi now came out openly against the princes and fasted at Rajkot in 1938. The carrot was a bait thrown out to the princes by the Congress that they would be welcome in the proposed federation if only they would take care to send representative men to the federal legislature. As soon as this was known, the Muslim League, which had so far paid lip-service to the idea of a federation, became openly inimical to it; and the British, who had hoped that they would be able to control the federation with the help of the Muslims, the princes, and others, became lukewarm about it. So the federation failed to materialize, not because the Congress opposed it, but because the Muslim League, the British and the princes lost interest in it.

Once the Muslim League adopted the demand for Pakistan in March 1940 and the Muslims all over the country began increasingly to rally to its support, Congress leaders prepared themselves for the unpalatable eventuality of partition. Their strategy was very simple. The Muslim League should have nothing but its pound of flesh. It should get nothing more than what Jinnah later described as 'a maimed, mutilated and moth-eaten Pakistan',[13] i.e. a smaller Pakistan (without Assam, west Bengal and east Panjab). The struggle for Indian freedom must continue unabated, and if unfortunately the Muslim League succeeded in getting the country partitioned, the unity of the rest of the country should be preserved.

The British were still playing the crescent card; but the more they played the Muslim card now, the more difficult it became for them to play the state card effectively. The Indian problem now became more and more a Hindu-Muslim or a Congress-Muslim League problem. The British accepted the principle of Pakistan publicly for the first time in the famous Cripps proposals of March 1942 which said that any province which did not wish to accede to the future Union of India could stay out of it and enjoy the same status. And what applied to the British Indian provinces also applied—and with greater effect—to the Indian states.

If you read carefully the reaction of the Congress Working Committee to the Cripps proposals, dated 2 April 1942,* you

*'The complete ignoring of ninety millions of people in the Indian States, and their treatment as commodities at the disposal of their rulers, is a negation both of democracy and self-determination. While the representation of an Indian State in the constitution-making body is fixed on a population basis, the people of the State have no voice in choosing those representatives, nor are they to be consulted at any stage while decisions vitally affecting them are being taken. Such States may in many ways become barriers to the growth of Indian freedom, enclaves where foreign authority still prevails, and where the possibility of maintaining foreign armed forces has been stated to be a likely contingency and a perpetual menace to the freedom of the people of the States as well as of the rest of India.

'The acceptance beforehand of the novel principle of non-accession for a Province is also a severe blow to the conception of Indian unity and an apple of discord likely to generate growing trouble in the Provinces, and which may well lead to further difficulties in the way of the Indian States merging themselves into an Indian Union. The Congress has been wedded to Indian freedom and unity, and any break of that unity especially in the modern world when peoples' minds inevitably think in terms of even larger federations would be injurious to all concerned and exceedingly painful to contemplate. Nevertheless, the Committee cannot think in terms of compelling the people of any territorial unit to remain in an Indian Union against their declared and established will. While recognizing this principle, the Committee feel that every effort should be made to create conditions which would help the different units in developing a common and co-operative national life. Acceptance of this principle inevitably involves that no changes should be made which would result in fresh problems being created and compulsion being exercised on other substantial groups within that area.

would notice that the Congress implicitly conceded the possibility of the partition of India, but it opposed the proposals because it feared that they might give the Muslim League the bigger Pakistan which it demanded, and also lead to the independence of many states or unions of states. Incidentally, if Jinnah wanted the smaller Pakistan which he ultimately got in association with India, he could have got it any time after 1942.

By 1946 the British were anxious to withdraw from India as early as possible. There were so many reasons for their anxiety. One of these was that they feared that there was going to be 'a revolution'[14] in the subcontinent.

If the British had tried to fulfil their obligations to everybody in India, they would have never been able to leave the country. There is no convenient time for dying or withdrawing. They decided to divide and quit. They fulfilled their obligations to the Muslim League to a large extent, but they had to ditch the princes.

The British had a curious love-hate relationship with the princes. I do not intend to examine it here. But one point I would like to make. The British gravely overestimated the power and authority of the Indian princes. Many of them hoped—even until 1947—that the bigger states might have an autonomous existence and some of the smaller ones could do the same by forming unions. The British had clear obligations of honour to the princes. They had nostalgic notions of the 'gorgeous east' and a belief in the stability of autocratic rule. But basically the belief of the British in the stability of the princes sprang from their long indulged preoccupation with the tactics of a triangular or quadrangular situation in India.

On the eve of the transfer of power the British government spelled out its policy towards the Indian states in the Cabinet Mission memorandum of 12 May 1946[15] (actually published on 22 May 1946). It was reiterated by Lord Mountbatten on 3 June 1947.[16] Briefly stated, the British policy towards the Indian states on the eve of the transfer of power was as follows:

'Each territorial unit should have the fullest autonomy within the Union consistently with a strong national state.' M. Gwyer and A. Appadorai (eds.), *Speeches and Documents on the Indian Constitution 1921-47* (O.U.P., Bombay, 1957), vol. ii, p. 525.

when the British withdraw from India, paramountcy would lapse and the rulers of the Indian states would become technically and legally independent: they could enter into any relationship with the successor government or governments; or they could remain independent; and they were free to decide all this at their convenience.

Lord Mountbatten made two qualifications to this general statement of policy. He advised the rulers to take their history, geography and composition of the population into account while deciding their future. And he also advised them to make up their minds before the date of the transfer of power (which was later announced to be 15 August 1947).[17]

The Congress denounced this statement of British policy. It argued that paramountcy came into existence as a fact and not by agreement and that on the British withdrawal from India the successor authority must inherit the fact along with the rest of the context. It also insisted that no state should be allowed to declare independence, and that the princes must make up their minds to accede to India or 'Pakistan', taking into account their geographical situation, before 15 August 1947.[18]

If Jinnah and the Muslim League wanted partition in a peaceful and friendly way, they should have supported the Congress on all these points. I would go further and say that had Jinnah made up his mind before 15 August 1947 that the only Indian state—outside the territory of the would-be Dominion of Pakistan—which he wanted, or could get, was Kashmir, he could have easily got it. There could have been some straightforward horse-trading. He could have asked the Indian leaders to keep out of Kashmir by promising himself to keep out of Hyderabad.

Kashmir was hardly a bone of contention between the Congress and the League leaders before 1947. Indian leaders had enough problems on their hands. Of the 562 princely states, all but a dozen were contiguous to Indian territory. In June 1947 Mountbatten had gone to Kashmir with the promise of Sardar Patel in his pocket that if Kashmir acceded to Pakistan before 15 August 1947 India would have no objection.[19]

I am not trying to argue that Kashmir was no problem. It was a problem—and a problem full of complications. Kashmir was contiguous to both India and Pakistan. Its strategic importance was great. The Maharaja was a Hindu. He was in a good bargaining position. He had evil counsellors of all races. One part of the state had a Hindu majority, the other had a Muslim majority, and the third had a Buddhist majority. And there was Sheikh Abdullah to make confusion worse confounded. But despite all these complications, I am inclined to think that if Jinnah would have satisfied himself with Kashmir alone, he could have easily bargained with the Congress leaders. He could have supported the Congress stand about paramountcy and about the desirability of all states acceding to one dominion or the other before 15 August 1947, taking into account their geographical position and the composition of their population.

Why did Jinnah not do this? Why did he come out with the astounding statement that the rulers had absolute freedom of decision: they could join either dominion; they could become independent; and they could make up their minds leisurely?[20] Some say that Jinnah was a barrister and he was being very legalistic. But this explanation is not entirely satisfactory. Jinnah was not only a barrister, he was also a politician. Had he such a great regard for legal forms he would have quietly accepted Kashmir's legal accession to India or at least not countenanced the invasion of Kashmir by Pakistani tribals. The second explanation often given is that Jinnah was annoyed because he got only 'a maimed, mutilated and moth-eaten Pakistan'. This is a plausible explanation, but not a sufficient one. The real reason, in my opinion, was very different. Jinnah was playing for high stakes. He knew that Pakistan had no problem of princely states. Almost all the princely states were in India or contiguous to Indian territory. And a good many of these princely states had Muslim rulers. He had his eye on Hyderabad, Bhopal, Rampur and Junagarh. There was not one scheme of Pakistan drawn up ever since the early 1930s which did not include Indian states with Muslim rulers within the orbit of Pakistan.

Jinnah had very little to lose and he had much to gain. Kashmir, after all, was predominantly Muslim. He would easily get it. Why forego the chance of acquiring other states? So he ran after the birds in the bush, leaving the bird in hand.

Now, I won't say that Jinnah was just being greedy. No, there was a lot of sentiment attached to states like Hyderabad. But I would insist that Jinnah's move was based on a very clear and cool calculation. Anybody who knew anything about the Indian problem in those days realized that India could easily survive the surgical operation of Pakistan, but it could not survive without the Indian states. Sir Reginald Coupland had already pointed out in 1945: 'An India deprived of the States would have lost all coherence. They stand between all four quarters of the country. If no more than the Central Indian States and Hyderabad and Mysore were excluded from the Union, the United Provinces would be almost completely cut off from Bombay, and Bombay from Sind. The strategic and economic implications are obvious. India could live if its Moslem limbs in the north-west and the north-east were amputated, but could it live without its midriff?'[21] (Sardar K. M. Panikkar later remarked. 'Hindustan is the elephant . . . and Pakistan the two ears. The elephant can live without the ears.')[22]

The easiest way to destroy India was to encourage the Indian states to become independent or to accede to Pakistan. Jinnah knew this full well. So did Conrad Corfield, the anti-Indian head of the Political Department of the government of India in 1947. And so Jinnah began to tempt Jodhpur, Bikaner, Jaisalmer, Hyderabad, and even far-off Travancore to become independent or to accede to Pakistan.

No sooner did Congress leaders learn of Jinnah's moves than they concentrated all their efforts on defeating him in his own game. Jinnah found more than a match in Sardar Patel. It was no treachery or duplicity. It was a simple game of power politics in which the Sardar defeated the Qaid-e-Azam by his firm and tactful handling of the problem of the Indian states. Before 15 August 1947 he persuaded almost all the rulers to accede to the Dominion of India. The notable exceptions were Hyderabad, Kashmir and Junagarh. Every schoolboy knows how they, too, later on acceded to India. What India lost by way of Pakistan, she more than made up by the accession of the states.

When Sardar Patel was born in 1875 the whole country was agog with the problem of one state: Gaikwar Malharrao of Baroda had tried to poison his Resident and the British government had instituted an inquiry against him. The strongest supporters of the Gaikwar were to be found in Poona, Calcutta and Madras. Today there is no problem of the states. And those who were born after 1947-8 would hardly imagine what a difficult and complex problem it was. For this happy situation our thanks are due largely to Sardar Patel.

But while we rightly pay tribute to Sardar Vallabhbhai Patel, who by his firm and tactful handling of the problem succeeded in integrating the Indian states and consolidating the unity of our country, we must not forget the help given by Lord Mountbatten. You probably know how when Bikaner was vacillating in 1947, it was Mountbatten who steadied him. You may have also read about the prime minister of a state coming to Mountbatten with the excuse that his master was away and he had no means of knowing what he would like to do, and Mountbatten took up a glass paper-weight and after a few seconds of crystal-gazing told the prime minister that his master wanted him to join the Dominion of India.[23]

Nor should we, while paying our tribute to the great Sardar, forget to commend the patriotism and self-sacrifice of many of our Indian princes. It is not easy to part with property and status. When Jinnah signed on a piece of paper and handed it over to the rulers of Jodhpur, Bikaner and Jaisalmer to write whatever conditions they wanted to write on it, it was the young ruler of Jaisalmer who refused to be fooled by Jinnah.[24] Similarly, when in June-July 1947 the Nawab of Bhopal was playing his tricks and creating confusion all around, it was the enlightened leadership provided by Baroda, Bikaner and Patiala which tilted the balance in favour of the states joining the Dominion of India by signing instruments of accession (in regard to defence, foreign affairs and communications).[25] The world is full of emigres working against their own countries. Not one Indian ruler really turned traitor and tried to harm his country.

13

THE DEVELOPMENT OF THE INDIAN OUTLOOK ON WORLD AFFAIRS BEFORE 1947

Indian Interest in World Affairs before 1914
Eighteenth-century India was, by and large, isolationist and inward-looking. It was the establishment of British rule and the spread of English education which broke her isolation and turned her eyes outward again. The beginning of this change in the Indian outlook is vividly illustrated in the career of Raja Rammohun Roy (1772-1833) who is well known as 'the first modern Indian'. Unlike the vast majority of his countrymen who lived, to use an Indian expression, the life of a frog in the well, Roy was, through his close contact with Englishmen and his knowledge of the English language, stimulated to take a keen interest in political developments all over the world. It would be worth while to give here a few instances of Roy's wide outlook and cosmopolitan sympathies. When the news reached India that the people of Naples after extorting a constitution from their despotic king were crushed back into servitude by the Austrian troops, Roy felt it so keenly that he wrote to his friend James Silk Buckingham, the editor of the *Calcutta Journal*, on 11 August 1821: 'From the late unhappy news I am obliged to conclude that I shall not live to see liberty universally restored to the nations of Europe, and Asiatic nations, especially those that are European colonies, possessed of a greater degree of the same blessing than what they now enjoy. Under these circumstances I consider the cause of the Neapolitans as my own, and their enemies as ours. Enemies to liberty and friends of despotism have never been and never will be ultimately successful.'[1]

The woes of Ireland evoked Roy's sympathy and in October

1822 he wrote an article on 'Ireland, the Causes of Its Distress and Discontents' in which he dwelt on the evils of absentee landlordism and the injustice of maintaining Protestant clergymen out of the revenues wrung from the Irish Catholics.[2] On receipt of the news of the successful rising of the Spanish colonies in South America in 1823, he celebrated the event by illuminations and by giving a public dinner in Calcutta.[3] Roy's interest in Unitarian Christianity led him into correspondence with several of its votaries in England and America. In a letter, dated 2 February 1824, to the Reverend Henry Ware, Unitarian minister of Harvard College, Cambridge, Massachusetts, he expressed his fervent desire for the maintenance of American federal unity—'for what I cannot but deem essential to its prosperity—the perpetual union of all the States under one general government'.[4] When he learnt of the July (1830) Revolution in France, 'so great was his enthusiasm that he could think and talk of nothing else'.[5] On his epoch-making voyage to England[6] (November 1830-April 1831), when his boat touched the Cape of Good Hope, though seriously injured and made lame by an accident, Roy insisted on being carried to the two French frigates which were lying in Table Bay and over whose decks he saw the glorious tricolour flying so that he might he able to do homage to the revolutionary flag, and as he left the frigates he shouted, 'Glory, glory, glory to France'.[7]

While in England (1831-33), Roy became so anxious about the fate of the Reform Bill then hanging in the balance in Parliament that he publicly avowed that in the event of the Bill being defeated, he would renounce his connexion with England and transfer himself and his allegiance to the United States.[8] He viewed the struggle between the reformers and the anti-reformers as one 'between liberty and oppression throughout the world; between justice and injustice; and between right and wrong'.[9] When the Reform Bill finally passed the Lords in June 1832, his delight knew no bounds and he wrote to his English friend William Rathbone, 'Thank Heaven, I can now feel proud of being one of your fellow subjects, and heartily rejoice that I have the infinite happiness of witnessing the salvation of the nation, nay, of the whole world.'[10]

Towards the end of 1832 Roy realized his long-cherished desire of visiting France. Before making the visit, however, he was informed that he could not set his foot on French territory without previously obtaining an express permission from the French ambassador in London. This provoked Roy to write a most remarkable letter to the foreign minister of France in which he said: 'Such a regulation is quite unknown even among the Nations of Asia (though extremely hostile to each other from religious prejudices and political dissensions), with the exception of China, a country noted for its extreme jealousy of foreigners and apprehensions of the introduction of new customs and ideas. I am, therefore, quite at a loss to conceive how it should exist among a people so famed as the French are for courtesy and liberality in all other matters. It is now generally admitted that not religion only but unbiassed common sense as well as the accurate deductions of scientific research lead to the conclusion that all mankind are one great family of which numerous nations and tribes existing are only various branches. Hence enlightened men in all countries feel a wish to encourage and facilitate human intercourse in every manner by removing as far as possible all impediments to it in order to promote the reciprocal advantage and enjoyment of the whole human race.'[11] In the same letter Roy advocated the establishment of a 'Congress' to which 'all matters of difference, whether political or commercial, affecting the Natives of any two civilized countries' might be submitted and 'settled amicably and justly to the satisfaction of both and profound peace and friendly feelings might be preserved between them from generation to generation'.[12]

Roy was in many ways an extraordinary man, but, as students of modern Indian history know, his cosmopolitan interests and sympathies were by no means untypical of 'Young Bengal' which had already in his own lifetime, and largely as a result of his efforts to promote English education, come into existence. With the rapid advance of English education all over India in the nineteenth century, with the development of a free press, and with increased communication with Europe, a steadily growing number of Indians acquired knowledge of and interest in the outside world. For long the eyes of the world had turned to India, now the eyes of India were turned to the world.

The first and foremost interest of Indians in the nineteenth century was in the country of their new rulers. Eagerly they sought knowledge of English history, literature, law, and economic and political institutions. Anxiously they watched the progress of events and ideas in England. The vicissitudes of political parties and the gradual extension of political liberties at 'home', the resistance to English rule in Ireland, the progress of the white colonies, England's doings in Europe, Asia and Africa—all engrossed their attention. England became an obsession with educated Indians, whether they liked her or not. Most Indians knew no other modern foreign language but English. Their knowledge of foreign countries was through English. Most of the news which they got of the wide world came to them via England—through the English press, through Reuter or through their London-based correspondents. They had few independent sources of information of their own. English thus became India's only window on the world. This was a fact of great consequence. The nascent Indian outlook on world affairs was in a subtle but profound way influenced by the English. For example, the Indian admiration for the French revolutionary tradition was tempered by the English criticism of it, their knowledge of European history and politics was confined to what was available in the English language, and they looked on Russia for a long time through English spectacles. True, the sources of information available in English were vast and varied, but the language through which Indians imbibed their ideas could not fail to colour their thoughts. True also, that England spoke in many voices, but it was the voice of English radicalism which appealed to Indians generally, and for all its radicalism it was basically English. Alike in their appreciation and criticism of men and events, Indians tended to follow the English. Not only did they absorb English standards and values, in their approach to problems, in their method of work and in their style of expression, they, consciously or unconsciously, imitated Englishmen. Even at the meetings of the committee of the League against Imperialism at Brussels in 1927, Jawaharlal Nehru usually found himself on the side of 'the Anglo-American members' on matters of argument, for, as he wrote: 'There was a certain similarity in our outlook in regard to method at least.'[13] And after his first interview in 1953 with the then secretary-general of the external affairs ministry in New Delhi, the late Sir Girja Shankar Bajpai, Adlai Stevenson exclaimed: 'I closed my eyes and it could have been Anthony Eden! The very same words, the very same way of approaching the problem!'[14]

Next only in importance to their interest in England was the interest of educated Indians in Europe. France, 'liberty-loving and liberty-giving', 'the traditional enemy of England', attracted their attention. Most Indian students and visitors to England made it a point to take a trip to France. Filled with ardent aspirations for the ultimate freedom and unity of their own country, Indian nationalists naturally admired the movements for national unification in Italy and Germany. Mazzini and Garibaldi were the heroes of 'Young India'. More than the work of Bismarck in Germany, it was the work of German scholars in Indian literature and philosophy which won admiration in India. 'The nations struggling to be free' in eastern Europe evoked sympathetic references in the Indian press. The Russia of the Tsars, 'barbaric and despotic', menacingly advancing towards the frontiers of India, was disliked, though her treatment of subject races, especially as regards social relations and employment in high offices, was often favourably compared with that of England. Turkey as an Asiatic power commanded the respect and sympathy of most Indians, educated or uneducated, Muslim or Hindu, though she was not very popular with the intellectuals of the latter community brought up on the pure milk of Gladstonian liberalism. The news of the Russo-Turkish war in 1877-8 created a stir in the *bazaars* of India. 'All our native subjects,' wrote the viceroy, Lord Lytton, 'from the highest to the lowest and without distinction of creed, have for the last six months, been watching with an interest which is, my most experienced officers and advisers assure me, quite unprecedented,—the process of the Russo-Turkish war...'[15] In 1897 the demonstrative enthusiasm of the Indian Muslims for the Sultan of Turkey and their severe condemnation of Britain for her pro-Greek attitude in the Greco-Turkish war gave the authorities in India grave cause for anxiety.[16]

The United States of America was too distant and known for long mainly through books, but as the first nation in modern times to have revolted successfully against British imperial power she had great attraction for educated Indians. Every schoolboy in India was familiar with the story of the Boston Tea Party and with the names of Washington, Jefferson and Lincoln. American missionaries such as C.H.A. Dall and R.A. Hume earned respect for themselves and their country in India by sympathizing with Indian political aspirations. The American Theosophist leader

Col. H.S. Olcott identified himself so completely with India that he came to be venerated almost like a Hindu *rishi*. America was known not only as the land of liberty but also as the land of enterprise and industry and from the 1880s on the Indian press repeatedly discussed the desirability of sending Indian students there for technical training. Beginning with a mere trickle in the latter half of the nineteenth century, the number of Indian visitors to America substantially increased in the first two decades of the present century, and whether they were religious leaders like P.C. Mozoomdar and Vivekanand, or politicians like B.C. Pal and Lajpat Rai, or princes like Sayajirao Gaikwar of Baroda, or industrialists like J.N. Tata, or mere students, they all felt the impact of the New World. American policy towards the Philippines was acclaimed by Indian nationalists and encouraged them to demand that Britain should pursue a similar policy in India. The cause of Indian freedom soon found American champions such as Myron H. Phelps, William J. Bryan, J.T. Sunderland and Henry Hotchner, and the growing volume of anti-British propaganda in the United States began to worry the American and British governments early in the twentieth century.[17] In 1903 the London correspondent of the *Hindu* (William Digby?) advised Indians to make 'an appeal to the United States against British Indian rule'.[18] The advice appears to have gone home, for Indian agitators soon became active in the United States, where they found a sympathetic hearing for their case against Britain, and in 1917 the veteran Indian nationalist leader Sir S. Subramania Iyer addressed a letter to president Wilson,[19] inveighing against British 'misrule and oppression in India' and expressing the hope that he would 'convert England to your ideals of world liberation'.

Nationalism and continentalism often go hand in hand. With the awareness of India came the awareness of Asia. 'Asia seems to be awaking from the sleep of ages,' wrote the *Bengalee* in 1875.[20] Appreciative references to Japan's progress began to appear in the Indian press early in the 1880s. Japan's victory over China in 1894 and that over Russia in 1905 made her the cynosure of Indian eyes. But very soon Indian enthusiasm for Japan began to cool as the realization grew that she was too intent on pursuing her own selfish ends and had no real sympathy with fellow Asians. The internal troubles of China and foreign encroachments on her soil elicited Indian sympathy. Indians, however, had little direct contact with China or first-hand information about her. Typical of their ignorance about their northern neighbour was the comment of a prominent Indian newspaper in 1900 that 'intellectually and spiritually China is the daughter of our own loved motherland'.[21] If the triumph of Japan over Russia demolished the myth of the invincible west, the adoption of a parliamentary constitution in Persia (1907), the Young Turk revolt (1908) and the establishment of the Chinese Republic (1911) demolished the myth of the unchanging east. 'It is not impossible that the twentieth century may see the complete withdrawal of Europe from Asia,'[22] remarked prophetically a famous Anglo-Indian administrator and author —Sir Alfred Lyall—shortly before his death in 1911. While these extraordinary developments in Asia were naturally greeted with enthusiasm in India—itself in political turmoil at the time—there were a few Indians who saw in them a possible threat to the security of their country in the future. 'Our real menace', wrote B.C. Pal in 1913, 'will come not from Europe but from Asia, not from Pan-Europeanism but from Pan-Islamism and Pan-Mongolianism . . . . The sixty millions of Mohomedans in India, if inspired with Pan-Islamic aspirations, joined to the Islamic principalities and powers that stand both to our West and our North-West, may easily put an end to all our nationalist aspirations, almost at any moment, if the present British connection be severed. The four hundred millions of the Chinese Empire can not only gain an easy footing in India, but once that footing is gained, they are the only people under the sun who can hold us down by sheer superior physical force. There is no other people who can do this. The awakening of China is, therefore, a very serious menace —in the present condition of our country, without an organized and trained army and a powerful navy of our own—to the maintenance of any isolated, though sovereign, independence of the Indian people.'[23]

Africa began to make news in India in the last quarter of the nineteenth century. Political developments in Egypt were closely watched by Indian nationalists. 'The scramble for Africa' among the European powers was deprecated. Indian traders became increasingly interested in East Africa. Early in the 1890s the attention of educated Indians was drawn to the maltreatment of their countrymen in South Africa. With the passage of time and the growth of national consciousness, Indian protests against racial discrimination in South Africa—and elsewhere in the British dominions and dependencies—grew in volume and intensity and became a powerful factor in their desire to break away from the British Empire.

Ties of religion had always made the Indian Muslims take a keen interest in the Muslim countries in the west. This interest was intensified by the Pan-Islam movement which began towards the end of the nineteenth century. Through its emphasis on the solidarity of Islam and opposition to western encroachments on Muslim states, Pan-Islamism came to acquire a anti-Christian and anti-imperialist character. The uncertainty about the allegiance of the Indian Muslims in case of an attack by Afghanistan, or by Russia in conjunction with Afghanistan, was always a cause of concern to the British government in India. The problem was further complicated by the presence of 300,000 unruly Pathans on the north-western frontier. Hence the increased necessity of maintaining friendly relations with Afghanistan. One of the main considerations which had made the Indian Muslims loyal to the British Raj was that the latter was friendly towards the Muslim states, especially towards Turkey, whose Sultan was the Caliph of Isam and as such enjoyed their deep reverence. The Indian Muslims had ever since the days of Gladstone hated the Liberal party in England for its anti-Turkish bias. They were seriously disturbed when that party came into power at the end of 1905. The foreign policy of Sir Edward Grey soon confirmed their worst apprehensions. They frankly disliked the Anglo-Russian Convention of 1907, for it disturbed their traditional belief that Russia was the enemy and Turkey the friend of Britain. In 1911, when Italy went to war with Turkey over Tripoli and Britain remained neutral, the Muslims in India felt aggrieved. They desired that in defence to the religious susceptibilities of her seventy million Muslim subjects in India Britain should have supported Turkey. Early in 1912 Russia, now the friend of Britain, perpetrated massacres in Persia. The event shocked the Muslims in India and the cry of 'Islam in danger' was raised.

The Balkan Wars in 1912-13 caused widespread anxiety amongst the Indian Muslims. Following upon the conquest of Morocco by France, the seizure of Bosnia-Herzegovina by Austria, the declaration of independence by Bulgaria and the Italian brigandage in Tripoli, the Balkan Wars confirmed them in their belief that there was a sinister conspiracy amongst the western countries to dismember and swallow Turkey. The sentiment of cohesion, always strong amongst the Muslims, blazed into a rapid flame. The Balkan Wars came to be regarded as 'a struggle between the Cross and the Crescent',[24] 'the ultimatum of Europe's temporal aggression'.[25] Poets and writers, religious and political leaders vied with one another in arousing sympathy for the cause of Turkey and Islam. Funds were raised to support Turkey and prayers were offered in mosques for her success. A medical mission, led by Dr M.A. Ansari, was dispatched to her aid in December 1912. In the summer of 1913, the Pan-Islamists in India founded an organization called the Anjuman-i-Khuddam-i-Kaaba, whose members took an oath to sacrifice life and property in defence of the holy shrine against non-Muslim aggressors. Its secretary, Shaukat Ali, also planned to send volunteers to fight for Turkey. Muslim loyalty to the British Raj was severely strained when Turkey joined the war against the Allies in November 1914, and it was in order to steady Muslim opinion in India that the British government was forced to give public assurances about the future of the Caliphate and the Turkish empire, which the Indian Muslims later accused it of dishonouring.

While the press in India—both Indian and Anglo-Indian—generally devoted a good deal of space to foreign news and comments thereon and educated Indians formed their own views on foreign affairs through their study of newspapers, periodicals and books, and, in some cases, through travel abroad, the Indian National Congress did not, until towards the end of the First World War, attempt to focus these views. The reasons for this apparent lapse on the part of the premier national organization in India are not difficult to understand. During the first thirty-five years or so of its existence, the Congress conceived its role to be merely that of a friendly critic of the British administration in India. It confined its attention almost exclusively to the questions of internal politics. It aimed at the ultimate achievement of self-government for India on the dominion model within the British Empire, which naturally excluded the conduct of foreign policy. If the proceedings of the Congress before 1918 were almost barren of pronouncements on international affairs, it was not—as is sometimes suggested—because Congressmen took no interest in the world outside or that their energies were wholly absorbed by the nationalist struggle, but because the Congress did not yet think that international affairs fell within its purview. There were only two subjects not strictly related to internal politics which attracted the attention of the Congress during this early period: the expeditions undertaken by the British beyond India's borders and the anti-Asiatic legislation passed by some of the British dominions. But the Congress condemned the first mainly on the ground that they tended to swell the already huge military expenditure incurred by the government of India. The second affected people of Indian origin and the status of Indians as equal subjects of the Empire and was, therefore, a matter of legitimate concern to the Congress.

The First World War and After

The First World War further stimulated Indian interest in world affairs. There was widespread sympathy in India for the cause for which the Allies were fighting. The dispatch of Indian troops to the western front was welcomed as affording Indians an opportunity to play their part on a wider stage. The events of the war and the new ideas to which it gave birth could not fail to affect India profoundly. India's loyal and generous response and her immense contributions in men, money and munitions to the war effort earned for her from a grateful British government the promise of ultimate 'responsible government' and dominion status within the Empire. She was represented at the Imperial War Cabinet and the Imperial War Conferences of 1917-18. At the conclusion of the war, India, like the dominions, signed the Peace treaties and was represented at the League of Nations in her own right. India's membership of the Imperial Conference and of the League of Nations gave her prestige, collective self-esteem and moral influence. It enabled her to know the world and to be known in turn. It gave at least a few Indians the opportunity of familiarizing themselves with the wider international problems and co-operating in their solution, and of establishing personal contacts with representatives of other countries. The knowledge and experience thus gained stood India in good stead when she became independent. But the rise in India's status in the intra-Commonwealth and international spheres, though highly significant and valuable for India in many ways, was in a certain sense unreal. The government of India, even after the reforms of 1919, continued to remain responsible to the British government and Parliament. Foreign affairs were never allowed to be debated in the Indian legislature. The viceroy of India, as an agent of the British government, retained exclusive control of India's foreign relations. Indian delegates to the Imperial Conference and to the League of Nations and other international organizations were nominated by the secretary of state in consultation with the government of India, and their briefs were prepared in London. Though in private the government of India, being geographically differently situated and subject to different local pressures, did not always see eye to eye with the home government on matters of foreign policy, it could not, constitutionally, have a separate foreign policy of its own, much less avow it publicly. In 1922, for example, when the secretary of state for India, E.S. Montagu—giving a rather exaggerated importance to India's new status—published the telegram of the government of India containing the latter's views on the proposed treaty with Turkey, which were at variance with those of the home government, he was forced to resign and Lord Curzon, as foreign secretary, dismissed the government of India as 'a subordinate branch of the British Government 6,000 miles away'.[26]

It was hardly to be expected that a growing self-conscious and self-assertive Indian nationalism would for long acquiesce in British foreign policy. In the years following the end of the First World War a marked cleavage occurred between British foreign policy and the nascent Indian outlook on world affairs. This was aided by two factors: an acute dissatisfaction in India with the constitutional reforms granted in 1919; and a growing realization in India that British foreign policy was reactionary and interventionist, as witnessed in Britain's dealings with the Middle East, the Soviet Union and China.

The Montagu-Chelmsford reforms of 1919 disappointed Indians. They considered them to be an inadequate recompense for India's sacrifices during the war and a breach of earlier British promises about granting India self-government. To this was added the bitterness caused by certain unfortunate occurrences in India immediately after the war, especially the notorious Amritsar massacre. The memory of these unhappy days was to be an important factor in determining the attitude of Indian nationalists when the Second World War came twenty years later.

Soon after the First World War, the policy of the Allies towards the defeated Turkish empire created consternation amongst the Muslims in India and gave rise to the Caliphate movement. Inspired by Pan-Islamic sentiments and obviously concerned with the future of the Caliphate, the movement had a political aspect inasmuch as it opposed the extension of western (non-Muslim) influence over the Middle East. Indian troops, of which the Muslims formed a fair portion, had taken a prominent part in the Middle Eastern campaigns during the war. There was a feeling of guilt and shame and anger in numerous Muslims hearts in India when they reflected on how their men and money had gone to bring about the dismemberment of the Caliph's empire and the extension of western influence over their co-religionists. They accused Lloyd George of breach of faith and were loud in their condemnation of Britain and France. Silly as it was in parts, the Caliphate movement was the first conscious linking-up of Indian nationalist struggle (for Gandhi associated the Congress with it) with international events. It created serious difficulties for the British government in India and the Foreign Office in London. Its supporters declared that they could not give their loyalty to a government which was inimical to Islam or Islamic countries. They asserted that the British Empire was as much Muslim as British and that its foreign policy could not be dictated merely by the governing classes of British birth and Christian faith. They claimed that the interests and sentiments of the seventy million Muslims of India were as much entitled to be heard as those of any other part of the Empire. The demand of the Indian Muslims for a revision of the treaty with Turkey, however unreasonable, could not be neglected with impunity. In September 1922, when the British government threatened to go to war with Turkey over the Chanak incident, it was warned by the viceroy that in any such contingency India would be 'ungovernable'.[27] The government of India, voicing the demands of its Muslims, also influenced considerably the making of the final settlement with Turkey at Lausanne in July 1923.[28] Fortunately for the British, Kemal Pasha abolished the Sultanate in 1922 and the Caliphate in 1924 and thereby dealt a *coup de grace* to the Caliphate agitation in India.

Pan-Asianism

The Muslim emphasis on Pan-Islamism was both suspect and

unsatisfactory to many Hindus. Their vision soared higher and embraced the idea of Pan-Asianism. Historians had already discovered 'the Greater India' that existed in the remote past. That Islam or Buddhism was the religion of most Asians seemed to provide the cultural links. And, above all, there was the fact of western dominance over Asia. Year after year the Indian National Congress conveyed its sympathies to other Asian countries struggling against western imperialism and emphasized the need for developing closer contacts with their peoples and the establishment of 'a Pan-Asiatic Federation'.[29] Little, however, was done to give effect to these oft-pronounced sentiments, besides meeting in an occasional conference, the most impressive being the Asian Relations Conference organized by the Indian Council of World Affairs in New Delhi in March 1947, which only served to reveal the immense difficulties of promoting an Asian federation.

The sentiment of Pan-Asianism increased Indian interest in China, more so as their disillusionment with Japan grew. China, like India, had a rich ancient civilizaion, to which India had in part contributed through her gift of Buddhism. She, too, was engaged in a struggle to throw off foreign yoke and achieve national freedom and unity. A resurgent India was, therefore, naturally drawn to a resurgent China. To the attraction of old China as the land of Fa-Hien and Yuan Chwang[30] was added the attraction of new China as the land of Sun Yat Sen. And many Indian nationalists looked forward hopefully to the day when the two largest and most populous countries of Asia would be free and co-operate with each other in shaping the history of the world. Geography had been a traditional barrier to enmity between the two neighbours and history provided inducement to their future friendship. Meeting together, probably for the first time, at the Brussels Congress against Imperialism in February 1927, Indian and Chinese nationalists issued a joint declaration which recalled 'the most intimate cultural ties' which had, before the establishment of British rule in India, united the people of India and China 'for more than three thousand years' and stressed the need to revive them.[31] It condemned the British use of 'Indian mercenary troops' in China and expressed the hope 'that the leaders of the Indian movement will do all in their power to co-ordinate their struggle with that of the Chinese people so that by simultaneously engaging British imperialism on two of its most vital fronts, China may receive active support in her present struggle and the final victory of both peoples may be secured'.[32] The Brussels joint declaration inaugurated a new era of Sino-Indian friendship—later summed up in the slogan 'Hindi-Chini Bhai Bhai'—which was brought to a tragic termination in 1962 by the Chinese invasion of India.

Indian Pacifism

A certain pacifism and quietism have perhaps been traditional to Hinduism. Gandhi's personality and his creed of non-violence did much to re-emphasize them. Gandhi also brought into special prominence the humanitarian and universal ideal which had inspired the Indian nationalist movement from the very beginning. Besides, a revived interest in ancient Hindu ideals made most educated Indians prone to speak of the new message of peace and spiritualism that India could deliver to a world given to the worship of false gods. Wholly ignorant of the realities of power politics, having no lot or part in the responsible administration of their country, with defence and foreign policy a sealed book to the highest in the land, preoccupied with the nationalist struggle, and with only a superficial knowledge of foreign countries, is it to be wondered that educated Indians developed an academic and ethical approach to international issues? India had enjoyed almost absolute security and peace for about a century. The much-dreaded invasion by Russia never came to pass. It was natural, therefore, for most Indians to dismiss all threats to the security of their country as imaginary. Any possible threat to India's security arose, it was instead argued, from the fact that she was being ruled by the British, who had rivals all over the world, and once India was free she would cut down her military expenditure drastically and live at peace with all her neighbours, for she had no designs on them nor did they have any on her. This tendency to treat any possible danger to India's security as wholly unreal and a bogey invented by the British to keep India perpetually in bondage was also prompted by the fact that many British politicians and publicists placed an undue emphasis on the immensity and peculiarity of the problem of Indian defence and turned it into an argument for delaying the grant of political independence to India.

Opposition to the Use of Indian Troops Abroad

Indian opposition to the frequent use of Indian troops by the British government for imperial purposes abroad became pronounced soon after the end of the First World War. In 1920 the publication of the Esher Committee Report aroused a storm of protest in India. The Esher Committee Report had not only recommended an increased control by the War Office of the Indian army with a view to having an integrated imperial defence policy and organization, it had looked forward, with unblushing frankness, to underprop British policy in the Near and the Middle East by the Indian army.[33] This provided an easy target for Indian attack. They accused the British government of attempting hegemony over the Near and the Middle East with the Indian army as its sword and buckler. They protested against the large-scale employment of Indian troops in these regions[34] as derogatory to India's position, self-respect and fair name. They demanded that Indian troops should not be used for purposes of offence and 'imperial aggrandizement'. Even the Indian Liberals,[35] generally very loyal, were heard to assert: We recognize our imperial obligations and shall not fail in our duty when actual danger threatens the British Empire, but we should be satisfied that those dangers are not of your seeking. If the United Kingdom wants to play high games of international politics, to dictate the fates of countries in Europe, to parcel out kingdoms everywhere in the world, or to create or solve problems in the Near or the Middle East, to carve out new spheres of influence, or to spread the benefits of western civilization, then we shall not encourage you by any promise of support with our manpower.

This was affirmed with full knowledge of the fact that the Indian legislature had no control over defence or foreign policy. But Indians had become very sensitive about their prestige and status[36] and were not without hope that they could exercise some influence over the Indian government. In October 1921 a manifesto, signed by forty-eight Indian leaders, was issued condemning the use of Indian soldiers 'for crushing the liberty of the Arabs, the Egyptians, the Turks and other nations who have done no harm to India'.[37] Early in 1927, when it was learnt that Indian troops had been dispatched to China, public resentment once again flared up. A protest resolution was tabled in the Indian Legislative Assembly, but it was disallowed by the viceroy. A sense of helplessness only increased the feeling of bitterness in nationalist circles.

India and the Soviet Union

The emergence of the Soviet Union was hailed with delight in India. Her early struggle against formidable odds, her liberal policy towards China and Persia, and her experiments in economic planning and social welfare evoked sympathy and admiration. Soviet methods were not always liked, nor was there any widespread approval of communism, but a growing number of young men in India were attracted to socialist thought. To ardent nationalist imagination it was tempting to accept the facile division of the world into imperialist and anti-imperialist—the former western, capitalistic, reactionary, exploitative and warlike; the latter standing for socialism, progress, national freedom and peace. Many in India and Asia had little doubt that Britain was the leader of the first group and the Soviet Union of the second. The frankly opportunist policy pursued by the Soviet Union in the early years of the Second World War, however, caused serious disillusionment in India, and the Indian communists by supporting the British government in India during the war discredited not only themselves but also the Soviet Union, whose orders they had blindly followed, in the eyes of Indian nationalists.

India and the United States

American prestige in India probably stood at its highest during the Wilsonian era. But then it suffered a sharp decline. This was due to several reasons. Indians considered American isolationism to be a serious dereliction of duty and rather selfish. As the richest capitalist country in the world, America was already in the eyes of many Indians the symbol of 'the materialist west'. Some of the emotional antipathy of Indians to the west because of colonialism was also gradually transferred to the United States. The increasing tendency of Indian intellectuals to view the world in Marxist terms made them look upon the United States as an incipient imperialist power. This was reinforced by the latter's delay in granting independence to the Philippines and her attempts to dominate Latin America. The negro problem in the United States was regarded by Indians—highly sensitive to any form of racial discrimination—as a continuing reproach to American professions of democracy and equality. Indian efforts to secure American sympathy for their cause did not prove to be much of a success. The Indian press bewailed the death of Wilsonian idealism in the United States. In 1927 an American woman, Katherine Mayo, published a book entitled *Mother India*, containing scurrilous remarks about Indians, which caused widespread resentment in India and provoked angry and bitter rejoinders such as K.L. Gauba's *Uncle Sham* (1929).

It was not until the coming of the Second World War that the Indian image of the United States brightened again. The inspiring leadership of president Roosevelt aroused fresh hopes in India. 'India is far from America,' wrote Nehru in an article published in the *Atlantic Monthly* in April 1940, 'but more and more our thoughts go to this great democratic country, which seems, almost alone, to keep the torch of democratic freedom alight in the world given over to imperialism and fascism, violence and aggression, and opportunism of the worst type.'[38] But Indian hopes of America were raised only to be dashed to the ground again. The Atlantic Charter did not apply to India and president Roosevelt's half-hearted attempts to intercede with prime minister Churchill merely resulted in the abortive Cripps Mission of 1942. At the San Francisco Conference of the United Nations in April 1945, the open Soviet support for the independence of subject countries in Asia and Africa stood in sharp contrast with American silence on the subject. Indians noticed the contrast and drew their own conclusions from it. Nehru referred to it on 28 October 1945[39] and remarked that during the last few years there had been 'some disillusionment in India in regard to American championship of freedom'.[40] He accused American policy in regard to India of being 'strangely subservient to British policy' and added, almost in warning: 'India's reactions to other powers will be governed by their policy to India. It should be clear to anyone that India will function independently before very long and that independent India will play an important role in world events. That role will be influenced by the attitude of other powers to Indian freedom.'[41]

Nehru's Contribution

Indian pronouncements on foreign affairs in the nineteen twenties consisted largely of denunciations of British foreign policy. This was natural enough. Britain not only held India in subjection, she was the greatest imperialist power in the world. Indian opposition to British imperialism was extended from the internal to the international sphere. Indians had as yet no clear or well-defined outlook on foreign affairs, nor was there any general and sustained interest in events outside India. The Liberal party did not bother about them as its ideal was dominion status for India. The Muslim organizations watched uneasily developments in the Middle East and occasionally passed resolutions sympathizing with the Arabs in Palestine or congratulating King Amanullah of Afghanistan for his reforms. Developments in Turkey, Egypt and Iran were watched, often with apprehension, for they did not always accord with the principles of Islamic orthodoxy. Even the Congress did little beyond expressing sympathy with the movements for national freedom in Asia and uttering pious platitudes about an Asian federation.

The development of a definite Indian outlook on world affairs owed much to Jawaharlal Nehru. It was he who gradually educated his party and his people to become increasingly conscious of international developments and view their national struggle in the context of world forces. Nehru attempted to integrate the diverse strands of thought, emotion and aspiration of his countrymen into a coherent outlook on world affairs.

Nehru first made his influence felt in this matter at the Madras session of the Indian National Congress held in December 1927. He had just returned from Europe after attending the Congress against Imperialism at Brussels and a visit to the Soviet Union. At Nehru's initiative the Madras Congress passed a number of resolutions. The first declared India's goal to be the achievement of complete independence.[42] The second spoke of the danger of war and affirmed that India would not be a party to any imperialist war waged by Britain in the future.[43] The third sent greetings to the Chinese people, 'the comrades of the Indian people in their joint struggle against imperialism',[44] and assured them of India's sympathy. It also condemned the government of India for the dispatch of Indian troops to China and its refusal to allow a Congress medical mission to go to that country.

The Congress and its provincial conferences kept on reiterating for a few years the resolution of the Madras Congress on the danger of war and India's determination to keep clear of it. Its avowed purpose was twofold: to affirm that India should not be involved in any war without the consent of her people; and to warn Britain off any rash imperialist ventures. From numerous platforms Nehru incessantly preached his views to the Indian people in the subsequent years.[45] His invariable theme was as follows: We must think and act internationally. The Indian probem is a world problem. Britain's policy in China, Persia, Mesopotamia and Egypt shows conclusively that she is opposed to the freedom of nations. Imperialism is the enemy. British imperialism is the strongest and the most far-reaching, and India is its corner-stone. Many parts of Asia and Africa have suffered domination because British imperialism wanted to strengthen its hold over India. The liberation of India is an essential step in the full emancipation of the peoples of Asia and Africa. We should ally ourselves with the anti-imperialist and progressive forces of the world. We are neither against Britain nor against the British people. We are against the imperialist system. When we are free we can develop contacts with other countries, including Britain, as we like. We stand for internationalism and do not want independence in a narrow sense, but the British Empire does not stand for true international co-operation. The League of Nations has come to be dominated by the imperialist powers. India's representation at the League is a farce, for her delegates do not represent the people. Imperialism and war are concomitant phenomena and India should not allow herself to be dragged into any war waged by Britain for her imperialist interests. The problem of India's defence is magnified by the British government to keep India in subjection. There is no danger to India's security if the British withdraw. We have a large army and no dangerous enemies. Moreover, the security of a country does not depend only on its defence force but also on the international situation and the balance of power.

India and the British Policy of Appeasemen*

Nehru's frequent visits to Europe in the 'thirties enabled him to keep in close contact with the changing currents of the international situation. At his insistence the Congress established a 'Foreign Department' in 1936 to act as a liaison with the outside world. It was mainly due to him that the Congress took a vigo rous stand against imperialism, Fascism, Nazism and Japanese militarism in the years immediately preceding the outbreak of the Second World War. In 1936 the Congress condemned Italian aggression in Ethiopia and upbraided the League of Nations and the great powers for looking on with indifference.⁴⁶ Sympathy was extended to republican Spain and the British government was criticized for following a policy of non-intervention which 'in effect aided' the Fascist rebels.⁴⁷ In 1937 and 1938 the Congress condemned Japanese aggression in China, called upon the people of India to boycott Japanese goods as a mark of sympathy with the Chinese people, and decided to send a medical mission to China as a token of Indian support.⁴⁸ In 1938 the Congress stated afresh the policy of the Indian people in regard to war and foreign affairs. It condemned increasing Fascist aggressions and the British foreign policy of appeasement, and reiterated that India would not join any war without the express consent of her people.⁴⁹

It is not to be supposed that the Congress blindly followed Nehru in these declarations. There were many in the Congress—and at their head was the then president of the Congress itself, Subhas Chandra Bose—who objected to India's lining up with republican Spain, China, Ethiopia and Czechoslovakia. They doubted the wisdom of antagonizing Italy, Germany and Japan, and would have liked to treat every enemy of Britain as India's friend. In private they ridiculed Nehru's idealism and his 'theses' —as the resolutions drafted by him were called—on foreign policy. It is, however, a tribute to the good sense of the Congress and to Nehru's leadership that the detractors never dared to carry their opposition to the public.

Early in 1939 the Congress disapproved of the Munich pact, the Anglo-Italian agreement and the recognition of rebel Spain, and regretted the decline in international morality.⁵⁰ When about the middle of 1939, it came to be known that Indian troops had been dispatched to Egypt and Singapore, the Congress protested at this being done without any reference to the representatives of the people in the Indian legislature.⁵¹ Early in August 1939—three weeks before the outbreak of the war—the Congress Working Committee declared: 'In this world crisis the sympathies of the Working Committee are entirely with the people who stand for democracy and freedom and the Congress has repeatedly condemned Fascist aggression in Europe, Africa, and the Far East of Asia, as well as the betrayal of democracy by British imperialism in Czechoslovakia and Spain.'[52] But, it added: 'The past policy of the British Government, as well as the recent developments, demonstrated abundantly that this Government does not stand for freedom and democracy and may at any time betray these ideals. India cannot associate with such a Government or be asked to give her resources for democratic freedom which is denied to her and which is likely to be betrayed.'[53]

The policy of the Congress had thus come to be clearly formulated. There was, on the one hand, consistent and vigorous opposition to Fascism, Nazism and Japanese militarism; there was sympathy with the victims of aggression, a strong dislike of the policy of appeasement and a willingness to join up in any attempt to stop this aggression. On the other hand, there was a deep-seated distrust of British intentions and an emphasis on the freedom of India, both as a fundamental objective of national policy and an essential prerequisite to any wholehearted co-operation with Britain in a war. This 'dualism' the Congress could never resolve.

India and the Second World War

When Great Britain declared war on Germany on 3 September 1939, the viceroy of India declared India also be at war automatically. Constitutionally the viceroy had acted within his rights in taking this step. But his action in thus committing India to war without even the formality of consultation with Indian leaders, either in the legislature or outside, in spite of repeated assertions by them to the contrary during the past two decades, was widely resented in India. 'One man', wrote Nehru later, 'and he a foreigner and a representative of a hated system could plunge four hundred millions of human beings into war without the slightest reference to them.'[54] The neglect was treated as an insult and a humiliation and was never forgiven.

Ignoring the slight, however, for the time being, the Congress Working Committee stated on 14 September 1939: 'If the war is to defend the *status quo*, imperialist possessions, colonies, vested interests and privileges, then India can have nothing to do with it. If, however, the issue is democracy and a world order based on democracy, then India is intensely interested in it . . . . If co-operation is desired in a worthy cause, this cannot be obtained by compulsion and imposition....A free democratic India will gladly associate herself with other free nations for mutual defence.. [but] co-operation must be between equals and by mutual consent for a cause which both consider to be worthy...their sympathy is entirely on the side of democracy and freedom. But India cannot associate herself in a war said to be for democratic freedom when that very freedom is denied to her....The Working Committee, therefore, invite the British Government to declare in unequivocal terms what their war aims are in regard to democracy and imperialism and the new order that is envisaged, in particular how these aims are going to apply to India and to be given effect to in the present.'[55]

Briefly stated, the Congress stand, which became clearer later on, was: India is prepared to co-operate wholeheartedly in a war for democracy and freedom but only as a free nation, and for this substantial power must be transferred at once to Indian hands and definite assurances given about the future.

It was not easy for the Congress to make this gesture. Many people in India had insufficient appreciation of the international issues involved in the war. There was division even amongst the Congress ranks. For a nationalist organization, with its long history of distrust of and opposition to British rule and with its creed of non-violence, it was undoubtedly a bold move to take such a clear and definite stand on an international issue involving active co-operation in war with an alien government. The fact, however, that the Congress attitude towards the war had necessarily to be defined in the light of the past and the present policy of the British government in India brought with it its inevitable limitations and contradictions.

The viceroy offered to include more Indians in his executive council but dismissed the Congress demand for an immediate transfer of substantial power as impracticable. About the future, he expressed willingness to consult with the communities, political parties and princes at the end of the war with a view to making modifications in the 1935 Act. The Congress considered the response to be inadequate and disappointing, called upon its ministries in the provinces to resign and decided not to have anything to do with the war.

The Congress repeated its conditional offer many a time in subsequent years. British responses were increasingly bolder and more reassuring, but they, in their turn, were circumscribed by the exigencies of the war and the basic difficulties of the Indian political problem, especially the need to take into account the views and the interests of the Muslims and the princes. The result was that the gap remained and the Congress non-co-operated.

India and the Post-War World

Hardly had the war ended when the rift between the wartime allies became visible. The shadow of the future cold war worried India's future prime minister. From his prison cell in 1944 he tried to peer into the future of world affairs and wrote: 'Much will inevitably depend on American and Soviet policy and on the degree of co-ordination or conflict between the two and Britain. Everybody talks loudly about the necessity for the Big Three to pull together in the interests of world peace and co-operation, yet rifts and differences peep out at every stage, even during the course of the war. Whatever the future may hold, it is clear that the economy of the U.S.A. after the war will be powerfully expansionist and almost explosive in its consequences. Will this lead to some new kind of imperialism? It would be yet another tragedy if it did so for America has the power and opportunity to set the pace for the future. The future policy of the Soviet Union is yet shrouded in mystery, but there have been some revealing glimpses of it already. It aims at having as many friendly dependent or semi-dependent countries near its borders as possible. Though working with other powers for the establishment of some world organization, it relies more on building up its own strength on an unassailable basis. So, presumably, do other nations also, in so far as they can. That is not a hopeful prelude to world co-operation. Between the Soviet Union and other countries there is not the same struggle for export markets as between Britain and the U.S.A. But the differences are deeper, their respective viewpoints further apart, and mutual suspicions have not been allayed even by joint effort in the war. If these differences grow, the U.S.A. and Britain will tend to seek each other's company and support as against the U.S.S.R. group of nations.'[56] But for Nehru the more immediate and important issue was: 'Where do the hundreds of millions of Asia and Africa come in this picture?... For them, inevitably, the test of each move or happening is this: Does it help towards our liberation? Does it end the dominion of one country over another? Will it enable us to live freely the life of our choice in co-operation with others? Does it bring equality and equal opportunity for nations as well as groups within each nation? Does it hold forth the promise of an early liquidation of poverty and illiteracy and bring better living conditions?'[57]

In a broadcast to his people on 7 September 1946,[58] as vice-president of and member for external affairs and Commonwealth relations in the interim national government, Nehru laid down the basic principles of India's future foreign policy which faithfully reflected the Indian outlook on world affairs as it had evolved over the years. They were: close co-operation with other nations in the furtherance of world peace and freedom 'as a free nation with our own policy and not merely as a satellite of another nation'; non-alignment with power blocs, 'which have led in the past to world wars and which may again lead to disasters on an even vaster scale'; 'the emancipation of colonial and dependent countries and peoples'; the repudiation of racialism; 'in spite of our past history of conflicts... friendly and co-operative relations with England and the countries of the British Commonwealth'; friendship with 'the people of the United States of America to whom destiny has given a major role in international affairs' and with 'that other great nation of the modern world, the Soviet Union, which also carries a vast responsibility for shaping world events', especially close ties with the countries of Asia, notably with China, 'our friend through the ages'; and the long-range goal of 'a world commonwealth'.

Some Concluding Reflections

This brief historical survey may well serve to reveal the main factors which determined the Indian approach to world affairs before 1947. During the long period of British rule Indians were subjected to influences and acquired their own images of foreign countries which could not fail to affect them profoundly. As opposition to the alien government developed strength, it was extended from the internal to the international sphere and anti-imperialism came to be its keynote. The fact of western dominance over Asia reinforced personal experience and made imperialism synonymous with the west for them. That a feeling of sympathy and solidarity should develop amongst the dominated was natural.

This was encouraged by the ties of religion and culture. Foreign domination also indirectly contributed to the absence of any legacy of conflict and vested interests between Asians themselves. Experiences of racial exclusivism at home and abroad rankled and, added to the humiliation and bitterness occasioned by foreign rule, made Indians sensitive about equality of status. The security against outside aggression provided for by British rule made Indians look on potential dangers as non-existent. Russia became covered with the glories of socialism and anti-imperialism and China was looked upon as the land of Fa-Hien and Yuan Chwang. The merits of British foreign policy were taken for granted or minimized, its drawbacks were exaggerated and resented. A habit of virtuous deprecation, which comes easy to distant onlookers, became common. The idealism generated by the nationalist movement and, especially, the influence of Gandhi are clearly visible. Above all, there is the imprint of the personality of Nehru—the man who did most to mould the outlook of his people on foreign affairs.

Differences in geographical situation, racial origins and cultural background alone would have made the foreign policy of independent India diverge from that of the countries belonging to what is generally known as 'the western bloc'. Their utterly different experiences in the recent past served to accentuate the divergence. The policy of promoting regional defence agreements which the leading western powers adopted in the post-war period was, to no small extent, dictated by their bitter experience in the 'thirties, by the memory of the well-nigh disastrous consequences of appeasement, and by their determination that the mistake should not be repeated and the aggressor never again allowed to pick off its victims one by one. The Indian people and their leaders had, fortunately, had no such experience. The dominant element in their recent experience had been the prolonged struggle for freedom from British rule, and the immense and arduous task of national reconstruction awaited them immediately after gaining independence. They, therefore, thought less of the risks of Communist aggression than of the evils of colonialism and naturally attached more importance to the raising of living standards, which could bring security within, than to military alliances, intended to bring security without. Moreover, they were inspired by the conviction that India, after coming to her own would have a distinct contribution to make to world problems. For long years Indians had been mere passive spectators of events, the playthings of others. They were anxious to make the history of their choice and they believed that this could not be done either in isolation or in an exclusive alliance.

BIOGRAPHICAL NOTES

ABDULLAH, SHEIKH MOHAMMAD (1905-   ). Organized National Conference in Kashmir 1938; president of All-India States' People's Conference 1946; prime (later chief) minister of Jammu and Kashmir 1948-53, 1975- .
ALI, MUHAMMAD (1878-1931). Journalist and politician; prominent Khilafat leader; president of Indian National Congress 1923.
ALI, RAHMAT (1897-1951). Author and politician.
ALI, SHAUKAT (1873-1938). Prominent Muslim League and Khilafat leader.
ANDREWS, C.F. (1871-1940). Joined Cambridge brotherhood in Delhi 1904; teacher, author and social reformer.
ARUNDALE, G.S. (1878-1945). Author and teacher; prominent Theosophist.
ATTLEE, C.R., FIRST EARL (1883-1967). Labour M. P. 1922-55; undersecretary for war 1924; member of Indian statutory commission 1927-30; prime minister of Britain 1945-51.
AUCKLAND, FIRST EARL OF (GEORGE EDEN) (1784-1849). Governor-general of India 1836-42.
AZAD, MAULANA ABUL KALAM (1888-1958). Author, journalist and politician; president of Indian National Congress 1923, 1939-46; minister in Indian government 1947-58.
BANERJEA, SURENDRANATH (1848-1925). Entered Indian civil service 1871; dismissed from Indian civil service 1874; teacher and journalist at Calcutta; president of Indian National Congress 1895, 1902; minister in Bengal government 1921-3.
BARODA, MAHARAJA GAIKWAR OF (SAYAJI RAO) (1863-1939). Chosen to replace unsatisfactory ruling prince (Malhar Rao) 1875; invested with ruling powers 1881.
BASU, BHUPENDRANATH (1859-1924). Lawyer and politician at Calcutta; president of Indian National Congress 1914; member of secretary of state's council 1917-24.
BAYLEY, E.C. (1821-84). Joined Indian civil service 1842; served in North-Western Provinces and Panjab; foreign secretary 1862-72; member of

governor-general's council 1873-8; vice-chancellor of Calcutta university 1869-74.
BENTINCK, LORD (WILLIAM CAVENDISH) (1774-1839). Governor of Madras 1803-7; governor-general of India 1828-35.
BESANT, ANNIE (1847-1933). Theosophist, educationist and politician; came to India 1893; president of Theosophical Society 1907-33; president of Indian National Congress 1917.
BHAU DAJI (1821-74). Physician and antiquarian at Bombay.
BHOWNAGGREE, M.M. (1851-1933). Lawyer and politician; Conservative M.P. 1895-1906.
BIRKENHEAD, FIRST EARL OF (F.E. SMITH) (1872-1930). Conservative M.P. 1906-18; attorney-general 1915-19; lord chancellor 1919-22 secretary of state for India 1924-8.
BLAVATSKY, HELENA PETROVNA (1831-91). Born in Russia; became American citizen 1873; founded, with Colonel H.S. Olcott, Theosophical Society at New York 1875.
BONNERJEE, W.C. (1844-1906). Lawyer at Calcutta; president of Indian National Congress 1885, 1892; member of Bengal legislative council 1893; later settled in England.
BOSE, SUBHAS CHANDRA (1897-1945). President of Indian National Congress 1938, 1939; escaped to Germany 1942; formed Indian National Army 1943.
BRADLAUGH, CHARLES (1833-91). British freethought advocate and politician.
BRIGHT, JOHN (1811-89). Liberal statesman.
BUCKINGHAM, JAMES SILK (1786-1855). Journalist; deported from India 1823; M.P. 1832-7.
BURKE, EDMUND (1729-97). Irish author, orator and statesman.
BUTT, ISAAC (1813-79). Irish politician; founded Home Rule Association 1870.
CANNING, EARL (CHARLES JOHN). Governor-general of India 1856-62.
CHARLU, P. ANANDA (1843-1908). Lawyer at Madras; president of Indian National Congress 1891.
CHATTERJI, BANKIMCHANDRA (1838-94). Appointed deputy magistrate in 1858 and rose to be assistant secretary to Bengal government; man of letters.
CHELMSFORD, FIRST VISCOUNT (F.J.N. THESIGER) (1868-1933). Governor of Queensland 1905-9 and of New South Wales 1909-13; governor-general of India 1916-21; first lord of admiralty 1924.
CHINTAMANI, C.Y. (1880-1941). Journalist and politician; editor of *Leader* (Allahabad); member of United Provinces legislative council 1916-23, 1927-36; minister in United Provinces government 1921-3; president of National Liberal Federation of India 1920, 1931.
CHIPLONKAR, S.H. (1851-94). Journalist and lawyer at Poona.
CHIROL, VALENTINE (1852-1929). Traveller, journalist and author; in charge of *The Times* foreign department 1896-1912; visited India seventeen times; member of commission on Indian public services 1912-14.

Biographical Notes 279

CHURCHILL, WINSTON SPENCER (1874-1965). Under-secretary for colonies 1906-8; president of board of trade 1908-10; home secretary 1910-11; first lord of admiralty 1911-15; minister of munitions 1917; secretary of state for war 1919-21; colonial secretary 1921-2; chancellor of exchequer 1924-9; first lord of admiralty 1939-40; prime minister of Britain 1940-5, 1951-5.

COLVIN, AUCKLAND (1838-1908). Entered Indian civil service 1858; comptroller-general in Egypt 1880-2; financial adviser to the Khedive 1882-3; finance member of governor-general's council 1883-7; lieutenant governor of North-Western Provinces 1887-92.

CONGREVE, RICHARD (1818-99). Positivist philosopher.

COTTON, HENRY JOHN STEDMAN (1845-1915). Entered Indian civil service 1867; chief commissioner of Assam 1896-1902; president of Indian National Congress 1904; Liberal M.P. 1906-10.

COUPLAND, REGINALD (1884-1952). Author and teacher.

CRIPPS, STAFFORD (1889-1952). Solicitor-general in Labour government 1930-1; British ambassador at Moscow 1940-2; minister of aircraft production 1942-5; president of board of trade 1945-7; chancellor of exchequer 1947-50.

CROSS, RICHARD ASSHETON, FIRST VISCOUNT (1823-1914). Conservative politician; home secretary 1885-6; secretary of state for India 1886-92; lord privy seal 1895-1900.

CURZON, GEORGE NATHANIEL, MARQUESS CURZON OF KEDLESTON (1859-1925). Under-secretary for India 1891-2; governor-general of India 1898-1905; lord president of council and member of war cabinet 1916-18; foreign secretary 1919-24.

DALHOUSIE, TENTH EARL AND FIRST MARQUESS OF (JAMES ANDREW BROUN RAMSAY) (1812-60). Governor-general of India 1848-56.

DALL, C.H.A. (1816-86). Unitarian missionary at Calcutta.

DAS, C.R. (1870-1925). Lawyer and politician at Calcutta; president of Indian National Congress 1921; formed, with Motilal Nehru, Swaraj party 1923.

DATTA, MICHAEL MADHUSUDAN (1824-73). Baptized 1843; author and lawyer.

DAYANAND (1824-84). Founder of Arya Samaj (1875).

DEY, LAL BIHARI (1824-94). Baptized 1843; teacher and journalist at Calcutta.

DIGBY, WILLIAM (1849-1904). Journalist and politician.

DOKE, JOSEPH J. (1861-1913). Baptist missionary; first biographer of Mahatma Gandhi.

DUFFERIN, FIRST MARQUESS OF (FREDERICK TEMPLE HAMILTON-TEMPLE BLACKWOOD) (1826-1902). Under-secretary for India 1864-6; governor-general of Canada 1872-8; ambassador at St. Petersburg 1879-1 and at Constantinopole 1881-2; special commissioner to Egypt 1882-3; governor-general of India 1884-8; ambassador at Rome 1889-91 and at Paris 1891-6.

DUTT, R.C. (1848-1909). Entered Indian civil service 1871; president of Indian National Congress 1899; in Baroda state service 1904-9.

DYER, REGINALD EDWARD HARRY (1864-1927). Brigadier-general; responsible for Amritsar massacre 13 April 1919.

EDEN, ASHLEY (1831-87). Joined East India Company's service 1852; secretary to Bengal government 1862-81; chief commissioner of Burma 1871-7; member of governor-general's council 1875; lieutenant-governor of Bengal 1877-82; member of secretary of state's council 1882-7.

ELGIN, NINTH EARL OF (VICTOR ALEXANDER BRUCE) (1849-1917). Governor-general of India 1894-8; colonial secretary 1905-8.

ELLENBOROUGH, FIRST EARL OF (EDWARD LAW) (1790-1871). Governor-general of India 1842-4.

GANDHI, MOHANDAS KARAMCHAND (1869-1948). Called to bar 1889; went to South Africa 1893; returned to India 1915; leading figure of Indian National Congress till his assassination.

GHOSE, AUROBINDO (1872-1950). Passed written examination for Indian civil service but did not take riding test 1890; teacher at Baroda 1893-1906; leader of Bengali extremists 1906-10; retired to Pondicherry in 1910 and devoted himself to spiritualism.

GHOSE, M.M. (1844-96). Barrister of Calcutta high court.

GHOSE, RAM GOPAL (1815-68). Merchant, author and social reformer; member of Bengal legislative council 1862-4.

GHOSE, RASH BEHARI (1845-1921). Lawyer and scholar; president of Indian National Congress 1907, 1908.

GHOSE, SHISHIR KUMAR (1840-1911). Began life as teacher but later took to journalism; proprietor and editor of *Amrita Bazar Patrika*.

GLADSTONE, W.E. (1809-98). Prime minister of Britain 1868-74, 1880-5, 1886, 1892-4.

GOKHALE, G.K. (1866-1915). Teacher and journalist at Poona; member of Bombay legislative council 1899-1901 and of imperial legislative council 1901-15; president of Indian National Congress 1905.

HAMILTON, LORD GEORGE FRANCIS (1845-1927). Conservative politician; under-secretary for India 1874-80; first lord of admiralty 1885-6, 1886-92; secretary of state for India 1895-1903.

HARDINGE, CHARLES, BARON HARDINGE OF PENSHURST (1858-1944). Entered Foreign Office 1880; assistant under-secretary of state 1903-4; ambassador at St. Petersburg 1904-6; permanent under-secretary of state 1906-10, 1916-20; governor-general of India 1910-16.

HARTINGTON, MARQUESS OF (SPENCER COMPTON CAVENDISH) (1833-1908). Chief secretary for Ireland 1870-4; secretary of state for India 1880-2; secretary of state for war 1882-5; lord president of council 1895-1903.

HASAN, SYED WAZIR (1874-1947). Lawyer and politician at Lucknow; secretary of Muslim League 1912-19; chief judge of Avadh chief court 1930-4; president of Muslim League 1936; joined Indian National Congress 1938.

HASTINGS, FIRST MARQUESS OF (FRANCIS RAWDON) (1754-1826). Goveror-general of India 1813-23.

HASTINGS, WARREN (1732-1818). Governor-general of India 1773-85.
HOARE, SAMUEL JOHN GURNEY (1880-1959). Secretary of state for India 1931-5; created Viscount Templewood 1944.
HUGHES, THOMAS (1822-96). Author; Christian Socialist; M.P. 1865-74.
HUME, ALLAN OCTAVIAN (1829-1912). Joined East India Company's service 1849; secretary to government of India 1870-9; general secretary of Indian National Congress 1885-1906; returned to Britain 1892; visited India last time 1893-4.
HUME, JOSEPH (1777-1855). In East India Company's medical and political service 1797-1807; M.P. 1812-55; leader of Radical party.
HUQ, A.K. FAZLUL (1873-1962). Lawyer and politician; member of Bengal legislative council 1913-35; founded Krishak Proja party 1927; chief minister of Bengal 1937-43; migrated to Pakistan 1947.
HYNDMAN, H. M. (1842-1921). British socialist leader.
IBRAHIM, HAFIZ MUHAMMAD (1889-1967). Lawyer and politician; minister in United Provinces government 1937-9, 1947-58 and in Indian government 1958-63; governor of Panjab 1964-6.
IQBAL, MUHAMMAD (1876-1938). Poet and philosopher; president of Muslim League 1930.
IYER, S. SUBRAMANIA (1842-1924). Lawyer and politician at Madras; member of Madras legislative council 1884-8; judge of Madras high court 1895-1907.
IYER, V. KRISHNASWAMI (1863-1911). Lawyer and politician at Madras; judge of Madras high court 1909-11; member of governor's council 1911.
JANG, SALAR (1829-83). Prime minister of Hyderabad 1853-83.
JINNAH, M.A. (1876-1948). Lawyer and politician; president of Muslim League 1916, 1920, and from 1934 until his death; governor-general of Pakistan 1947-8.
JOSHI, GANESH VASUDEV (1828-80). Lawyer and politician at Poona; founder and secretary of Poona Sarvajanik Sabha 1870-80.
KELKAR, N.C. (1872-1947). Lawyer, journalist and politician at Poona.
KHALIQUZZAMAN, CHAUDHRY (1889-1973). Lawyer and politician at Lucknow; migrated to Pakistan 1947.
KHAN, SYED AHMED (1817-98). Joined East India Company's service as clerk 1837; retired as subordinate judge 1876; founded Muhammadan Anglo-Oriental College at Aligarh 1877; member of Indian legislative council 1878-80, 1881-3; knighted 1888.
KIMBERLEY, FIRST EARL OF (JOHN WODEHOUSE) (1826-1902). Lord privy seal 1868-70; colonial secretary 1870-4, 1880-2; secretary of state for India 1882-5, 1886; foreign secretary 1894-5.
KITCHENER, HORATIO HERBERT, FIRST EARL (1850-1916). Soldier; commander-in-chief in India 1902-9; secretary of state for war 1914.
KRISHNAVARMA, SHYAMJI (1857-1930). Scholar, journalist and politician.
KRUGER, STEPHANUS JOHANNES PAULUS (1825-1904). President of Transvaal republic 1883-1900.

LANSDOWNE, FIFTH MARQUESS OF (HENRY CHARLES KEITH PETTY-FITZMAURICE) (1845-1927). Under-secretary for war 1872-4; under-secretary for India 1880; governor-general of Canada 1883-8; governor-general of India 1888-94; secretary of state for war 1895-1900; foreign secretary 1900-5.

LINLITHGOW, SECOND MARQUESS OF (VICTOR ALEXANDER JOHN HOPE) (1887-1952). Chairman of royal commission on Indian agriculture 1926-8; chairman of joint select committee on Indian constitutional reform 1933-4; governor-general of India 1936-43.

LLOYD GEORGE, DAVID (1863-1945). Liberal M.P. 1890-1945; president of board of trade 1905-8; chancellor of exchequer 1908-15; prime minister of Britain 1916-22, created earl 1945.

LYALL, ALFRED COMYN (1835-1911). Entered Indian civil service 1856; lieutenant-governor of North-Western Provinces 1882-7; member of secretary of state's council 1887-1902.

LYTTON, FIRST EARL OF (EDWARD ROBERT BULWER) (1831-91). Author and diplomatist; governor-general of India 1876-80.

MACAULAY, THOMAS BABINGTON, FIRST BARON (1800-59). Historian and jurist; secretary to board of control 1833-4; member of governor-general's council 1834-8; secretary of state for war 1839-41.

MACDONALD, J. RAMSAY (1860-1937). Labour leader and statesman; prime minister of Britain 1924, 1929-31.

MAHMUD, SYED (1889-1971). Lawyer and politician at Patna; minister in Bihar government 1937-9, 1946-52.

MALAVIYA, MADAN MOHAN (1861-1946). Lawyer and educationist; president of Indian National Congress 1909, 1918; founder and vice-chancellor of Banaras Hindu University 1919-40.

MAYO, SIXTH EARL OF (RICHARD SOUTHWELL BOURKE) (1822-72). Chief secretary for Ireland 1852-69; governor-general of India 1869-72.

MEHTA, PHEROZESHAH M. (1845-1915). Lawyer and politician; member of Bombay legislative council 1887-9, 1893-4 and of Indian legislative council 1894-6, 1898-1901; president of Indian National Congress 1890.

MENON, V.P. (1894-1966). Indian civil servant.

MINTO, FOURTH EARL OF (GILBERT JOHN MURRAY KYNYMOND ELLIOTT) (1845-1914). Governor-general of Canada 1898-1904; governor-general of India 1905-10.

MITRA, RAJENDRALAL (1824-91). Scholar; director of Wards' Institution of Calcutta 1856-60; leading member and later president of British Indian Association.

MOHANI, HASRAT (FAZL-UL-HASAN) (1877-1951). Journalist and politician at Kanpur; president of Muslim League 1921.

MONTAGU, EDWIN SAMUEL (1879-1924). Liberal M.P. 1906-22; under-secretary for India 1910-14; financial secretary to treasury 1914-16; chancellor of Duchy of Lancaster 1915; minister of munitions 1916; resigned December 1916; secretary of state for India 1917-22.

MORLEY, JOHN, VISCOUNT (1838-1923). Author and statesman; chief

Biographical Notes

secretary for Ireland 1886, 1892-5; secretary of state for India 1905-10; created viscount 1908.

MOUNTBATTEN OF BURMA, FIRST EARL (LOUIS FRANCIS ALBERT VICTOR NICHOLAS MOUNTBATTEN) (1900-   ). Chief of combined operations 1942-3; supreme Allied commander, South-East Asia 1943-6; governor-general of India 1947-8.

MOZOOMDAR, P.C. (1840-1905). Brahmo missionary.

NAIR, C. SANKARAN (1857-1934). Lawyer; president of Indian National Congress 1897; judge of Madras high court 1908-15; member of governor-general's council 1915-19 and of secretary of state's council 1920-1.

NAOROJI, DADABHAI (1828-1917). Businessman, journalist and politician; first Indian member of British Parliament 1892-5; president of Indian National Congress 1886, 1893, 1906.

NATESAN, G.A. (1873-1949). Journalist and politician at Madras.

NATH, AJODHIA (1840-92). Lawyer; member of North-Western Provinces legislative council 1886-90; joint general secretary of Indian National Congress 1889-92.

NEHRU, JAWAHARLAL (1889-1964). Man of letters and statesman; president of Indian National Congress 1929, 1936, 1937, 1946, 1951-4; prime minister of India 1947-64.

NORTHBROOK, FIRST EARL OF (THOMAS GEORGE BARING) (1826-1904). Under-secretary at India Office 1859-64, at War Office 1861, 1868, at Home Office 1864; secretary to admiralty 1866; governor-general of India 1872-6; first lord of admiralty 1880-4; special commissioner to Egypt 1884.

O'CONNELL, DANIEL (1775-1847). Irish national leader.

OLCOTT, H. S. (1832-1907). Founded, with H. P. Blavatsky, Theosophical Society 1875; arrived in India 1879.

PAL, BIPIN CHANDRA (1852-1932). Author and journalist.

PAL, KRISTODAS (1838-84). Assistant secretary and later secretary of Calcutta British Indian Association 1857-84; member of Bengal legislative council 1874-82 and of Indian legislative council 1883-4; editor of *Hindoo Patriot* 1861-84.

PANIKKAR, K. M. (1895-1963). Author, administrator and diplomatist.

PARNELL, CHARLES STEWART (1846-91). Irish national leader.

PATEL, SARDAR VALLABHBHAI (1875-1950). Lawyer and politician at Ahmedabad; president of Indian National Congress 1931; deputy prime minister of India 1947-50.

PRASAD, RAJENDRA (1884-1963). Lawyer and politician at Patna; president of Indian National Congress 1934, 1939, 1947-8; president of Indian Constituent Assembly 1946-50; president of India 1952-62.

RAI, LAJPAT (1865-1928). Author, lawyer and social reformer; president of Indian National Congress (special session at Calcutta) 1920.

RANADE, M.G. (1842-1901). Entered Bombay judicial service 1871; author and social reformer; member of Bombay legislative council 1885-7, 1891-2; judge of Bombay high court from 1893 until his death.

RAO, MADHAV (1828-91). Prime minister of Travancore 1858-72, of Indore 1873-5 and of Baroda 1875-82.

RAU, B. N. (1887-1953). Indian civil servant and jurist.
REAY, ELEVENTH BARON (DONALD JAMES MACKAY) 1839-1921). Governor of Bombay 1885-90; under-secretary of state for India 1894-5.
REDMOND, JOHN EDWARD (1856-1918). Irish political leader.
RIPON, FIRST MARQUESS OF (GEORGE FREDERICK SAMUEL ROBINSON) (1827-1909). Secretary of state for India 1866; governor-general of India 1880-4; colonial secretary 1892-5; lord privy seal 1905-8.
ROY, RAMMOHUN (1772-1833). Author, journalist and social reformer; in East India Company's service 1803-13; founded Brahmo Samaj 1828; sailed for England November 1830; died at Bristol 1833.
SEN, KESHAVACHANDRA (1838-84). Brahmo missionary.
SMUTS, JAN CHRISTIAN (1870-1950). Statesman; prime minister of South Africa 1919-24.
STRACHEY, JOHN (1823-1907). Entered Bengal civil service 1842; lieutenant-governor of North-Western Provinces 1874-6; member of governor-general's council 1876-80; member of secretary of state's council 1885-95.
TAGORE, RABINDRANATH (1861-1941). Poet and philosopher; awarded Nobel prize for literature 1913.
TATA, J.N. (1839-1904). Pioneer of Indian industries.
TELANG, K.T. (1850-93). Lawyer, author and social reformer at Bombay; member of Bombay legislative council 1886-9; judge of Bombay high court from 1889 until his death.
THIERS, LOUIS ADOLPHE (1797-1877). French statesman and historian.
THOMPSON, RIVERS (1829-90). Joined East India Company's service 1850; secretary to Bengal government 1869-75; chief commissioner of Burma 1875-8; member of governor-general's council 1878-2; lieutenant-governor of Bengal 1882-7.
TILAK, BAL GANGADHAR (1856-1920). Teacher and journalist at Poona; jailed for sedition 1897-8, 1908-14.
TREVELYAN, C. E. (1807-86). Joined East India Company's service 1826; retired as secretary to board of revenue 1838; secretary to British treasury 1840-59; governor of Madras 1859-60; finance member of governor-general's council 1863-5.
VIDYASAGAR, ISHWARCHANDRA (1820-91). Educationist and social reformer.
VIVEKANAND (NARENDRANATH DATTA) (1863-1902). Hindu missionary; disciple of Ramakrishna and founder of Ramakrishna order.
WACHA, D.E. (1844-1936). Businessman, journalist and politician; president of Indian National Congress 1901.
WAVELL, ARCHIBALD PERCIVAL, FIRST EARL (1883-1950). Commander-in-chief, Middle East 1939-41; commander-in-chief, India 1941-3; governor-general of India 1943-7.
WEBB, ALFRED JOHN (1834-1908). Irish author and politician; president of Indian National Congress 1894.

WEDDERBURN, WILLIAM (1838-1918). Entered Indian civil service 1860; judge of Bombay high court 1885; officiating chief secretary to Bombay government 1886-87; M.P. 1893-1900; president of Indian National Congress 1889, 1910.

WELLESLEY, RICHARD COLLEY, MARQUESS (1760-1842). Governor-general of India 1798-1805.

WILLINGDON, FIRST MARQUESS OF (FREEMAN FREEMAN-THOMAS) (1866-1941). Governor of Bombay 1913-18, of Madras 1919-24; governor-general of Canada 1926-30; governor-general of India 1931-6.

WOOD, CHARLES (1800-85). M.P. 1832-65; chancellor of exchequer 1846-52; president of board of control 1852-5; first lord of admiralty 1855-8; secretary of state for India 1859-66; created Viscount Halifax 1866.

YULE, GEORGE (1828-92). Businessman at Calcutta; president of Indian National Congress 1888.

ZETLAND, SECOND MARQUESS OF (LAWRENCE JOHN LUMLEY DUNDAS) (1876-1961). Governor of Bengal 1917-22; secretary of state for India 1935-40.

NOTES

CHAPTER 1

[1] J. Strachey, *India* (London, 1888), p. 5.
[2] *Ibid.*, p. 8.
[3] *Friend of India*, 22 January 1857. The term 'Anglo-Indian' is used in this chapter as a synonym for the British resident in India.
[4] See R. K. Mookerji, *The Fundamental Unity of India* (London, 1914), pp. 14 ff.
[5] *Ibid.*, pp. 70 ff.
[6] *Hindoo Patriot*, 21 May 1857.
[7] E. Bevan, *Indian Nationalism* (London, 1913), pp. 45-6.
[8] *Friend of India*, 25 January 1855.
[9] E. Arnold, *The Marquis of Dalhousie's Administration*, vol. ii (London, 1865), pp. 341-2.
[10] *Madras Times*, 29 July 1885.
[11] R. C. Dutt, *Rambles in India during Twenty-Four Years, 1871 to 1895* (Calcutta, 1895), p. 1.
[12] *Amrita Bazar Patrika*, 13 August 1880.
[13] Ripon's address to the Edinburgh Philosophical Institution, 10 November 1885, supplement to *Voice of India*, December 1885, p. v.
[14] *Indian Daily News*, 22 November 1870.
[15] C. E. Trevelyan, *On the Education of the People of India* (London, 1838), pp. 187 ff.
[16] S. R. Mehrotra, *The Emergence of the Indian National Congress* (Delhi, 1971), p. 140.
[17] W. Edwards, *Reminiscenes of a Bengal Civilian* (London, 1866), pp. 308-9.
[18] W. Knighton, *The Policy of the Future in India* (London, 1867), pp. 20-1.
[19] *Copy of Correspondence between the Government of India and the Secretary of State for India on the Subject of Act No. IX of 1878*, 'An Act for the Better Control of Publications in Oriental Languages', Parliamentary Papers, 1878, vol. lvii, C. 2040, pp. 66-7.
[20] J. R. Seeley, *The Expansion of England* (London, 1883), p. 227.
[21] *Poona Observer*, 7 December 1876.
[22] Mehrotra, *op. cit.*, pp. 201-5.
[23] *Ibid.*, pp. 168-9, 265-7, 408-9.

CHAPTER 2

[1] *Second Report from the Select Committee of the House of Lords...*, Parliamentary Papers, 1852-3, vol. xxxii, no. 627-I), p. 170.
[2] *On the Education of the People of India* (London, 1838), pp. 187 ff.
[3] *Parliamentary Papers*, 1852-3, vol. xxxii, no. 627-I, pp. 170-1.
[4] *Ibid.*, p. 171.
[5] On the growth of modern politics in India in the 19th century, see S. R. Mehrotra, *The Emergence of the Indian National Congress* (Delhi, 1971) and A. Seal, *The Emergence of Indian Nationalism* (Cambridge, 1968).
[6] 'Oriental Patriotism', *Spectator* (London), 17 June 1882.
[7] Throughout this paper the term 'Anglo-Indians' is used in its original sense of British persons residing or having resided in India.
[8] *Hindoo Patriot*, 21 May 1857.
[9] *Friend of India* (Serampore), 4 June 1857. See also the same correspondent's letter to the editor, *Hindoo Patriot*, 25 June 1857.
[10] The phrase is Lord Dufferin's. See *Statesman and Friend of India*, 31 November 1888.
[11] Speech at the sixteenth annual general meeting of the British Indian Association, Calcutta, 27 February 1868. *Englishman*, 10 March 1868. See also N. N. Ghose, *Indian Views of England: The Effects of Observation of England upon Indian Ideas and Institutions* (Calcutta, 1877), pp. 45-7.
[12] *Englishman* (Calcutta), 28 February 1870.
[13] For some interesting reflections on the 'alienation' of English-educated Indians from their society and their anxiety to mitigate it, see a speech by Madhav Rao at Madras in *Native Opinion* (Bombay), 18 May 1884.
[14] *Hindoo Patriot*, 23 October 1876.
[15] *The Fifth Report from the Select Committee on the Affairs of the East India Company, Parliamentary Papers*, 1812, vol. vii, no. 377, p. 536.
[16] *Calcutta Courier*, 25 November 1840.
[17] G. Thompson, *Addresses; Delivered at Meetings of the Native Community of Calcutta, and on Other Occasions* (Calcutta, 1843), pp. 127-8.
[18] R. Tagore, *Crisis in Civilization* (Santiniketan, 1941), p. 2.
[19] *Report of the Thirteenth Indian National Congress*, 1897, p. 15.
[20] *Bombay Times*, 13 October 1859.
[21] *Report of the Second Indian National Congress*, 1886, p. 107.
[22] Cited in J. Morley, *Recollections* (London, 1917), vol. i, p. 122.
[23] Manifesto of the Deccan Sabha, 1896, allegedly drafted by M. G. Ranade, quoted in M. R. Palande (ed.), *Source Material for a History of the Freedom Movement in India* (Collected from Bombay Government Records), vol. ii, 1885-1920 (Bombay, 1958), pp. 848-9.
[24] *Mahratta* (Poona), 4 July 1897.
[25] In 1883, Sir Courtenay P. Ilbert, the law member of the governor-general's council introduced a bill to remove certain judicial disqualifications based on race distinctions. It was vehemently opposed by the British community in India and had substantially to be withdrawn.
[26] 'The Agitation in regard to the Native Magistrate's Jurisdiction Bill', *Quarterly Journal of the Poona Sarvajanik Sabha*, April 1883, pp. 29-30.

27 *Indu Prakash*, 8 June 1883.
28 *Ibid.*, 23 July 1883.
29 *Ibid.*, 30 July 1883.
30 *Speeches of Gopal Krishna Gokhale* (Madras, 1920), p. 1006.
31 The Charter Act of 1883 (3 & 4 Will. 4, c. 85) laid down that no native of India 'shall by reason only of his religion, place of birth, descent, colour, or any of them be disabled from holding any Place, Office or Employment' under the East India Company. For the full text see R. Muir (ed.), *The Making of British India 1756-1858* (Delhi, 1971 ed.) pp. 301-4.
32 The Queen's proclamation of 1 November 1858 said, among other things, that 'so far as may be, our subjects, of whatever race or creed, be freely and impartially admitted to office in our service, the duties of which they may be qualified, by their education, ability, and integrity, duly to discharge'. For the full text see *ibid.*, pp. 381-4.
33 See R. Coupland, *India: A Re-Statement* (London, 1945), pp. 291-3.
34 *Speeches and Writings of Dadabhai Naoroji* (Madras, 1910), p. 18.
35 *Ibid.*, p. 210.
36 Cited in *Report on Native Papers Published in the Bombay Presidency*, 25 April 1885.
37 *Bombay Times*, 13 October 1859.
38 *Indian Reformer* (Serampore), 25 January 1861.
39 *Athenaeum and Daily News* (Madras), 20 August 1864.
40 B. C. Pal, *The National Congress* (Lahore, 1887), p. 9.
41 *Report of the Thirteenth Indian National Congress*, 1897, pp. 14-15.
42 *Report of the Fifteenth Indian National Congress*, 1899, p. 11.
43 Letter, dated 17 May 1888, to the editor of the Allahabad *Morning Post*, reproduced in the *Indian Mirror* (Calcutta), 23 May 1888. In a private letter to Dadabhai Naoroji, dated 12 December 1887, Hume wrote that 'though we do not thus designate them—and do not aim at any such radical separation—even in a pretty distant future—as do the Irish—after all our efforts are directed towards Home Rule [for India].' Dadabhai Naoroji Papers, Nehru Memorial Museum and Library, New Delhi.
44 See letter issued by K. P. Gadgil and G. K. Gokhale, secretaries to the Poona Congress Committee, reproduced in the *Hindu* (Madras), 6 November 1895.
45 Quoted in R. P. Masani, *Dadabhai Naoroji: The Grand Old Man of India* (London, 1939), pp. 400-1.
46 *Ibid.*, p. 401.
47 For the Indian criticism of British economic policies in India in the 19th century, see Bipan Chandra, *The Rise and Growth of Economic Nationalism in India* (New Delhi, 1966).
48 See, for example, *Amrita Bazar Patrika*, 12 January, 29 November, 20 December 1888; 10 January, 5 December 1889; 9 January, 2 October, 11, 24 December 1890.
49 See, for example, *Mahratta*, 25 April, 20, 27 June, 4 July, 12 December 1886; 4 September, 13 November, 4, 11, 25 December 1887; 29 January, 5 February, 3 June, 15 July, 19 August, 11 November 1888; 17 March, 14 April, 5 May, 6 October 1889; 5 January 1890; 15, 22, 29 November 1891.

Notes

⁵⁰ The articles are reproduced in Haridas and Uma Mukherjee, *Sri Aurobindo's Political Thought* (Calcutta, 1958), pp. 63-123, and in *Sri Aurobindo* (Sri Aurobindo Birth Centenary Library—De Luxe Edition, Pondicherry, 1972), vol. i, pp. 5-56.
⁵¹ *Sri Aurobindo*, p. 9.
⁵² *Ibid.*, p. 16.
⁵³ *Ibid.*, p. 18.
⁵⁴ *Ibid.*, p. 20.
⁵⁵ *Ibid.*, pp. 22-5.
⁵⁶ *Ibid.*, p. 15.
⁵⁷ *Ibid.*, pp. 12-13.
⁵⁸ *Ibid.*, p. 45.
⁵⁹ *Ibid.*, p. 54.
⁶⁰ *Ibid.*
⁶¹ 152 H. C. Deb. 4s., col. 844.
⁶² 161 H. C. Deb. 4s., col. 587.

CHAPTER 3

¹ Gordon Johnson, *Provincial Politics and Indian Nationalism: Bombay and the Indian National Congress 1880-1915* (Cambridge, 1973), p. 5.
² Herbert Butterfield, *History and Human Relations* (London, 1951), p. 169.
³ Hume to Ripon, 11 January 1884, Ripon Papers, British Museum, London.
⁴ *Ibid.*
⁵ S. R. Mehrotra, *The Emergence of the Indian National Congress* (Delhi, 1971), pp. 45-7.
⁶ For Hume's early career see *National Guardian*, 17 May, 7 June 1889, and William Wedderburn, *Allan Octavian Hume, C.B.* (London, 1913), pp. 3-24.
⁷ G. O. Trevelyan, *The Competition Wallah* (London, 1864), p. 288.
⁸ Hume to Northbrook, 1 August 1872, Northbrook Papers, India Office Library, London.
⁹ See, for example, *Englishman*, 2, 5, 9 December 1870, *Hindoo Patriot*, 5 December 1870, and *Pioneer*, 2, 7 December 1870.
¹⁰ *Pioneer*, 4 October 1870.
¹¹ Hume to Northbrook, 1 August 1872, Northbrook Papers.
¹² S. R. Mehrotra, *op. cit.*, p. 310.
¹³ 'I never had a son; this though I have carefully hid it for my dear old wife's sake, has been a great grief to me, and has altered the whole course of my life....' Hume to Dufferin, 28 October 1886, Dufferin Papers, India Office Library, London.
¹⁴ *Pioneer*, 16 December 1879.
¹⁵ E. J. Buck, *Simla: Past and Present* (Calcutta, 1904), p. 118.
¹⁶ Mehrotra, *op. cit.*, pp. 297-381, *passim*.

17 Ripon to Thomas Hughes, 9 January 1883, Ripon Papers.
18 Hume to S. H. Chiplonkar, 16 November 1884, Chiplonkar Papers. By courtesy of Shri S. B. Bhat of Dhulia.
19 Mehrotra, *op. cit.*, pp. 396-7.
20 *Ibid.*, pp. 397-8.
21 Ananda Charlu, 'The Indian National Congress: A Suggestive Retrospect', *Hindustan Review*, July-August 1903, p. 21.
22 *Pioneer Mail*, 7 November 1888.
23 A. O. Hume, *A Speech on the Indian National Congress: Its Origins, Aims and Objects, Delivered at Allahabad, 30 April 1888* (Calcutta, 1888), p. 13.
24 See, for example, Hume's letter, dated 17 May 1888, to the editor of the Allahabad *Morning Post*, reproduced in the *Indian Mirror* (Calcutta), 23 May 1888, and Hume's letter to Dadabhai Naoroji, 12 December 1887, Dadabhai Naoroji Papers, Nehru Memorial Museum and Library, New Delhi.
25 Hume to Wedderburn, 30 January 1906, Gokhale Papers, National Archives of India, New Delhi.
26 *India*, 13 May 1892.
27 *Ibid.*; also *Mahratta*, 3 April-5 June 1892.
28 *Mahratta*, 27 December 1891.
29 *Hindustan Review*, December 1903, p. 480.
30 *Report of the Twenty-Seventh Indian National Congress*, 1912, p. 51.

CHAPTER 4

1 The first expressly political association was the Landholders' Society established in Calcutta in 1838. This was followed in 1843 by the Bengal British India Society. These two societies were amalgamated in 1851 to form the Bengal British Indian Association. In 1852 were established the Bombay Association, the Madras Native Association and the (Poona) Deccan Association. These early associations represented local interest groups of landlords (e.g., the Bengal British Indian Association) or merchants (e.g., the Bombay Association). The English-educated middle classes, though they often participated in the activities of these associations, formed their own organizations (e.g., the Indian League or the Indian Association of Calcutta) much later in the seventies.
2 Charles Dilke, Herbert Gladstone, John Morley and Edward Blake were also offered the presidency of the Congress, but could not accept it. Ramsay MacDonald was prevented by the death of his wife from presiding over the Congress in 1911.
3 Ananda Charlu, 'The Indian National Congress: A Suggestive Retrospect', *Hindustan Review*, July-August 1903, p. 21.
4 Ajodhia Nath (1889-91), W. C. Bonnerjee (1892), S. N. Banerjea (1891); Ananda Charlu (1893); D. E. Wacha (1895-1913); G. K. Gokhale

(1904-6); D. A. Khare (1908-13); N. Subba Rao (1914-17); Syed Mohammed (1914-17); Kesava Pillai (1918); C. P. Ramaswami Aiyer (1918), G. M. Bhurgri (1918); G. N. Misra (1919-20); Fazlul Huq (1919); V. J. Patel (1919-20); M. A. Ansari (1920).

5

Year	Venue	President	Number of delegates
1885	Bombay	W. C. Bonnerjee	72
1886	Calcutta	Dadabhai Naoroji	434
1887	Madras	Badruddin Tyabji	607
1888	Allahabad	George Yule	1248
1889	Bombay	W. Wedderburn	1889
1890	Calcutta	P. M. Mehta	702
1891	Nagpur	P. Ananda Charlu	812
1892	Allahabad	W. C. Bonnerjee	625
1893	Lahore	Dadabhai Naoroji	867
1894	Madras	Alfred Webb	1163
1895	Poona	S. N. Banerjea	1581
1896	Calcutta	R. M. Sayani	784
1897	Amraoti	C. Sankaran Nair	692
1898	Madras	A. M. Bose	614
1899	Lucknow	R. C. Dutt	740
1900	Lahore	N. G. Chandavarkar	567
1901	Calcutta	D. E. Wacha	896
1902	Ahmedabad	S. N. Banerjea	471
1903	Madras	L. M. Ghose	535
1904	Bombay	H. J. S. Cotton	1010
1905	Banaras	G. K. Gokhale	756
1906	Calcutta	Dadabhai Naoroji	1663
1907	Surat	R. B. Ghose	1675
1908	Madras	R. B. Ghose	626
1909	Lahore	M. M. Malaviya	243
1910	Allahabad	W. Wedderburn	636
1911	Calcutta	B. N. Dhar	446
1912	Bankipur	R. N. Mudholkar	207
1913	Karachi	Syed Mohammed	550
1914	Madras	B. N. Basu	866
1915	Bombay	S. P. Sinha	2259
1916	Lucknow	A. C. Mazumdar	2301
1917	Calcutta	Annie Besant	4967
Aug. 1918 (special session)	Bombay	Hasan Imam	
1918	Delhi	M. M. Malaviya	4881
1919	Amritsar	M. L. Nehru	7031
Sept. 1920 (special session)	Calcutta	Lajpat Rai	
1920	Nagpur	C. Vijayaraghavachari	14582

[6] Nehru wrote of the first Congress he attended in 1912: 'It was very much an English-knowing upper class affair where morning coats and well-pressed trousers were greatly in evidence.' Jawaharlal Nehru, *An Autobiography* (London, 1942), p. 27.

[7] See *Report of the Fourth Indian National Congress*, 1888, p. 63. This assurance was also embodied in the Congress constitutions of 1908 and 1920.

[8] Besides occasionally electing Muslims as presidents and general secretaries, the Congress laid down in its constitution of 1908 that one-fifth of the total number of representatives on the All-India Congress Committee should be Muslims, that the president could nominate five delegates to the subjects committee to represent minorities, and that 'in any representations which the Congress may make or in any demands which it may put forward for the larger association of the people of India with the administration of the country, the interests of minorities shall be duly safeguarded'. See *Report of the Twenty-Third Indian National Congress*, 1908, pp. xxi, xxiv.

[9] In 1887, the Congress declined to take up the question of cow-killing. In 1900, it annoyed the Panjabi Hindus by its refusal to discuss the Panjab Land Alienation Act and even accepted their secession from the Congress for a few years. The Congress offended many Hindus in northern India in 1913 by dropping its previous resolution deprecating the extension of the principle of communal representation to local bodies, and again in 1914 by negativing the election of Lajpat Rai to the presidency. In 1916, the Congress entered into a pact with the Muslim League which allowed the Muslims excessive representation in the legislative councils of certain provinces, in the teeth of opposition by the Hindus of those provinces.

[10] *Report of the First Indian National Congress*, 1885, p. 3.

[11] *Sudharak*, 12 December 1892.

[12] W. Wedderburn, *Allan Octavian Hume* (London, 1913), p. 86.

[13] When the draft constitution of the Congress was sent to the British Indian Association in 1888, the latter took serious objection to it on the ground that it aimed at transforming the character of the Congress from a casual gathering into a permanent organization and at doing away with the autonomy of the existing public associations. See letter from the secretary of the British Indian Association, dated 6 December 1888, to the general secretary of the National Congress Committee, *Publications of the British Indian Association*, 1888-92, vol. vi., pp. 10-13, British Indian Association, Calcutta. For similar objections raised by the British Indian Association in 1896, see the editorial of the *Hindoo Patriot*, 5 October 1896, entitled 'Is the Congress an Institution?'

[14] *Report of the Fifteenth Indian National Congress*, 1899, p. xxviii.

[15] *Ibid.*, p. xxix.

[16] *Report of the Twenty-Third Indian National Congress*, 1908, Appendix B, p. xix.

[17] *Ibid.*, pp. xxi-ii.

[18] G. K. Gokhale to Mrs Besant, 21 November 1914, Gokhale Papers, National Archives of India, New Delhi.

[19] B. N. Basu to G. K. Gokhale, 21 December 1914, *ibid.*

Notes

[20] G. K. Gokhale to B. N. Basu, 25 December 1914, *ibid.*
[21] B. G. Tilak, *A Step in the Steamer* (Bombay, 1918), p. 36.
[22] 'Indian Political Development', *New India* 4 November 1915.
[23] 'Vanavasi Arjun' in *Indu Prakash*, quoted in *New India*, 19 December 1916.
[24] *Report of the Thirty-Fifth Indian National Congress*, 1920, Appendix F, p. 6.
[25] *Ibid.*, p. 12.

CHAPTER 5

[1] *Petition to Parliament from the Members of the British Indian Association and other Native Inhabitants of the Bengal Presidency, relative to the East India Company's Charter* (Calcutta, 1852), p. 15.
[2] W. C. Bonnerjee, 'Representative and Responsible Government for India', *Journal of the East India Association*, September 1867, pp. 157-78.
[3] *Amrita Bazar Patrika*, 1, 8 September, and 10 November 1870.
[4] *Hindoo Patriot*, 24 August 1874.
[5] R. C. Palit (ed.), *Speeches of Babu Surendranath Banerjea, 1876-80* (Calcutta, 1880), p. 224.
[6] *Quarterly Journal of the Poona Sarvajanik Sabha*, April 1883, pp. 29-30.
[7] *Report of the First Indian National Congress*, 1885, p. 3.
[8] *Ibid.*, p. 8.
[9] *Ibid.*, p. 29.
[10] *Report of the Third Indian National Congress*, 1887, p. 2.
[11] *Ibid.*, pp. 4-6
[12] Hume to Naoroji, 12 December 1887, Naoroji Papers, Nehru Memorial Museum and Library, New Delhi.
[13] Reproduced in *Indian Mirror* (Calcutta), 23 May 1888.
[14] *Pioneer Mail*, 7 November 1888.
[15] B. C. Pal, *The National Congress* (Lahore, 1887), p. 9.
[16] *Report of the Sixth Indian National Congress*, 1890, p. 2.
[17] *Report of the Thirteenth Indian National Congress*, 1897, pp. 14-15.
[18] *Report of the Fifteenth Indian National Congress*, 1899, p. 11.
[19] *Report of the Eleventh Indian National Congress*, 1895, p. 51.
[20] *Report of the Fifteenth Indian National Congress*, 1899, p. 29.
[21] *India*, 10 June 1904, pp. 281-2.
[22] *Ibid.*, p. 282.
[23] *Report of the Twentieth Indian National Congress*, 1904, p. 37.
[24] 'Constitution of the Servants of India Society' in *Speeches of Gopal Krishna Gokhale* (Madras, 1920 ed.), p. 915.
[25] See *India*, 6 October-24 November 1905.
[26] *Speeches and Writings of Dadabhai Naoroji* (Madras, 1910), p. 652.
[27] *Report of the Twenty-First Indian National Congress*, 1905, p. 13.

28 John Morley to Lord Minto, 2 August 1906, Morley Papers, India Office Library, London.
29 Aurobindo Ghose, *The Doctrine of Passive Resistance* (Pondicherry, 1952 ed.), p. 16.
30 *Ibid.*, p. 3.
31 See Arthur Griffith's speech at the convention held under the auspices of the National Council in the Dublin Rotunda, reproduced in *Indian Review*, July 1906, pp. 534-6, and B. G. Tilak's speech at Calcutta on 'The Tenets of the New Party', in *Indian Review*, January 1907, pp. 58-60.
32 Aurobindo Ghose, *The Doctrine of Passive Resistance*, pp. 69-70.
33 H. and U. Mukherjee, *'Bande Mataram' and Indian Nationalism* (Calcutta, 1957), p. 85.
34 *Ibid.*
35 H. and U. Mukherjee, *Sri Aurobindo's Political Thought* (Calcutta, 1958), pp. 175, 181.
36 B. C. Pal, *Swadeshi and Swaraj* (Calcutta, 1954 ed.), pp. 149-67.
37 *Ibid.*, p. 162.
38 *Ibid.*, pp. 165-6.
39 *Kesari*, 22 January 1907. See also H. W. Nevinson, *The New Spirit in India* (London, 1908), pp. 72, 75.
40 H. and U. Mukherjee, *Sri Aurobindo's Political Thought*, p. 37.
41 E. Bevan, *Indian Nationalism: An Independent Estimate* (London, 1913), p. 107.
42 *Ibid.*, pp. 112-14.
43 Morley to Minto, 27 July, 2 August 1906, Morley Papers.
44 'Divided Counsels in the Congress', *The Times*, 16 October 1906.
45 *Report of the Twenty-Second Indian National Congress*, 1906, p. 21.
46 *Ibid.*, pp. 17-18.
47 *Ibid.*, p. 19.
48 *The Times*, 2 January 1907, thus commented on Naoroji's speech: 'Mr. Naoroji contends that, because the inhabitants of India are British citizens, they are entitled to all the political rights, privileges, and franchises which the inhabitants of England enjoy.... But the contention has no more root in history or in law than it has in common sense. We have won India be by the sword, and in the last resort we hold it by the sword.'
49 *Report of the Twenty-Second Indian National Congress*, 1906, pp. ii-iii. The reforms demanded were: simultaneous examinations for higher services in England and in India; adequate representation of Indians in the council of the secretary of state and in the executive councils of the viceroy and governors; the expansion of the legislative councils; increased representation of Indians thereon and larger control over administration and finances; and the extension and liberalization of local self-government.
50 *Speeches of Gopal Krishna Gokhale* (Madras, 1920 ed.), pp. 947-57.
51 See *Aurobindo on Himself and on the Mother* (Pondicherry, 1953), pp. 78-82.
52 *Report of the Twenty-Third Indian National Congress*, 1908, p. 17.
53 *Ibid.*, Appendix B, p. xix.
54 *Ibid.*

Notes

⁵⁵ H. and U. Mukherjee, *'Bande Mataram' and Indian Nationalism*, pp. 77-80.
⁵⁶ *Ibid.*, pp. 80-8.
⁵⁷ Gokhale to Besant, 5 January 1915, Gokhale Papers, National Archives of India, New Delhi.
⁵⁸ *Indian Social Reformer*, 5 May 1907.
⁵⁹ *Report of the Thirty-Fifth Indian National Congress*, 1920, p. 46; *Times of India*, 29 December 1920.
⁶⁰ S. C. Bose, *The Indian Struggle, 1920-34* (London, 1936), p. 58.

CHAPTER 6

¹ The Congress was organized in December 1885.
² The main demands of the Congress during this period were: examination for the I.C.S. in India; separation of the executive and the judiciary; fixity and permanence in land revenue; increased grants for education; reduction in military expenditure; increase in the representative element in the legislative councils; reform of the India Council; periodical inquiry into the administration of India; and the appointment of Indians to the executive councils of the governor-general and the governors.
³ Morley to Minto, 6 August 1906; Minto to Morley, 13, 20 December 1905, Morley Papers, India Office Library, London.
⁴ Minto to Morley, 20 December 1905, *ibid.*
⁵ Minto to Morley, 15 August 1906, *ibid.*
⁶ Morley, 26 February 1906, 152 H. C. Deb, 4s., col. 844.
⁷ Morley, 20 July 1906, 161 H. C. Deb. 4s., col. 589.
⁸ Minto to Morley, 28 May 1906, Morley Papers.
⁹ Minto to Morley, 28 May 1908, *ibid.*
¹⁰ Minto to Morley, 28 May 1908, *ibid.*
¹¹ Minto to Morley, 29 May 1907, *ibid.*
¹² Morley to Minto, 30 November 1906, *ibid.*
¹³ Morley to Minto, 6 June 1906, *ibid.*
¹⁴ This contained, among other things, proposals for the creation of imperial and provincial advisory councils composed of princes and notables.
¹⁵ This was Morley's favourite appellation for the bureaucrats.
¹⁶ Morley set out his views later on in detail on this subject in an article, 'British Democracy and India', *Nineteenth Century and After*, February 1911, pp. 189-209.
¹⁷ Morley to Minto, 7 May 1908, Morley Papers.
¹⁸ Minto to Morley, 28 May 1908, *ibid.*
¹⁹ Morley to Minto, 26 March 1908, *ibid.*
²⁰ Morley to Minto, 5 November 1908, *ibid.*
²¹ Morley to Minto, 16 May 1907, *ibid.*
²² Morley to Minto 15 November 1906, *ibid.*
²³ Morley to Minto, 14 March 1907, *ibid.*
²⁴ Minto to Morley, 2 April 1907, *ibid.*

[25] The number of additional members was increased to a maximum of 50 in the larger and 30 in the smaller provinces. The nominated plus official members still had a majority over the elected. Only in Bengal there was a clear elective majority, but here European representation held the balance.

[26] Out of the total membership of 68 in the imperial legislative council, there were 36 officials and 32 non-officials; 41 seats were filled by nomination and 27 by election.

[27] Morley's oft-quoted remark: 'If it could be said that this chapter of reforms led directly or necessarily up to the establishment of a Parliamentary system in India, I, for one, would have nothing at all to do with it.... If my existence, either officially or corporeally, were prolonged twenty times longer than either of them is likely to be, a Parliamentary system in India is not the goal to which I for one moment would aspire.' 17 December 1908, 198 H. L. Deb., 4s., col. 1985.

Minto remarked at the opening of the new imperial legislative council on 25 January 1910: 'I commit no breach of confidence in indicating the lines which the Government of India has endeavoured to follow. We have distinctly maintained that representative government in its Western sense is totally inapplicable to the Indian Empire.... We have aimed at the reform and enlargement of our councils, but not at the creation of parliaments.' *Proceedings of the Council of the Governor-General of India*, 1909-10, vol. xlviii, p. 50-1.

[28] *Despatch of the Secretary of State to the Governor-General*, 27 November 1908, Cd. 4426, p. 47.

[29] *Ibid.*, p. 50.

[30] There were 4,818 electors for the 27 elective seats in the imperial legislative council. Of these 2,406 were directly landlords and 1901 Muslims, 13 of the 27 elected members were elected by the non-official members of the provincial legislative councils, 6 by Muslims, and 2 by the chambers of commerce. 8 electors chose the Muslim representative from Bombay and 9 the one from Burma.

[31] Morley to Minto, 3 May 1907, Morley Papers.

[32] Minto to Morley, 17 June 1908, *ibid.*

[33] Morley to Minto, 2 August 1907, *ibid.*

[34] Minto to Morley, 13 May 1909, *ibid.*

[35] 'If we can hatch some plan and policy for half a generation that will be something; and if for a whole generation, that would be better. Only I am bent, as you assuredly are, on doing nothing to loosen the bolts.' Morley to Minto, 17 April 1907, *ibid.*

[36] Morley to Minto, 15 July 1909, *ibid.*

[37] Lord Crewe best summed up the attitude of his contemporaries when he remarked: 'What will be the future of India fifty, sixty, or a hundred years hence need not, I think, trouble us. It is on the knees of the gods, and all we have to do is to provide, as best as we can, for the conditions of the moment, having, of course, an eye to the future, but not troubling ourselves about what many happen in days when to use Sheridan's words "all of us are dead and most of us are forgotten".' 24 February 1909, 1 H. L. Deb. 5s., col. 215.

38 Morley to Minto, 27 July, 2 August 1906, Morley Papers.
39 *Report of the Joint Select Committee*, 1919, H. C. 203, vol. ii, p. 223.
40 Evidence of Sir Claude H. Hill, ex-member of the executive council of the governor of Bombay and of the governor-general's executive council, before the Joint Select Committee, 1919, *ibid.*, p. 31.
41 Morley, 17 December 1908, 198 H. L. Deb. 4s., col. 1984.

CHAPTER 7

1 For example, in October 1822, Rammohun Roy had written an article, entitled 'Ireland, the Causes of Its Distress and Discontents', in which he had dwelt on the evils of absentee landlordism and the injustice of maintaining Protestant clergymen out of the revenues wrung from Irish Catholics. See S.D. Collet, *The Life and Letters of Raja Rammohan Roy* (London, 1900), pp. 64-5.
2 S. R. Mehrotra, *The Emergence of the Indian National Congress* (Delhi, 1971), p. 16.
3 See, for example, R. C. Palit (ed.), *Speeches of Babu Surendranath Banerjea, 1876-80* (Calcutta, 1880), 89, and *Bengalee*, 18 June 1881.
4 Mehrotra, *The Emergence of the Indian National Congress*, pp. 327-31.
5 *Report of the Twenty-Third Indian National Congress*, 1908, Appendix B, p. xix.
6 E. Norman, *A History of Modern Ireland* (London, 1971), p. 227.
7 Cited in M. S. Kamath, *The Home Rule Leagues* (Madras, 1918), pp. 7-9. See also *New India*, 18 October 1915.
8 N.C. Kelkar, *Home Rule and the Home-Rule League* (Poona, 1916), pp. 6-8.
9 *Mahratta*, 30 August 1914.
10 S. Wolpert, *Tilak and Gokhale* (Berkeley, 1962), pp. 265-9.
11 *New India*, 25 September 1915.
12 *Report of the Thirtieth Indian National Congress*, 1915, p. 161.
13 *Ibid.*, pp. 115-38.
14 *Mahratta*, 30 April, 7 May 1916.
15 *New India*, 4 September 1916.
16 *Bal Gangadhar Tilak, His Speeches and Writings* (Madras, 1918), pp. 141-2.
17 *Ibid.*, pp. 142-58.
18 *Ibid.*, p. 178.
19 *Ibid.*, pp. 179-80.
20 *Ibid.*, pp. 233-5.
21 *Ibid.*, pp. 163.
22 *Ibid.*, p. 217; also D. V. Tahmankar, *Lokamanya Tilak* (London, 1956), p. 286.
23 B. C. Pal, *Why I Advocate Home Rule for India* (Adyar, 1918), p. 6.

24 Cited in Judith M. Brown, *Gandhi's Rise to Power: Indian Politics 1915-1922* (Cambridge, 1972), pp. 27-8.
25 Cited in D. P. Karmarkar, *Bal Gangadhar Tilak: A Study* (Bombay, 1956), p. 260.
26 Cited in Ram Gopal, *Lokamanya Tilak* (Bombay, 1956), p. 397.
27 Cited in *ibid.*, pp. 398-9.
28 *Mahratta*, 14 July 1918; S.R. Mehrotra, *India and the Commonwealth 1885-1929* (London, 1965), p. 152.
29 H. F. Owen, 'Organizing for the Rowlatt Satyagraha of 1919', in R. Kumar (ed.), *Essays in Gandhian Politics* (Oxford, 1971), p. 74.
30 Judith M. Brown, *op. cit.*, p. 28. See also H. F. Owen, 'Towards Nation-Wide Agitation and Organisation: The Home Rule Leagues, 1915-18', in D. A. Low (ed.), *Soundings in Modern South Asian History* (London, 1968), pp. 180-6.

CHAPTER 8

1 Joseph J. Doke, *M. K. Gandhi: An Indian Patriot in South Africa* (London, 1909). The book also carried an 'Introduction' by Lord Ampthill, who had been governor of Madras (1900-6) and acting governor-general of India (1904).
2 The phrase in Gandhi's. See, for example, *The Collected Works of Mahatma Gandhi* [hereinafter referred to as *Collected Works*] (Delhi, 1958-), vol. xii, pp. 523, 536, 565.
3 *Ibid.*, vol. xxix, p. 268.
4 *Ibid.*, vol. i, p. 187; vol. viii, p. 246; vol. ix, p. 101; vol. xii, p. 565; vol. xiv, pp. 436, 442; vol. xv, p. 16.
5 *Ibid.*, vol. i, p. 289.
6 *Ibid.*, vol. ii, pp. 47, 365; vol. vi, p. 251.
7 *Ibid.*, vol. i, pp. 200, 235, 286, 290, 306; vol. ii, pp. 33, 50, 106, 230, 289, 333, 336; vol. iii, pp. 51, 125, 163, 167, 172, 248, 294, 340, 363, 400, 403, 426, 437, 449; vol. iv, pp. 100, 113, 135, 190, 402; vol. v, pp. 150, 193, 248, 250; vol. viii, pp. 475-6; vol. ix, pp. 28-9, 516, 521, 538, 542; vol. x, pp. 78, 84, 461; vol. xi, pp. 112-14; vol. xii, pp. 72, 198, 476, 505; vol. xiii, pp. 110, 464.
8 *Ibid.*, vol. ii, pp. 286, 328; vol. iii, p. 254; vol. ix, p. 515.
9 *Ibid.*, vol. vii, p. 469.
10 C. P. Lucas, 'Empire and Democracy', in *The Empire and the Future* (London, 1916), p. 18. In a letter to J. B. Petit, dated 16 June 1915, Gandhi remarked: 'We fought [in South Africa] to keep the theory of the British Constitution intact so that practice may some day approach the theory as near as possible.' *Collected Works*, vol. xiii, p. 110.
11 *Collected Works*, vol. xxix, p. 31.
12 *Ibid.*, vol. ix, p. 409.
13 *Ibid.*, vol. i, pp. 200, 290, 306; vol. ii, pp. 33, 106; vol. iii, pp. 163, 167, 437.

Notes

¹⁴ *Ibid.*, vol. viii, p. 400. Two other early definitions of this kind are: 'to suffer in order to put an end to suffering' (*ibid.*, vol. ix, p. 96); and 'suffering in our own persons until our opponents see the error of their ways and cease to harass us by imposing their will on us' (*ibid.*, vol. x, p. 121).

¹⁵ *Ibid.*, vol. ix, p. 28.

¹⁶ *Ibid.*, p. 489.

¹⁷ C. F. Andrews, *Mahatma Gandhi's Ideas* (London, 1929), p. 249. In a letter to his son Devdas, dated 5 March 1919, Gandhi wrote: 'An Englishman will not be argued into yielding; he yields only under compulsion of events. He is not worried about the result, and bears what he must. Knowing that events will take their course, he remains unconcerned and goes his way resolutely. He is very much in love with the strength of his body and with armed might, is even proud of them a great deal. He readily yields to such strength and respects it. However, he recognizes moral force and, voluntarily or involuntarily, perhaps even against his will, yields to it. It is this moral force we are employing and, if it is genuinely moral, we shall win.' *Collected Works*, vol. xv, p. 126. Again, on 7 January 1920, he wrote in *Young India:* '. . . as they [Englishmen] always wish to appear to be just even when they are in reality unjust, it is easier to shame them than others into doing the right thing.' *Ibid.*, vol. xvi, p. 376.

¹⁸ *Collected Works*, vol. iv, p. 113.

¹⁹ *Ibid.*, vol. pp. 258-9. Even as late as 31 December 1919 Gandhi wrote: 'Under the British Constitution no one gets anything without a hard fight for it.' *Ibid.*, vol. xvi, p. 360.

²⁰ Dr. Judith M. Brown in her book *Gandhi's Rise to Power: Indian Politics 1915-1922* (Cambridge, 1972) obviously conveys a wrong impression when she says (p. 7) that Gandhi 'only read Thoreau's essay on civil disobedience when he was in prison for that very offence [in 1908]'. Gandhi was already familiar with the views of Thoreau in 1907. See *Collected Works*, vol. vii, pp. 212, 217-18, 228-30, 304-5. For Gandhi's much longer familiarity with the views of Tolstoy and Ruskin, see *ibid.*, vol. i, pp. 89-90; vol. iv, pp. 290, 320; vol. v, pp. 56, 57, 326; vol. vi, p. 198; vol. xxxix, pp. 239, 246, 248.

²¹ *Collected Works*, vol. x, p. 301.

²² For example, the Sinn Fein movement in Ireland, the Suffragette movement in England, and the boycott movement in Bengal. See *ibid.*, vol. v, pp. 44, 92, 114, 121-2; vol. vi, pp. 17, 30, 87-7, 223, 269, 335-6; vol. vii, pp. 6-7, 65-6, 73-4, 213-14; vol. viii, p. 188; vol. ix, pp. 303, 324; vol. xxix, pp. 93-4. Gandhi was also familiar with the ancient Indian practice of *dharna* (*ibid.*, vol. vii, pp. 86-7; vol. x, p. 51).

²³ *Ibid.*, vol. v, p. 175.

²⁴ *Ibid.*, vol. x, p. 83.

²⁵ *Ibid.*, vol. ix, p. 97. As early as 1903 Gandhi had written: 'South Africa ought to be to the British Indians a great Puri [place of pilgrimage] where all divisions are abolished and levelled up. We are not, and ought not to be, Tamils or Calcutta men, Mahomedans or Hindus, Brahmans or Baniyas, but simply and solely British Indians, and as such as we must sink or swim together.' *Ibid.*, vol. iii, p. 412.

26 *Ibid.*, vol. ix, p. 385.

27 *Ibid.*, p. 506. A little later Gandhi wrote: 'It is now necessary for every Indian to understand what the struggle is about and how important are the issues involved. We are carrying a burden on behalf of the whole of India.' *Ibid.*, p. 521. See also *ibid.*, vol. v, p. 417; vol. ix, pp. 113, 464.

28 Gandhi to Gokhale, 11 November 1909, *ibid.*, vol. ix, p. 532.

29 *Ibid.*, vol. x, p. 97.

30 *Report of the Twenty-Eighth Indian National Congress*, 1913, pp. 67-8.

31 *Collected Works*, vol. ix., p. 452. On 22 November 1907 Gandhi had written to Gokhale: 'May I draw your attention to the fact that the struggle we are undergoing here has resulted in making us feel that we are Indians first and Hindus, Mahomedans, Tamils, Parsees, etc., afterwards?' *Ibid.*, vol. vii, p. 376.

32 *Times of India*, 30 December 1908. See also *Report of the Twenty-Fifth Indian National Congress*, 1910, p. 39.

33 *Collected Works*, vol. ix, p. 507.

34 *Ibid.*, p. 529.

35 *Indian Mirror*, 26 January 1902. For an equally laudatory estimate of Gandhi by the editor of the Calcutta *Indian Mirror*, N. N. Sen, see *ibid.*, 21-3 January 1902.

36 *Report of the Twenty-Fourth Indian National Congress*, 1909, pp. 88-9.

37 Andrews to Gokhale, 27 December 1914, Gokhale Papers, National Archives of India, New Delhi.

38 Gandhi to V.S. Srinivasa Sastri, 18 March 1920, *Collected Works*, vol. xvii, p. 96.

39 *Ibid.*, vol. xiii, p. 200; vol. xxxiv, pp. 306-7. See also B. R. Nanda, *Mahatma Gandhi: A Biography* (London, 1958), pp. 131, 133, and *Gokhale: The Indian Moderates and the British Raj* (Delhi, 1977), p. 467.

40 *Collected Works*, vol. x, p. 139.

41 *Ibid.*, vol. xii, p. 462.

42 *Ibid.*, vol. xxxix, p. 314.

43 Gandhi to A. H. West, 23 December 1914, *ibid.*, vol. xii, p. 566. Later in his autobiography Gandhi wrote: '. . . it may be said that God has never allowed any of my own plans to stand. He has disposed them in His own way.' *Ibid.*, vol. xxxix, p. 202. Gandhi was very fond of the following hymn by Cardinal Newman:

> Lead, Kindly Light, amid the encircling gloom,
>   Lead Thou me on;
> The night is dark, and I am far from home,
>   Lead Thou me on,
> Keep Thou my feet; I do not ask to see
> The distant scene; one step enough for me.

44 *Collected Works*, vol. iv, pp. 116-17.

45 *Ibid.*, vol. vii, pp. 6-7.

46 *Ibid.*, vol. vi, p. 269.

47 *Ibid.*, vol. viii, p. 246.

48 '. . . the immutable maxim that government of the people is possibl

only so long as they consent either consciously or unconsciously to be governed.' *Ibid.*, vol. xii, p. 461. 'No government has ever yet come into existence which could successfully resist the will of the people. When the people are determined to get their rights, they will have them.' *Ibid.*, vol. xiv, p. 400. See also *ibid.*, pp. 328-9, 339, 379.

[49] *Ibid.*, vol. xi, 112-14; vol. xiii, pp. 59-60, 66.

[50] *Ibid.*, vol. vii, p. 334.

[51] *Ibid.*, vol. viii, p. 224.

[52] *Ibid.*, vol. x, pp. 65, 313; vol. xix, p. 28.

[53] *Ibid.*, vol. i, p. 289; vol. iv, p. 285.

[54] *Ibid.*, vol. ix, pp. 476, 479; vol. x, p. 24; vol. xii, p. 412.

[55] *Ibid.*, vol. xxxix, p. 277.

[56] *Ibid.*, vol. vi, p. 264; vol. vii, pp. 6-7; vol. xiv, p. 442; vol. xviii, p. 373.

[57] *Ibid.*, vol. xviii, pp. 414, 418, 421, 435-6, 442, 452; vol. xix, pp. 27-8, 30, 32, 49, 80, 95, 178, 250, 251, 284.

[58] J. R. Seeley, *The Expansion of England* (London, 1883), pp. 227-8.

[59] *Collected Works*, vol. i, p. 289; vol. iii, p. 383.

[60] *Ibid.*, vol. x, pp. 22-3. 'The governance of India is possible only because there exist people who serve.' *Ibid.*, vol. v, p. 132. See also the views of Shyamji Krishnavarma reproduced by Gandhi in *ibid.*, vol. vi, p. 84.

[61] *Ibid.*, vol. xi, p. 351; vol. xxxix, p. 304. See also B. R. Nanda, *Mahatma Gandhi*, pp. 124, 131, and *Gokhale*, pp. 415, 416.

[62] *Collected Works*, vol. xii, pp. 360-1, 401, 565; vol. xiii, pp. 2, 16, 55, 250.

[63] *Ibid.*, vol. xii, pp 360, 401.

[64] In a letter dated 25 September 1917 and addressed to the editor of the *Leader*, Gandhi wrote: 'I have now been in India for over two years and a half after my return from South Africa. Over one quarter of that time I have passed on the Indian trains travelling 3rd class by choice. I have travelled north as far as Lahore, down south up to Tranquebar, and from Karachi to Calcutta.' *Ibid.*, vol. xiii, p. 547. Again, on 15 December 1917 he wrote: 'Half of my time is passed in the Indian trains.' *Ibid.*, vol xiv, p. 108.

[65] *Ibid..*, vol xii, pp. 478, 565.

[66] *Ibid*, vol. xi, p. 351; Gokhale to C. Y. Chintamani, 26 October 1911, Gokhale Papers; Nanda, *Gokhale*, pp 416-17.

[67] Speaking at the 1914 Congress at Madras, F. G Natesan, a delegate from Trichinopoly, remarked that but for his continued preoccupation with the question of the Indians in South Africa, 'the genius, the fire, the enthusiasm and the consuming sacrifices of a Gandhi, would have been available to us, nearer home, in our own country to expedite the construction and consolidation of the Indian Nation, and lead her on triumphantly in the path of progress and advancement, in a manner which would satisfy the highest aspirations of united India and the ardent, impatient throbbings of Young India', *Report of the Twenty-Ninth Indian National Congress*, 1914, p 125.

[68] *Collected Works*, vol. xxxix, p. 304.

[69] This Act authorized the government of India in 1919 to retain the

summary powers vested in them during the First World War. It was based upon the recommendations of a committee which inquired into seditious activities in India and was presided over by Sir Sidney Rowlatt of the King's Bench in England.

[70] *Collected Works*, vol. xiv, pp. 427-8, 436-8.

[71] K. Dwarkadas, *Gandhiji through My Diary Leaves* (Bombay, 1950), pp. 10-11.

[72] *Collected Works*, vol. xiv, p. 378.

[73] E. S. Montagu, *An Indian Diary* (London, 1930), p. 58.

[74] *Collected Works*, vol. xiv, p. 380.

[75] *Ibid.*, p. 470. As early as 1895 Gandhi had quoted with obvious approval the following remark of a writer on Indian affairs (W. W. Hunter?) in *The Times*: 'The battlefield has always formed the short cut to an honourable equality among races.' *Ibid.*, vol. i, p. 255.

[76] *Ibid.*, vol. xiv, p. 410.

[77] *Ibid.*, vol. xv, p. 15; also pp. 26, 29, 30, 31, 40.

[78] *Ibid.*, vol. xii, p. 70; vol. xiv, p. 48.

[79] *Ibid.*, vol. xv, p. 29.

[80] See, for example, excerpts in Government of India, Home (Political) Department Proceedings, January 1918, nos. 487-90; February 1918, no. 216; August 1918, no. 28, National Archives of India, New Delhi, and N. R. Phatak (ed.), *Source Material for a History of the Freedom Movement in India* (Bombay, 1965), vol. iii, pt. i, pp. 45, 53, 108, 134, 147, 203, 204, 209.

[81] *Collected Works*, vol. xiv, p. 114.

[82] *Ibid.*, vol. xv, p. 152.

[83] *Ibid.*, p. 121.

[84] 'The Government want to show that they can afford to disregard public opinion. We must show that they cannot do so.' Gandhi to H. S. L. Polak, 30 May 1919, *ibid.*, p. 335. See also *ibid.*, vol. xvi, pp. 23-40.

[85] *Ibid.*, vol xv, p. 179.

[86] *Ibid.*, vol. xvi, pp. 307-12; vol. xxxix, pp. 380-4. See also S. R. Mehrotra, *India and the Commonwealth 1885-1929* (London, 1965), pp. 192-3.

[87] *Collected Works*, vol. xvi, p. 360.

[88] *Report of the Thirty-Fourth Indian National Congress*, 1919, p. 123.

[89] *Ibid.*, pp. 65-8.

[90] For a different point of view, see P. H. M. Van Den Dungen, 'Gandhi in 1919: Loyalist or Rebel?', in R. Kumar (ed.), *Essays on Gandhian Politics* (Oxford, 1971), pp. 43-63.

[91] The terms of the Treaty of Sevres proposed to deprive Turkey of her control over Thrace, Smyrna, Syria, Palestine and Mesopotamia. The treaty was concluded in August 1920, but it was not ratified and was later superseded by the Treaty of Lausanne in 1923.

[92] *Report of the Committee Appointed by the Government of India to Investigate the Disturbances in the Punjab, etc.* [Presided over by Lord Hunter, lately Solicitor-General for Scotland], Cmd. 681 (1920).

[93] *Collected Works*, vol. xviii, p. 89.

[94] *Ibid.*, vol. xxiii, p. 230; vol. xxxix, pp. 397-8; D. G. Tendulkar,

Mahatma: Life of Mohandas Karamchand Gandhi (Bombay, 1951-4), vol. ii, p. 12.
95 *Report of the Thirty-Fifth Indian National Congress*, 1920, p. 85.
96 *New India*, 19 March 1915.
97 J. Nehru, *The Discovery of India* (Bombay, 1961 ed.), p. 368.
98 Rajni Kothari, *Politics in India* (Delhi, 1970), p. 51.
99 Viscount Samuel, 'The Fruits of True Leadership', in S. Radhakrishnan (ed.), *Mahatma Gandhi* (London, 1931), p. 259.
100 J. Nehru, *Mahatma Gandhi* (Calcutta, 1949), p. 168.
101 J. Nehru, *An Autobiography* (London, 1942), p. 418.
102 For example, Stanley Reed, *The India I Knew* (London, 1952), p. 57.
103 Quoted in A. Campbell-Johnson, *Mission with Mountbatten* (London, 1951), p. 353.
104 Gokhale's speech at Bombay on 14 December 1912, reproduced in *Collected Works*, vol. xi, p. 579.
105 *Ibid.*, vol. xiv, p. 460.
106 J. Nehru, *Mahatma Gandhi*, p. 162.
107 See, for example, J. Halliday, *A Special India* (London, 1968), p. 52.
108 J. Nehru, *Mahatma Gandhi*, p. 160.

CHAPTER 9

1 Ramsay Muir, *The Making of British India 1756-1858* (Delhi, 1971 ed.), pp. 133-9.
2 *Ibid.*, pp. 170-8.
3 *Ibid.*, pp. 301-4.
4 S. R. Mehrotra, *The Emergence of the Indian National Congress* (Delhi, 1971), pp. 62-7.
5 A.C. Banerjee (ed), *Indian Constitutional Documents 1737-1947* (Calcutta, 1961), vol. i, pp. 299-305.
6 H. L. Singh, *Problem and Policies of the British in India 1885-1898* (Bombay, 1963), pp. 76-7; R. J. Moore, *Sir Charles Wood's Indian Policy 1853-66* (Manchester, 1966), pp. 49-52.
7 Minute, dated 16 March 1860, of Bartle Frere, then member of viceroy's council, quoted in H. L. Singh, *op. cit.*, pp. 77-8.
8 Mehrotra, *The Emergence of the Indian National Congress*, pp. 230-5.
9 C. H. Phillips (ed.), *The Evolution of India and Pakistan 1858 to 1947* (London, 1962), pp. 35-8.
10 C. P. Ilbert, *The Government of India* (Oxford, 1898), pp. 102-6; M. Maclagan, *'Clemency' Canning* (London, 1962), pp. 268-71; H. L. Singh, *op. cit.*, pp. 76-83; R. J. Moore, *Sir Charles Wood's Indian Policy 1853-66*, pp. 61-4; and S. Gopal, *British Policy in India 1858-1905* (Cambridge, 1965), pp. 18-20.
11 Ripon to Hartington, 31 December 1881, Ripon Papers, British Museum, London.
12 Hartington to Ripon, 26 December 1882, *ibid*.

[13] Dufferin to Kimberley, 21 March, 6, 26 April 1886, Dufferin Papers, India Office Library, London.
[14] *Ibid.*, 26 April 1886.
[15] Kimberley to Dufferin, 22 April 1886, Dufferin Papers.
[16] Dispatch of the Government of India, Home Department, Public No. 67 of 1888, dated 6 November 1888, Public Letters from India, 1888, vol. 9, pp. 171-203, India Office Library. See also Dufferin to Cross, 20 October, 11 November 1888, Cross Papers, India Office Library.
[17] Cross to Dufferin, 21 December 1888, Cross Papers; also Viscount Cross, *A Political History* (privately printed, 1903), p. 121, quoted in R. J. Moore, 'The Twilight of the Whigs and the Reform of the Indian Councils, 1886-1892', *Historical Journal*, December 1967, p. 410.
[18] Philips (ed.), *op. cit.*, pp. 66-7.
[19] For the text of the Indian Councils Act, 1909, see *ibid.*, pp. 88-90.
[20] *Proposals of the Government of India and Dispatch of the Secretary of State*, 1908, Cd. 4426, p. 47.
[21] C. H. Philips, *India* (London, 1949), p. 107.
[22] Morley to Minto, 31 October 1907, Morley Papers, India Office Library, London.
[23] Beni Prasad, *The Hindu-Muslim Questions* (Allahabad, 1941), p. 45.
[24] 97 H. C .Deb. 5s., coll. 1295-6.
[25] Philips (ed.), *op. cit* , pp. 273-85.
[26] *Letter from the Government of India to the Secretary of State for India, dated 5 March 1919* ..., Cmd. 123, 1919, p. 47.
[27] 109 H. C. Deb. 5s, col. 1162.
[28] C. Ilbert and. J Meston, *The New Constitution of India* (London, 1923), p. 138.
[29] Viscount Midleton: 37 H. L. Deb. 5s., col. 1029.
[30] C. R. Das: cited in Marquess of Zetland, *'Essayez'* (London, 1956), p. 135.
[31] E. S. Montagu, *An Indian Diary* (London, 1930), p. 236.
[32] *Report on Indian Constitutional Reforms*, 1918, Cd. 9109, p. 232.
[33] 157 H C Deb. 5s., col. 1513.
[34] 61 H. L. Deb. 5s., col. 1087.
[35] Malcolm Hailey: *Legislative Assembly Debates*, 1924, vol. iv, pt. i, p. 363.
[36] C. S. Ranga Iyer says in his book *How to Lose India*? (Lahore, 1935), p. 83, that Lord Winterton, for long under-secretary of state for India, once told him 'that he could not think of a day when the Indian Government consisting of Indians and responsible to India would be endowed with the same powers which... the Dominions have in regard to the Army. He could only think of giving India autonomy in Civil Affairs such as Rhodesia enjoyed.'
[37] The Report of the Commission described the north-west frontier as 'an international frontier of the first importance from the military point of view for the whole Empire' and remarked: 'India and Britain are so related that Indian defence cannot, now or in any future which is within sight, be regarded as a matter of purely Indian concern.' It recommended that the

control and direction of the Indian army 'must rest in the hands of agents of the Imperial Government' and 'should not be regarded as a function of an Indian Government in relation with an Indian legislature'. See *Report of the Indian Statutory Commission*, vol. ii—*Recommendations*, 1930, Cmd. 3569, pp. 173-4.

[38] Philips (ed.), *op. cit.*, pp. 320-35.

[39] H. V. Hodson, *The Great Divide* (London, 1969), p. 60.

[40] *Ibid.*, p. 48.

[41] 297 H. C. Deb. 5s., col. 1167.

[42] A. B. Keith, *A Constitutional History of India* (Allahabad, 1961 ed.), pp. 473-4.

[43] Quoted in N. Srinivasan, *Democratic Government in India* (Calcutta, 1954), pp. 63-4.

[44] *Ibid.*, p. 63; also *Indian Annual Register*, 1936 (Calcutta, 1936), vol. i, pp. 248-9; vol. ii, p. 205.

[45] *Indian Annual Register*, 1936, vol. i, pp. 295-300; S. R. Mehrotra, *India and the Commonwealth 1885-1929*, pp. 197-203; R. J. Moore, *The Crisis of Indian Unity 1917-1940* (Delhi, 1974), pp. 22-5, 34-9, 218-23, 309-10.

[46] Quoted in R. J. Moore, 'The Making of India's Paper Federation', in C. H. Philips and M. D. Wainwright (eds.), *The Partition of India* (London 1970), p. 65.

[47] Quoted in *ibid.*, pp. 65-6.

[48] Quoted in R. J. Moore, *The Crisis of Indian Unity 1917-1940*, pp. 155-6.

[49] Linlithgow to Zetland, 28 December 1939, quoted in Zetland, *op. cit.*, p. 277.

[50] M. Gwyer and A. Appadorai (eds.), *Speeches and Documents on the Indian Constitution 1921-47*. (Bombay, 1957), vol. i, p. 323.

CHAPTER 10

[1] For the attitude of the Congress to the Act of 1935 see *Indian Annual Register*, 1936 (Calcutta, 1936), vol. i, pp. 248-9; vol. ii, p. 205.

[2] *Ibid.*, vol. ii, p. 205.

[3] For the results of the 1937 elections see *Return Showing the Results of Elections in India*, 1937, Cmd. 5589.

[4]

Provinces	Total number of seats in the Legislative Assembly	Seats won by the Congress in the elections of 1937
Assam	108	35
Bengal	250	54
Bihar	152	95
Bombay	175	88
Central Provinces	112	71
Madras	215	159

Provinces	Total number of seats in the Legislative Assembly	Seats won by the Congress in the elections of 1937
N. W. Frontier Province	50	19
Orissa	60	36
Panjab	175	18
Sindh	60	8
United Provinces	228	133

5 Provinces	Total number of seats allotted to Muslims in the Legislative Assembly	Seats won by the Muslim League in the elections of 1937
Assam	34	9
Bengal	117	39
Bihar	39	—
Bombay	29	20
Central Provinces	14	—
Madras	28	10
N. W. Frontier Province	36	—
Orissa	4	—
Panjab	84	1
Sindh	33	3
United Provinces	64	27

[6] Maurice Gwyer and A. Appadorai (eds.), *Speeches and Documents on the Indian Constitution, 1921-47* (Bombay, 1957), vol. i, pp 392-3.

[7] Jinnah's famous Fourteen Points of March 1929 had proposed that 'no cabinet, either central or provincial, should be formed without there being a proportion of at least one-third Muslim ministers'. At the Round Table Conference some Muslim delegates had urged that the representation of minorities should be specifically provided for in the constitution. This demand was indirectly rejected by the Joint Parliamentary Committee in criticizing an earlier draft of the Instruments of Instructions, which seemed to fetter the discretion of governors by making it obligatory that they should select ministers from minority communities and vitiated the principle of joint responsibility of ministers. Nothing was said on the subject in the Act of 1935 and the governors were only told, in the instructions issued to them, 'to appoint those persons (including as far as practicable members of important minority communities) who will best be in a position to command the confidence of the legislature', but in so acting they should 'bear constantly in mind the need for fostering a sense of joint responsibility' among their ministers. See Gwyer and Appadorai (eds.), *op. cit.*, vol. i, p. 379.

[8] See, for example, R. Coupland, *Indian Politics, 1936-1942* (Oxford, 1943), pp. 110-12, 179, and Beni Prasad, *India's Hindu-Muslim Questions* (London, 1946), pp 61-2.

[9] *Statesman*, 4 January 1937.

[10] *Ibid.*, 9 January 1937.

Notes

11 In the United Provinces, for example, of the 14 Muslim candidates run by the Congress no less than 4 were pitted against Muslim Leaguers. See *Leader* and *Poineer*, 9-20 February 1937. The alleged 'agreement' or 'understanding' between the Congress and the Muslim League does not appear to have gone beyond the support extended by certain individual Congressmen to a few progressive Muslim League candidates in the 1937 elections.

12 *Statesman*, 4 January 1937.
13 *Leader*, 15 March, 3 May 1937.
14 *Ibid.*, 4 May 1937.
15 *Ibid.*, 12 May 1937.
16 *Ibid.*, 4 May 1937.

17 In Bombay some informal soundings about a possible coalition between the Congress and the League appear to have been made, but no reliable information about them is available.

18 See, for example, the statement of Syed Muhammad Hussain in *Leader*, 21 April 1937.
19 *Ibid.*, 28-9 April 1937.
20 *Ibid.*, 28 April 1937.
21 *Ibid.*, 6 May 1937.
22 *Ibid.*
23 *Ibid.*, 9-10 May 1937.
24 *Ibid.*, 10 May 1937.
25 *Pioneer*, 27 March 1937.
26 *Leader*, 19 May 1937.
27 *Ibid.*, 5 June 1937.
28 *Ibid.*, 25 July 1937; *Pioneer*, 24 July 1937.

29 See, for example, Nehru's statement in *Leader*, 3 July 1937, and his letter to Khaliquzzaman in *A Bunch of Old Letters* (Bombay, 1959), pp. 258-60.

30 *Pioneer*, 18 July 1937.

31 For the terms offered by Maulana Azad on behalf of the Congress, see *Leader*, 4 August 1937. There were only two main conditions laid down by the Congress for a coalition with the League, namely, that the 'Muslim League group in the United Provinces Legislature shall cease to function as a separate group' and that the 'Muslim League Parliamentary Board in the United Provinces will be dissolved, and no candidates will thereafter be set up by the said Board at any by-election'. As regards the first condition, all that needs to be said is that it is difficult to see how a Congress-League coalition government could function effectively in the United Provinces if the Muslim League group in the local legislature continued to function as a separate group. As regards the second condition, it is necessary to point out that the Congress had already dissolved its own Parliamentary Board and all that it was asking the League to do was to follow suit, with the sole object of avoiding a confrontation between the Congress and the League in any future by-election. It is significant that none of these two conditions was specifically objected to by Khaliquzzaman in his public statement of 30 July 1937.

[32] See Khaliquzzaman's statement in *Leader*, 4 August 1937.

[33] See the statement of Maulana Ahmad Said in *ibid.*, 10 November 1937. Also, A. K. Azad, *India Wins Freedom* (Bombay, 1959), pp. 160-1, and Khaliquzzaman, *Pathway to Pakistan* (Lahore, 1961), pp. 160-3. It seems that the objection of Congress leaders to the inclusion of Nawab Muhammad Ismail Khan in the ministry was due not merely to the fact that he was a Nawab. They wanted to have a cabinet of six ministers in the United Provinces, at least one of whom was a Congress Muslim. They were, therefore, unwilling to admit more than one Muslim Leaguer in the cabinet. Khaliquzzaman, on the other hand, demanded that one-third of the members of the cabinet should belong to the Muslim League. As he says in his *Pathway to Pakistan* (p. 160): 'Pandit Pant . . . asked me how many seats in the Cabinet I would demand in case of a coalition between the Congress and League. I replied: Three in nine and two in six, i.e., one-third of the total strength of the Cabinet whatever it may be.' Had Congress leaders conceded Khaliquzzaman's demand, they would have been required either to have no Congress Muslim in the cabinet or to have fifty per cent Muslims in the cabinet. In either case, a precedent would have been created which was not welcome to Congress leaders. As Yakub Hasan, a leading Congress Muslim from Madras, wrote later ('The Hindu-Muslim Situation', *Indian Review*, April 1940, p. 218): 'If the Congress had been short-sighted enough to agree to the proposed arrangement, the Congress-League cabinets would have been today ruling over all the 11 provinces . . , . The two-nation formula that has been propounded lately would not have come before the public as a pet theory of Mr. Jinnah, for it would have already become an accomplished fact and threby a legitimate demand would have been created for the inclusion of the two-nation principle in the new constitution of India.'

[34] *Leader*, 4 August 1937.

[35] See Marquess of Zetland, *'Essayez'* (London, 1956), pp. 254-5.

[36] Cited in V. P. Menon, *The Transfer of Power in India* (Bombay, 1957), p. 57.

[37] See *Indian Annual Register*, 1922 (Calcutta, 1922), vol. i, Appendices, pp. 71-2; also S. R. Mehrotra, *India and the Commonwealth 1885-1929* (London, 1965), pp. 197-8.

[38] Gwyer and Appadorai (eds.), *op. cit.*, vol. ii, p. 437.

[39] See Choudhary Rahmat Ali, *Paksitan: The Fatherland of the Pak Nation* (Cambridge, 1947), p. 225.

[40] *Letters of Iqbal to Jinnah* (Lahore, 1956), pp. 17-19.

[41] *Ibid.*, pp. 23-4.

[42] *Ibid.*

[43] For some well-known schemes see Coupland, *op. cit.*, pp. 199-206, and Gwyer and Appadorai (eds.), *op. cit.*, vol. ii, pp. 444-65.

[44] *Leader*, 20 October 1937. The question of an alternative to federation was discussed at this session, but no definite conclusion was reached.

[45] *Ibid.*, 19 October 1937.

[46] *Pioneer*, 7 November 1937.

[47] *Ibid.*, 19 October 1937.

[48] *Leader*, 11 October 1938.

49 *Ibid.*
50 *Times of India*, 10 October 1938.
51 *Ibid.*, 11 October 1938.
52 *Statesman*, 12 October 1938.
53 *Ibid.*, 11 October 1938. See also *Times of India*, 5 and 10 October 1938.
54 *Pioneer*, 15 October 1938.
55 *Statesman*, 14 October 1938. Similarly in early 1937 Jinnah had sarcastically wished Nehru 'long life' in order to be able to realize his dream of political independence for India in his own lifetime (*Leader*, 3 May 1937). These remarks lead us to conclude that in 1937-8 Jinnah still believed that the British had no intention of withdrawing from India in the near future. It was the assurance given by the British government after the outbreak of the war—especially that contained in the viceroy's statement of 10 January 1940—that India would be granted dominion status as soon as possible after the war, which probably convinced Jinnah that the transfer of power could not be far off. In his presidential address to the Lahore session of the Muslim League in March 1940 Jinnah made a pointed reference to 'the termination of the British regime, which is implicit in the recent declaration of His Majesty's Government' (*Leader*, 24 March 1940). This fact has some relevance to the timing of the Muslim League's demand for Pakistan.
56 *Statesman*, 29 December 1938.
57 *Pioneer*, 28 March 1939.
58 *Indian Annual Register*, 1939 (Calcutta, 1939), vol. i, p. 374.
59 Gwyer and Appadorai (eds.), *op. cit.*, vol. ii, p. 443.
60 *Leader*, 21 March 1940.
61 D. G. Tendulkar, *Mahatma* (Bombay, 1952), vol. v, pp. 334-5.
62 *Ibid.* pp. 333-4.
63 *Ibid.*, pp. 336-7.
64 *Leader*, 15 April 1940. On another occasion Nehru was reported to have remarked: 'Many knots of the Hindu-Muslim problem had been merged into one knot, which could not be unravelled by ordinary methods, but would need an operation ... he would say one thing very frankly that he had begun to consier them [Muslim Leagues] and people like himself, as separate nations.' *Leader*, 16 April 1940.
65 Cited in *Statesman*, 5 May 1940.
66 *Ibid.*, 16 June 1940.
67 Gwyer and Appadorai, *op. cit.*, vol. ii, p. 505.
68 Lord Linlithgow to Lord Zetland, 28 December 1939, cited in Zetland, *op. cit.*, p. 277.
69 *Statesman*, 26 March 1940.
70 Gwyer and Appadorai (eds.), *op. cit.*, vol. ii, p. 525. Italics added.
71 *Ibid.*, pp. 549-50.
72 *Ibid.*, pp. 550-1.
73 *Ibid.*, p. 443.
74 *Ibid.*, pp. 554-5.
75 *Ibid.*,
76 *Ibid.*, p. 577.

[77] In the elections to the central legislature the Congress secured 91 per cent of the votes cast in non-Muslim constituencies and won 57 seats; the Muslim League secured 86 per cent of the votes cast in Muslim constituencies and won 30 seats. In the elections to the provincial legislatures the Congress increased its strength to 930 seats; it gained an absolute majority in 8 provinces (including Assam and the N.W. Frontier Province) and constituted the second largest party in the remaining three. The Muslim League won 427 of the 507 Muslim seats, but it could form ministries only in Bengal and Sindh. See *Indian Annual Register*, 1946 (Calcutta, 1946), vol. i, pp. 229-31.

[78] Jamil-ud-Din Ahmad, *Some Recent Speeches and Writings of Mr. Jinnah* (Lahore, 1947), vol. ii, p. 578.

[79] Gwyer and Appadorai (eds.), *op. cit.*, vol. ii, p. 578.

[80] *Ibid.*, p. 579.

[81] *Ibid.*, p. 578.

[82] The description is that of Sir Stafford Cripps (18 July 1946). See 425 H. C. Deb., col. 1397.

[83] For the text of the proposals, dated 16 May 1946, see Gwyer and Appadorai (eds.), *op. cit.*, vol. ii, pp. 577-84.

[84] *Ibid.* pp. 667-9.

[85] *Ibid.* pp. 669-70.

[86] Michael Brecher, *Nehru: A Political Biography* (Oxford, 1959). p. 345.

[87] V. P. Menon, *op. cit..* p. 361 and Alan Campbell-Johnson. *Mission with Mountbatten* (London. 1951). p. 89.

[88] V. P. Menon, *op. cit..* pp. 406-7.

[89] *Ibid.* pp. 357-67. For the text of the plan see Gwyer and Appadorai (eds.). *op. cit..* vol. ii. pp. 670-5.

[90] See V. P. Menon, *op.cit..* pp. 406-7.

[91] See, for example, Nehru's statement in *Leader*, 16 June 1947.

[92] See *Leader*, 18 June 1947.

[93] *Ibid.*, 16 June 1947.

[94] Gwyer and Appadorai (eds.), *op. cit.*, vol. ii, p. 682.

[95] *Leader*, 6 June 1947.

[96] *Ibid.*, 7 June 1947.

CHAPTER 11

[1] R. J. Moore 'The Making of India's Paper Federation, 1927-35', in, C. P. Philips and M. D. Wainwright (eds.), *The Partition of India* (London 1970), p. 63.

[2] M. Gwyer and A. Appadorai (eds.), *Speeches and Documents on the Indian Constitution 1921-47* (Bombay, 1957) vol. i, p. 323.

[3] See above, pp. 178-9, 198-200; also S. R. Mehrotra, *India and the Commonwealth 1885-1929* (London, 1965), pp. 197-8.

[4] R. J. Moore, 'The Making of India's Paper Federation, 1927-35', and 'British Policy and the Indian Problem, 1935-40', in C. H. Philips and M. D. Wainwright (eds.), *op. cit.*, pp. 59-94.

⁵ *Statesman*, 4 January 1937.
⁶ *Ibid.*, 9 January 1937.
⁷ A. K. Azad, *India Wins Freedom* (Bombay, 1959), p. 144.
⁸ *Ibid.*
⁹ Gwyer and Appadorai (eds.), *op. cit.*, vol. ii, pp. 520-1.
¹⁰ Quoted in B. R. Nanda, *Gokhale, Gandhi and the Nehrus: Studies in Indian Nationalism* (London, 1974), p. 169.
¹¹ Azad, *op. cit.*, p. 138.
¹² Gwyer and Appadorai (eds.), *op. cit.*, vol. ii, pp. 586-8.
¹³ According to Sir Francis Wylie, then governor of the United Provinces, Sir Stafford Cripps, a member of the Cabinet Mission, told him in early 1946: 'There is going to be a revolution here [in India] and we must get out—quick.' Francis Wylie, 'Federal Negotiations in India 1935-1939, and after', a paper presented in 1966 at the Seminar on the Partition of India, School of Oriental and African Studies, University of London.
¹⁴ Quoted in H. V. Hodson, *The Great Divide* (London, 1969), p. 113.
¹⁵ Gwyer and Appadorai (eds.), *op. cit.*, vol. ii, pp. 577-84.
¹⁶ H. Tinker, *Experiment with Freedom: India and Pakistan 1947* (London, 1967), p. 45.
¹⁷ 425 H. C. Deb.5s., col. 1397.
¹⁸ Compare 15(5) with 19(v) of the Cabinet Mission plan: Gwyer and Appadorai (eds.), *op. cit.*, vol. ii, pp. 580-3.
¹⁹ Penderel Moon (ed.), *Wavell: The Viceroy's Journal* (London, 1973), Appendix IV, p. 485.
²⁰ Cited in G. K. Gokhale to A. Vamanrao Patwardhan, 30 October 1908, Gokhale Papers, National Archives of India, New Delhi.

CHAPTER 12

¹ J. Hutchinson and J. Ph. Vogel, *History of the Panjab Hill States* (Lahore, 1933), vol. i, p. 62.
² See William Lee-Warner, *The Protected Princes of India* (London, 1894), ch. iii.
³ Quoted in H. H. Dodwell (ed.), *The Cambridge History of India* (Delhi, 1963), vol. v, p. 570.
⁴ Quoted in T. R. Metcalf, *The Aftermath of Revolt. India, 1857-1870* (Princeton, 1965), pp. 31-2.
⁵ S. R. Mehrotra, *The Emergence of the Indian National Congress* (Delhi, 1971), pp. 83, 85.
⁶ T. R. Metcalf, *op. cit.*, p. 219.
⁷ Dispatch no. 43A of 30 April 1860, quoted in *ibid.*, p. 224.
⁸ Quoted in M. Gwyer and A. Appadorai (eds.), *Speeches and Documents on the Indian Constitution 1921-47* (Bombay, 1957), vol. ii, pp. 759-60.
⁹ R. Coupland, *India: A Restatement* (London, 1945), pp. 38, 278.
¹⁰ V. P. Menon, *The Story of the Integration of the Indian States* (Bombay, 1961), pp. 34-5; U. Phadnis, *Towards the Integration of Indian States 1919-*

1947 (Bombay, 1968), pp. 98-101.

[11] Quoted in H. V. Hodson, *The Great Divide* (London, 1969), p. 48.

[12] See above, pp. 178-9.

[13] Quoted in Hodson, *op. cit.*, p. 113.

[14] See chapter 11, note 13.

[15] Gwyer and Appadorai (eds.), *op. cit.*, vol. ii, pp. 767-9.

[16] Alan Campbell-Johnson, *Mission with Mountbatten* (London, 1951), Appendix,. p 367.

[17] *Ibid.*, p. 141; Gwyer and Appadorai (eds.), *op. cit.*, vol. ii, pp. 773-5.

[18] See, for example, Nehru's statement in *Leader*, 16 June 1947.

[19] A. Campbell-Johnson, *op. cit.*, p. 120.

[20] See *Leader*, 18 June 1947.

[21] R. Coupland, *India: A Restatement*, p. 278; also R. Coupland, *The Future of India* (London, 1943), pp. 151-2.

[22] Quoted in A. Campbell-Johnson, *op. cit.*, p. 47.

[23] *Ibid.*, pp. 141-2.

[24] L. Mosley, *The Last Days of the British Raj* (London, 1961), pp. 177-8; Hodson, *op. cit.*, pp. 379-80; Menon, *op. cit.*, pp. 112-13.

[25] Menon, *op. cit.*, pp. 113-14, 118, 231, 398-9.

CHAPTER 13

[1] S. D. Collet, *The Life and Letters of Raja Rammohun Roy* (London, 1900), p. 48.

[2] *Ibid.*, pp. 64-5.

[3] See B. N. Banerji, 'English Impressions of Rammohun Roy before His Visit to England', *Modern Review*, March 1932, p. 283.

[4] Collet, *op. cit.*, p. 59.

[5] *Ibid.*, pp. 119-20.

[6] Roy was not the first Indian to visit England, but he was the first Hindu of eminence who dared to cross the ocean and thus set a conspicuous precedent to the host of educated Hindus who later studied and travelled in Europe. Collet rightly considered Roy's visit to England to be a landmark in the history of modern civilization and said: 'The West had long gone to the East. With him the East began to come to the West.' *Ibid*'

[7] *Ibid.*, p. 120.

[8] *Ibid.*, p. 134.

[9] *Ibid.*, p. 133.

[10] *Ibid.*, p. 133.

[11] See B. N. Banerji, 'Rammohun Roy on International Fellowship', *Modern Review*, October 1928, pp. 467-8.

[12] *Ibid.*

[13] J. Nehru, *An Autobiography* (London, 1942 ed.), p. 163.

[14] Cited by Selig S. Harrison, 'Leadership and Language Policy in India', in R. L. Park and H. Tinker (eds.), *Leadership and Political Institutions in India* (Princeton, 1959), p. 151.

Notes

15 Lytton to Northbrook, 25 April 1187, Lytton Papers, India Office Library, London.

16 See, for example, A.P. MacDonnell, the lieutenant-governor of the North-Western Provinces, to Elgin, the viceroy, 16 July and 22 August 1897, Elgin Papers, India Office Library, and a memorandum on the Pan-Islamic movement enclosed with the dispatch of the government of India to the secretary of state, Foreign Department, No. 110 of 1890, Political and Secret Letters and Enclosures from India, vol. 114, India Office Library.

17 James Bryce, as British ambassador at Washington (1907-13), repeatedly drew the attention of the home government to the anti-British propaganda being carried on in America by Indian agitators, in alliance with the Clanna-Gael. On 23 April 1908 Morley, the secretary of state for India, wrote to Minto, the viceroy: 'I am slowly beginning to think that a tide of strong opinion may one day swell in the U.S.A about our rule in India, of the same kind as has prevailed here about Austria, Russia, the Turks, etc.' Morley Papers, India Office Library.

In a speech at Washington on 18 January 1909, President Theodore Roosevelt came out openly in defence of British rule in India 'as there were foolish people here ... who looked with mischievous pleasure on that [anti-British] agitation'. (Roosevelt to Bryce, 21 January 1909, Bryce Papers, Bodleian Library, Oxford) Roosevelt's speech earned for him the gratitude of the British government, but it brought forth an open letter of protest signed by eighteen pro-Indian Americans. (For the text of the letter of protest, see M. R. Palande (ed.), *Source Material for a History of the Freedom Movement in India* (Bombay, 1958), vol. ii, pp. 547-51.

18 *Hindu*, 18 May 1903.

19 D. V. Gundappa (ed.), *Speeches and writings of Dr. (Sir) S. Subramania Iyer* (Madras, 1918), pp. 389-94.

20 'Asiatic Revival', *Bengalee*, 25 September 1875.

21 'The Chinese Fiasco', *Bengalee*, 6 September 1900.

22 Cited by Lord Courtney in the House of Lords on 29 July 1912. See 12 H. L. Deb. 5s., col. 750.

23 B. C. Pal, 'Nationalism and Politics', *Hindu Review*, March 1913, pp. 223-4; also his *Nationality and Empire* (Calcutta, 1916), pp. 93-4.

24 *Report on Indian Constitutional Reform*, Cd. 9109 (1918), p. 22.

25 Mohamed Ali, *My Life: A Fragment* (Lahore, 1942) p. 57.

26 49 H. L. Deb. 5s., col. 467.

27 See Earl Winterton, *Orders of the Day* (London, 1953), p. 116, and *Fifty Tumultuous Years* (London, 1955), p. 55.

28 See Second Marquess of Reading, *Rufus Isaacs, First Marquess of Reading* (London, 1945), vol. ii, p. 232.

29 See Warner Levi, *Free India in Asia* (Minneapolis, 1952), pp. 32-3, and Bimla Prasad, *The Origins of Indian Foreign Policy* (Calcutta, 1962 ed.), pp. 74-84.

30 Fa-Hien and Yuan Chwang were Chinese pilgrims who visited India in the fifth and seventh centuries A.D. respectively.

31 *Indian Quarterly Register*, 1927, vol. i, p. 209.

32 *Ibid.*

33 *Report of the Committee Appointed by the Secretary of State for India to Inquire into the Administration and Organization of the Army in India* Chairman: Viscount Esher] Cmd 943 (1920), pp. 3-4.

34 There were as many as 97,000 Indian troops employed in Egypt, Mesopotamia and Persia early in 1921, See *Legislative Assembly Debates*, 1921, vol. i, pt. ii, p. 1712.

35 See, for example, the speech of Sir Sivaswamy Aiyer on 17 February 1921 in the Indian Legislative Assembly, *Legislative Assembly Debates*, 1921, vol. ii, pt. i, p. 97.

36 Nehru later recalled the bitter remark of an Egyptian: 'You have not only lost your own freedom but you help the British to enslave others' J. Nehru, *The Discovery of India* (London, 1956 ed.), p. 430.

37 *Indian Annul Register*, 1922, vol. i, p. 270.

38 J. Nehru, 'India's Demand and England's Answer', *Atlantic Monthly*, April 1940, p. 455,

39 In an interview with a special correspondent of the Associated Press at Lucknow. See J. S. Bright (ed.), *Before and after Independence* (New Delhi, 1950), pp. 375-7.

40 *Ibid.*, p. 376.

41 *Ibid.*

42 *Indian Quarterly Register*, 1927, vol. ii, p. 380.

43 *Ibid* , p. 379.

44 *Ibid* , p, 378.

45 For Nehru's views on foreign affairs in the late 'twenties and the early 'thirties, see R.M. Lal (ed.), *Jawaharlal Nehru, Statements, Speeches and Writings* (Allahabad, 1929); R. Dwivedi (ed.), *The Life and Speeches of Pandit Jawaharlal Nehru* (Allahabad, 1930); J. Nehru, *Soviet Russia* (Bombay, 1929), *Recent Essays and Writings* (Allahabad, 1934), *Glimpses of World History* (Allahabad, 1934-5), *India and the World* (London, 1936) and *An Autobiography* (London, 1936).

46 *Indian Annual Register*, 1936, vol. i, p. 248.

47 *Ibid.*

48 *Ibid*, 1937, vol .ii, p. 322 and 1938, vol. i, p. 296.

49 *Ibid.*, 1938, vol. i, pp. 296-7.

50 *Ibid*, 1939, vol. i, pp. 341-2.

51 *Ibid.*, vol. i, p. 351; vol. ii, p. 214.

52 *Ibid.*, vol. ii, p. 214.

53 *Ibid.*

54 J. Nehru, *The Discovery of India* (London, 1956 ed.), p. 433.

55 *Indian Annual Register*, 1939, vol. ii, pp. 226-8.

56 J. Nehru, *The Discovery of India* (London, 8956 ed.), pp. 560-1.

57 *Ibid.*, p. 561.

58 The text of the broadcast is in J. Nehru, *India's Foreign Policy* (Delhi, 1961), pp. 1-3,

INDEX

Abdullah, Sheikh, 248
Afghanistan, 258, 268
Africa, 254, 257, 267, 269, 273
Ahrars, 189
Ali, Muhammad, 217
Ali, Rahmat, 199
Ali, Shaukat, 194, 203, 259
Aligarh, 6
Allahabad, 49, 53, 96, 108, 110, 193
All-India Congress Committee, 70, 90, 129, 130, 185
All-India Muslim League, 88, 113, 178, 182-222, 224-32, 243-7
All-India States' People's Conference, 239, 244
America. See United States of America
Amraoti, 79
Amrita Bazar Patrika, 7, 40, 91
Amritsar, 53, 76
Amritsar massacre, 113, 150, 152, 155
Andrews, C. F., 137, 142, 143, 147
Ansari, M. A., 259
Ansari, Suleman, 190, 193
Anti-Corn Law League, 78
Arabs, 265, 268
Arnold, Edwin, 6
Arundale, G. S., 133
Asia, 3, 115, 222, 254, 256, 263, 267, 269, 271, 273, 274, 275
Asian Relations Conference, 263
Assam, 167, 173, 174, 184, 186, 214, 216, 217, 218, 220, 231, 232, 245
Atlantic Charter, 267
Atlantic Monthly, 267
Attlee, C. R., 177, 219-20, 232

Auckland, Lord, 236
Australia, 92
Austria, 251, 258-9
Avadh, 13, 234, 235, 237
Azad, Abul Kalam, 193, 206, 222, 229, 230
Aziz, Shah Abdul, 197

Baghat, 236
Bajpai, G. S., 254
Balkan Wars, 258-9
Baluchistan, 214
Banaras, 53, 101
Bande Mataram, 111
Banerjea, S. N., 7, 33, 91, 98
Bankipur, 86
Baroda, 234, 235, 238, 239, 250, 256,
Basu, B. N., 58, 86
Bayley, E. C., 25
Belgaum, 129
Bengal, 1, 10, 16, 21, 43, 45, 76, 86, 107, 110, 115, 116, 158, 159, 161, 166, 167, 168, 173, 174, 179, 184, 198, 200, 214, 216, 217, 218, 220, 227, 231, 232, 234, 245; partition of (1905), 58, 115, 116
Bengalee, 256
Bentham, J., 39
Bentinck, William, 18, 236
Besant, Annie, 69, 88, 89, 111, 112, 113, 126, 127-34, 148, 149, 151
Bevan, Edwyn, 5, 105-6
Bhat, S. B., 52
Bhau Daji, 7, 28, 36
Bhopal, 248, 250
Bhownaggree, M. M., 56
Bihar, 11, 86, 167, 173, 174, 184, 186, 231, 232

Bikaner, 249, 250
Birkenhead, Lord, 171
Blavatsky, H. P., 9
Boers, 99, 108
Boer War, 136
Bombay, 1, 6, 10, 14, 23, 31, 53, 54, 63, 68, 81, 92, 107, 129, 133, 158, 159, 161, 166, 167, 168, 173, 174, 184, 186, 189, 231, 232
Bonnerjee, W. C., 54, 79, 91, 92, 93
Bose, S. C., 270
Boycott movement, 110, 115
Bradlaugh, Charles, 79
Bright, John, 39
British Committee of the Congress, 57, 58, 76, 77, 80, 81, 136
British Commonwealth, 113, 260, 274; see also British Empire
British constitution, 136-7
British Empire, 35, 86, 90, 91, 101, 104, 108, 109, 110, 111, 118, 125, 126, 136, 137, 144, 145, 148, 234, 237, 258, 259, 260, 262, 265; see also British Commonwealth
British Indian Association of Calcutta, 81, 91
British Indian Association of the Transvaal, 137
Brussels, 254, 263, 268
Bryan, W. J., 256
Buckingham, J. S., 251
Burke, E., 34, 39, 124
Burma, 165, 222
Butt, Isaac, 124
Butterfield, H., 44

Cabinet Mission, 216-19, 230-2
Calcutta, 6, 7, 10, 14, 16, 20, 23, 45, 89, 107, 110, 133, 141, 147, 151, 158, 159, 161, 203, 249, 252, 253
Calcutta Courier, 26
Calcutta Journal, 251
Caliphate. See Khilafat
Cambridge University, 1, 14, 233
Canada, 37, 91, 92, 96, 108
Canning, Lord, 238

Canning College, 13
Carnatic, Nawab of, 236
Catholic Association, 124
Central Provinces (and Berar), 129, 158, 165, 167, 173, 174, 184, 186, 189, 231, 232
Chamber of Princes, 242
Champaran, 149
Chanak, 262
Charlu, P. Ananda, 55
Charter Act 1833, 10, 34, 119, 158-9
Charter Act 1853, 159-60
Chartist movement, 45
Chatterji, Bankimchandra, 24
Chelmsford, Lord, 148, 167, 168
Chhatari, Nawab of, 190
China, 253, 256-7, 261, 263, 264, 266, 268, 269, 270, 274, 275
Chintamani, C. Y., 177
Chirol, Valentine, 119
Christians, 2, 9, 168, 174, 175, 182
Churchill, W. S., 177, 243, 267
Cobden, R., 39
Coleridge, S. T., 223
Colonies, 100, 101, 103, 104, 107-8; see also Dominions
Colvin, Auckland, 55, 96
Commonweal, 127
Comte, Auguste, 39
Congress against Imperialism, 263, 268
Congress Working Committee, 213, 219, 245, 270-2
Conservative Party (British), 80, 115, 179, 188
Constituent Assembly, 201-2, 208, 219, 227
Corfield, Conrad, 249
Cotton Henry, 69, 100
Coupland, R., 249
Cripps Mission, 212-14, 229-30, 267
Cripps, Stafford, 230-1
Cross, Lord, 163
Curzon, Lord, 43, 100, 101, 115, 119, 261
Czechoslovakia, 270, 271

Index

317

Dacca, 53, 227
Dalhousie, Lord, 45, 236, 237
Dall, C. H. A., 255
Das, C. R., 150
Datta, M. Madhusudan, 24
Dayanand, 42
Delhi, 4, 10, 20, 53, 169
Delhi Darbar 1877, 4, 15, 16
Dey, Lal Bihari, 36
Digby, William, 79, 99, 100, 146, 256
Doke, Joseph J., 135
Dufferin, Lord, 37, 53, 54, 56, 68, 98, 163
Dutt, R. C., 36-37, 98, 116
Dyarchy, 171, 176
Dyer, General, 149, 150

East Africa, 257
East India Company, 4, 22, 107, 158, 234, 235
Eden, Anthony, 254
Eden, Ashley, 49
Edwards, William, 13
Egypt, 3, 257, 265, 268, 269, 270
Elgin, Lord, 119
Ellenborough, Lord, 236
Elphinstone, Mountstuart, 34
England, 34, 38, 68, 70, 80, 92, 95, 98, 99, 115, 118, 122, 134, 135, 252, 253-4, 255, 274; *see also* Great Britain; United Kingdom
Esher Committee Report, 265
Etawah, 46, 47
Ethiopoia, 270
Eurasians, 73, 168, 174, 175
Europe, 2, 106, 115, 253, 254, 255, 269
Europeans, 168, 174, 182
Extremists, 83-9, 101-13, 122, 126, 127, 128, 136, 149,

Fa-Hien, 263, 275
Faizpur, 182
Fascism, 270-1
Fergusson College, 55
Filipinos, 99

France, 41, 102, 252, 254, 258
French Canadians, 108
French Revolution 1789, 12; 1830, 252
Friend of India, 3, 6, 21

Gaikwar, Malharrao, 238, 249
Gaikwar, Sayajirao, 256
Gandhi-Jinnah talks, 214-15
Gandhi, M. K., 73, 79, 114, 133, 134, 135-57, 207, 214, 242, 262, 264, 275
Garibaldi, Giuseppe, 255
Gauba, K. L., 267
Germany, 255, 271
Ghose, Aurobindo, 41, 42, 101, 102, 103, 104, 109, 110, 153
Ghose, M. M., 97
Ghose, Ram Gopal, 45
Ghose, Rashbehari, 109, 110
Ghose, S. K., 7
Gladstone, W. E., 39, 40, 99, 125, 258
Gladstonian liberalism, 50, 80, 115, 255
Gokhale, G. K. 55, 56, 70, 85, 100, 101, 108, 109, 110, 111, 112, 116, 121, 128, 129, 136, 139, 141, 142, 143, 146, 147, 151, 152, 156
Government of India Act 1919, 150, 167-71, 173; *see also* Montagu-Chelmsford reforms
Government of India Act 1935, 172-80, 181-2, 184, 185, 201-2, 223-5, 234, 244, 272
Great Britain, 11, 29, 30, 40, 43, 47, 100, 103, 106, 127, 128, 131, 212, 258, 269, 273; *see also* England; United Kingdom
Gujarat, 11, 151

Haileybury, 45
Hakim, Abdul, 193
Hamilton, Lord George, 100
Hardinge, Lord, 127, 242
Harijan, 209, 210
Haroon, Sir Abdulla, 203
Hartington, Lord, 162, 163

Hasan, Syed Wazir, 193
Hastings, Lord, 235
Hastings, Warren, 124
Hindoo Patriot, 4, 20, 25, 91
Hind Swaraj, 136, 146
Hindu, 256
Hindus, 2, 9, 18, 22, 74, 197, 207, 225
Hoare, Samuel, 179
Home rule, 91, 96, 124-34, 148, 149
Home Rule Leagues, 88, 113, 128, 129-34
Home rule movement in Ireland, 124-6
Hotchner, H., 256
House of Commons, 58, 99, 117, 125
House of Lords, 18, 99, 120, 126
Hughes, Thomas, 51
Hume, A.O., 26, 37, 44-66, 67, 70, 80, 81, 93, 96, 122
Hume, James, 45
Hume, Joseph, 45, 67
Hume, R. A., 255
Hunter Committee, 150
Huq, A. K. Fazlul, 189, 203
Hutchinson, J., 233
Hyderabad, 175, 195, 221 225, 234, 235, 238, 240, 243, 248, 249
Hyndman, H. M., 38

Ibrahim, Hafiz Muhammad, 190, 193
Ilbert Bill, 13, 30, 46, 51, 120
Imperial Conferences 1917-18, 260
Imperial War Conferences 1917-18, 260
India, 63, 77, 80
Indian Civil Service, 11, 13, 45, 56, 80, 170, 176
Indian Congress Committee, 69, 81-2
Indian Council of World Affairs, 263
Indian Councils Act 1861, 160-2
Indian Councils Act 1892, 163-4
Indian Councils Act 1909, 166-7; *see also* Morley-Minto reforms

Indian Daily News, 10
Indian National Congress, 1, 8, 16, 27, 29, 35, 37, 38, 40, 42, 43, 44, 54, 56, 57, 58, 67-90, 91-114, 115, 117, 112, 127, 135, 139, 142, 150, 151, 163, 177-8, 181-222, 224, 226-32, 245-6, 259-60, 263, 268-73
India Office, 176
Indian Opinion, 139
Indian Parliamentary Committee, 80
Indian Political Agency, 79
Indian Social Reformer, 112
Indian (princely) states, 2, 171, 174, 178, 212-13, 216, 225-6, 230, 232, 233-50
India Wins Freedom, 229
Indu Prakash, 31, 33, 41
Iqbal, Muhammad, 199
Iran. *See* Persia
Ireland, 37, 40, 41, 99, 102, 124, 125, 126, 222, 251-2
Italy, 41, 102, 255
Iyer, S. S., 256
Iyer, V. K., 110

Jaisalmer, 249, 250
Jamiat-ul-Ulema, 189, 190, 193
Jang, Salar, 238
Japan, 43, 99, 104, 115, 164, 256, 257, 263, 270
Jefferson, Thomas, 255
Jhansi, 236, 237
Jinnah, M. A., 114, 122, 149, 184, 190, 194, 195, 196, 198, 201, 202, 203, 205, 211, 215, 216, 226-8, 230-1, 244, 246-9
Jodhpur, 249, 250
Jones, W. B., 14
Joshi, G. V., 7
Junagarh, 221, 248, 249
Jung, Mahmudulla, 202

Karachi, 139, 179, 203
Karnatak, 130
Kashmir, 221, 225, 239, 240, 243, 247, 248, 249

Index

Keith, A. B., 177
Kelkar, N. C., 128
Kemal Pasha, Mustafa, 262
Kesari, 35, 104
Khaliquzzaman, Chaudhry, 189, 190-4, 228
Khan, Nawab Muhammad Ismail, 194
Khan, Saiduddin, 190, 193
Khan, Syed Ahmed, 6, 197
Kheda, 148, 149
Khemchand, Thakurdas, 139
Khilafat, 113, 149, 151, 152
Khilafat movement, 259, 262
Kimberley, Lord, 163
Kitchener, Lord, 123
Knighton, William, 13
Kothari, Rajni, 153
Krishak Proja Party, 189
Krishnavarma, Shyamji, 56
Kruger, S. J. P., 136
Kukas, 48

Lahore, 53, 57, 142, 205, 208, 209, 214-16
Landholders' Society, 14
Lansdowne, Lord, 119, 163
Latin America, 266
League against Imperialism, 254
League of Nations, 260, 261, 269, 270
Liberals, British, 80, 115-16, 258
Liberals, Indian, 223-4, 242, 265
Lincoln, Abraham, 255
Linlithgow, Lord, 179, 180, 185, 211, 243
Lloyd George, David, 262
London, 79, 158, 172
London India Society, 99
Lucas, C. P., 136
Lucknow, 10, 13, 36, 88, 89, 113, 130
Lucknow Pact, 227
Lyall, Alfred, 119, 257
Lytton, Lord, 15, 49, 50, 242

Macaulay, T. B., 19, 34, 159
MacDonald, Ramsay, 169

Madras, 1, 5, 6, 10, 14, 23, 74, 76, 78, 86, 88, 104, 127, 131, 133, 158, 159, 161, 167, 168, 173, 174, 184, 186, 189, 231, 232, 249, 268
Maharashtra, 6, 129, 130
Mahmud, Syed, 193
Mahratta, 41
Maine, Henry, 39
Majid, Sheikh Abdul, 203
Malaviya, Madan Mohan, 29, 110, 114
Malcolm, John, 34
Manchester Guardian, 178
Mansergh, Nicholas, 223
Mayo, Katherine, 267
Mayo, Lord, 47, 48, 162
Mazzini, Giuseppe, 12, 39, 255
Mehta, P. M., 33, 73, 88, 109, 110, 112, 128, 129, 152
Menon, V. P., 220, 231
Mesopotamia, 269
Metcalf, T. R., 237
Middle East, 261, 265, 268
Mill, J. S., 12, 39
Milton, John, 12
Minto, Lord, 115-23, 127, 164-6
Mitra, Rajendralal, 24
Moderates, 83-9, 101-13, 121, 126, 127, 128, 136, 149
Mohani, Maulana Hasrat, 199
Momins, 189, 190
Montagu-Chelmsford reforms, 134, 150, 167-71, 242, 261; *see also* Government of India Act 1919
Montagu-Chelmsford Report, 113, 167, 169
Montagu, E. S., 123, 133, 148, 167, 168, 169, 179, 261
Mookerjee, G. B., 63
Moore, R. J., 225
Morley, John, 39, 43, 101, 106, 116-23, 164-6
Morley-Minto reforms, 115-23, 126, 164-6; *see also* Indian Councils Act 1909
Morning Post, 96
Morocco, 258

Mother India, 267
Mountbatten, Lord, 52, 219-20, 246-7, 250
Mozoomdar, P. C., 256
Munro, Thomas, 34
Muslim League. *See* All-India Muslim League
Muslims, 2, 9, 18, 73-4, 106, 121, 122, 149, 165, 166, 167, 168, 182, 188, 195, 207, 208, 227, 228, 241, 258, 259
Mutiny. *See* Revolt of 1857
Mysore, 175, 236, 249

Nagpur, 72, 76, 89, 109, 113, 151, 236, 237
Nair, C. Sankaran, 28, 36, 97
Nana Sahib, 236
Naoroji, Dadabhai, 6, 34, 38, 57, 73, 80, 93, 96, 99, 100, 107, 146
Naples, 251
Natesan, G. A., 78, 139, 140
Nath, Ajoodhia, 63
National Agriculturist Party, 190
Nazism, 270, 271
Near East, 265
Nehru, Jawaharlal, 152, 155, 156, 157, 188, 189, 209, 227, 230, 239, 254, 267-75
New Delhi, 254, 263
New India, 127, 132, 151
Northbrook, Lord, 48, 49
North-Western Provinces, 46, 55, 158, 159, 161; *see also* United Provinces
North-West Frontier Province, 172, 173, 174, 179, 183, 186, 195, 198, 214, 231, 232
Norton, E., 79
Nundy, Alfred, 71

O'Connell, Daniel, 124
Olcott, H. S., 49, 256
Orange River Colony, 43
Orissa, 167, 172, 173, 174, 184, 186, 189, 231, 232, 234

Paine, Thomas, 39

Pakistan, demand for, 197, 205, 206, 208, 209-11, 215-21, 229-32, 243-7
Pal, B. C., 36, 97, 101, 104, 131, 256, 257
Pal, K. D., 91
Palestine, 268
Palmerston, Lord, 1
Pan-Asianism, 262-4
Panikkar, K. M., 249
Pan-Islamism, 197, 257, 258, 262
Panjab, 1, 10, 11, 77, 116, 122, 150, 158, 161, 165, 167, 173, 174, 179, 183, 198, 200, 214, 216, 217, 218, 220, 231, 232, 237, 245
Parliament (British), 37, 45, 58, 80, 91, 93, 125, 158, 169
Parnell, C. S., 126
Parsis, 2, 9, 73
Patel, Vallabhbhai, 233, 247, 249-50
Patiala, 250
Patna, 204
People's Friend, 46
Persia, 13, 257, 258, 266, 268
Peterhof, 50
Phelps, Myron H., 256
Philippines, 99, 266
Philips, C. H., 166
Pitt's India Act 1784, 158
Poona, 7, 14, 35, 53, 235, 249
Poona Pact, 173
Poona Sarvajanik Sabha, 15, 52, 112
Prasad, Rajendra, 196
Punjab. *See* Panjab

Qasim, Muhammad bin, 197, 203
Quarterly Journal of the Poona Sarvajanik Sabha, 17, 92
Queen's proclamation of 1858, 34, 119

Rai, Lajpat, 101, 256
Ramgarh, 206
Rampur, 248
Rana, S. R., 56
Ranade, M. G., 29-30, 33, 112, 232

Index

321

Rangachari, S., 36
Rao, Madhav, 6
Rathbone, William, 252
Rau, B. N., 231
Reay, Lord, 54
Redmond, John, 125-6
Regulating Act 1773, 173
Renan, E., 223
Revolt of 1857, 4, 9, 19, 20, 21, 22, 47, 56, 155, 162, 237-9
Ripon, Lord, 10, 13, 50, 52, 53, 67, 92, 119, 162, 163
Round Table Conference, 172, 179, 242
Roosevelt, F. D., 267
Rothney Castle, 50
Rowlatt Act, 113, 148, 149, 150, 152
Roy, Rammohun, 25, 251-3
Ruskin, John, 138
Russia, 2, 11, 27, 40, 43, 99, 115, 164, 254, 255, 257, 258, 264, 275; see also Soviet Union
Russian revolution of 1905, 118
Russo-Turkish War, 255

Sambhalpur, 236
Samuel, Lord, 155
San, Aung, 222
Satara, 236, 237
Satyagraha, 90, 137, 138, 143, 145, 146, 147, 148, 149, 153, 154
Scheduled castes, 174-5, 178-9
Seeley, J. R., 14, 146
Sen, K. C., 7
Servants of India Society, 100, 142-3
Sevres, Treaty of, 150
Shia Political Conference, 189, 190
Sikhs, 2, 13, 168, 174, 182
Simla, 50, 51, 53, 55, 56
Simon Commission, 171, 172
Sindh, 172, 173, 174, 179, 183, 198, 214, 231, 232
Sindh Provincial Muslim League Conference, 203-4
Singapore, 270

Singh, Ranjit, 237
Sinn Fein, 43, 80, 110, 125
Smith, Adam, 39
South Africa, 99, 108, 135, 138, 139, 140, 141, 144, 145, 146, 147, 148, 152, 257-8
South Africa British Indian Committee, 136
Soviet Union, 261, 266, 273
Spain, 270, 271
Spencer, Herbert, 39
Statesman, 211
Stead, W. T., 131
Stevenson, Adlai, 254
Strachey, H., 26
Strachey, John, 1
Subsidiary alliances, 234-5
Sudharak, 77
Suffragettes, 137
Suhel, Aqbal, 193
Sunderland, J. T., 256
Sun Yat Sen, 263
Surat, 70, 87, 109, 112, 116
Swadeshi (movement), 10, 102, 115, 151
Swaraj, 89, 104, 107, 110, 113, 154
Sylhet, 220

Tagore, Rabindranath, 28, 149
Tanjore, Raja of, 236
Tata, J. N., 256
Telang, K. T., 63
Theosophical Society, 127
Theosophy, 49
Thiers, Louis Adolphe, 137
Thompson, George, 26
Thompson, Rivers, 47
Thoreau, Henry David, 138
Tilak, B.G., 42, 88, 101, 104, 105, 106, 109, 111, 112, 127, 128, 132, 133, 149, 150, 152, 153
Times, The, 106
Times of India, 140
Tolstoy, Leo, 138, 141
Townsend, Meredith, 20
Transvaal, 43, 139
Travancore, 5, 14, 232, 249
Tripoli, 258

Trevelyan, C. E., 12, 18, 19
Trevelyan, G. O., 46
Turkey, 113, 149, 150, 169, 255, 258, 259, 262, 265, 268

Udaipur, 236
Uncle Sham, 267
United Kingdom, 107, 150; *see also* England; Great Britain
United Nations, 220, 267
United Provinces, 77, 86, 122, 167, 173, 174, 184, 186, 189, 192, 193, 226-9, 231, 232
United States of America, 41, 99, 100, 102, 255, 256, 266-7, 273, 274

Victoria, Queen, 4, 15
Vidyasagar, Ishwarchandra, 6, 24
Vivekanand, 42, 256
Vogel, J. Ph., 233

Wacha, D. E., 71, 73, 110
Wadia, B. P., 133
Wahabis, 48
Waliullah, Shah, 197

Wardha, 185, 190
Ware, Henry, 252
War of American Independence, 12
Washington, George, 255
Wavell, Lord, 217, 219, 232
Webb, Alfred, 69
Wedderburn, William, 57, 58, 79, 80, 81, 122
Wellesley, Lord, 234
Willingdon, Lord, 179, 243
Wilson, T. W., 256
Wood, Charles, 161
World War, First, 126, 148, 152, 167, 181, 186, 198, 259, 260, 261, 265
World War, Second, 179, 226, 261, 266, 267, 270, 271-2, 273

Young Bengal, 21-2
Young Turk Revolt, 43, 257
Yuan Chwang, 263, 275
Yule, George, 63, 69

Zaheer, Ali, 190
Zetland, Lord, 180
Zulu Rebellion, 136